Managing Politics and Islam in Indonesia

Managing Politics and Islam in Indonesia examines the politics of Islam and the state in Indonesia over recent decades, during which time there has been a notable resurgence of Islamic political movements. It argues that after the state had consistently worked to restrict and exclude political Islam from power, in the late 1980s and 1990s, there was a change whereby Suharto courted the support of, and began to incorporate, Muslim interests within the political system.

One unintended consequence of this was to raise Muslims' political expectations and to mobilise Muslim political interests in the context of broadening 'pro-democracy' opposition which contributed to the downfall of Suharto's regime. Based on extensive original research, including interviews with participants, this book charts the shifts in relations between Islam and the Indonesian state over time, assessing the impact on other groups, and on the overall cohesion of Indonesia.

Donald J. Porter completed his PhD at the Australian National University and is currently engaged at the Southeast Asia and Pacific branch of the Australian Department of Defence.

Managing Politics and Islam in Indonesia

Donald J. Porter

RoutledgeCurzon
Taylor & Francis Group

LONDON AND NEW YORK

First published 2002
by RoutledgeCurzon, an imprint of Taylor & Francis
2 Park Square, Milton Park, Abingdon, Oxfordshire OX14 4RN

Simultaneously published in the USA and Canada
by RoutledgeCurzon
711 Third Avenue, New York, NY 10017

RoutledgeCurzon is an imprint of the Taylor & Francis Group

First issued in paperback 2011

Typeset in Times by BC Typesetting, Bristol

British Library Cataloguing in Publication Data
A catalogue record for this book is available from the British Library.

Library of Congress Cataloging in Publication Data
Porter, Donald J.
Managing politics and Islam in Indonesia/Donald J. Porter.
p. cm.
Includes bibliographical references and index.
ISBN 0-7007-1736-6
1. Islam and politics-Indonesia. 2. Indonesia-Politics and
government 20th century.
3. Islam-Indonesia-Societies, etc.-History-20th century. I. Title.

BP63.15 P68 2002
959.803'9-dc21   2002068008

ISBN 978-0-700-71736-1 (hbk)
ISBN 978-0-415-51538-2 (pbk)

Contents

Contents

Contents

Foreword

Indonesia is the world's largest predominantly Muslim country but its government has never been in the hands of leaders determined to identify the state with Islam. On the contrary, the state ideology of *Pancasila* (Five Principles) embodies a vision of a pluralist state in which no particular religion is endowed with special privileges. Although 87 per cent of the population is Muslim, popular support for the demand that some form of an Islamic state be established and *shar'iah* law implemented has never been widespread. Nevertheless part of the Muslim community has been mobilised from time to time behind Islamic issues. Although radical Muslims have never been near to toppling the government, they have considerable capacity to 'cause problems' by mobilising their supporters. Under the governments of President Sukarno and, especially, President Suharto, political Islam was therefore usually seen as a threat. Today, in the democratic conditions following the fall of Suharto's New Order regime, vigorous Muslim parties have re-emerged calling for expanded Muslim influence in the government and the introduction of *shar'iah* law but these parties have failed to win extensive electoral support.

In this study, Don Porter examines the way in which the government, especially during the three decades of authoritarian military-backed rule under President Suharto, dealt with Islamic political challenges. Suharto relied in part on straightforward repression and many radical Muslims spent years in jail. But Suharto used carrot as well as stick. In a regime that was as corrupt as any in the world, the president tied the competing segments of the national and regional elites to his regime by distributing material benefits that rewarded loyalists, attracted former opponents and punished those who 'betrayed' him. Suharto's pyramid of patronage worked in part through corporatist political institutions that provided representation for the elites of various sectors of society.

Porter shows how corporatist strategies can be used by authoritarian regimes to tame potential opposition, in this case from the Islamic camp. For several decades Suharto successfully tied favoured Islamic interests to his regime while excluding others. Muslim students and other radicals could occasionally demonstrate in the streets but the regime was able to maintain its hold over key sections of the Islamic elite. Through incorporation they were able to ensure that their voice was at least heard and obtain a few crumbs from the ruler's table. While many authors have used a corporatist framework to explain how governments have kept a balance between economic groups, Porter's contribution is to apply this framework to understanding how an authoritarian government has used corporatist methods to keep political Islam under control.

Porter's book, however, is not limited to examining how an authoritarian regime maintained itself in power but also looks at the way its power was undermined and how it finally collapsed. In other words, corporatism does not always work for rulers. In this case, Suharto opted to move from exclusionary to inclusionary corporatism by allowing his favourite minister, Professor B. J. Habibie, to establish in 1990 a new Islamic organisation to attract not only Muslims who had previously been unenthusiastic about the regime but also those who had been vociferous dissidents. Some allowed themselves to be convinced that the leopard really had changed its spots while others, more realistically, grasped what they saw as an opportunity to entrench Islamic influence in preparation for the inevitable succession—as Suharto passed his seventieth year. Porter, of course, does not focus on Islamic politics alone but shows how Suharto played 'the Islamic card' by inserting a new Muslim organisation into an already complex balance of incorporated interests involving the military, business, the regions and others. According to Porter, Suharto hoped to 'maintain a shifting disequilibrium of forces' in which political Islam would play an enhanced role. But, the foundation of the Islamic organisation, ICMI, in fact failed to incorporate smoothly the new element into the political elite. On the contrary, it stimulated sharper rivalries with other segments.

This political struggle, of course, was played out against a background of a transformed society created by three decades of steady—to some extent, oil-financed—economic growth. Indonesia in 1998 was very different to the Indonesia of 1968 when Suharto finally achieved the 'full' presidency after serving in an acting capacity for a year and holding effective power since 1966. The Indonesian economy had become increasingly integrated into the world economy and a still small, but growing, middle class had appeared, among whom Muslims were much more prominent than they had been in the past. The Indonesian political elite, however, was still sharply divided when disaster, in the form of the Asian Monetary Crisis, struck in 1997. No longer backed by a cohesive political elite, Suharto had few political resources left at his disposal when massive rioting broke out and forced him to resign in May 1998.

In the conclusion to his study, Porter asks whether Suharto made a fatal political error when he decided to incorporate the Islamic forces that had previously opposed his regime. Did corporatism contain the seeds of its own destruction or was it just an error of judgement on the president's part? Porter's answer is that Suharto's turn to inclusionary corporatism in 1990 contributed to his fall eight years later but does not provide the full explanation. In any case the corporatist structures that Suharto had built soon unravelled, ironically under President Habibie, the man appointed by Suharto to head ICMI, the organisation that contributed much to the elite disunity that proceeded the regime's fall. Coming to office with a divided elite, Habibie's presidency was short and he was succeeded by Indonesia's first democratically (more or less) elected president, Abdurrahman Wahid, who had occasionally allowed himself to be dragged into the corporatist framework but never became fully entrapped. Abdurrahman's tenure, too, was short, but that is a different story.

This book makes an important contribution to the literature on corporatism by applying the concept to a government's strategies to control a potential political challenge—in this case a political challenge emanating from a religious community. It also shows in considerable detail how different sections of Indonesia's Islamic community responded to that effort. And it shows that the corporatist strategy ultimately failed. Porter's study has focused on an important aspect of authoritarianism in Indonesia and provides significant insights applicable to other countries with similar forms of government. I recommend it not only to readers with a special interest in Indonesian politics or a special interest in Islamic politics but also to those seeking to understand authoritarian government in general.

Harold Crouch
October 2001
Director, Indonesia Project, International Crisis Group, Jakarta

Preface

The book is the product of detailed study in fulfilment of my doctorate, which included two years of fieldwork of various Islamic organisations in their interactions with other key elements of state and society, carried out in the years 1994, 1996, and 1997. I interviewed a wide spectrum of Muslim political and organisational leaders, scholars, intellectuals and national political leaders (both Muslim and non-Muslim). My interests in this line of inquiry began with an attempt to understand the possible connection between the political, ideological and intellectual posturing of Indonesian Muslim leaders and the institutional and power structures of the Suharto regime. In the first year of my research, I interviewed these people regarding current and past political events, as well as documented people's political and religious stances and attitudes on the implementation of Islamic law in Indonesia. I became particularly interested in how a Muslim leader's location as a member of an independent organisation, or as someone more closely aligned to the state, might have affected their stance on certain issues.

Political developments in Indonesia began to unfold so rapidly in the second year of my research that it caused a shift in the focus of my inquiry. By this stage of the research, I became keenly interested in the role of the Suharto regime in organising Muslim interests. However, the mounting challenges to Suharto's rule led me also to consider the role of the state in organising Muslim interests against anti-regime forces. Subsequent political developments leading to Suharto's resignation in May 1998 reinforced my desire to understand the relationship between the state, political Islam, and other social interests during Suharto's last years.

Acknowledgements

I would like to acknowledge several people in Australia and Indonesia for the contribution they made to the book. First, and foremost, I would like to thank my supervisor, Dr Harold Crouch, for his considerable assistance at important moments of the book. I would also like to thank my advisers, Prof. Anthony Milner and Prof. Jim Fox for their specific contributions. Special acknowledgment must go to Dr Greg Fealy, who advised on chapter six concerning the Islamic traditionalist organisation, Nahdlatul Ulama. Prof. Anthony Johns offered good advice at early stages of my research on the literary history of Islam, as well as took a personal interest in my progress. Prof. Ben Kerkvliet, Dr Ron May, Dr Edward Aspinall, and Dr Sinclair Dinnen also gave helpful input into the final writing of the book. There are many other academic colleagues and Ph.D. candidates who helped provide a stimulating intellectual environment during my time at the Department of Political and Social Change within the Research School of Pacific and Asian Studies at the Australian National University. Special thanks must also go to the Faculty of Asian Studies for kindly providing me with an office for the final manuscript preparation.

The Indonesian President, KH Abdurrahman Wahid, when he was still chairman of Nahdlatul Ulama, was of great assistance to me in 1993–1994 and 1996–1997. He provided me with accommodation both in his household and in other locations and gave me access to, as well as advice on, his organisation and its leaders. I would like to thank the many government officials, politicians, and community leaders cited in the book for permitting me to interview them. I would also like to acknowledge for their assistance the following organisations: the Department of Religion, the Indonesian Association of Muslim Intellectuals (ICMI), the Centre for Information and Development Studies (CIDES), the Indonesian Council of Ulama (MUI), the Dewan Dakwah Islam Indonesia, the Jakarta campus of the State Islamic Tertiary Institute (IAIN), the journal *Studia Islamika*, the Paramadina Foundation and the Association for Pesantren and Community Development (P3M). Finally, I would like to thank Mayasari and her family for their immense moral and material support, which they gave during much of my research.

Abbreviations

abangan	Nominal Muslims
ABRI	*Angkatan Bersenjata Republik Indonesia* (Armed Forces of the Republic of Indonesia)
AJI	Alliance of Independent Journalists
Akrab	*Aksi Rakyat Bersatu* (Unified People's Action)
aliran kepercayaan	mystical belief systems
AMPI	*Angkatan Muda Pembangunan Indonesia* (Indonesian Development Generation of Youth)
azas tunggal	sole ideological foundation or unifying principle
BAIS	*Badan Inteljin Strategis* (Strategic Intelligence Agency)
BAKIN	*Badan Kordinasi Intelijen Negara* (State Intelligence Coordinating Agency)
BAKOMUBIN	*Badan Koordinasi Mubaligh se-Indonesia* (Indonesian Co-ordinating Body of Muslim Preachers)
Bakorstanas	*Badan Kordinasi Pemantapan Stabilitas Nasional* (Coordinating Agency for the Maintenance of National Stability)
Banser	paramilitary wing of GP Ansor
Bapilu	*Badan Pengendalian Pemilu* (General Election Controlling Body)
Bappenas	*Badan Perencanaan Pembangunan Nasional* (National Development Planning Agency)
Bernas	*Barisan Nasional* (National Front)
BIA	*Badan Inteljin ABRI* (ABRI Intelligence Agency)
BKPRMI	*Badan Komunikasi Pemuda Remaja Masjid Indonesia* (Communication Board of Indonesian Mosque Youth)

BKSPP	*Badan Kerja Sama Pondok Pesantren* (Pondok Pesantren Co-operation Body)
BMI	*Bank Mualimat Islam*
BMOIWI	*Badan Musyawarah Organisasi Islam Wanita Indonesia* (Indonesian Islamic Women's Consultation Body)
BPPMI	*Badan Pembina Perpustakaan Masjid Indonesia* (Indonesian Agency for the Promotion of Mosque Libraries)
BPPT	*Badan Penkajian dan Penerapan Teknologi* (Agency of Applied Technology Research)
Bulog	*Badan Urusan Logistik* (Logistic Affairs Agency)
CIDES	Centre for Information and Development Studies
CPDS	Centre for Policy Development Studies
CSIS	Centre for Strategic and International Studies
dakwah	Islamic propagation
DDII	*Dewan Dakwah Islam Indonesia* (Indonesian Islamic Dakwah Council)
DEMA	*Dewan Mahasiswa* (University Student Councils)
Depdagri	*Departmen Dalam Negeri* (Department of Home Affairs)
Dephankam	*Departmen Pertahanan Keamanan* (Department of Defence and Security)
Dewan Pembina	Supervisor's Council
Dharma Wanita	Women's Service/Duty—an official association of wives of civil servants
DI/TII	*Darul Islam/Tentara Islam Indonesia* (Darul Islam/Indonesian Islamic Army)
DMI	*Dewan Mesjid Indonesia* (Indonesian Mosque Council)
DPA	*Dewan Pertimbangan Agung* (Supreme Advisory Council)
DPKSH	*Dewan Penegakan Keamanan dan Sistem Hukum* (Security and Law Council)
DPR	*Dewan Perwakilan Rakyat* (Parliament)
Dwi-fungsi	Dual Function—ABRI doctrine stipulating a dual role of defence and politics
F-ABRI	*Fraksi ABRI* (ABRI fraction in the parliament)
Famred	*Front Aksi Mahasiswa untuk Reformasi dan Demokrasi* (Student Action Front for Reform and Democracy)
Fatayat	Younger women's wing of NU
fatwa	Pronouncement or ruling by Islamic authority
FBSI	*Federasi Buruh Seluruh Indonesia* (All-Indonesian Labour Federation)

FKLD	*Forum Komunikasi Lembaga Dakwah* (Communication Forum for Dakwah Institutes)
FKOI-KK	*Forum Komunikasi Ormas Islam* (Islamic Communication Forum for Mass Organisations)
FKPPI	*Forum Komunikasi Putra-Putri Purnawirawan Indonesia* (Communication Forum for Sons and Daughters of ABRI Veterans)
FKSMJ	*Forum Komunikasi Senat Mahasiswa Jakarta* (Jakarta Communication Forum of Student Senates)
Forum Kota	City Forum
FUNGSI	*Forum Ummat Islam Pendukung Konstitusi* (Forum of Muslim Supporters of the Constitution)
Furkon	*Forum Ummat Islam untuk Keadilan dan Konstitusi* (Forum for Upholding the Constitution and Justice)
GBHN	*Garis-Garis Besar Haluan Negara* (Broad Outlines of State Policy)
GMKI	*Gerakan Mahasiswa Kristen Indonesia* (Indonesian Christian University Student Movement)
GMNI	*Gerakan Mahasiswa Nasional Indonesia* (Indonesian Nationalist University Student Movement, the students' wing of the former Indonesian Nationalist Party, PNI)
Golkar	*Golongan Karya* (Government party)
GP Ansor	*Gerakan Pemuda Ansor* (NU's Ansor Youth Movement)
GPII	*Gerakan Pemuda Islam Indonesia* (Movement of Indonesian Islamic Youth)
GPK	*Gerakan Pengacau Keamanan* (Security Disturbance Movement)
GUPPI	*Gabungan Usaha Perbaikan Pendidikan Islam* (Union of Efforts to Improve Islamic Education)
halal	permitted
Hankam	*Pertahanan Keamanan* (Defence and Security—Dwifungsi's first function)
Hansip	*Pertahanan Sipil* (Civil Defence)
haram	prohibited
HIP	*Hubungan Industri Pancasila* (Pancasila Industrial Relations)

HKTI	*Himpunan Kerukunan Tani Indonesia* (Indonesian Farmers' Harmony Association)
HMI	*Himpunan Mahàsiswa Islam* (the Association of Islamic University Students)
HNSI	*Himpunan Nelayan Seluruh Indonesia* (All-Indonesian Fishermen's Association)
IAIN	*Institut Agama Islam Negari* (State Islamic Tertiary Institutes)
ICKI	*Ikatan Cendekiawan Kebangsaan Indonesia* (Association of Indonesian Nationalist Intellectuals)
ICMI	*Ikatan Cendekiawan Muslim Indonesia* (Association of Indonesian Muslim Intellectuals)
IPPNU	*Ikatan Putri-Putri Nahdlatul Ulama* (Association of Daughters of NU)
Iptek	*Ilmu pengetahuan dan teknologi* (science and technology)
IPTN	*Industri Pesawat Terbang Nusantara* (National Aircraft Industry)
KADIN	*Kamar Dagang dan Industri* (the Indonesian Chamber of Commerce and Industry)
KAHMI	*Korps Alumni HMI* (Corps of HMI Alumni)
KAMMI	*Kesatuan Aksi Mahasiswa Muslim Indonesia* (Muslim University Students Action Front)
Kassospol	*Kepala Staf Social Politik* (ABRI's Chief of Social-Political Affairs)
KAWI	*Kesatuan Aksi Wanita Indonesia* (Indonesian Women's Unified Action)
KBB	*Keluarga Bulan Bintang* (Crescent Moon and Star Family—supporter organisations for Masyumi)
kekaryaan	Sending ABRI personnel to non-military posts
kelompok sempalan	religious splinter groups
kerukunan	(harmony: a key word in the state's Pancasila discourse, which refers to an 'organic' or hierarchically ordered harmony of social relations)
keterbukaan	Political Openness
kewaspadaan	(Vigilance: the concept refers to ABRI's approach or 'doctrine' of vigilance)
KIPP	*Komite Independent Pemantau Pemilu* (Independent Election Monitoring Committee)

KISDI	*Komite Indonesia untuk Solidaritas Dunia Islam* (Indonesian Committee for Solidarity of the Islamic World)
KND	*Koalisi Nasional untuk Demokrasi* (National Coalition for Democracy)
KNPI	*Komite Nasional Pemuda Indonesia* (National Committee of Indonesian Youth)
Kokar	*Korps Karyawan* (Corps of Functionaries)
Kokarmendagri	*Korps Karyawan Menteri Dalam Negeri* (Corps of Functionaries for the Ministry of Internal Affairs)
Komando Jihad	Islamic Holy War Command
Komnas HAM	*Komisi Nasional untuk Hak Asasi Manusia* (National Human Rights Commission)
Komrad	*Komite Mahasiswa dan Rakyat untuk Demokrasi* (Student and People Committee for Democracy)
Kopassus	Komando Pasukan Khusus (Special Forces Command)
Kopkamtib	*Komando Operasi Pemulihan Keamanan dan Ketertiban* (Operational Command for the Restoration of Security and Order)
Korpri	*Korps Pegawai Republik Indonesia* (Corps of Civil Servants of the Republic of Indonesia)
Kosgoro	*Koperasi Serba Gotong Royong* (Total Self-help Cooperative)
Kostrad	*Komando Cadangan Strategis Angkatan Darat* (Army Strategic Reserve Command)
KOWANI	*Kongres Wanita Nasional Indonesia* (Indonesian Women's National Congress)
KPRP	*Komite Perjuangan Rakyat untuk Perubahan* (People's Struggle Committee for Change, a front organisation for PRD)
KUD	*Koperasi Unit Desa* (Village Cooperative Unit)
kyai	(religious scholars who run a system of traditional Islam boarding schools mainly in rural Java—also written KH as the designated title)
LDII	*Lembaga Dakwah Islam Indonesia* (Indonesian Institute of Islamic Propagation)
LDK	*Lembaga Dakwah Kampus* (Campus Dakwah Institutes)
Lemhanas	*Lembaga Ketahanan Nasional* (National Resilience (or Defence) Institute)

LIPI	*Lembaga Ilmu Pengetahuan Indonesia* (Indonesian Institute of Sciences)
LMMY	*Liga Mahasiswa Muslim Yogyakarta* (Yogyakarta League of Muslim University Students)
LP3ES	*Lembaga Penelitian, Pendidikan, dan Penerangan Ekonomi dan Sosial* (Social and Economic Research, Education, and Information Institute)
LPPTKA	*Lembaga Pembinaan dan Pengembangan Taman Kanak-Kanak Al-Qur'an Indonesia* (*Al-Qur'an* Kindergarten Guidance and Development Institute)
LSM	*Lembaga Swadaya Masyarakat* (Self-reliant Community Institution)
Malari	*Malapetaka 15 Januari* (15 January (1974) Affair)
MARI	*Majelis Rakyat Indonesia* (The Council of Indonesian People)
Masyumi	*Majelis Syuro Muslim Indonesia* (Consultative Council of Indonesian Muslims)
MAWI	*Majelis Agung Wali-Gereja Indonesia* (Indonesian (Catholic) Council of Bishops)
MDI	*Majelis Dakwah Indonesia* (Indonesian Dakwah Council)
Mimbar Bebas	Free Speech Forums
MKGR	*Musyawarah Kekeluargaan Gotong Royong* (Self-help Family Association, a founding organisation of Golkar)
MPR	*Majelis Permusyawaratan Rakyat* (People's Consultative Assembly)
Mubaliq/dai	Islamic preacher
Muhammdiayah	organisation representing the modernist wing of Indonesian Islam
MUI	*Majelis Ulama Indonesia* (Indonesian Council of Ulama)
Munas	*Musyawarah Nasional* (National (Consultative) Congress)
Muslimat	Elder women's wing of NU
NKK	*Normalisasi Kehidupan Kampus* (Normalisation of Campus Life)
NU	*Nahdlatul Ulama* (Revival of the Religious Scholars—Indonesia's largest Islamic 'traditionalist' organisation)
Opsus	*Operasi Khusus* (Special Operations)

OTB	*Organisasi Tanpa Bentuk* (Formless Organisation)
P3M	*Perkumpulan Pengembangan Pesantren dan Masyarakat* (Association for Pesantren and Community Development)
P4	*Pedoman Penghayatan dan Pengamalan Pancasila* (Guidelines for the Comprehension and Implementation of Pancasila)
Pam Swakarsa	*Pengamanan Swakarsa* (Civilian Security Militia)
PAN	*Partai Amanat Nasional* (National Mandate Party)
Pancasila	the five (*panca*) guiding principles (*sila*) of the Republic of Indonesia
Parkindo	*Partai Kristen Indonesia* (the Indonesian Christian Party)
Parmusi	*Partai Muslimin Indonesia* (Indonesian Muslim Party)
PBB	*Partai Bulan Bintang* (Crescent Moon and Star Party)
PCPP	*Persatuan Cendekiawan Pembangunan Pancasila* (Association of Pancasila Development Intellectuals)
PDI	*Partai Demokrasi Indonesia* (Indonesian Democracy Party)
PDI-P	*Partai Demokrasi Indonesia—Perjuangan* (Indonesian Democracy Party of Struggle)
PDR	*Partai Daulat Rakyat* (People's Sovereignty Party)
pembangunan	development
pembinaan	guidance, supervision
Persis	*Persatuan Islam* (Unity of Islam)
Perti	*Persatuan Tarbiyah Islam* (Association of Islamic Education)
pesantren	school of Koranic studies for Muslim students, mostly boarders
Petisi 50	Petition of 50 Group—an opposition group consisting of fifty members of retired officers and civilians
PGI	*Persekutuan Gereja-Gereja di Indonesia* (Communion of Indonesian Churches)
PGRI	*Persatuan Guru Republik Indonesia* (Teachers' Union of the Republic of Indonesia)
PII	*Pelajar Islam Indonesia* (Organisation of Indonesian Islamic Secondary School Students)

PK	*Partai Keadilan* (Justice Party)
PKB	*Partai Kebangkitan Bangsa* (National Awakening Party)
PKI	*Partai Komunis Indonesia* (Indonesian Communist Party)
PKK	*Pembinaan Kesejahteraan Keluarga* (Association for Promoting Family Welfare)
PKP	*Partai Keadilan dan Persatuan* (Justice and Unity Party)
PKU	*Partai Kebankitan Umat* (Community Awakening Party)
PMII	*Pergerakan Mahasiswa Islam Indonesia* (Indonesian Muslim University Students Movement—NU's university students associations)
PMKRI	*Persatuan Mahasiswa Katolik Republik Indonesia* (Catholic University Students Association of the Republic of Indonesia)
PMP	*Pendidikan Moral Pancasila* (Pancasila Moral Education)
PNI	*Partai Nasional Indonesia* (Indonesian National Party)
PNU	*Partai Nahdlatul Ulama* (Nahdlatul Ulama Party)
PPBI	*Pusat Perjuangan Buruh Indonesia* (Indonesian Centre for Labour Struggle)
PPP	*Partai Persatuan Pembangunan* (United Development Party)
PRD	*Partai Rakyat Demokrasi* (People's Democratic Party)
PSII	*Partai Syarikat Islam Indonesia* (Islamic Union Party)
PUDI	*Partai Uni Demokrasi Indonesia* (Union of Indonesian Democracy Party)
PUI	*Partai Umat Islam* (Muslim Community Party)
Rais Aam	Chairman of the Central Syuriah; effectively president-general of NU
Rapat Akbar	mass meeting
Ratih	*Rakyat Terlatih* (Trained People—civilian militia established by ABRI)
Repelita	*Rencana Pembangunan Lima Tahun* (Five Year Development Plan)
RMI	*Rabithalul Mai'ahidil Islamiyah* (NU's *pesantren* organisation)

santri	devout Muslims
SBSI	*Serikat Buruh Sejahtera Indonesia* (Indonesian Workers' Welfare Association)
Shar'iah	Islamic law
SI	*Sarekat Islam* (United Islam)
SKU	*Satuan Karya Ulama* (Ulama Functional Union)
SMID	*Solidaritas Mahasiswa Indonesia Demokrasi* (Solidarity of Indonesian University Students for Democracy)
SOKSI	*Sentral Organisasi Karyawan Sosialis Indonesia* (Central Organisation for Indonesian Socialist Functionaries)
SPSI	*Serikat Pekerja Seluruh Indonesia* (All-Indonesian Workers' Union)
Syuriah	NU's supreme Islamic law council
Tanfidziah	Executive board of NU
tut wuri handayani	a Javanese expression to describe how a father supports his young children from behind as they learn to walk
ulama	Muslim religious scholar
umat	the Muslim community
wadah	Literally means 'container' for facilitating activities. *Wadah tunggal* can be translated as 'peak organisation' or 'umbrella organisation'
WALUBI	*Perwakilan Umat Budha Indonesia* (Representation of the Indonesian Buddhist Community)
WMAB	*Wadah Musyawarah Antarumat Beragama* (Inter-Religious Consultation Forum)
Yayasan Abdi Bangsa	Foundation of Devotion to the Nation
YKPK	*Yayasan Kerukunan Persaudaraan Kebangsaan* (National Brotherhood Reconciliation Foundation)
YLBHI	*Yayasan Lembaga Bantuan Hukum Indonesia* (Indonesian Legal Aid Institute)

Chapter 1

Islamic Revival and State Control

Indonesia is the world's largest Muslim country, with 87 per cent of the population adhering to the faith. The country has been widely regarded as home to a moderate brand of Islam compared to the more assertive political and militant Islamic revivals that have taken place in the Middle East. Much of the population of the main island of Java has long adhered to a blend of Javanese–Hindu beliefs combined with Islamic belief and ritual practices. However, for the past two decades, there has been a shift in the religious landscape, as increasing numbers of so-called 'statistical' or nominal Muslims have sought to deepen their faith and adhere more closely to the prescriptions of Islam. There has been a steady rise in Muslim consciousness and ritual formalism, especially among the urban middle classes and student population. University campuses have become fertile ground for an Islamic awakening, with students being recruited into a diverse range of disciplined organisational cells. Some of these cells have taken their inspiration from fundamentalist thought and organisational models of radical Islamic movements in the Middle East.

In recent years there also has been a notable Islamic political revival and, at the fringes of society, an increase in Islamic militancy. Between March and May 1998, Muslim students played an important role in forging cross-campus networks and protest actions against Suharto in his final weeks of office. In November of the same year, Muslim militias mobilised in the streets of Jakarta to defend the Habibie government and 'legitimate' political authority against pro-democracy student demonstrators who were marching on parliament. Several Islamic political parties were established to contest democratic general elections in 1999 after President Habibie lifted curbs imposed by President Suharto on political organisation during his thirty-two-year period of authoritarian rule. In a dramatic shift in political fortunes, the Muslim cleric, Abdurrahman Wahid, who led the largest Islamic mass organisation, was elected to the presidency after Muslim political leaders had been excluded from power for decades. Although he stood for a liberal brand of Muslim nationalism, Muslim leaders belonging to the 'Central Axis' (an informal alignment of Islamic political parties) initially viewed the election of Abdurrahman as a significant gain for Islamic politics. In turn, Abdurrahman's Muslim supporters

1

mobilised in the streets in defence of his presidency when parliament, including the Muslim opposition, sought to censure and impeach him. Recent developments have also included Muslim militia departing from the shores of Java to fight a *Jihad* against Christians in the war-torn Moluccas. Over the last decade, there has been a significant escalation of Muslim mob attacks on churches and the property and persons of the Chinese (mostly Christian) ethnic minority.

This political resurgence of Islam can be traced back to the policies towards Islam pursued by Suharto's so-called 'New Order' regime (1966–1998). In his first two decades of rule, Suharto set in place strict controls on Islamic political organisation and ideology and repressed political dissent. He did this as part of a de-politicisation of society and emasculation of the political party system. Schwarz argues that the Islamic political resurgence was due to the Suharto government's 'efforts to de-politicise Indonesia', which drove 'many to look to Islam as an alternative political arena'.[1] There is some evidence for this argument, at least as far as student politics was concerned. In the late 1970s, Suharto set in train a program of campus 'normalisation' aimed at de-politicising campus life through restrictions on student organisations. The policy of campus normalisation forced student activities underground as students joined a proliferating number of unmediated Islamic organisational cells and study groups. Mosques, both on and off campus, became a new focus of religious-political activities and discussion groups and helped fuel an Islamic awakening. Although the campus normalisation coincided with the Islamic revolution in Iran, which influenced some of the intellectual and ideological trends in Indonesia, the surge of Islamic activities on campus in the 1980s and 1990s appears to have been, at least partly, a product of New Order policy.

However, it is clear that for much of the New Order period, far from sparking an Islamic political resurgence, Suharto's heavy restrictions on Islamic political organisation successfully prevented a political resurgence of Islam. Muslim political interests were channelled into, and kept largely subservient within, an emasculated political party system that was dominated by the government's election machine-cum-party, Golkar. Although, during the first two decades of the New Order, state–Islamic relations were largely antagonistic, Suharto faced little organised Islamic opposition or dissent. The military's intelligence services kept Muslim organisational activities under close surveillance and the military repressed any signs of Islamic militancy, with a prominent example being the crushing of an alleged Islamic rebellion in Lampung in 1989. In 1984, in Jakarta's port district of Tanjung Priok, the military also shot hundreds of Muslim demonstrators.

There was a shift in state–Islamic relations in the 1990s, with a state–Islamic accommodation emerging as Suharto sought to co-opt the Muslim middle classes and Muslim critics as a new base of support for his regime. As part of this accommodation, Suharto agreed to the establishment of the Association of Indonesian Muslim Intellectuals (ICMI) in 1990. The establishment of ICMI drew considerable domestic criticism and raised expectations among many

2

Muslim leaders that they would gain greater access to power and representation in the political institutions. The state–Islamic accommodation coincided with a regime-initiated political opening, which was the product of an intra-elite rivalry and provided the impetus for growing pluralist challenges to Suharto's rule. In seeking to stave off such challenges, Suharto drew on the support of incorporated Muslim interests. An outcome of the state-Islamic accommodation and Suharto's reliance upon Muslim support was the politicisation of Islam, after two decades of concerted efforts to 'de-Islamise' politics. However, it needs to be stressed that the re-politicisation of Islam occurred within the context of a re-politicisation of group interests more generally, as a growing number of people sought to organise outside the state's restrictive political framework.

This book examines the shift in Suharto's management of state–Islamic relations during the New Order period from his efforts to restrict Islamic politics to the phase of state–Islamic accommodation. An assessment is also made of state–Islamic relations during the presidency of B.J. Habibie (May 1998– October 1999), when curbs on Islamic political organisation were lifted. The study seeks to explain the re-politicisation of state–Islamic relations in the 1990s, in the context of intra-elite rivalries and pluralist challenges to Suharto. Some of these challenges came from disaffected elements in the military and from elite members of the government, who had been sidelined by the rise of new civilian and Muslim groups. A key issue discussed is the changing nature of state regulation of Islam as part of institutional and political adaptation to new challenges arising both from within and outside the state.

'Corporatism' (for an exploration and definition of this concept see chapter two) is the main analytical framework used to examine these institutional linkages and interactions between the state, the Islamic community and other political interests. The cornerstone of the corporatist framework was the Golkar-dominated party system, which included two subordinate parties representing Muslims (the United Development Party or PPP) and non-Muslims (the Indonesian Democracy Party or PDI). Suharto also channelled group interests into non-party national peak bodies representing different occupations and 'functional' categories for labour, farmers, women, civil servants and the like. Labour, in particular, was channelled increasingly into monolithic peak organisations, which represented the interests of the state and employers rather than the interests of workers. Organisations like the Indonesian Council of Ulama (MUI), the Indonesian Mosque Council (DMI), the Indonesian Dakwah Council (MDI), and ICMI sought to channel different organisational segments of the Muslim community.

A corporatist framework of analysis provides us with an important starting point for understanding how Suharto's regime managed state–Islamic relations. However, such a framework does not explain an entire social-political reality. Deeper historical and socioeconomic factors are responsible for the development, strength and diversity of organisation in a given society. For Suharto, channelling interests into corporatist structures was a means of limiting organised pluralism in society. The aim was to keep political participation and interest-demands low by channelling group interests into state-supervised structures and effectively locking them out of power sharing arrangements. During the 1970s and 1980s, the strategy of containing social-political organisation and suppressing opposition appeared to be largely successful. However, by the mid-to-late 1990s, corporatist forms of organisation were proving incapable of containing societal interests as increasing demands were being made for political participation and the right to organise independently of the state. During Habibie's administration, corporatist structures were largely dismantled or rendered irrelevant in an emerging multiparty system.

Thus, the book goes beyond a purely corporatist framework of analysis and addresses broader considerations concerning regime maintenance and survival, and regime decay, under authoritarian systems of rule. The argument is made that state management of Islamic political interests demonstrated a shift in the pattern of corporatism being applied from a strategy based on the restrictive exclusion of interests (1970s–1980s) to a more inclusionary one (1990s)—albeit with key exclusionary mechanisms still in place. This partial shift in strategy reflected the need, as part of regime maintenance, to respond to the demands of an expanding pluralism of social-political organisation. However, the shift in strategy, which aimed to keep political interests within the corporatist net, ultimately was unable to contain the burst of organised activity.

BOOK LAYOUT

The book is organised into two main sections and is set out roughly in chronological order. The first section (chapters two to six) provides a theoretical overview and an analysis of initiatives taken by the Suharto regime to place corporatist constraints on political organisation. Chapter two assumes the form of a literature review and explores scholarship on corporatism and regime transitions in developing countries. Chapter three examines the establishment of corporatism in Indonesia and the ideological rationales and institutional structures that underwrote the state's organisation of group interests. Chapters four to six analyse Suharto's strategies for the management of Muslim political and social organisation.

Chapter seven represents an introduction to the second section of the book as it examines growing intra-elite rivalry which created conflict between corporatised Muslim interests and segments of the state (parts of the military and civilian bureaucracy). Chapters eight and nine look at the mounting pluralist (elite-level and societal) challenges to Suharto's rule, which led to his resignation. Chapter ten analyses Habibie's presidency both in terms of continuity with, and departure from, Suharto's regime and examines the unravelling of corporatist arrangements. The conclusion draws the themes together concerning the regulation of state–Islamic relations, regime maintenance, pluralist challenges, and regime decay.

Although many authors have scrutinised the Suharto regime's policies towards Islam, and regime manipulations of Islamic political organisation, not much attention has been given to specific strategies adopted by the regime to structure state–Islamic relations. Authors such as Boland, Noer, van Dijk, and Buyung Nasution have outlined historical developments in the political and ideological struggle of Indonesian Muslim organisations as they have sought to build and define the nation-state in rivalry with other Muslims and non-Muslim interests.[2] A number of scholars have studied political interactions between the state, Islam, and non-Muslim group interests during the New Order period of President Suharto. For example, Kamal, Vatikiotis, McVey, Jones, Samson, Ward, Hefner, Schwarz, Ramage and Syamsuddin have looked at Muslim political, ideological, intellectual and organisational responses to nation-state building and government policy concerning Islam.[3] Studies by Fealy, van Bruinessen, Feillard, Nakamura, Noer, Tanja, and Federspiel have analysed in detail major Islamic organisations, including their relationship with larger political structures of the state.[4]

In particular, the studies of Hefner, Schwarz, and Ramage have explored some of the issues that have led to my examination of state–Islamic relations. Hefner argues that Suharto's efforts in the 1990s to co-opt Islam were a response to the changing composition of society, which was characterised by a notable rise in the educated Muslim middle classes and a deepening Islamisation of society and the government bureaucracy. Schwarz also acknowledges changing social composition as a factor influencing Suharto's decision to try to bring Muslim critics into the 'establishment fold' and neutralise them as a source of opposition. Hefner, Schwarz and Ramage canvas a range of opinions held by government officials and Muslim and non-Muslim community leaders in order to identify the composition of the Muslim middle classes, their value-orientations and lines of cleavage between political groups. Much of the analysis of these scholars concerned how and why the state–Islamic accommodation came about and what implications this had for Indonesian politics and developments in Islam.

However, these early studies, because of the time that they were made, were unable to explore in depth the outcomes of Suharto's strategy of co-optation and what implications this had for broader state–society relations. With the advantage of hindsight, my study examines some of the outcomes and implications of the state–Islamic accommodation. By applying a corporatist framework of analysis to Suharto's management of Muslim interests, the study identifies the specific linkages and structures of power that tie the state and Islamic political interests into a series of complex relations. The study provides further insights into the shifting patterns of repression, co-optation, accommodation, and conflict between the state and Islam. Although scholars have applied a corporatist framework to their analyses of Indonesian politics, there is no single substantial study on the corporatisation of Muslim interests.[5] Schwarz, in particular, does not look far beyond the idea that Suharto repressed Islamic politics. My study identifies less repressive forms of compliance that required a degree of consent and co-operation by the Muslim political community. The book also examines the inter-relationship between Suharto's management of state–Islamic relations and pluralist challenges to Suharto's rule. This part of the study provides original analysis and a new perspective on recent developments in Indonesian politics. Finally, the book also provides a useful comparison with the strategies adopted by other leaders of developing countries in their dealings with the political resurgence of Islam.

NOTES

1. Schwarz, *A Nation in Waiting*, p.174.
2. Boland, *The Struggle of Islam*; van Dijk, *Rebellion Under the Banner of Islam*; Nasution, *The Aspiration for Constitutional Government*.
3. Kamal, *Muslim Intellectual Responses*; Vatikiotis, *Indonesian Politics under Suharto*; McVey, 'Faith as the Outsider'; Jones, 'The Contraction and Expansion'; Samson, 'Islam and Politics'; Samson, 'Conceptions of Politics'; Ward, *The 1971 Election*; Hefner, 'Islam, State, and Civil Society': Schwarz, *A Nation in Waiting*; Syamsuddin, 'Religion and Politics'; Ramage, *Politics in Indonesia*; Syamsuddin, 'The Muhammadiyah'.
4. Fealy, 'The 1994 NU Congress'; van Bruinessen, *NU: Tradisi*; Feillard, 'Traditionalist Islam'; Nakamura, 'NU's Leadership Crisis'; Noer, *Partai Islam*; Tanja, *HMI*; Federspiel, *Persatuan Islam*; Federspiel, 'The Muhammadiyah'.
5. See chapter three concerning literature on corporatism in Indonesia.

Chapter 2

State Corporatism and Pluralist Challenge

The purpose of the following review of literature is to set the parameters of analysis and argumentation of the book. We begin with some concepts and definitions and then develop argumentation and review of literature on corporatism and regime transitions.

CONCEPTS/DEFINITIONS

State and Society

One definition of the state is 'a set of organisations invested with the authority to make binding decisions for people and organisations, juridicially located in a particular territory and to implement decisions using, if necessary, force'.[1] The state consists of its formal-legal institutions and office-holders (the bureaucracy, the executive, the legislature, the police, the courts, the military, and intelligence). However, one of the problems in defining the state is that the boundaries between state and society are somewhat blurred because of interpenetration between state agencies, officials, and other social groups and individuals. For example, do we consider private clients of state patrons part of the state or part of society? Where do we situate quasi-public organisations and institutions (e.g., television networks and airlines with part-state ownership)? Where do we locate private individuals and groups that sit on government advisory bodies and commissions and have direct input into policy-making? Are corporatist organisations a function of state or society? In short, the state consists not only of its formal-legal institutions, but also of informal institutions and non-office holders.[2]

Migdal conceives of the state as a differentiated and complex organisation 'imbedded' in society. He argues that different parts of the state and society engage, and disengage, each other in a mutually transforming manner in multiple social arenas of domination, opposition, accommodation, and co-optation. Different parts of the state tend to pull in different directions; 'one component of the state might align itself to an affiliated or linked social group

7

against another component of the state'.[3] In short, state and society interpenetrate one another, as well as contest who makes the binding rules and norms of society. This study uses Migdal's concept of state and society in its analysis of political interactions and change.

Despite interpenetration of state and society, society consists of formal and informal organisations, movements, networks, and cells, which are not directly part of the state. In advanced liberal democracies the concept of 'civil society' is frequently applied to denote a vigorously organised, pluralistic and autonomous society with its rich array of private professions and associations, which stand midway between communities and the state. Civil society supplements political parties in a multiparty democracy, as it independently informs and participates (through lobby, forum, petition, and organised protest) in the political system.[4] This study uses the concept of 'societal pluralism' in the sense just described of the independent array of private associations not directly linked to the state.

States are discussed in terms of their degree of autonomy from other social organisations, or the degree to which society penetrates the state, or how penetrative states are of society. East Asian states are seen as highly interventionist, controlling states, which deeply penetrate society and retain a high degree of autonomy; many African states are considered as weak and penetrated, with low autonomy. However, what constitutes a 'strong' or 'weak' state, or whether an authoritarian regime, which relies on violence against its citizenry, is in command of a strong or weak state is still a matter of debate.[5]

Authoritarianism

Although there has been a wide variety of authoritarian regimes historically (including one-party systems, military regimes, and personal dictatorships), they all tend to be deficient in key institutional features present in liberal democracies. In greater or lesser degree, they lack well-institutionalised and peaceful competition (including institutionalised opposition parties) for political office through regular free and fair elections. Semi-opposition and regular (often-manipulated) elections are a feature of some authoritarian political systems, while they are denied in others. In authoritarian systems, power is concentrated in the executive with limited, if any, separation or differentiation of powers between the executive, the legislature and the judiciary. Authoritarian systems are short on responsive and accountable government (and commonly suffer from endemic corruption of the bureaucracy), lack a transparent legal system, and tend (in varying degree) to infringe citizens' liberties and rights. Authoritarian regimes are noted for enforcing 'limited pluralism', by denying legal scope to civil associations and parties, and restricting the participation and competition of citizens.[6]

Corporatism

Broadly speaking, corporatism is a system of interest representation that results in the 'planned integration' of society's associational interests into the decision-making structures and policy arena of the state. The state plays a leading role in regulating, creating, and setting the ground rules for the organised internal activities of given interest categories, and the external interactions between groups and between those groups and the state. In its ideal-typical form, corporatism, through the recognition, licensing, and compulsory membership of designated categories by the state, ensures the controlled emergence, and numerical limitation, of organised interest demands, rather than the spontaneous and autonomous expansion of interests as in pluralist political systems.

To borrow, mostly, from Schmitter's often quoted definition: it is an interest system in which the membership is organised into a 'limited number of singular', constituent units, or functional categories, whose 'internal structure of authority' and decision-making is hierarchically ordered. These categories are fragmented (to weaken their autonomous capacities) through a kind of 'vertical pillaring', with the objective of destroying cross-class loyalties. They remain 'non-competitive' within and between 'sectorally compartmentalised' categories (e.g., trade union, peasants' association, religious organisation, and guild-like professional associations).[7] Typically, state-chartered associations of professional categories at their different levels of activity (branch, sub-branch, factory unit) belong, automatically, to their respective peak organisations at the national level and, sometimes, are linked to a bureaucratic centre of government. The designated professional associations and producer organisations become agents of the state, and are given a 'representational monopoly' over their constituent members. They act to enforce political decisions, and discipline and control the behaviour of the membership in accordance with the imperatives and goals of the socioeconomic order (promoted by the state). It is here that they acquire their prescriptive designation as intermediaries in channelling the two-way traffic of state directives and societal messages. The state also 'subjects' the associations to 'controls' both on their 'leadership selection' and on the articulation of autonomous interest inputs. It does this in order to discourage challenges to the state from 'popular and particularistic' demands, and especially to guarantee the suppression of class conflict.[8]

Before proceeding with the analysis, the question arises as to the explanatory value of corporatism in describing social-political relationships. Chalmers offers a succinct answer to this question and is therefore worth quoting at length. Chalmers explains

1) Corporatism starts with the state and defines group interests in terms of their relations to the state. Corporatism's heuristic contribution has been to emphasise the central importance of state-group ties for explaining a variety of outcomes.

2) Corporatism requires one to look not only at the interests of the state, but also at the structure that defines the relationships between various interests, the organisations that represent them, and the bureaucracy.

3) Corporatists also consider the 'state' not as a single entity with a single interest, but rather as a 'naturally' divided entity, made up of particular relationships with the major economic groups and professions (or however interests are defined). The state cannot be isolated from civil society: it is defined by the series of links that form both the state and the societal groups.

4) By focusing attention on the importance of state-initiated structuring of state-group relationships, corporatism draws attention to the choices being made by those who design those links.[9]

I am using corporatism in the structuralist sense just described—as an explanation of the shifting state–societal linkages and political contests and accommodations therefrom—as well as the policy implications of corporatism. I am also using corporatism as an interpretative tool of the many fluid inter-relationships of state–societal political actors and their choices.

REVIEW OF LITERATURE AND ARGUMENTATION
Varieties of Corporatism

Recent theorists have identified corporatism as branching out into at least two main varieties. Williamson distinguishes these as 'consensual-licensed' and 'authoritarian-licensed';[10] Schmitter categorises them as 'societal corporatism' and 'state corporatism';[11] O'Donnell calls them 'privatising' and 'statising'.[12] These two varieties have their roots in early theorising and in the divergent paths taken by corporatist systems in continental Europe and further afield. The consensual-licensed type corresponds to advanced liberal-capitalist countries such as Great Britain, West Germany, France, Canada, Australia, the US, and new democracies in the Third World. The statising type corresponds to countries under dictatorship or authoritarian rule at different points of history, including Petainist France, Fascist Italy, Nazi Germany, and Greece, Portugal, Spain, Brazil, Chile, Peru, Mexico, and some of the countries of Africa and Asia.[13]

In consensual-licensed (societal) corporatism the impetus for organisation largely comes from society, as semi-autonomous, self-regulating professions manage their preserve of activity but within a broad framework of principles and rules stipulated by the central state. This variety of corporatism is the culmination of an evolutionary process as it gradually, and unevenly, supplants the decaying institutions of pluralism within liberal democratic polities. It follows an organisational process and logic, whereby interests of society penetrate the state, as these interests open up to their representation 'institutional areas of the state'.[14] It, therefore, corresponds to strategies of co-optation and inclusion of interests as state and society 'seek each other out' for the sake of establishing a mutually beneficial socioeconomic environment. Theorists and advocates of this variety, with varying emphasis, tend to place defined limits on state intervention in the crafting of a non-pluralist political order.[15]

By contrast, the studies of O'Donnell, Schmitter, and Williamson show that authoritarian-licensed (state) corporatism is imposed from above by a highly interventionist state noted for its bureaucratic centralism, which seeks to deeply penetrate society and thereby control it by strictly subordinating it to the state. Under authoritarian-licensed systems, interest associations become 'auxiliary and dependent organs' of the state apparatus, often through the linking of them to the relevant bureaucratic centres of government that have jurisdictional authority over their respective preserves of activity.[16] Authoritarian regimes introduce corporatist devices, write Silvio Baretta and Helen Douglas, 'under conditions of high mobilisation, in which the demands of the popular sector cannot be kept in bounds simply by indiscriminate use of coercion'.[17] The regime captures the organisational bases of independent activity, demobilises them, and then reintegrates them into a strictly subservient, and neutralised, position within the newly constructed socioeconomic and political order. To quote Schmitter, regime leaders seek to fill the 'resulting organisational vacuum with compliant worker syndicates [in the case of labour]'[18] which, through sole license, are established to pre-empt any alternative, future independent organisational activity. Finally, Baretta and Douglas identify three principal purposes of state corporatism: 1) to provide a means of control or active domination of social groups; 2) to provide a channel of communication between state organs and social groups, and 3) to secure support for the regime.[19]

Inclusionary–Exclusionary Corporatism

The idea that an authoritarian-licensed (state) variety of corporatism can be distinguished as a unique category has gained strong currency in literature on developing countries of the Third World. Building upon O'Donnell's distinction between 'incorporating populist-authoritarian' systems and 'excluding bureaucratic-authoritarian' systems, Stepan has identified two subtypes of 'inclusionary' and 'exclusionary' corporatism within authoritarian political systems.[20] Inclusionary forms of corporatism are tied to authoritarian populism and the exclusionary variety to bureaucratic-authoritarian regimes. As with all analytical categories, a great deal of variation occurs between these ideal sub-types, and this depends on the country under analysis, given their diverse political histories and institutional systems.[21] Nonetheless, some common features and patterns of behaviour could be found in many countries of the periphery (in Latin America, East Asia, and Africa).[22]

Populist leaders of authoritarian states tended to establish inclusionary corporatist arrangements in order to install their regimes. They did this through the controlled mobilisation of cross-class popular support, and by organising its incorporation and subordination into the structures of the state, behind their leadership. They tended to draw on nationalism as a means of rallying support to their cause and destroying old economic classes (whether they were land-owning classes or colonial capitalists) and creating new ones. Consequently, they introduced programs of nationalisation of industry and the application of heavy state protectionism of domestic producers with which to underwrite rapid industrialisation. The combination of political activation, which tended to get out of hand, and protectionist industrial policy often resulted in rapid deterioration of the economies of Third World countries and caused widespread social-political instability. In particular, mass mobilisation of social interests, linked to competing demands of the incorporated groups on the state, weakened the populist state and eroded its ability to mediate conflicts.[23] In Huntington's analysis, the pre-existing authoritarian structures lacked sufficient institutional capacity to cope with the high level of societal activation, or to absorb and regulate the diversifying and conflicting demands of society.[24]

This, according to O'Donnell and Stepan caused a 'drastic defensive reaction' that led to the installation of the bureaucratic-authoritarian state and/or new institutional arrangements for the exclusion of the popular classes.[25] In collaboration, stability-minded military leaders and technocrats typically responded to these crises by seeking to stabilise the economies, to bring about a new social-political order, and to expand the state apparatus in terms of its 'scope, penetration, and coercive capacity'.[26] They embarked on ambitious reconstruction of the political system, and dismantling of the old party-linked institutions. They did this in support of programmatic, guided economic development as they tried to convince international donor agencies and investors to inject much needed capital into the ailing economies. They installed their regimes through a combination of strategies, including the often ruthless suppression of left-wing forces and the demobilisation of politically activated popular classes, including the peasantry and labour. They introduced exclusionary-corporatist institutions as an integral part of their de-politicisation campaigns, to serve as structural barriers against any future re-activation of the left and opposition. In particular, Stepan argues, in response to the breakdown of previous patterns of domination, these regimes drew on so-called 'organicist' principles—postulating an organic unity between state and society—with which to construct new legitimacy formulas.[27] They did this both in rejection of liberal ideas of procedural democracy and competition and Marxist notions of class conflict, and in support of the new mode of domination.[28] In the transformation to exclusionary arrangements in non-communist countries, the 'communist threat', the need to eradicate 'subversion', and to create national security and stability, were the most common rationales given for the installation of the new, anti-communist, military-technocratic regime.[29]

It appears, however, that the presence of inclusionary and exclusionary subtypes of corporatism is not necessarily dependent on authoritarian regime types, and elements of these subtypes can be found at different stages of political development and appear in varying order. One reason for this is that regimes seeking renewal alternate between different policy instruments, with inclusionary mechanisms sometimes being engaged when exclusionary ones lose efficacy and the ruling elite decides to incorporate new social groups in support of the regime.[30]

Pluralist Challenges to State Corporatism

As the last points suggest, state–society interactions tend to be fluid, with regime leaders needing to readjust management strategies vis-à-vis other social organisations in order to adapt successfully to changing social reality. In Migdal's terms, state and society transform one another as different segments of state and society interact in multiple arenas of struggle and accommodation.[31] Components of the state may successfully capture parts of society or segments of society might, alternatively, capture parts of the state as different social organisations interpenetrate one another. Typically, state corporatism is established in order to maximise state autonomy from society and minimise penetration of key state agencies by other social organisations. However, given the fluidity and complexity of social relations, the question arises as to how long regime leaders can maintain state corporatist strategies of capture or under what specific circumstances state corporatism might disappear.

Thus, a central issue for consideration is tensions that occur in the relationship between the inhibiting state corporatist structures and the pluralist tendencies in a given society. Authoritarian regimes, by definition, permit (or tolerate) islands of pluralism that are not directly linked to, or regulated by, the corporatist framework. Schmitter observes that 'interest inter-mediation systems', within a single polity, can have 'legal heterogeneity', with regimes 'regularly' enforcing 'discriminatory norms' upon different group interests, affecting their freedom to associate. The regime tolerates, and sometimes encourages, the 'spontaneous and autonomous collective action for some groups, while repressing, co-opting, or channelling it for others'. For example, labour unions might be repressed and channelled. Meanwhile, business and entrepreneurial associations might be allowed a high degree of autonomy and self-regulation. Similarly, single target constituencies might be subject to varying degrees of regulation and autonomy with, for instance, some parts of a religious establishment finding themselves subject to tight regulation, and other sections seemingly escaping, or resisting, the purview of the state. State corporatist (re)structuring can be characterised as one of a shifting relationship in which the state seeks to extend its control over society, through its increasing capture of independent organisational bases. Meanwhile some segments of society develop strategies to evade capture, and/or exist on a continuum of unincorporated, partially co-opted, to more fully co-opted categories. Possible tensions can arise from this associational heterogeneity, and particularly arise from two main distorting tendencies of corporatism, which are located at its inclusionary and exclusionary poles.

To begin with, at its inclusionary pole, if corporatism becomes too incorporative, competing interests can use their acquired positions in the state structure to increase their demands on the state. Bianchi, in his study of corporatism in Egypt, and Ding, in his examination of China, contend that the risk is that incorporated interests can extend their influence and veto powers over state policy, as well as hijack the policy goals of their intended incorporation and supplant them with their own 'private' objectives.[33] In this way, the growing intrusion and penetration of 'external' interests threaten the autonomy of the state and its leaders. As occurs with authoritarian populist regimes, the state is rendered less able to mediate the conflicting interest demands and is confronted with erosion of its institutional integrity by the diffusion of multiple interests within the state. Ding calls this phenomenon 'institutional parasitism'. He records how a 'counter-elite' of intelligentsia—incorporated perhaps, but by no means co-opted into the state's institutional structures—attacked the policy goals, power relations, and institutional apparatus of the communist state from within the state.[34] Corporatism, which over incorporates, or is too inclusionary, can behave in a similar manner to Ding's 'institutional parasitism'.

Schmitter identifies a similar problem confronted by societal corporatism. He argues that incorporated interests tend to call for much greater participation than permitted by the established arrangements, as these arrangements are revealed as providing only 'pseudo-participatory' mechanisms. Inclusionary arrangements are 'bombarded with demands for more direct and authentic forms of participation, undermining both the stability of their established internal hierarchies of authority and their claim to democratic legitimacy'.[35]

Regime leaders can react to 'institutional parasitism', and to pressures for participation, by seeking to maintain an 'imbalance' of forces between dominant, aspiring elites, and the subordinate excluded forces. Regime leaders play off against one another corporatised and pluralist interests in an eminently divide-and-rule strategy. Bianchi argues that heterogeneous systems of 'representation', which combine corporatist and pluralist components, in fact, can provide authoritarian leaders with a more flexible mixture of strategies. It offers them adaptability in dealing with interest demands in a manner that will help preserve the power and autonomy of the state. Regime leaders can stimulate antagonistic contests between corporatised and pluralist sectors by an adjustable range of incentives and disincentives that will alternately favour one sectional interest over the other.[36] The incentives could be in terms of providing or denying legal scope for an organisation's activities. They might include giving unequal access to economic and political resources, such as promotion to higher office and status, access to patronage and economic opportunities, furnishing of contracts and licenses, and the like. Legal recognition and access might be conditioned by the extent to which either of the contending interests demonstrates loyalties to the ruling elite, provides useful services, complies to state directives, and/or threatens the autonomy and interests of the state leaders.[37]

Thus, Bianchi contends, 'pluralism' (non-incorporation) can 'serve as a form of punishment for group leaders who refuse to collaborate in state-controlled corporatist arrangements and as a vivid reminder of the marginal, precarious, and impotent roles awaiting collaborators who might try to exploit the privileges of corporatism in an independent manner'. This might include regime leaders choosing to expel, or marginalise, to paraphrase Bianchi, those over ambitious 'allies' who, through their incorporation, aspire to becoming 'full coalition partners'.[38] Regime leaders therefore exploit heterogeneous interest systems as a way of ensuring a permanent, but shifting, asymmetry of contending classes and group interests (both state and non-state).

In the long term, however, such a strategy is limited in its utility. On the one hand, according to Bianchi, this kind of facilitation of controlled competition can get out of hand. State offers of special treatment and concessions to one associational constituency generates resentment among the neglected groups, which then organise to demand greater participation (inclusion) in the public decision-making processes and power-sharing arrangements. This results in a tendency for contending interests to vie for political predominance, which, in turn, can trigger a 'chain reaction' of organisation and counter-organisation of differentially affected group interests (especially between pluralist and corporatist ones).[39]

On the other, at its exclusionary pole, corporatism tends to alienate broad classes and categories of people. These classes have no strong attachments or commitment to the established institutional arrangements or official ideologies, and therefore eventually organise outside of the formal political system and mobilise independently against it. One consequence of state policies of exclusion, in fact, is the creation of significant islands of unmediated, unincorporated, and therefore, relatively autonomous activity. Once the resentment and disaffection of broad sections of society finds common cause, either through unforeseen triggering events, or through cumulative processes that engender extended group awareness and shared goals, the isolated islands of autonomous activity can crystallise into co-ordinated group actions. The actions tend to focus on the deep structural inequalities caused by policies of exclusion and the attendant maldistribution of political and economic resources. They often call for an end to the established political and economic order and its incumbents in power.[40]

In a nutshell, the highly discriminatory and exclusionary structures of the state engender different levels of disaffection with the political status quo, and eventually bring pluralist societal forces into conflict with the established and corporatised forces of the authoritarian state.

Scholarship on regime transitions has sought to explain the phenomenon of expanding pluralism in authoritarian polities, and the attendant trend away from undemocratic systems of governance to more democratic-pluralist ones during the late twentieth century. There are divergent approaches to the subject, with different explanations, but also a significant degree of overlap, about how this pluralism came about and impacted on authoritarian structures. One line of argument, with Huntington's book 'The Third Wave: Democratization'[41] making an important contribution, and including authors like Diamond, Lipset, Linz, Pei, Ethier, Chazan and Shue, maintains that socioeconomic development and market forces in much of the Third World were responsible for the rapid expansion of civil associations and interest groups in those societies.[42]

The increasing complexity and diversification of a national economy, set within the specific context of a deregulated global economy, produces pressures for market reforms domestically. The introduction of outward-oriented market reforms, often in response to economic crisis, accelerates the overall process of interdependence and interrelation between local and global economies. Sustained market forces depend on devolution of economic decision-making and generate new, expanding sources of non-governmental power and wealth outside the direct regulatory control of the state. Greater resources are made available for distribution throughout society resulting in major gains for private interests vis-à-vis the state. With a significant gain in resources come commensurate political leverage and influence and 'countervailing capabilities' of society against the state. Sustained industrialisation, accelerated market forces, intensification of inequalities, and economic crisis, especially if occurring simultaneously, serve to raise the political consciousness of broad sections of society. It stimulates their mobilisation into politics as social groups increase their demands on government for social justice and participation. The expanding pluralism and associated demands tend to cause a power shift in the upper levels of society and requires a renegotiation of social relations to meet the more complex social realities.[43]

Although not disagreeing with 'transition' literature concerning the link between the existence of vigorous civil association and democracy, Schmitter argues that 'transition from authoritarian rule is clearly not merely a matter of economic development or societal complexity, as earlier literature on the "social requisites of democracy" put it'.

> What is relevant to an understanding of these differences [between different countries] are the obscure historical conditions that have given rise to independent territorial communities, especially towns and cities, and to distinctive functional identities, especially of social classes, economic sectors, and professions. Ethnic and linguistic groups, religions and sects, voluntary associations and social service organizations, gender and generational groupings have also prominently contributed to the institutionalized social pluralism that supports a strong civil society.[44]

According to this line of argument, a country with a strong history of civil associations independent of the state, which has subsequently come under authoritarian rule, stands a much better chance of democratising than do countries lacking viable civil associations.[45] (However, a word of caution is in order, as vigorous civil society might be a pre-requisite of functioning democracy but not a sufficient condition. Functioning and stable political institutions [legislatures, the judiciary, and political parties] need to link civil society to the state and competition needs to be institutionalised, as well as involve moderation, compromise and widespread respect for civil liberties and human rights.)

Other scholars give an additional explanation of growing pluralism in authoritarian polities. Hoogvelt argues that people's experience with the structures of political exclusion and poverty, combined with structural adjustment programs (economic reform), sparked urban movements and militant protest actions against social injustice and authoritarianism. In particular, regime-led economic reform made under structural adjustment agreements with international funding agencies caused an upsurge in associational activism in developing societies, as urban populations were deprived of state support, urban services, and subsidies.[46] Chazan argues in the case of many countries in Africa that there was a growing diversity of associational activism since the adoption of structural adjustment.[47] In their study of China, Unger and Chan note that economic reform policies 'jeopardised' workers' benefits and led to organised worker resistance and militant actions by the 1990s.[48]

Thus, middle-class and entrepreneurial elements of society, and to some extent labour, increasingly conduct their activities outside the tutelage of the existing corporatist structures, which originally were instituted to contain societal pluralism, and they compete with, and exploit, the weaknesses of the authoritarian institutions.[49] With respect to labour, regimes that initiate reforms commonly devolve authority within the centralised corporatist structures to local-level organisations, partly in response to new economic imperatives and partly in response to an upsurge in complaints against the unrepresentative arrangements. Whereas the goal of the regime invariably is to extend its corporatist net over social organisation by becoming, or appearing, more responsive to target constituencies, relaxation of controls tended to have the opposite effect. Chazan notes that in Africa 'specific groups carved out their own spheres of autonomous action…[and] several officially controlled social institutions detached themselves from state control'.[50] Unger and Chan argue that, as China's central leadership gradually devolved authority to the regions, corporatist arrangements showed signs of shifting from state to societal corporatism. They began to parcel out into more numerous, semi-independent entities and reflect the concerns and demands of their designated membership. In particular, during the mid-1990s, 'local union branches broke loose of central control and led strikes'.[51] Overall, the different studies addressing regime transition indicate that, whereas in the 1960s and 1970s central state (corporatist) controls stunted the development of autonomous associational life, increasing associational capacity during the 1980s and 1990s was undermining authoritarianism and state corporatist structures in many developing countries.

Scholars have given different weight to factors responsible for transitions such as economic liberalisation, crisis, intra-elite rivalry, political reform, social mobilisation, and foreign intervention. There is also debate on the prospect of democracy deepening, consolidating and/or suffering reversal in former non-democracies.[52] Nonetheless, there is considerable agreement on certain empirically observable phenomena. First, economic liberalisation typically is followed by the introduction of some civil liberties and (if somewhat limited) renegotiation of social relations between components of state and society. Second, economic liberalisation acts to politicise state–society linkages and produces pressures for political reform or political openings. Increasing internal complexity of the state affects the state's organisational integrity, especially as the state undergoes a 'pluralisation of departmental perspectives' and 'rivalries'. Correspondingly, regimes often experience internal division, or rupture of consensus, among the top leadership and its key supporters concerning the policy orientation and power-sharing arrangements of the regime. At the same time, there occurs mounting pressure for change from below.[53] According to Huntington, liberal reformers seek to defuse the growing opposition to the regime by introducing minor changes, as they want to 'create a kinder, gentler, more secure and stable authoritarianism without altering fundamentally the nature of the system'.[54] These changes can include a loosening of repression, introduction of some civil liberties, greater toleration of criticism and public debate, reduction of censorship, and allowing civil society greater scope to conduct its affairs.[55]

Third, if industrialisation and market processes produce latent social forces that progressively impinge on the political process and challenge state autonomy, political reform unleashes those forces at an accelerating speed. Initial political openings, as a side effect, produce escalating levels of social-political mobilisation. This is largely because:

1) The lifting of controls provides opportunities for opposition groups to exploit, and within which to operate and grow in organisational size, autonomy and strength, as they begin to test the limits of regime toleration of their activities.

2) Decline in repression results in a widespread loss of fear on the part of society, and a consequent preparedness to intensify demands on the system, and mobilise against it if those demands are not met, at the risk of persecution of its individual members.

3) Limited reforms raise considerably people's expectations that more, far-reaching liberalisation will be forthcoming, as well as increase aspirations for a fuller inclusion into a re-fashioned, or new, political system.[56]

Pei argues that, with few exceptions (e.g., the Meiji Restoration, Bismark's Germany, Attaturk's modernising reforms), authoritarian rulers lose control of the regime-initiated reforms. The institutions of authoritarianism suffer decay, because they no longer are able to absorb, co-opt, channel, counter, or neutralise the diversifying demands and challenges of society.[57] On the other hand, Ethier contends that an absence of compromise on, or commitment to, reform on the part of the regime and interest groups can result in only provisional and arbitrary reforms, which can be 'annulled at any time by the regime'.[58] Huntington also argues that rising expectations for further change can lead to 'instability, upheaval, and even violence; [which] in turn, could provoke an antidemocratic reaction and replacement of the liberalising leadership'.[59]

Moreover, the ability of society based movements to dictate, or significantly influence, political developments in the transition process depends on various factors. These factors, together, constitute the strengths and weaknesses of social opposition groups relative to state resources and power. Such factors, writes Pei, include the organisational size, strength, autonomy, and value orientations of societal interests that constitute an opposition force. Autonomy is gauged in terms of a social group's capacity to undertake independent collective actions, in pressing its demands on the state, and to resist total 'assimilation or co-optation' into the official (corporatist) structures and value orientations. A measure of a group's strength, among other things, is its 'membership size, organisational and entrepreneurial capacity, and access to political and economic resources'—which includes its influence in the mass media. Value orientations refer to the commitment of a group to principles of participation and democracy, in contrast, for instance, to those groups that give priority to legitimate governmental order at the expense of such principles.[60]

According to Pei, important to societal activation is the initial size and arena of reform. In particular, 'the size of the opening matters less than the arena of the opening...a relatively small or weak opening in a significant or strategic area [e.g., NGOs, the Press, Labour] may unleash, after a short period, enormous amounts of stored energy in that particular area'. Liberal elements capture significant parts of the Press, NGO advocates and student dissidents are emboldened to take up the cause of labour and exploited classes, and independent labour unions begin to flourish and organise industrial actions. What begin as specific demands, reflecting local grievances for improvement in welfare provisions, land and labour rights, and better wages and working conditions broaden out into larger-scale democracy movements calling for an end to oppressive authoritarian rule.

These emerging cells of civil society grow into a torrent of opposition coalitions that can coalesce into a major movement. Members of the intelligentsia, student activists, NGO advocates, and anti-regime dissidents start to identify with each other's causes and build cross-class, cross-sectional linkages that serve to undermine the hierarchical ordering of state corporatist structures. However, the dismantling of exclusionary corporatist institutions does not necessarily result in their replacement with viable democratic institutions. If a new regime succeeds in replacing the old authoritarian regime, it still needs to build a new linkage system between state and society; one that will open new channels of participation to those groups seeking or demanding inclusion in the political system without undermining the system's stability.

There is no logical point at which we should end analysis and review of literature and there is much that can be added about regime transitions towards more democratic-pluralist political systems. However, the main purpose of the discussion concerning transitions is to provide some background observations to subsequent analysis in chapters. This discussion now turns to chapter three and a consideration of how the Suharto regime implemented state corporatist arrangements and strategies.

NOTES

1. Migdal, 'The State in Society', p.11; Ruechmeyer and Evans, 'The State and Economic Transformation', quoted in Migdal, pp.46–7.
2. Kohli and Shue, 'State Power and Social Forces', p.294; Migdal, 'Why Do So Many States?', pp.19–35; Nordlinger, 'Taking the State Seriously', pp.353–98.
3. Migdal, 'The State in Society', pp.8–9; Chazan, 'Engaging the State', pp.256–7.
4. Diamond et al., 'Introduction: Comparing Experiences', pp.21–2.
5. Dauvergne, 'Weak States', pp.1–9; Migdal, 'Strong States', pp.391–430; Crouch, 'Indonesia's "Strong" State', pp.93–110.
6. Diamond, 'Beyond Authoritarianism', pp.143–7; Diamond et al., 'Introduction: Comparing Experiences', pp.10–14; Linz, 'An Authoritarian Regime'.
7. Schmitter, 'Still the Century of Corporatism?', pp.86–103.
8. Schmitter, 'Still the Century of Corporatism?', pp.93–104; Williamson, *Varieties of Corporatism*, pp.8–23: O'Donnell, 'Corporatism', p.49.
9. Chalmers, 'Corporatism', pp.67–8.
10. Williamson, *Varieties of Corporatism*, p.16.
11. Schmitter, 'Still the Century of Corporatism?', pp.104–5.
12. O'Donnell, 'Corporatism', p.48.
13. Williamson, *Varieties of Corporatism*.
14. O'Donnell, 'Corporatism', p.48.
15. Williamson, *Varieties of Corporatism*, pp.22–9; Schmitter, 'Still the Century of Corporatism?', pp.105–26.
16. O'Donnell, 'Corporatism', pp.48–65; Schmitter, 'Still the Century of Corporatism?', pp.105–24; Williamson, *Varieties of Corporatism*.
17. Baretta and Douglas, 'Authoritarianism', p.522.
18. Schmitter, 'Still the Century of Corporatism?', p.124.
19. Bretta and Douglas, 'Authoritarianism', pp.520–1.
20. Stepan, *The State and Society*, pp.74–82; O'Donnell, *Modernization*.

21. Schmitter, 'Southern European Transitions', p.4; Giner, 'Political Economy'.
22. O'Donnell, *Modernization*; Bianchi, *Unruly Corporatism*; Unger and Chan, 'Corporatism in China'; Shue, 'State Power and Social Organization'; Chazan, 'Engaging the State'.
23. Stepan, *The State and Society*; O'Donnell, *Modernization*.
24. Huntington, *The Third Wave*.
25. O'Donnell, 'Corporatism'; Stephn, *The State and Society*; Malloy, 'Authoritarianism', pp.464–81; Collier and Collier, 'Who Does What', pp.503–4.
26. Stepan, *The State and Society*, p.79.
27. See chapter three for an explanation of 'organicist' principles.
28. Stepan, *The State and Society*, p.58.
29. Hadiz, *Workers and the State*, pp.26–32; O'Donnell, 'Corporatism', p.57.
30. Bianchi, *Unruly Corporatism*; MacIntyre, 'Organising Interests', pp.12–18; Hadiz, 'Challenging State Corporatism', pp.198–200.
31. Midgal, 'The State in Society', pp.7–29.
32. Schmitter, 'Modes of Interest Intermediation', p.69.
33. Bianchi, *Unruly Corporatism*, pp.24–57; Ding, *The Decline of Communism*, pp.30–1.
34. Ding, *The Decline of Communism*, pp.22–31
35. Schmitter, 'Still the Century of Corporatism?', p.127.
36. Bianchi, *Unruly Corporatism*, pp.21–4.
37. Chalmers notes that in 'Latin America and elsewhere in the Third-World...the military could claim that their unequal treatment of various groups in society was to correct the imbalances of the prior regime. In other words, the contrast in treatment accorded different segments of the population under corporatism is not only possible, but expected'. Chalmers, 'Corporatism', p.63.
38. Bianchi's usage of 'pluralism' can be misleading in this context and perhaps too loosely applied. I understand him to actually mean that the regime can deliberately exclude groups from incorporation in the existing state arrangements and thereby deny them access to state facilities and patronage. These groups then constitute part of an under-organised and relatively impotent associational pluralism. 'Non-incorporation' or 'exclusion' might have been more appropriate words to use than pluralism in this context. Bianchi, *Unruly Corporatism*, p.24.
39. Bianchi, *Unruly Corporatism*, p.21.
40. Stepan, *The State and Society*, pp.43–81; Bianchi, *Unruly Corporatism*, pp.12–25; Hoogvelt, *Globalization*, pp.233–4; Pei, *From Reform to Revolution*, pp.54–6.
41. Huntington, *The Third Wave*.

42. The underlying assumption is that modernisation, with significant levels of industrialisation and economic development, creates new pluralist and autonomous forces within an increasingly complex, differentiated, and competitive society. Society's standards of living rise dramatically, as do literacy rates, education, and urbanisation. The middle-class sections of society expand, the working class becomes more combative, and new social groups and organisations emerge. Diamond et.al, 'Introduction: Comparing Experiences', pp.18–23; Pei, *From Reform to revolution*, pp.1–58; Ethier, 'Processes of Transition', pp.10–18; Chazan, 'Engaging the State', pp.272–6; Shue, 'State Power and Social Organization', pp. 74–83.

43. Diamond, 'Beyond Authoritarianism', pp.146–9; Diamond et al., 'Comparing Experiences', p.19; Huntington, *The Third Wave*, pp.59–72; Pei, *From Reform to Revolution*, pp.42–60; Ethier, 'Processes of Transition', pp.10–18; Chazan, 'Engaging the State', pp.272–6; Shue, 'State Power and Social Organization', pp.82–5.

44. Schmitter, 'Southern European Transitions', p.6.

45. Recent literature on regime transitions, largely, is in agreement with Schmitter's point, as this literature takes into account the specific configuration of civil societies and state in the countries under study. Diamond, *Developing Democracy*; Huntington, *The Third Wave*; Pei, *From Reform to Revolution*; Shue, 'State Power and Social organization'; Chazan, 'Engaging the State'.

46. Hoogvelt, *Globalization*, pp.229–34.

47. Chazan, 'Engaging the State', pp.272–3.

48. Unger and Chan, 'Corporatism in China', pp.121–2.

49. Pei, *From Reform to Revolution*, p.49.

50. Chazan, 'Engaging the State', p.274.

51. Unger and Chan, 'Corporatism in China', p.122.

52. Diamond, *Developing Democracy*; Ethier, 'Processes of Transition'; Pei, *From Reform to Revolution*; Hoogvelt, *Globalization*; O'Donnell and Schmitter, *Transitions from Authoritarian Rule*; Chazan, 'Engaging the State'; Shue, 'State Power and Social Organization'; Acharya, 'Southeast Asia's Democratic Moment'; Huntington, *The Third Wave*.

53. Huntington, *The Third Wave*, p.122; O'Donnell and Schmitter, *Transitions from Authoritarian Rule*; Pei, *From Reform to Revolution*, p.71; Ethier, 'Processes of Transition'; Migdal, 'Why Do So Many States?', p.19.

54. Huntington, *The Third Wave*, p.129.

55. Huntington, *The Third Wave*, p.129.

56. Huntington, *The Third Wave*, pp.134–6; Pei, *From Reform to Revolution*, pp.21–55; Ethier, 'Processes of Transition', pp.7–8.

57. Pei, *From Reform to Revolution*, pp.50–51.

58. Ethier, 'Processes of Transition', p.12.

59. Huntington, *The Third Wave*, p.134.

60. Pei, *From Reform to Revolution*, pp.54–6.
61. Pei, *From Reform to Revolution*, p.53.

Chapter 3

State Corporatism and Indonesia under Suharto

ESTABLISHING A CORPORATIST FRAMEWORK IN INDONESIA

Several scholars have applied corporatist frameworks to their analyses of Indonesian politics. What follows are a review of this literature and an explanation of state corporatist organisation, with emphasis on its development under the New Order regime of President Suharto.

Reeve, in his book entitled 'Golkar of Indonesia: An Alternative To The Party System', has made a major contribution to scholarly understanding about the development of non-party, functional group representation in Indonesia.[1] Reeve has shown how Indonesia's first president, Sukarno, motivated by his vision for a one-party state, and by the need to create a broad base of support with which to underwrite his executive control over a newly defined political system, promoted functional group representation as an alternative to party based democracy.[2] From 1956–1959, Sukarno promoted the idea of establishing a 'guided democracy', which, in one formulation was to include a national front as a co-ordinating body for functional groups under his leadership. The thinking behind functional groups was that all groups and interests that comprised the nation would be incorporated and linked to the state according to the function and/or profession they performed. A major part of Sukarno's strategy entailed coaxing voluntary mass organisations (*ormas*) to sever their ties with their mother parties and to enter the parliament and other institutions as members of functional groups. Together with regional and other non-party professional categories, the *ormas* would be drawn into a single national party or council based on common 'functional' interest. On 5 July 1959, Sukarno introduced by presidential decree an authoritarian order called 'Guided Democracy', which formalised greater presidential power and reduced to ten the number of political parties.[3]

In the late 1950s, army leaders began to form their own functional groups in rivalry with Sukarno. From 1957 to 1959, they established a number of co-operation-bodies (BKS) with the aim of de-linking mass organisations from

24

affiliation with the political parties and bringing them under army control.[4] In 1964, they brought the various BKSs into a Joint Secretariat of Functional Groups (Sekber Golkar), which was primarily intended as an anti-communist/ anti-labour front and as a mechanism to assist the army integrate into the political structure.[5] The leaders pursued strategies of counter-mobilisation against the left, as well as the demobilisation of labour in contrast to Sukarno's populist mobilisations.

The installation of Suharto's military-backed New Order regime exhibited many of the features attributed to countries undergoing a change of regime-type from authoritarian populist to bureaucratic-authoritarian regime.[6] After an abortive coup of 1965, which Suharto blamed on the communists, the army ruthlessly eliminated its main rival, PKI, in a bloody massacre followed by a counter coup. The army moved against Sukarno and his radical nationalist supporters, and purged the civil service, military, and political institutions of 'old order' forces. The army leadership transformed Golkar in accordance with its new strategy to demobilise and pre-empt the re-emergence of autonomous political organisation and left-wing movements that Sukarno had activated during the previous populist phase. Their exclusionary strategies created a de-politicised environment to help prepare the ground for accelerated economic development.[7]

Ward, Emmerson, Suryadinata and others have shown how the Suharto regime re-fashioned Golkar into the regime's electoral machine and, together with the introduction of new election and party laws, vote rigging, and manipulations ensured that it would achieve landslide victories at general elections. Ali Murtopo (a military officer), a close adviser to Suharto and member of the president's personal staff (SPRI), was the main strategist who developed Golkar's election strategy and the corporatist framework. Murtopo exerted considerable influence from the mid-1960s to the late-1970s, after which his political fortunes declined. He had worked under Suharto's command during the West Irian campaign as a member of Special Operations (OPSUS, an informal intelligence section of the Army Strategic Reserve, Kostrad). He used OPSUS as a base for conducting his election strategy and Golkar interventions, and established the General Election Controlling Body (Bapilu) as his main vehicle for managing the general election of 1971. The Intelligence Coordinating Agency (BAKIN) was also a power base for Murtopo.[8]

Ward describes how Murtopo gathered around himself intelligence personnel and a number of modernising intellectuals and technocrats, including Catholics, intellectuals from Gadja Madah University in Yogyakarta (Central Java), and a group of intellectuals from Bandung (West Java). In 1971, the Murtopo group established the largely Chinese-Catholic run think-tank, the Centre for Strategic and International Studies (CSIS). Together these modernisers elaborated upon an OPSUS-led scheme of political restructuring with which to underwrite programs for economic development. Part of their strategy included obtaining a clear victory for Golkar at the first general election of 1971 so that Golkar could then implement the planned institutional reconstruction.[9]

Emmerson illustrates how the Minister of Internal Affairs, Amir Machmud (also a military general) implemented the Golkar strategy, beginning within his own department, as part of a broader effort to eliminate party influence from the government bureaucracy. The aim was to create a new cadre of de-politicised civil servants and to imbue them with internal discipline and undivided loyalty to a centralised chain of command, presided over by President Suharto (the supreme commander of the armed forces). In line with the Golkar strategy, Machmud required staff at the Ministry to join a Corps of Functionaries for the Ministry (Korps Karyawan Menteri Dalam Negeri, Kokarmendagri), or face the threat of dismissal.[10]

During the 1971 election campaign, Ali Murtopo organised rival Korps Karyawan (Kokar) in governmental departments, ministries and institutions and, after the election, they were fused into a single organisation, the Corps of Civil Servants of the Republic of Indonesia, Korpri. Machmud issued Governmental Regulation (PP No.6/1970), requiring civil servants to swear their sole allegiance ('mono-loyalty') to the government and cut their ties with the political parties. In practice, at general elections, civil servants were organised into voting for Golkar, and faced dismissal if they refused to comply.[11]

The Korpri strategy undermined the strength of some of the political parties and the trade unions, by depriving them of substantial bases of support. For example, the Indonesian National Party (PNI) had drawn much of its support from the bureaucracy, and the Islamic party, Nahdlatul Ulama (Awakening of Religious Scholars), had entrenched itself in the Department of Religion. Under the new provisions, independent trade unions also were refused access to Korpri members, and therefore were greatly weakened. In reality, however, state leaders were unable to enforce rigidly mono-loyalty provisions, as some government employees (especially from the Department of Religion) continued to vote for the parties.[12]

The Korpri initiative was part of a wider strategy of the 'Big Golkar Family (Golkar, Korpri, and ABRI)', to enable the military and the bureaucracy to penetrate all levels of Indonesian society from the national level downward to the province, district, sub-district and village levels. This coincided with greater military intrusion into the government bureaucracy, with military officers holding civilian office as governors, and district heads. These officials were charged with bringing about a Golkar victory at local and national elections. Before the 1982 election, village chiefs became Korpri members under a new regulation, which effectively linked village headmen to the national government and helped facilitate the mobilisation of rural populations behind Golkar.[13]

Complementing this militarisation and Golkarisation of state and society, was the introduction of the 'floating mass' concept in 1971, whereby the political parties were denied access to their traditional constituencies below the district level. Golkar established non-party functional and professional organisations with which to re-channel the interests of the rural population.

Between 1973 and 1974, the government required various professional and community organisations to merge into state-dominated, non-competitive national peak organisations (*wadah tunggal*) to represent the respective community interests in relation to the state. For instance, the army-controlled Central Coordinating Body for Farmers' Mass Organisations (BKS Tani) was transformed into a more centralised and unified Indonesian Farmers' Harmony Association (HKTI) and six fishermen's organisations were amalgamated into the All-Indonesian Fishermen's Association (HNSI). After several trial attempts, the All-Indonesian Federation of Labourers (FBSI) was established as the sole association for the labour movement. In 1985, FBSI was transformed into a more centralised and monolithic organisation called the All-Indonesian Workers' Association (SPSI). The state gave license to a re-defined Congress of Indonesian Women (KOWANI) and a re-defined Teachers' Union of the Republic of Indonesia (PGRI).[14]

The functional groups system gave the government bureaucracy the means to by-pass the political parties and make direct links with society. Antlov, Cederoth and Sullivan argue that in reality there was a sharp discontinuity between the peak organisations and rural communities, which were organised into a plethora of village-level cooperative and vigilance bodies along quasi-military lines. Instead of having their interests channelled upward through these functional institutions, rural communities were shut-off from national politics and decision-making above the sub-district level. Instead, the functional institutions acted as mechanisms for sending state directives downward, and for managing and supervising lower-level social activities.[15]

Suharto's regime sought to contain the political parties within the corporatist framework, resulting in the law on party simplification of 1973, wherein the existing nine political parties were forced to merge into two state-sponsored parties. Four Muslim parties joined a new amalgam, the United Development Party (PPP) and two nationalist, two Christian, and a 'socialist' party entered the Indonesian Democracy Party (PDI). PPP and PDI were the only two parties officially permitted to contest the five-yearly general elections against the much stronger Golkar machine. Ward, Liddle and Suryadinata have demonstrated that military and bureaucratic backing of Golkar, interventions in party leaderships, security vetting of party candidates, election fraud, vote-buying and intimidation all helped ensure that Golkar obtained landslide victories at the polls and that the parties remained fragmented and weak.[16]

The general elections aimed to garner for the New Order rulers a modicum of legitimacy, and Golkar's dominance was seen as a test of Suharto's ability to impose his will on the political system. One year after each general election, a People's Consultative Assembly (MPR) would convene to 'elect' the president and vice president and decide on the broad outlines of state policy (GBHN) for the next five-year term. The initial composition of the MPR was 920 members, consisting of the 460 members of the DPR (People's Representative Council) and 460 appointees (including a quota of regional, special and functional representatives). At that time, the DPR comprised of 360 elected members from

Golkar and the parties in accordance with their share of the votes at general elections, seventy-five ABRI appointees, and twenty-five *karyawan* (civilian) appointees. In 1984, the membership of the MPR inceased to 1000 and the DPR to 500, with ABRI increasing its seats to one hundred in both. Overwhelming victories for Golkar at elections, and the system of appointees, many of them handpicked by the president, ensured that the MPR remained stacked in favour of the New Order rulers and the legislative bodies behaved as rubber stamp institutions for the passing of laws. It also guaranteed President Suharto's unchallenged re-election to the country's top job every five years.[17]

The development of a corporatist framework overseen by Golkar occurred over a protracted period, as these institutions experienced repeated reorganisations, which were directed toward achieving more monolithic structures under the centralising control of the state.[18] Suharto retained control of Golkar and progressively offset the military's influence within it. For example, at Golkar's second national congress in October 1978, he became chairman of the supervisors' council, and active military officers were no longer permitted to hold office in Golkar. At the third national congress in October 1983, the supervisors' council became the supreme council with veto rights over the policies and decisions of the central executive board, the right to freeze the board, and the right to appoint leaders of other boards. Sudharmono (a close confidant of Suharto and Secretary of State) became chairman of the organisation. He presided over a new strategy for Golkar based on supplementing indirect membership through affiliate (functional) organisations of Golkar with the registration of individual membership. The aim of the strategy was to build a cadre party with a mass membership as a support base for Suharto. Golkar began to look like a ruling party, with the injection of a greater civilian membership.[19]

Robison argues that Golkar's transformation, which was well in process by the fourth national congress in 1988, was part of a strategy to shift 'the nature of state corporatism from one dominated by the officials and institutions of the state to one dominated by new social groups',[20] represented by Suharto's family. The intention was that the military and civilian bureaucracies were to become subservient primarily to the family interests of Suharto and a new oligarchy within the reorganised structures. In the face of Suharto's declining support from the military, another objective was to recruit strategic members of the rising middle classes into the regime and convince them that the existing corporatist structures served their career ambitions and interests.

However, Golkar never attained the status of a mass-based party and its aggressive recruitment of party cadres fell well short of projected targets.[21] At Golkar's fifth national congress in 1993, Suharto replaced some military leaders in Golkar with civilian figures, with a compliant Harmoko becoming the first civilian chairman of Golkar. Another civilian leader, and Suharto protégé, the Minister of Science and Technology, B.J. Habibie, headed a seven-person committee of formateurs, which was responsible for selecting the new Golkar chairman and its executive board.[22]

Robison explains that an important aspect of the new arrangements was that state-sponsored mass organisations, such as the youth fronts KNPI (National Committee of Indonesian Youth) and AMPI (Indonesian Development Generation of Youth), as well as mass organisations outside of the state apparatus and functional groups were cultivated as support groups for Golkar. For example, two of Suharto's children, Siti Rukmana and Bambang Trihatmodjo, who held senior positions in Golkar, had their own supporting youth fronts.[23] Both the Golkar chairman and Siti Rukmana dispensed massive patronage to constituencies in the race for grassroots support. New regulations introduced in 1995 brought about regeneration within Golkar. Fealy notes that the regulations aimed to displace about 60 per cent of its older, long-serving Golkar members of the DPR with 'younger high-profile leaders from mass organisations who can maximise Golkar's appeal to the under-40s voters who constitute the majority of the electorate'.[24]

The changes to Golkar brought about not only a shift in the balance of power in favour of civilian family interests of Suharto and his close associates. It also created a ruling party that sought to draw upon increasingly heterogeneous sources of support that was, at face value, more inclusionary in nature and, to some extent, outside of the corporatist structures. MacIntyre argues that there would most likely occur a shift from the New Order's exclusionary corporatist framework to a more inclusionary one, rather than a shift to democracy, given the mounting pluralist pressures for change in the 1990s.[25] Nonetheless, under Suharto, Golkar continued to preside over a political system organised along exclusionary lines, which denied the right of Indonesians to organise independently and did not open new channels of participation in the formal political system. It appears that Suharto's strategy from the late-1980s until the late-1990s was directed towards securing his unchallenged dominance over the political system, and reducing the political influence of ABRI, rather than making Golkar more responsive to the grassroots. It was also a strategy directed towards absorbing and deflecting the growing demands within society for democratic participation and change, by co-opting strategic middle classes into existing political structures.

Studies by Hadiz, Lambert and others on the New Order regime's structuring of labour reinforce this general picture of corporatist organisation. Despite a short period in the early-to-mid-1990s of a relaxation of controls on labour and the introduction of some reforms, which devolved limited authority to industry sector unions, the overall corporatist structure remained exclusionary in nature.[26]

IDEOLOGICAL AND STRUCTURAL UNDERPINNINGS OF CORPORATISM IN INDONESIA

The State Philosophy of *Pancasila*

Bourchier illustrates how European-derived corporatist thought found its way to Indonesia. Mostly European-trained Indonesian law scholars adapted major strands of corporatist thought to local circumstances. Corporatist values of 'organic-statism' were written into Indonesia's Constitution of 1945 and found strong expression in the state philosophy of *Pancasila* (five principles). New Order strategists turned *Pancasila* into an 'ideological' project for the containment and exclusion of alternative ideologies deemed as threatening to the political fabric and stability of the nation. Communism, Islamic ideology, and liberalism were identified as antithetical to a collectivist ideal of organic-statism as contained in *Pancasila*, which was to provide a single political culture to underwrite the new corporatist arrangements. During the 1970s, state leaders introduced *Pancasila* Moral Education (PMP) and Guidelines for the Comprehension and Implementation of *Pancasila* (P4) indoctrination courses. Through these courses, the state leadership sought to instill in military personnel, civil servants, teachers, students and broader society the main values contained in the official political culture. The courses emphasised a so-called 'integralist' conception of state–societal relations that placed great emphasis on the family unit as the nucleus of paternalistically guided, hierarchically 'ordered' and 'harmonious' society. Like Stephn's 'organic-statism', integralism was a conception of state and society constituting an organic unity with the state having a strong role in establishing social order. The courses and 'integralism' stressed inter-connecting duties and obligations of citizens to their immediate family, which tied Indonesians in ever-wider concentric circles of allegiance and loyalty to the state, itself conceived as the larger family. The 'integralistic' conception of the state became an underlying functional logic of Golkar, and 'the whole idea of the collectivity of the nation' was 'expressed through functional groups' of the 'Big Golkar Family'.[28] These values were also a central part of European, Latin American, and East Asian corporatist thought.

In Indonesia, the state and society conceived as a family meant that there was little room for dissent. Dissent was seen, at best, as an act of disobedience of a naughty child deserving of punishment and scorn. At worst, dissent was viewed as subversion that required heavy stricture and removal from the family (imprisonment or worse). These organicist values were used as an instrument of ideological persuasion.[29] In the mid-1980s, the state mandated *Pancasila* as the sole ideological foundation of all organisational life in Indonesia, effectively prohibiting organisations from adhering to alternative ideologies in their party platforms and programs. *Pancasila* Industrial Relations (HIP) codified the ideal of harmonious relations between state, employer, and worker conceived as a mutually beneficial partnership in which all parties sought industrial peace and productivity. Workers' strikes were regarded as being in 'contradiction with the principles' governing HIP.[30] Both ABRI and Golkar became purveyors and defenders of state ideology and political culture.

The Armed Forces

This analysis would not be complete without examining the military institutions and doctrines that underwrote Indonesia's exclusionary social-political order after 1965. The armed forces (ABRI) and the Department of Defence and Security (Dephankam), developed a number of rationales and structures giving sanction to their expanding role in civilian affairs, some of them dating back to Sukarno's years. Although these rationales were developed outside of a corporatist framework, Dephankam brought some of them into Golkar, corporatist institutions and the broader community as it intensified its indoctrination of civilian society and militarisation of civilian institutions.

ABRI's propaganda machine constantly reminded Indonesians of the military's indispensable role as a saviour and creator of an independent Indonesia during the revolutionary struggle against the Dutch. ABRI claimed the right to a special role in civilian affairs based on this period as a people's army fighting guerrilla warfare and as the effective government in many parts of rural Java.[31] Army leaders developed a major doctrinal rationale for ABRI's role in civilian affairs called the 'dual function' or *dwi-fungsi* doctrine.[32] The doctrine encompassed a security and defence role as a military organisation and a 'social-political' role in ideological, political, social, economic, cultural and religious spheres of national life.

It was, however, through the development of an elaborate territorial command structure that the military exerted its pervasive influence on society. From 1958 to 1962, army leaders developed the doctrines of 'territorial warfare (*perang wilayah*)' and 'territorial management (*pembinaan wilayah*)' as a justification for its expanding role under martial law.[33] During the New Order period, the military extended this structure until its tentacles intruded into virtually all aspects of national life at the national, provincial, and district levels. The territorial structure paralleled the government bureaucracy and party apparatus at each administrative level, providing Indonesia with elaborate 'double government'. ABRI realised its role in civilian affairs as *kekaryaan* (functionaries), through membership of Golkar, and as seconded personnel to state enterprises and governmental positions as ministers, senior officials, governors, regents, and as members of the national and local legislatures.[34]

Social-political (sospol) staff sections were brought into the territorial structure at all levels from ABRI headquarters to military district commands to regulate and monitor the political activities of ABRI's seconded personnel and the public. Sospol staff collaborated closely with military intelligence agencies and with the social-political directorate of the Ministry of Internal Affairs, whose minister was appointed from the military, in providing political management and training for officers in parliamentary factions and to Golkar functionaries. They were responsible for political education/indoctrination of

31

the public and for monitoring and regulating the development of political parties and organisations. Heading the sospol staff was the Chief of Social-Political Staff (Kassospol), a key post in ABRI headquarters.[35] Clearly the security-intelligence apparatus underwrote Indonesia's political institutions.

The many, overlapping political, intelligence, military and *kekaryaan*—Golkar structures provided ABRI with far-reaching supervision over the ABRI leadership, the bureaucracy and society. The military's extensive apparatus of territorial management was quite clearly directed towards internal-security objectives of protecting Indonesia domestically from 'ever-present actual or latent' threats. The internal-security approach had as one of its central projects to root out competing 'antagonistic' ideologies, identified at different points during the New Order as 'individualism and liberalism', 'communism', and 'religious fanaticism'.[36] New Order leaders commonly mobilised its security and social-political apparatus against political agitators, dissenters, and pro-democracy movements and sought to discredit them by branding them as the 'extreme left', the 'extreme right', 'anti-government subversives', or some other underground dark forces. Thus, the spectre of constant threat served not only the regime's legitimacy purposes, but also justified a more active policy of discrediting and eliminating opposition. ABRI also recruited and organised civilian militia under the auspices of 'total people's defence' and civil defence (*pertahanan* sipil, Hansip).[37]

The term most commonly applied for military management and supervision of society, as developed in its territorial doctrines, was *pembinaan*. *Pembinaan* carries the meaning 'to construct' or 'to develop' and is particularly associated with the meaning to give paternal guidance to subordinates through instructions or directives. A high-ranking civil servant is a *pembina*, or one who gives guidance and directives. *Pembinaan* became associated closely with projects for ideological and institutional reconstruction and indoctrination of society. Ideological guidance (*pembinaan mental*) began as a project to rehabilitate communists, who had been incarcerated after 1965, and bring them back into mainstream political culture developed by the New Order. This terminology was then adapted to projects for the management and reconstruction of political party life. For example, in his book entitled 'Strategi Politik Nasional (National Political Strategy: 1973)', Ali Murtopo explained the two-fold political strategy for the management of party life and of broader society. The first was to re-educate Indonesians and re-orient parties' programs away from the ideological and political predilections of Sukarno's guided democracy period towards a new consciousness and 'professionalism through programs oriented to the government's economic development goals'.[38] The second was to construct new political arrangements, as discussed (above).

Implicit in these two aims was continued vigilance against, and eradication of, rival ideologies. Dephankam's terminology found its way into Golkar, with the supervisors' council (Dewan Pembina) first being dominated by Hankam men, and into the other corporatist institutions. Murtopo noted that ABRI, through its *kekaryaan* role and as a *pembina*, would provide ideological and political re-education to the Indonesian community to enable its, and ABRI's, full participation in development.[39] Thus, as a dominant member of Golkar, ABRI had brought into its *kekaryaan* role some of the ideological baggage of its territorial management doctrine. *Pembinaan* sections were established within each of the corporatist institutions linking them directly to relevant (*pembinaan*) secretariats within government departments, which performed supervisory roles over the organisations' programs and activities. It appears that one of the objectives of *pembinaan* was to facilitate the controlled mobilisation of citizens into the political system, in aid of official development programs and for specific political projects, such as state-sponsored denouncements of rival ideologies and political movements.[40]

CONCLUSION

Although regime leaders put in place an exclusionary corporatist framework, the institutions did more than just exclude. They became important mechanisms of state (military) management and supervision of society, instruments of ideological re-orientation, and vehicles for the controlled mobilisation of Indonesians into state-guided political and economic projects. The military also was the primary institution that developed an exclusionary political framework and elaborated supporting doctrines and mentalities of exclusion. These were in line with its perceived security role of defending the Indonesian state and its people from antagonistic elements and ideologies, and were part of its ideological arsenal that provided legitimacy to the military's expanded role in civilian affairs.

It is important to stress that an analysis of corporatism does not provide explanation of the workings of the entire political system. The political system under Suharto can be characterised as 'exclusionary', with the manipulation of electoral politics, the stacking of political institutions with Suharto loyalists, and the use of repression against dissent also considerably reinforcing what might best be described as a policy of political exclusion. In particular, corporatist organisation of group interests provides authoritarian regimes with a means of reducing the need for indiscriminate coercion. Nonetheless, authoritarian leaders frequently resort to direct repression of dissent when corporatism fails to neutralise organised opposition.

NOTES

1. Reeve, *Golkar of Indonesia*.
2. Sukarno was not content with remaining a figurehead president, and parliamentary democracy had provided him with no formal channels to play the more central role he desired in shaping the political future of the nation.

33

Reeve, *Golkar of Indonesia*, pp.109–22; Feith, *The Decline of Constitutional Democracy*.

3. Reeve, *Golkar of Indonesia*, pp.164–5; Suryadinata, *Military Ascendancy*.

4. These included a Youth-Military Cooperation Body, a Labour-Military Cooperation Body, a Peasant-Military Cooperation Body and a Press-Military Contact Body. In January 1958, the army founded the National Front for the Liberation of West Irian (FNPIB), as a co-ordinating body for BKSs and subsequently promoted it as the sole national organisation for functional groups. This brought the army leaders into direct confrontation with Sukarno, who intervened in its choice of leaders and openly disparaged the organisation. Sukarno created the National Front in 1959 to replace FNPIB, and the army and PKI became major competitors in the Front. Sukarno leaned more and more to the left, and towards a pro-China/anti-West foreign policy, and PKI increased its militancy and influence until it virtually dominated the National Front. This led to a polarisation between pro-PKI and anti-PKI forces as the military prepared to retaliate. Reeve, *Golkar of Indonesia*, pp.119–48.

5. Sukarno's proclamation of martial law in March 1957 in order to combat secessionist rebellions, and the anti-western campaigns against the Dutch in West Irian and the British in Malaysia provided the army with an extensive role in civilian affairs. The army also took managerial control of Dutch estates and enterprises under a virulent program of nationalisation aimed at launching Indonesia on the path of an import-substitution phase of industrialisation. With the anticipated termination of martial law in 1962, the army leaders needed to find a rationale and legal basis for the military's continuing role in civilian affairs and to defend its economic interests.

6. I am not arguing that the Suharto regime was a bureaucratic-authoritarian one. My concern is not so much with regime types, as it is with explanations of internal structures and interactions of the political system. For an argument concerning the relevance of applying bureaucratic-authoritarianism to Suharto's New Order see the study by King, 'Indonesia's New Order as a Bureaucratic Polity'.

7. Crouch, *The Army and Politics*.

8. Ward, *The 1971 Election*, pp.2–49; Emmerson, 'The Bureaucracy in Political Context', pp.99–109; Suryadinata, *Military Ascendancy*, pp.23–41.

9. Murtopo promoted Golkar as the only social-political force that was capable of uniting functional groups under a single banner at the elections, and the only one oriented to the government's development program. As such, he tried to establish Golkar's monopoly of representation of community groups and cast the political parties in the role of ideologically divisive and anti-development forces. Murtopo, *Strategi Politik Nasional*, pp.67–101.

10. Emmerson, 'The Bureaucracy in Political Context', pp.105–6; Ward, *The 1971 Election*, pp.2–49.

11. Presidential Decision no. 82/1971 made membership of Korpri compulsory for civil servants, employees of state corporations and employees of private corporations in which the government held part ownership. Emmerson, 'The Bureaucracy in Political Context', pp.106–9; Ward, *The 1971 Election*, p.12.

12. Interview with Alamsjah Ratu Prawiranegara [Coordinator of Cabinet Presidium Personal Staff of the President (1966–1968); Secretary of State (1968–1972); Minister of Religious Affairs (1978–1983)], 22 September 1997.

13. Suryadinata, *Military Ascendancy*, pp.45–97.

14. Typical of the new emphasis on function, PGRI had to change its orientation from workers' union to professional organisation and its program, like those of the other peak organisations, had to support the government's five-yearly development plans (Repelita). Murtopo, *Strategi Politik Nasional*, pp.67–101; Suryadinata, *Military Ascendancy*, p.70.

15. Anlov and Cederroth, 'Introduction', Antlov, 'The Village Leaders', pp.7–96; Sullivan, 'Master and Managers', pp.52–76.

16. Ward, *The 1971 Election*; Liddle, 'The 1977 Indonesian Election'; Suryadinata, *Political Parties*.

17. Suryadinata, *Military Ascendancy*, pp.65–101.

18. After 1965, military officers loyal to Sukarno still dominated Sekber Golkar's central executive board, and hence reorganisations of Golkar were aimed partly at replacing these men with Suharto loyalists. Sekber Golkar changed from an unwieldy federation of almost 300 member functional organisations, to around 200 affiliates, and then in October 1969 to an amalgam of seven basic organisations (kinos), as party men also were purged from Golkar. For instance, Amir Machmud issued Permen 12 (December 1969), which was directed towards cleansing functional groups of party men and affiliations, and giving Sekber Golkar at least half the seats in provincial and regional legislatures. After the 1971 election, a change of name to the shortened title Golkar accompanied further reorganisation. Golkar's First National Congress in September 1973 witnessed a power struggle between its heterogeneous membership, especially between Murtopo's group and the Department of Defence, Dephankam. Amir Murtono (a Hankam man) became the new chairman preventing Murtopo's group from dominating Golkar. Golkar experienced another modification, including the creation of a dual structure of executive boards and supervisors' councils (Dewan Pembina) at central, provincial and regency levels. The supervisors' council (headed by military men) was the decision-making body and the central executive board implemented decisions. This dual structure enabled the military to supervise their civilian counterparts and to undertake 'cultivation, control and direction' of Golkar.

19. Suryadinata, *Military Ascendancy*, pp.107–27; Reeve, 'The Corporatist State', p.52.
20. Robison, 'Organising the transition', p.52.
21. Moreover, at the Golkar's fourth national congress in 1988, Suharto, in an apparent compromise with the military, approved the election of an army general, Wahono, as the new chairman of Golkar. ABRI also launched a successful campaign to install military personnel to head Golkar at the sub-national level.
22. Many of the civilian membership were drawn from a newly formed corporatist organisation, the Indonesian Association of Muslim Intellectuals (ICMI), chaired by Habibie. Robison, 'Organising the Transition', p.53.
23. Robison, 'Organising the Transition', p.57.
24. Fealy, 'Indonesian Politics', p.21.
25. MacIntyre, 'Organising Interests'.
26. Hadiz, *Workers and the State*; Hadiz, 'Challenging State Corporatism'.
27. In line with historical developments, corporatist theorists appealed to an ideal that had existed in medieval European society of organic community, in which landlord and peasant coexisted and co-operated in a 'family-like' unity of harmonious and hierarchically ordered society. Each person had his/her ranking on the ladder of fixed social status and knew his/her station in life. The predominant economic activity was the guild system, in which each person was identified by the specialised occupation they performed. People assumed their duties and privileges from their respective location within this integrated social order. Contributing to the debate, Stepan, in his book entitled *State and Society* (1978), showed that the idea of organic community/state belonged to a corpus of political thought, which he called 'organic-statism'. He traced the origins of organic-statism to Aristotle, Roman law, and medieval law. European philosophers, who were predisposed to nationalism, contributed to this body of ideas, with contemporary Roman Catholic social philosophers (in the late-1970s) also becoming strong exponents of the theory. Organic-statism posited a strong role for the state in achieving social order and harmony, the common good and political community, and provided an abstract model of governance. In concrete terms, corporatism is an institutional pattern that sometimes draws its theoretical supports from organic-statism. Bourchier, 'Lineages of Organicist Political Thought'; Stepan, *The State and Society*, pp.27–41; for a comprehensive coverage of the European theoretical contributions to corporatist (organic-statist) thought see Williamson, *Varieties of Corporatism*, pp.20–103.
28. Reeve, 'The Corporatist State,' p.161; Bourchier, 'Lineages of Organicist Political Thought', pp.228–46.
29. Sullivan, *Local Government*, pp.97–207; Bowen, 'On the Political Construction'.

30. Hadiz, 'State and Labour', p.33; Cahyono, 'The Unjuk Rasa Movement', pp.109–13.
31. Lowry, *The Armed Forces*, pp.193–4; Suryadinata, *Military Ascendancy*, p.7.
32. The *dwi-fungsi* doctrine evolved from a speech made on 12 November 1958 by the then army chief of staff, Gen. Nasution, who declared that the Indonesian army would take a 'middle way' between two extremes. It would neither 'follow the course of Latin American armies [of military dictatorship]' nor take 'the passive role prescribed for the military establishments in Western Europe [under civilian control]'. Nasution provided the first public justification for the military's 'integration into the political theory and structure of Guided Democracy'. He talked of the military exerting a positive influence on the polity without overly dominating its institutions and processes. With the onset of the New Order, Nasution's 'middle way' was transformed into a doctrine of military domination. At the First Army Seminar in April 1965, the military began to outline its claim to a dual role or 'function,' which army leaders elaborated upon at the Second Army Seminar in 1966. Reeve, *Golkar of Indonesia*, p.144.
33. With the lifting of martial law in 1962, they supplemented their territorial doctrine with the concept of *operasi karya* ('civic mission') as justification for their continued role in civilian administration. *Operasi karya* provided the military with a central role in rural development projects reaching down to the village level, which was placed on a legal footing with the issuance of Presidential Decision no. 371/1962. During the Guided Democracy period, then, ABRI began to establish its territorial command structure.
34. Lowry, *The Armed Forces*, pp.187–8; Sundhaussen, 'The Military', pp.57–81.
35. Lowry, *The Armed Forces*, pp.184–6.
36. Reeve, *Golkar of Indonesia*, p.187.
37. Lowry, *The Armed Forces*, pp.111–150; Reeve, *Golkar of Indonesia*, p.191; Tanter, 'Totalitarian Ambition', pp.213–71.
38. Murtopo, *Strategi Politik Nasional*.
39. Murtopo, *Strategi Politik Nasional*.
40. This theme is explored in chapters four, five, and eight of the book.

Chapter 4

State Management of Muslim Associational Life

INTRODUCTION

Muslim associations became particular targets of the regime's corporatist strategy. However, because of the heterogeneous nature of autonomous Muslim associations, and the tendency for some segments of the Muslim constituency to resist regime initiatives, the regime's mechanisms were initially partial attempts to capture the Islamic sector in state structures. Although, in the short term, they were of an ad-hoc nature, usually starting as politically expedient responses to specific challenges and threats, they increasingly became determined attempts at coherent restructuring of Muslim interests. They represented recurring initiatives by state officials to exert regulatory control over politically recalcitrant segments of this heterogeneous religious sector as well as to bring Islam's social, religious and political life within state-defined parameters. In particular, state officials were concerned to capture Muslim interests and place them into state structures in order to exclude them from power sharing arrangements. They sought to remove people's attachment to Islamic political-ideological goals and activities, and to rechannel them in support of state-defined goals for economic development and political stability.

While bearing these objectives in mind, this chapter examines three targets of exclusionary strategies: the Islamic parties, Islamic education, and what can be called the government's religious 'harmonising' program. In each of the target areas discussed, the regime adopted a similar management approach insofar as the three areas were subject to the same set of policy objectives, political constraints, and organisational principles. That is, Suharto sought to contain and restrict independent political activities, religious movements, and rival ideologies that might challenge state autonomy, cause instability, and disrupt economic development.

The chapter begins with a study of Suharto's initiatives to bring the Islamic parties into state-chartered merger within corporatised party arrangements and, in doing so, to create a de-politicised environment conducive to stability and development. Second, the chapter examines measures to remove the influence of the Islamic parties and student organisations from university campuses and to reorient students' activities and education to development priorities. As part of mono-loyalty provisions aimed at cutting the ties of civil servants to political parties, academics were obliged to join the sole public service union, Korpri, and teachers had to join the compulsory teachers' union. Eventually, as part of de-politicisation of campuses, students were required to channel their activities through student co-ordinating bodies and through the university hierarchy in place of independent student organisations. Islamic student organisations were a major target of this reorganisation.

Third, the chapter considers how religious organisation, in many respects, assumed the form of corporatist mergers. That is, in pursuit of harmonising inter-religious relations and state–religious relations, Suharto gave recognition to state-chartered institutions representing the five officially sanctioned religions. Then he created a peak inter-religious council, which was intended as the sole consultation body between representatives of the religious institutions and the state. This part of the analysis also looks at the regime's initiatives to circumscribe what constituted religious orthodoxy and practice, to increase its regulatory control over Islam's community/religious affairs, and to discourage and eliminate unmediated religious movements, splinter groups and sects that threatened to disrupt economic development and cause instability. As a result, religious tendencies that fell outside of official definitions of religious interpretation and practice either were persuaded to join the mainstream religions, and find representation in the state-sanctioned institutions, or risk prohibition. In short, they were 'harmonised', through merger, into organisational structures representing mainstream religions to ensure that they did not become sources of political instability or opposition to the regime.[1]

The analysis also considers that, as a concomitant to the restructuring, Suharto progressively enforced ideological conformity of Islamic political parties, organisations, and the state-chartered religious institutions to the state's 'organicist' ideology of *Pancasila*. It is important to bear in mind that *Pancasila* was an ideology of containment and exclusion, which was antithetical to Marxism and Islamic political ideology.[2] Compulsory *Pancasila* courses emphasised the virtues of respect for authority, harmony of social relations, hierarchical order, patriotism and commitment to economic development. A common thread runs through each of these target areas discussed. That is, Suharto was concerned to establish political control over unmediated political, social, and religious organisation and to enforce ideological conformity either to *Pancasila* or to mainstream religious belief, as acknowledged by *Pancasila*. In other words, political-religious practice was brought into state-delineated parameters, and corporatist structuring played a role in the capture of unmediated organisation.

A final point needs to be made before proceeding with the analysis. That is, efforts to restructure Muslim interests spanned a thirty-year period, in which the relationship between the ruling coalition of state officials and independent Muslim groups shifted from an antagonistic one (1968–1987), to one of rapprochement from the late 1980s onwards. In the first period (the focus of this chapter), the objective of corporatist strategies was to demobilise and politically exclude Muslim interests from power sharing arrangements. In the second period (discussed in chapter five), President Suharto was behind initiatives to incorporate a hitherto neglected but increasingly important Muslim middle-class sector. We will discuss the implications of this shift in corporatist strategy in the following chapters.

ISLAMIC ORGANISATIONS

Before proceeding with the main analysis a brief account of Islamic organisations in Indonesia is necessary. The main trends and movements in Indonesian Islam belong to the *Sunni* branch of orthodoxy, originating in the Arab hinterlands, as opposed to the splinter branch of *Shi'ism*, which spread to parts of Persia. Indonesian orthodoxy has coalesced into two major movements: the *kaum muda* ('young group') or *santri moderen* (modernists) and *kaum tua* ('old group') or *santri kolot* (the traditionalists).

Islamic modernism in Indonesia grew out of an Egyptian reform movement and in response to early indigenous nationalism at the turn of the century. It drew substantial inspiration from the reform ideas of the anti-colonial, pan-Islamist Jamal al-Din al-Afghani (1839–1897) and the 'Father of Modernism' Muhammad Abduh (1845–1905). Representing Islamic modernism at home were organisations such as Sarekat Islam (United Islam, SI) and the Muhammidayah, both founded in 1912, and Persatuan Islam (Unity of Islam, Persis) founded in 1923. The modernist organisations mostly catered to a socioeconomic class of educated urban elites and merchant traders. They gave priority to education, social welfare programs and *dakwah* (religious propagation) activities.[3]

Muhammadiyah is the main modernist organisation today with an estimated 28 to 30 million members. It was founded in Yogyakarta (Central Java) by K.H. Ahmad Dahlan, a traditionalist scholar who became inspired by the reformist ideas of Muhammad Abduh. Muhammadiyah expanded to other urban centres first on Java and then onto the Outer Islands, with a strong presence in Sumatra. It now has an impressive network of organisational infrastructure, which includes youth and women's organisations, schools, teachers' academies and universities, medical clinics and hospitals, orphanages and other social welfare activities. After the declaration of independence by Indonesia's first president, Sukarno, modernist youth organisations were established. These included Gerakan Pemuda Islam Indonesia (the Indonesian Movement of Islamic Youth, GPII) in 1945, Pelajar Islam Indonesia (Indonesian Islamic Secondary School Students, PII) in 1946, and Himpunan Mahasiswa Islam (The Association of Islamic University Students, HMI) in 1947.[4]

Two prominent religious scholars (*kiai*), Wahab Chasbullah and Hasjim Asj'ari founded the Nahdlatul Ulama (Revival of the Religious Scholars, NU) in 1926 in order to protect the economic and social-religious interests of *pesantren* (religious boarding schools) and Islamic traditionalism from modernism at home and abroad.[5] In the last seventy years, NU has become a diverse and complex organisation with a decentralised structure largely based on the personalistic and informal networks and authority of individual *kiai* who run a system of traditional Islam boarding schools mainly in rural Java. Much of the authority of NU *kiai* has been hereditary. NU has an estimated membership of over 30 million people.[6]

Muhammadiyah, NU and other Islamic organisations joined the Masyumi party, founded in 1945, after the declaration of independence (17 August), to represent Muslim interests in competition with newly forming parties, especially the Indonesian National Party (PNI). NU withdrew from Masyumi in 1952 because of conflict with modernist politicians over leadership roles and Masyumi since was dominated by Muslim modernist leaders. Masyumi had a prominent role in the cabinets of parliamentary democracy of the 1950s. In 1960, President Sukarno banned Masyumi on the grounds that its leaders had supported a regional rebellion in Sumatra. Meanwhile, NU leaders were brought into Sukarno's 'Guided Democracy' government.[7] NU has a long history of rivalry with modernist organisations based on political and religious disputes, although Greg Barton argues that the traditionalist/modernist dichotomy and antagonisms are less relevant today.[8] However, to this day, organisational affiliation remains an important source of political cleavage between the modernists and traditionalists.

The discussion now turns to efforts by Suharto's New Order regime to restrict and contain the political participation of organised Islam.

MANAGING THE ISLAMIC PARTIES

The Modernists (Parmusi)

Politically activated Islam was a prominent target of Suharto's initiatives to de-politicise state and society. New Order leaders sought to dismantle Islam's party base and re-channel it into new vehicles within a corporatised party system. These initiatives first focused on Muslim modernist interests. Army leaders were concerned to undercut the autonomy of political modernism.[9] They were suspicious of politically organised Islam and were determined to prevent modernist leaders from re-establishing Masyumi. Masyumi party leaders had a popular grassroots following that potentially could mount a challenge to army power. Second, army leaders objected to Masyumi's political-ideological goals for the realisation of a state based on Islamic law, especially in constitutional struggles for inclusion of the so-called Jakarta Charter. (The Jakarta Charter required that all Indonesians of Muslim faith adhere to Islamic law.) Third, they suspected Masyumi of having given clandestine support to the Darul Islam revolt for a separate Islamic state in West Java. Fourth, they blamed Masyumi for the role performed by its most prominent leaders Muhammad Natsir,

Sjafruddin Prawiranegara and Burhanuddin Harahap in giving support to the regional rebellion in Sumatra.

Nonetheless, Suharto and army leaders, who were less anti-party than some segments of the military, viewed with sympathy calls by Muslim modernist leaders for the re-establishment of a political party to represent their interests. A modernist party made amenable to the Suharto regime could prove useful, as it would help counterbalance the considerable influence of NU at future general elections. Suharto settled on a strategy of permitting the formation of a new party, the Indonesian Muslim Party (Parmusi), which was registered as a political party by Presidential Decision No.70 of February 1968.[10]

Through a series of interventions in the selection of leaders, and manipulations of the party by Murtopo's OPSUS, Suharto ensured the effective emasculation of Parmusi as an independent political force. Suharto made it clear that party lists were to include no senior Masyumi leaders. The Muhammadiyah leaders, H. Djarnawi Hadikusomo and Lukman Harun, were appointed party leader and Secretary General respectively, as a temporary expedient. However, attempts by old guard modernists to establish Masyumi's control over Parmusi at its first congress in Malang in 1968, resulted in army interference in leadership selection. In 1969 the pro-army appointees to Parmusi, Jaelani Naro and Imran Kadir, instigated an internal party coup to oust Djarnawi's leadership. Both figures were known to be close to Ali Murtopo and the coup was thought to be part of Murtopo's OPSUS. The impasse that this created prepared the ground for Suharto to intervene and impose an amenable figure, M.S. Mintaredja (a state minister), as party chairman (Presidential Decision No.77/1970).[11]

Rising to leadership positions in Parmusi were young educated Muslims from Muhammadiyah Youth and HMI, who possessed educational and technical skills (in economics, engineering and law); skills, which, generally, were not held by older Masyumi leaders. These young Muslims were well placed to take advantage of the kinds of 'technocratic-dominated', 'construction-oriented' policies of the New Order and fitted in well with the government's preference of promoting into government positions administrators who had no party affiliation.[12]

Part of the regime's corporatist strategy also entailed the dismantling of Masyumi's party base—the array of supporter organisations called the *Keluarga Bulan Bintang* (the Moon and Star Family)—and re-attaching them to Parmusi. In doing so, the regime hoped to channel Muslim modernist energies into the new vehicle, whilst excluding Masyumi's senior politicians and cutting the *Bulan Bintang* masses from old party loyalties. During the 1971 election campaign, Parmusi allied itself to Golkar and the army against NU and PNI, which helped split the Muslim political community and dissipate its energies. Before the election, Muhammadiyah had announced its formal withdrawal from politics, disassociated itself from Masyumi and, together with HMI, withdrew its support from Parmusi. Muhammadiyah leaders, many of them ex-Masyumi figures, were disaffected by regime manipulations of Parmusi. Although Parmusi failed to become an effective vehicle of Muslim support for the regime, Suharto succeeded in emasculating Islamic modernism as an independent political force and transfering the electoral vote to Golkar. Consequently, Parmusi fared poorly at the election, gaining only 5.4 per cent of the vote compared to Masyumi's 20 per cent share at the last elections in 1955.[13]

In conclusion, Parmusi was a first tentative step in the direction of state-corporatised Muslim interests, which sought to fragment and weaken the political independence of modernism represented by Masyumi and pave the way for non-party-led economic development.

The Traditionalists (NU, PPP and General Elections)

Although state leaders emasculated modernist party politics, Ward argues that army–Golkar efforts to split NU initially were unsuccessful. For instance, initiatives by GUPPI (Union of Efforts to Improve Islamic Education)—a state backed merger of religious scholars and leaders—to win the allegiances of the *pesantren* community over to Golkar's election campaign aroused among NU members intense resentment and retaliations as they felt their own organisational base threatened by Murtopo's OPSUS.[14] Among the reasons for this failure was that NU's sprawling and decentralised organisation, and staunch independence of *ulama*, proved much more resistant to state intervention and co-optation than the Islamic modernist and nationalist organisations. Before the elections, NU was the only party left intact after army purges and party manipulations had eliminated PKI, emasculated PNI and sidelined the modernist parties. Although a dominant, pro-army faction in NU assisted Suharto's New Order to come to power, it soon became the party in opposition as it vigorously resisted Golkar's campaign and restrictions on the parties which hurt NU's electoral prospects. One of the younger NU leaders, Subchan, led NU as a party of opposition against Golkar and its unfair campaign tactics of intimidation and fraud in the lead up to, and during, the 1971 general election. NU's share of the vote (18.67 per cent), although insignificant in comparison to Golkar's landslide victory (62.8 per cent), convinced Suharto that the party represented an Islamic bloc that posed a future threat to the New Order's monopoly on power.[15]

This was the context of Suharto's introduction of the 'floating mass' concept, which ensured that NU, and other parties, could no longer organise politically below the district level where most of its constituency lived. Implementation of the 'floating mass' concept can be considered as a central plank of the state's exclusionary policy, which paved the way for, or at least complemented, a corporatist re-ordering of party organisation. In 1971, Golkar also launched the slogan, 'politics no, development yes' as a way of indicating the future direction of party organisation.[16]

Suharto had worked with caution, step-by-step to simplify the party system and forced them to reduce their number. In 1973, the Muslim parties, NU, Perti (Association of Islamic Education), Parmusi and PSII were merged as the

United Development Party (PPP). Thenceforth, PPP was part of the Golkar (plus-two-parties) system as a very unequal and distrusted partner in development. NU became the dominant element of PPP, with 61 per cent of the seats and effective veto over the other combined elements, particularly Parmusi (subsequently called Muslimin Indonesia, MI). As such, five years after state incorporation of the modernists, the traditionalist NU was included in the corporatist party arrangements.

Since the merger, PPP comprised opposing tendencies between the modernist and traditionalist camps, with the main battle-lines in the future drawn between the MI and NU factions. This appeared to be part of a deliberate strategy by Suharto to foster conflict within the parties in order to fragment them while seeking to minimise conflict between political parties and Golkar.[18] The pro-government Parmusi Chairman, Mintaredja, became PPP's first chairman.[19]

An immediate, unanticipated outcome of the party fusion was that, whereas the mergers seriously damaged PDI, between 1973 and 1978 PPP's Islamic identity provided the party with a degree of cohesion.[20] The 1977 general election brought PPP and the government's machine Golkar into direct conflict as they aggressively competed for the hearts and minds of Indonesians, with each party rallying support based on the two opposing claims of 'Islam' and 'development'. For instance, the Rais Aam of NU's Religious Council and Chairman of PPP's Religious Council, Bisri Sjansuri, declared that 'in order to uphold the religion and law of Allah, every Muslim who takes part in the 1977 general election, but especially a member of PPP, is legally obliged to vote PPP when the time comes'.[21] Sjansuri's religious opinions seemed to carry some influence within the party and Golkar failed to make a dent in traditional strongholds of the Islamic parties, such as Aceh, South Sumatra, South Kalimantan and East Java.[22]

In an effort to neutralise the Islamic appeal of PPP, the Minister of Internal Affairs, Amir Machmud, and the Commander of Kopkamtib, Admiral Sudomo, led a campaign alleging the existence of an anti-government conspiracy in the form of a *Komando Jihad* (Islamic Holy War Command). Party leaders interpreted statements made by Sudomo as offering a pretext for security forces to arrest Muslim party politicians at whim, as well as seeing in it an implied connection between PPP, although publicly denied by Sudomo at the time, and Muslim 'extremists' who seek to establish an Islamic state. According to Liddle, the 1977 elections were conducted along the lines of the 1971 elections insofar as the government continued to make use of intimidation, coercion, propaganda directed against the parties, security screening of candidates, arrests, manipulation of party organisations, election regulations, party laws and campaign restrictions.[23] In particular, screening of candidates by the state intelligence co-ordinating organisation, Bakin, was meant to ensure that the MPR/DPR would be stacked with loyalists, which would facilitate executive control over the passing of legislation. In short, government coercion, which aimed to cow and drive into retreat the opposition, was part of its policy of exclusion to ensure that it maintained preponderant control of the MPR and

DPR through an overwhelming Golkar victory. By contrast, the increasingly corporatised parties were locked into a system that, through engineered elections, greatly restricted their access to legislatures and government office. The mix of state strategies, including corporatism, to control the parties and elections represented an ongoing process that sought to ensure the two-way political exclusion of PPP from society and the state.

The government was concerned by PPP's increased vote, as Golkar's share of the vote dropped marginally to 62.1 per cent (down 0.7 per cent), while PPP gained 29 per cent (up 2.18 per cent) of the final vote.[24] Suharto was not willing to have a 'loyal opposition' party in parliament that could disrupt enactment of government legislation. Vindication of the government's concerns came in 1978, when the dominant faction of PPP, NU, led a walkout from the MPR general session in protest over two decrees. One decree gave religious status to mystical belief systems (*aliran kepercayaan*), equal to that of the official religions, and incorporated them into the broad outlines of state policy (GBHN). This decree was aimed at reducing the strength of Islam by offering an officially approved, alternative form of organisational representation to non-practising Muslims, who might otherwise have felt obliged to register under the religion of Islam. The other decree introduced *Pancasila* moral instructions called P4 (Guidelines for the Comprehension and Implementation of *Pancasila*). Muslims perceived the P4 courses as being an attempt to turn *Pancasila* into a religion, particularly as it could displace religious lessons in schools. NU staged a second walkout in 1980, as it refused to participate in the passing of new election laws in parliament, which NU leaders viewed as undemocratic.[25] At its national conference in 1981, NU unequivocally defied (the by now almost routine) national consensus by declining to endorse Suharto for a third presidential term, or to endorse his title of 'Father of Development'.[26]

The challenge posed by the NU faction of PPP convinced Suharto that more interventions were required to push NU further to the political margins. He began by replacing Mintaredja with Jaelani Naro, who had instigated the earlier coup in Parmusi, as chairman of PPP. Naro was imposed on PPP to discipline the party and to neutralise the influence of NU within it.[27] Corporatist restructuring of interests allows the state to manoeuvre itself into a position of greater autonomy and prevent potential challenges to its power, by readjusting an 'imbalance' of contending group interests. Naro's subsequent manipulations of PPP appeared to conform to this principle of reordering. Thus, Naro sought to resolve an ongoing dispute between the MI and NU elements over leadership of DPR commissions, by preparing a provisional candidate list for the 1982 general elections. He delivered the list on 27 October 1981 to the National Election Board, and unilaterally reallocated seats away from NU. NU lost seven of its seats to MI in the list of candidates for the next DPR election, which eliminated its commanding position of being able to over-rule the decisions of the other constituent members. These members now held a combined majority by one seat. The most outspoken government critics were placed at the bottom of the list of candidates effectively removing them as possible successful candidates for the 1982 elections. NU leaders threatened to withdraw from PPP, which elicited a harsh rebuke from Ali Murtopo, who accused them of seeking to replace *Pancasila* and the national flag.[28] At this point, the state leaders seemed unprepared to allow a large Islamic faction to extricate itself from the authorised party system, as NU's continued inclusion must have furnished the New Order political system with a semblance of legitimacy.

Both before and during the election campaign of 1982, the army and Golkar intensified their efforts to intervene in, and manipulate, the political process to defeat PPP. In September 1981, Ali Murtopo had pressured Korpri civil servants to vote for Golkar. More restrictive campaign regulations were introduced (Presidential Decision No.3/1982) and parties were severely circumscribed in what they could discuss at rallies. The army introduced a program to enter rural areas (called 'ABRI masuk desa') in order, among other things, to mobilise support for Golkar against alleged 'anti-*Pancasila* Forces'.[29] Meanwhile, PPP had been excluded from establishing branches in rural areas by the 'floating mass' policy. The measures constituted a reinforcement of the state's corporatist/exclusionary policy, as they sought to deny PPP what limited access it had to the electorate. Meanwhile, PPP supporters became increasingly militant with the belief that their election chances had improved, which resulted in frequent violent clashes between Golkar and PPP supporters. For example, the greatest conflict erupted at the Lapangan Banteng rally of 18 March in Jakarta, which turned into a riot with hundreds of students and youths being arrested. Religion was again the issue at stake; but this time, Golkar tried to project itself as Islamic as PPP. The Golkar emblem had Arabic characters, and the Minister of Internal Affairs and member of Golkar's supervisor's council, Amir Machmud, donated money for mosque building programs. The outcome of the election was that Golkar improved its landslide victory (64.34 per cent), while PPP's share of the vote declined (27.78 per cent).[30]

To sum up, Suharto's regime resorted to a mix of strategies aimed at weakening Islam's capacity for independent political activity and to garner a victory for Golkar at the general elections. Among these strategies were state interventions in the parties, electoral manipulations, intimidation and coercion. The restructuring of Islamic parties within a corporatised party framework— dominated by Golkar—helped ensure the political exclusion of Islamic parties from effective participation in power sharing arrangements. However, as we have seen, PPP (especially the NU faction) was not a completely submissive political force and did contest elections, but with no real hope of winning power. To some considerable extent, then, the regime's corporatist measures appear to have been responding to the challenges posed by NU and PPP, and therefore were ad-hoc in nature. The next section, which deals with post-1982 developments and the regime's enforcement of *Pancasila* ideology, looks at Suharto's increasingly determined attempts to restructure Muslim associational interests.

Replacing Islamic Identity with Corporatist Ideology

Bitter opposition of PPP at elections and in parliament led Suharto to implement measures aimed at separating Islamic organisational activity more firmly from its ideological base, although these efforts had been under way for, at least, the past decade. For example, before the PPP merger in 1973, the government obliged the Islamic parties to add '*Pancasila* and the 1945 Constitution' to their party constitutions. PPP had to reaffirm its 'double basis' of state ideology and Islamic identity, with the aim of diminishing the importance of the latter. The Minister of Internal Affairs tried to prohibit the use of PPP's party symbol (the *Ka'bah*) at the 1977 elections, but PPP refused to comply and threatened to boycott the election.[31] After the NU-led walkout in 1978, the government embarked on an aggressive campaign to induct civil servants, professionals, students and 'the masses' into indoctrination courses in the state ideology of *Pancasila*, co-ordinated nationally. In particular, the *Pancasila* (P4) courses sought to unify citizens' perceptions regarding state ideology, especially concerning development. In other words, the courses aimed to lessen people's identification with alternative ideologies such as Islam (and Marxism and Liberalism). Morfit argues that *Pancasila* (P4) was primarily an ideology of containment and exclusion, as it ensured that both communism and the political goals of Islam remained 'outside the arena of permissible political activity'.[32]

Chapter three has considered how the New Order leaders propagated 'state-organicist' notions of corporate harmony through Golkar channels and the state ideology of *Pancasila* and how this conformed to a pattern of corporatist ideology and organisation. The P4 courses represented such an attempt to underwrite Islam's organisational existence with 'organicist' ideologies as an adjunct to the corporatist reordering of organisational life. The connection between state ideology and organisation became clear when *Pancasila* was declared as the sole ideological foundation (*azas tunggal*) of all organisations in Indonesia. Before elaborating upon this connection, however, the chronology of the introduction of *azas tunggal* will be discussed.

The government viewed PPP's continued adherence to its 'double' basis, writes Faisal, as 'proof' that the Muslims were not completely committed to *Pancasila*.[33] Suharto announced his concerns in a speech before an ABRI leadership meeting at Pekanbaru, Sumatra in March 1980. In the speech, Suharto spoke of a national 'consensus' in 1966 between ABRI and the political parties concerning *Pancasila* as the state ideology. He maintained that the consensus had not been fully 'successful' because 'there was still a party [PPP] using other principles (*azas*) in addition to *Pancasila*. This led to a "question mark" with regard to their commitment to *Pancasila*.'[34] He referred to the (NU-led) walkout over the P4 policy in 1978 and the Election Law Amendment Bill in 1980, as two obvious points of tension between the government and PPP, although he did not mention the party by name.

The sole basis law was submitted to parliament in 1982, after the elections, and passed by the MPR general session of 1983 in Enactment No.II/1983. PPP held its first congress in Jakarta in 1984, eleven years after its founding, at which it announced three broad objectives. They were, 'to consolidate *Pancasila* as the sole foundation'; 'to conclude the process of the PPP merger' and 'to become more development oriented'.[35] *Pancasila* formally replaced PPP's ideology of Islam. In line with Law No.1/1985 passed in parliament, which prescribed the use of symbols related to *Pancasila* at the next elections, the party eventually substituted a new 'star' symbol for its Islamic *Ka'bah*.[36] (Although these changes appeared to reduce support for the party at the 1987 election they did not prevent party faithful from identifying PPP with Islam in the 1992 and 1997 general elections.) The parliament passed two other laws: Law No.3/1985 and Law No.8/1985, enforcing the *azas tunggal* on all social and political organisations, including Golkar.

It is worth studying the texts of the two laws for a moment as they outline priorities of the state leadership, and make important connections between these priorities, for the reorientation of Indonesia's organisational memberships. The two laws were concerned with achieving ideological conformity and corporatist reordering of Indonesia's associations. For example, Law No.8/1985, and Law No.18/1986 for the implementation of Law No.8, outlined the conditions for the corporatising of non-party, community organisations. The clauses read that, based on profession, function, or religion, community organisations of similar type were 'obliged' to gather together 'in merger or association' under *wadah pembinaan* (supervisory organisations). These compulsory peak organisations, at the national, provincial and district levels, would exercise sole representation of farmers through the Indonesian Farmers' Harmony Association (HKTI), youth through the Indonesian National Youth Committee (KNPI), women through the Indonesian Women's National Congress (KOWANI) and so forth.[37] The Indonesian Ulama Council (MUI), established in 1975, was intended as the single national organisation to represent the interests of *ulama vis-à-vis* the state. The state administration had finally legislated what had been *de facto* policy, which sought to shut off parties from their lines of communication with the grassroots and provide the bureaucracy with a near monopoly over channels of representation via corporatised non-party entities.

Pembinaan (guidance) was a key concept employed by state leaders and was defined (Laws 1985 and 1986 and elucidation of Laws cited above) as an initiative to 'guide, protect and urge' organisations to achieve an 'independent' and 'healthy' growth in the service of 'national objectives'. The main national objective was stated as gaining the 'increased' and 'active participation of all Indonesians in national development' with a view to achieving a '*Pancasila* society' underwritten by the 1945 Constitution. The peak organisations were to act as 'instruments' with which to 'channel the thoughts and opinions of citizens' for the realisation of national development, through state-directed education, 'thought training' and development of their memberships. Law No.18 outlined the functions, rights and duties of community organisations. These included the obligation of the leaderships to ensure their members attended *Pancasila* (P4) indoctrination courses and fostered national unity by placing national interests above those of individual or group interests. The government required each organisation to have a constitution, which had to include *Pancasila* as their sole (political) ideology, but did not interfere in the religious belief of established organisations. Organisations had to register with, and supply membership lists to, the Minister of Internal Affairs. The government authorised the minister, governors and regents to remove the leadership of, or disband any organisation as a last resort, if they engaged in 'harmful acts' and after the giving of 'positive guidance and education' had failed to establish compliance to the sole foundation law. Muslim organisations that refused to abide by the new regulations (PII and a breakaway faction of HMI) were prohibited under instructions from the Minister of Internal Affairs.[38]

The effect of these laws was that, from 1985 onwards, the ideological delineation of corporatism, which had started with Golkar and was applied to the parties, especially PPP, was now extended across to all organisations in Indonesia. The *azas tunggal* legislation was the pinnacle of the government's corporatist initiatives aimed at achieving ideological and associational conformity to state development goals.

PPP's congress of 1984 had included as one of its broad objectives, 'concluding the party merger', which, in practice, meant NU's exit from PPP. NU chose to withdraw from PPP because regime intervention in the party had proven too detrimental to NU's political and economic interests. At its 1984 congress in Situbondo, NU announced its formal withdrawal from PPP and its return to the NU's founding spirit of 1926 as a purely social-religious organisation. NU succumbed to regime pressure and at the congress passed a resolution accepting *Pancasila* as the organisation's *asaz tunggal*, or sole foundation. However, NU retained Islam as its undergirding religious conviction rather than ideology *per se*. NU also confirmed that it accepted the unitary Republic of Indonesia as the final form of the state and, by implication, no longer struggled for specific Islamic provisions.[39]

The withdrawal of NU freed its individual members to stay with PPP or join Golkar and PDI. The new president of NU, Achmad Siddiq, issued a *fatwa* (non-binding legal opinion) declaring that it was 'not the duty of NU members to choose PPP' and 'not forbidden to choose Golkar or PDI' at the polls.[40] (His ruling reversed Sjansuri's earlier *fatwa* of 1977, which obliged NU members to vote PPP.) Naro strengthened his position as party leader after the withdrawal of NU, with positions on PPP's leadership board allocated accordingly (twenty-three for MI, twelve for NU, four for Perti and two for PSII). In 1987, PPP removed references to Islam in its party constitution and struggle program. For instance, the reference to 'Islamic brotherhood' in PPP's constitution was replaced with a typically New Order phrase, 'fostering brotherhood' (*membina rasa persaudaraan*).[41]

PPP no longer held a monopoly of representation regarding the Muslim constituency, and its loss of specific Islamic identity and lack of clear program saw its political fortunes decline as Golkar picked up Muslim votes. The outcome of NU's withdrawal from PPP was that the party only received 16 per cent of the vote at the 1987 general elections, down 11 per cent from its 1982 results. Golkar achieved a phenomenal 73.17 per cent landslide victory. The Secretary General of Golkar called PPP's behaviour at the elections 'more Golkar than Golkar', as the party sought accommodation with the government.[42] PPP demonstrated the extent of its post-election submissiveness to Suharto by seeking government consultation concerning the choice of future party chairman. The final choice of PPP chairman, worked out between party leaders and the Minister of Internal Affairs, was Ismail Hasan Metareum of the MI faction, who went on to lead the party for two consecutive periods. The NU leader for Central Java, Matori Abdul Jalil became Secretary General and, despite his ouster, Naro managed to place three of his loyalists in leadership positions.[43]

Many NU leaders, especially politicians who had had their careers advanced through PPP, continued to identify with and support the party after NU's institutional withdrawal. Consequently, established patterns of rivalry between NU interests and the MI (modernist) faction continued to plague the party. In particular, at the next PPP congress Matori contested the party chairmanship, but was defeated by the regime's preferred candidate, Ismail Metareum. The NU Chairman, K.H. Abdurrahman Wahid (1984–1999), came into regular conflict with Ismail because of the former's efforts in the 1987 and subsequent election campaigns to weaken PPP. On more than one occasion, Abdurrahman sent signals to his constituency not to vote PPP. In 1988, Abdurrahman was appointed to the MPR as a member of the Golkar faction.[44] During the 1992 and 1997 general elections regular, violent clashes occurred between PPP and Golkar supporters from the NU support bases in Java. Thus, it seems that, as an outcome of corporatist reordering and *azas tunggal*, divisions were created between NU supporters of PPP and NU supporters of Golkar.[45]

In conclusion, the reordering of Islam's political, ideological and organisational existence involved a process that was at least two decades in the making. The analysis centred on the argument that implementing exclusionary corporatism was part of Suharto's strategy to undermine the autonomy of Muslim parties and organisations and severely restrict and delineate their participation in the political system. One of the functions of exclusionary corporatism is precisely that of capturing the organisational bases of independent group activity to politically demobilise, fragment and neutralise them within new, state controlled structures. The purpose of such reordering for the authoritarian regime is to create structural barriers to people's effective political participation and thus limit challenges to state power. This was the purpose of organisational restructuring in Indonesia. In addition, we considered how Suharto intensified his corporatist initiatives by demanding conformity to the state ideology of *Pancasila*. In doing so, he sought to reinforce state power, as this conformity was intended to discourage rival ideologies (in this case Islamic political ideology) from contending with state ideology for hegemony. Exclusionary corporatism also serves as an alternative to more direct forms of coercion and suppression, which might otherwise be required to keep societal demands low.

Moreover, regimes derive some legitimacy from the limited representation offered to selected interests by their incorporation in state-chartered organisations. Suharto was intent on obtaining political legitimacy for his regime, and corporatised party arrangements which locked political interests into the system but shut them out of power appeared to give the regime a semblance of legitimacy. However, NU withdrew from organisational membership of the corporatised PPP and its exclusion from state structures raised questions about the future viability of these arrangements. Would NU become a force of direct opposition to Suharto and to the political system? Or would Suharto find other means of alternately incorporating in, and excluding from, state structures significant components of NU, thereby fragmenting them and neutralising potential challenges to state autonomy?

A provisional answer to the (above) questions is that another purpose of exclusionary corporatism is to contain competition and conflict between rival interests within the tightly controlled boundaries of the political system. In this context, Bianchi argues that mixed systems of representation—in which there coexist significant corporatist and pluralist (unincorporated and semi-incorporated) components—can help preserve state autonomy, as the regime plays off the differently structured interests that contend for power. After its withdrawal did NU, then, constitute an unincorporated or semi-incorporated component brought into contest with corporatised modernist interests in PPP, in what Bianchi (and Schmitter) called 'mixed systems of representation'? It is true, as discussed, that in order to offset NU's strength, Suharto sought to readjust the balance between competing MI and NU factions in PPP. NU's withdrawal from PPP also seemed to create divisions between PPP and Golkar supporters in NU (see the discussion in chapter six). Although Suharto's political restructuring of Muslim interests might not have been responsible for all existing lines of conflict, the competing corporatised (PPP) and unincorporated (NU) components did seem to lend themselves to Suharto's divide-and-rule tactics. In addition, the corporatised party system seemed to provide the boundaries and context for future contest—including contests between those interests incorporated in state structures and unincorporated groups.

Following chapters elaborate upon these kinds of theoretical issues in the context of growing conflict between elite political interests, both within and outside of the state. Meanwhile, the analysis turns to a consideration of the regime's reorganisation of Islamic education, which was partially achieved through corporatist structures and ideological reorientation programs but also through direct forms of coercion.

MANAGING ISLAMIC EDUCATION

The de-politicisation of campus life—which corresponded with national trends for the removal of party influence from the political system—and reorientation of Islamic education went hand in hand. That is, the regime tried to develop a cadre of administrators and technocrats, both in the government bureaucracy and educational institutions, who would have no attachment to the political parties and would contribute to the state's development goals. The analysis will consider how New Order modernisers viewed both 'political' Islam and 'traditional' Islam as obstructions to their vision for a standardised, national system based on western models of education. In turn, education was an integral part of preparing citizens to become the next generation of 'construction-oriented' technocrats, intellectuals and administrators, who would share the anti-party bias of New Order leaders. Thus, by stages, the regime brought academic and, to a lesser extent, student life within the state's exclusionary corporatist arrangements, disengaged it from independent political and organisational activity, and sought to re-orient it to the New Order ideology of *Pancasila* and development.

The Problem of Islamic Education

Before proceeding with the main analysis, a very brief historical context of Islamic education under Suharto is in order. One of the most perplexing problems for Indonesian administrations was how to integrate Indonesia's 'dual' system of education, that had the Department of Religion overseeing religious education and the Department of Education and Culture administering general education. The historical process of establishing a common standard of education, in the cause of creating a distinctive national identity, national unity and patriotism, was a complex one. It entailed successive attempts to narrow the gap between the two systems, which included the accommodation of an increasing proportion of secular (science and general) subjects into the Islamic schools and tertiary institutes.[46]

By the 1970s, the Department of Religion's largest policy area of concern was that of modernising the Islamic education system to bring it more into line with western interdisciplinary curricula from primary and secondary through to tertiary levels. In March 1975, the Ministers of Education, Religion and Internal Affairs signed a joint decision on the universalisation and standardisation of education, with Islamic education thenceforth being based on the general curriculum. In seeking to standardise the education system, education ministers met with considerable resistance from Muslim political and community interests. For example, Daud Jusuf (the Minister of Education and Culture between 1978 and 1982) explained that, in the face of Muslim opposition, the regime shelved most of the minister's initiatives (discussed below) to standardise and secularise education. In June 1988, the next Minister of Education, Fuad Hasan, submitted to parliament a controversial draft bill on education,[47] which omitted any mention of religious education. The bill created a furore among the Muslim mainstream, and pressures from Muslim organisational and political interests led to compromise legislation in August. The legislation upheld a 1966 government decision on the compulsory nature of religious instructions in schools.[48]

However, on 27 March 1989 (Education Act No.2/1989), there occurred significant integration of the state-run education systems with the Ministry of Education and Culture assuming responsibility for the administration of most of the religious schools hitherto within the jurisdiction of the religious ministry. This included taking control of the State Tertiary Institutes for Islamic Studies (IAINs), numbering fourteen in total. Since then, the IAINs and other state Islamic schools concentrated on providing Islamic education, with general subjects being phased out of their curriculum.[49] Religious instructions were phased out of the general educational institutions.

The latest reorganisations coincided with a growing political rapprochement between the state and Islam. The regime, consequently, presented the reorganisation of education as a concession to mainstream Muslim interests, among other things, by upgrading religious sciences and studies at state-run Islamic institutions. The upgrading of religious sciences aimed to improve the quality of education at IAINs, by adopting the methodologies of Islamic sciences as taught in western centres of Islamic learning, including in Canada, Britain, the Netherlands and Australia. The regime sought to turn IAINs into a training centre for religious scholars (*ulama*) of the rural *pesantren* networks as a means of increasing the state's jurisdiction over Islamic educational and community affairs. By promoting western educated scholars into the government's religious bureaucracy and by sending some of them back to *pesantren*, the regime was hoping to orient the Muslim community away from attachment to Islamic political and ideological goals and towards active participation in development. Thus, the regime progressively developed IAINs and *pesantren* as centres of (often UNDP-funded) commercial enterprise in addition to being centres of Islamic learning.[50] By 1997, over 75 per cent of *pesantren* had come within the jurisdiction of the state education system.[51]

We now return to the main analysis of the regime's initiatives to remove the political and ideological influence of Islam from education, partially through corporatist restructuring and educational reorientation programs.

Reorienting Islamic Education

Removing the political influence of NU from education

New Order initiatives to reorient Islamic education were bound up with efforts to remove the influence of the NU party both from the Department of Religion and from the religious education system within the department's jurisdiction. We first consider the regime's moves to dislodge NU from the department. NU had turned the Department of Religion into a bureaucratic bastion for the traditionalists during a period of accommodation (late-1950s to mid-1960s) with President Sukarno's guided democracy government. This was at a time that modernists were agitating against Sukarno's government, resulting in the banning of Masyumi, and therefore they were greatly disadvantaged by new power relations. NU was thereby able to use the department as a major source of patronage and positions and exercise an enormous influence over the direction of Islamic education under the department's control during this period. Before the 1971 general election, New Order leaders, especially Ali Murtopo's OPSUS, initially sought to contain NU's influence in the department by co-opting its staff into Golkar as a means of separating them from their loyalties with the NU party. This was in line with national efforts to establish control of the civilian bureaucracy and remove the political influence of both NU and the PNI. Government decisions on compulsory membership of the Civil Service Corps (Korpri) for public servants, and mono-loyalty provisions prohibited all civil servants from having party allegiances or voting for them at the elections.[52] Teachers of Islamic educational institutes, like their secular counterparts, also were drawn further into the corporatist arrangements through their compulsory membership of the Teachers Association of the Indonesian Republic (PGRI). PGRI was formed in 1945 and brought into Golkar as a professional group in 1973.[53]

However, these efforts were initially unsuccessful as the department staff continued to identify with the NU party. The then Minister of Religious Affairs, K.H. Muhammad Dahlan (a NU figure), resisted the Golkar strategy of co-optation, including his refusal to apply legislation concerning mono-loyalty and the requirement that civil servants join Golkar. Instead, he placed NU figures in senior positions in the department and its tertiary institutes. He relieved from their posts non-NU affiliated staff, such as Mulyanto Sumardi (a graduate from Colombia University, USA), Harun Nasution (Dean of the post graduate program at IAIN in Jakarta and graduate from the Institute of Islamic Studies at McGill University), and Sunarjo (former Rector of IAIN Jakarta).[54]

Following this setback, Murtopo's OPSUS began to recruit technocrats and administrators into the religious bureaucracy with which to replace traditionalist bureaucrats. Sumardi and other displaced department staff at the IAIN in Jakarta were among the Muslim administrators recruited by Murtopo. They sought retaliation against Dahlan and joined forces with Murtopo in order to purge NU bureaucrats and establish Golkar's control of the department. Before the general election of 1971, Sumardi and his colleagues at IAIN founded a forum, the Golkar-linked Korps Karyawan Department Agama (Corps of Government Employees of the Department of Religion), to assist them with this strategy. They worked closely with the mostly Chinese-Catholic run Centre for Strategic and International Studies (CSIS), which Murtopo had turned into a centre for his OPSUS campaigns. In August 1970, Sumardi's group met with Murtopo and Sujono Humardani (another of President Suharto's personal assistants who was instrumental to GUPPI initiatives) in Bogor, West Java. There they agreed on the choice of Abdul Mukti Ali (a long-time department employee, a leading scholar in the educational field, and a known moderate with a background in the Muhammadiyah) as the next Minister of Religious Affairs to replace Dahlan.

After his appointment in 1971, Mukti Ali presided over the purging of NU-affiliated department staff. He placed Sumardi as director general of Islamic tertiary institutes in charge of IAINs nationally. Sumardi then implemented a process of institutional rationalisation by, among other things, replacing (NU-affiliated) IAIN rectors.[55] Thus, in the early 1970s, Golkar's strategy to establish 'mono-loyalty' in the Department of Religion and its tertiary institutes largely was directed towards the goal of removing the political and bureaucratic influence of NU, both before and immediately after the election.

New direction for Islamic education

The purge and corporatist reordering of institutional affiliation was to help pave the way for New Order administrators—mostly non-NU aligned Korpri members—to reorient Islamic education. Murtopo had outlined this New Order priority in his book, 'National Political Strategy', which aimed to attain political, institutional and ideological supervision of the Indonesian people, especially to gain people's full participation in national development. People's participation in 'accelerated modernisation' would be implemented through their membership of Golkar-linked professional organisations for youth, women, farmers, fishermen, labour unions, academics, teachers and civil servants.[56] In particular, Murtopo had pursued a strategy of recruiting non-NU graduates from western universities into academic positions, who shared the New Order's anti-party bias, its vision for a secular process of modernisation, and had no background of political activism.

Once appointed, the modernisers (such as Mukti Ali, Sumardi, Harun Nasution, and much later Munawir Sjadzali) embarked on a program to restructure Islamic education, partly in order to replace the 'legalistic' orientation of classical Islamic methodologies with a comparative, 'scientific' approach to Islamic studies viewed as more conducive to development goals. These modernisers regarded NU's jurisprudence-centred approach as being responsible for creating 'narrow-minded' scholars and graduates, who, it was thought, were not equipped to deal with the contemporary challenges thrown up by an industrialising and increasingly urban society. Suharto's administration also was concerned that this preoccupation with a 'legalistic' approach to Islamic education had encouraged psychological attachment to the ideological and political goals of establishing an Islamic state.[57]

As minister, Mukti Ali wished to bring about a reorientation of religious education in Indonesia, which dovetailed with the New Order's determination to modernise religious education and outlook.[58] He was the first in a line of ministers of religion to preside over policies for the creation of a cadre of western educated Muslim intellectuals to counter the practice of sending Muslim graduates to universities in the Middle East. A graduate from McGill University in 1957, studying under the eminent Islamicist, Professor Wilfred

Cantwell Smith, at the Institute of Islamic Studies, he pioneered the science of comparative religions in Indonesia.[59] As minister, he established a McGill unit within the department's research and development section in order to advance comparative religious studies. Programs for the sending of Muslim graduates of IAINs to western universities were intended to assist the government to create a de-politicised campus environment, in which students and academic staff focused their energies on academic pursuits and practical skills and training suitable for industrial occupations.[60] More generally, Ali outlined New Order religious policy, which would give the government a central role in protecting, supporting and guiding religious activities through programs aimed at 'strengthening' the faith of Indonesians providing they remained 'outside of politics'.[61]

Another McGill graduate, who was to implement and elaborate upon the comparative approach, was Harun Nasution. In 1973, Nasution became Rector of the IAIN campus in Jakarta serving under Mukti Ali. In 1973, at a meeting in Bandung, Nasution was assigned to write a textbook for a new IAIN curriculum, which was to be based roughly on the curriculum of the Institute of Islamic Studies at McGill. The result was a textbook entitled 'Islam Viewed From Various Aspects',[62] which sought to apply a 'comprehensive', comparative', and 'rational' understanding of Islamic knowledge, philosophy, theology, mysticism and history. In particular, Nasution sought to introduce *Mutazila* theology and *Shi'ite* ideas, which he viewed as more progressive and modern, to replace, in his opinion, the 'stagnant' teachings of traditionalist schools—*Asy'ariyah* (theology) and *Shafi'i* (jurisprudence)—of *Sunni* orthodoxy. His 'heterodox' curriculum was strongly opposed by orthodox Sunni staff at the IAIN in Jakarta. Although Nasution had strong backing from senior officials, including Mukti Ali and Sumardi, a compromise was reached in which a limited number of subjects on classical Islamic jurisprudence and doctrine were retained within the new curriculum at the Jakarta campus.[63]

Nasution's secular-oriented curriculum was related to the government's efforts to eliminate the psychological attachment of Indonesian Muslims to ideals for an Islamic state. Nasution therefore put forward arguments against political-ideological goals for an Islamic state, as both he and Mukti Ali contended that there was minimal historical justification for such goals. Nasution saw IAIN campuses at that time as a breeding ground for Islamic statist ideals and demands. He also argued that the Islamic party, PPP, had done nothing to advance the interests of Islam. Instead, he advised Indonesian Muslims to place their trust in Suharto and the New Order; they should make accommodations with state power, as Muslim interests would be served through such a strategy.[64] Nasution's statements were in reference to a government clampdown (under the auspices of a program called 'campus normalisation') on IAIN and university campuses in 1978, which sought to remove the political influence of PPP and student associations from tertiary institutes.

The analysis next discusses campus normalisation as an example of the regime's efforts to de-politicise campus life and to extend state control over unmediated Muslim student organisation. Normalisation policy also reinforced earlier efforts to orient the activities of staff and students away from politics and in support of modernisation.

Normalisation of campus life

After PPP's challenge at the 1977 election, waves of student unrest on Islamic and secular campuses in 1977 and 1978 elicited a harsh crackdown by the military and an intensification of coercive measures to contain political activism. In an atmosphere of heightened tension and antagonisms between Muslims and the government, in the weeks before the MPR general session, student demonstrators had called for Suharto's resignation and protested against the blatant manipulations of PPP at the election. Suharto had already taken a more repressive and exclusionary approach to political opposition since the Malari (disaster of 15 January) student riots in early 1974. On this occasion, with Kopkamtib orchestrating the repression, between January and March 1978 the army invaded the more rebellious campuses, such as Gajah Mada University in Yogkakarta and the IAIN in Jakarta. It crushed the protest and arrested student activists and lecturers.[65]

Following this, the government set in train a program of 'normalisation' of campus life (Minister of Education's Campus Normalisation Act of 1978) that required students to concentrate solely on academic pursuits and 'to eliminate harmful problems'. In this de-politicisation of campus life, the government also introduced the concept of the 'three duties of tertiary educational institutions' that stressed 'expertise', responsibility', and 'corporateness'.[66] It replaced independent student bodies, the university students' councils (DEMA), with administration-dominated activity co-ordination bodies and prohibited Islamic student organisations (especially HMI and the NU's PMII) and other student organisations from conducting their activities on the campuses. The co-ordinating bodies were to act as the sole organisational representation for students, who were required to channel their future concerns through the university administrations. The establishment of co-ordinating bodies was part of exclusionary corporatist strategy in that the bodies aimed to capture students' activities and create structural barriers to their participation in politics. With these arrangements, students were supposed to have no political access to the power holders as they became the most recent targets of exclusionary, 'floating mass' policy. The government placed all campus life under the tight control and supervision of the rectors, themselves directly answerable to the government. The university authorities also imposed a strict system of permits on student activities.[67]

According to the former student activist, Azyumardi Azra (currently the Rector of IAIN Jakarta), after the clampdown, Harun Nasution enforced Korpri membership on IAIN lecturers and obliged them to vote for Golkar in future elections.[68] Nasution was concerned that Suharto might do away with the IAIN system and his measures aimed to save the institutions and their education system from possible extinction. Nasution told how the IAIN in Jakarta was accused of being a centre of *Komando Jihad* and struggle for an Islamic state. 'We [the IAIN administration] held dialogues with students to convince them that an Islamic state was not the only acceptable form of state [according to Islamic political ideologies].'[69] In an intelligence operation to discredit the Muslim and student opposition, the Commander of Kopkamtib, Admiral Sudomo (1978–1983), in fact, spread the idea that 'political elements' had entered campuses to struggle for an Islamic state. One of the targets of the Kopkamtib campaign was clearly PPP. As Nasution noted, for example, the Islamic *Ka'bah* sign at the Jakarta IAIN campus had to be taken down because it was considered as being 'identical with PPP'.[70]

An Ali Murtopo protégé at CSIS, the Minister of Education and Culture (1978–1982), Daud Jusuf, was the chief architect of campus normalisation under Kopkamtib auspices. Although the 'normalisation' program was directed towards de-politicisation of campuses in general, Daud, a Muslim by faith, expressed a particular dislike for the Islamic student organisation, HMI. He explained that HMI had played a major role in the protests and riots. HMI 'dominated the student councils [DEMA]: I wanted to force them [HMI] out' of the campuses. Normalisation was also part of his program to reduce religious (Islamic) content at education institutions with the aim of creating a national education system, a goal that was yet to be attained. He regarded many 'Islamic' practices as being responsible for holding back Indonesian education from achieving international standards. He wanted to create on campus a 'scientific community' dedicated to scholarly pursuits. As minister, he therefore abolished the Muslim fasting month as a school holiday and refused Muslim requests to increase the religious content of instruction in schools. He also attracted controversy when he refused requests to build a mosque on the IAIN campus in Jakarta. He explained that he 'thought it was better to build a laboratory or library', given the poor level of educational facilities at the IAIN.[71] Thus, initiatives of the Education Minister to de-politicise campus life went hand in hand with efforts to de-Islamise and secularise education.

Reorienting education in line with Pancasila

This section discusses regime initiatives to reinforce the state's political control over unmediated student organisation and rival Islamic ideology by intensifying its campaign to win Muslim hearts and minds over to *Pancasila* and by seeking to increase its supervision of religious education.

To begin with, coinciding with the normalisation policy, in reaction to the PPP's walkout of the MPR general session of March over P4 and *aliran kepercayaan* legislation, Suharto appointed Gen. (ret.) Alamsjah Ratu Prawiranegara as his next Minister of Religious Affairs (1978–1983). This was in line with a general practice of placing senior army officers (and intelligence staff) in cabinet and government in order to monitor and maintain control over the activities of civilian bureaucrats. Alamsjah had been Coordinator of Cabinet Presidium Personal Staff of the President from 1966 to 1968 and Secretary of State (1968–1972). Suharto delegated Alamsjah the task of persuading Islamic organisations and educational institutions to accept the P4 instructions. According to Alamsjah, Suharto explained to him 'As long as *Pancasila* is unclear to Muslims, or some of them cannot accept it, national unity will always be fragile.'[72] Alamsjah formulated three basic program objectives of religious policy. The first was to get all religions to accept *Pancasila* (P4) instructions. The second was to get all religions to support the government's development programs. The third was to achieve harmony of religious life for the sake of national stability.[73]

He went on regular circuits of Islamic university campuses, IAINs and to Islamic organisational meetings and events and sought to win a commitment of Muslim students to the government's corporatist ideology by urging compliance to P4. He called on students to sharpen their intellectual and technical skills, to remove the 'bad image attached to Islam', and to participate in development. The P4 campaign on campuses was an intensification of earlier attempts to bring about an ideological reorientation of student life, which hitherto had focused on reducing the content of Islamic instructions that were based on classical texts and teaching methods.[75]

The next Minister of Religious Affairs, Munawir Sjadzali (serving for two terms, 1983–1993), stepped up efforts to win over Muslim adherence and conformity to *Pancasila* ideology. In support of these efforts, he called for the *reaktualisasi* ('reactualisation') of Islamic doctrine and its Scripture. *Reaktualisasi* was another word for the reinterpretation of Islam's classical texts in light of present contexts and issues to bring contemporary relevance to Islam's message and law. However, Munawir called for a re-actualisation of Islamic doctrine as part of his effort to convince Muslims that *Pancasila* was not antithetical to Islam.[76] Munawir sought to persuade the Muslim political community that they could implement Islamic values without having to establish a theocratic state, and that *Pancasila* did not threaten to replace Islam's religious existence, as some Muslim activists had claimed.

Munawir propounded his *reaktualisasi* ideas in response to a specific political context. That is, government efforts to enforce the sole foundation law had caused strident reactions from Muslim leaders and preachers. The leaders condemned *azas tunggal* as attacking Islam's religious base, and their protests culminated in riots in Jakarta's port district of Tanjung Priok. Suharto charged his Minister of Religious Affairs with the task of assisting to overcome the tensions and suspicions of *Pancasila*. Munawir explained that the government's main approach to overcoming 'Islamic political extremism' was through the introduction of educational programs that aimed to deepen people's understanding of the 'essence' or 'substance' of religion. In this way, it was hoped that Indonesian Muslims would be educated out of 'narrow' comprehension of scripture-based formalism, which had led them to attach great importance to the ideal of Islamic institutions regulating the affairs of the state.[77]

Munawir's *reaktualisasi* agenda coincided with government efforts to persuade Muslims to accept the P4 instructions. Persuasion was adopted only after the state had engaged its repressive instruments as security forces shot hundreds of protesters at Tanjung Priok and arrested and imprisoned outspoken opponents of *azas tunggal*. The state's repressive instruments were invariably at the ready to underwrite, or prepare the ground for, institutional and ideological systems of compliance.

Munawir also re-instituted the policy began by Mukti Ali and Sumardi (but also dropped by them because of opposition to the policy within the IAINs) of sending IAIN graduates to western institutions. He shared with his predecessors the vision of developing IAIN graduates, who would 'broaden their academic horizons and learn the critical approach to science, including religious science'.[78] He presided over the pedagogical approach that acknowledged Islam as an important source of moral values for state and society. Thus, in 1987, he launched a new type of senior Islamic high school that provided 70 per cent religious and Arabic studies in its curriculum and only 30 per cent secular subjects. This initiative was a partial reversal of earlier policy that saw Islamic schools offer 30 per cent religious subjects and 70 per cent secular subjects respectively.[79] Ministerial Decree No.122 of July 1988, saw the reorganisation of studies at the 14 IAINs and marked the phasing out of general subjects taught at the institutes and the closure of general teachers' training departments. From the late-1980s through to the 1990s, the IAINs increasingly became centres of the Islamic sciences, developed according to models borrowed from Islamic centres of learning in the West. The IAINs provided regular, short-term intensive courses to independent *ulama* in order to upgrade their comprehension of the Islamic sciences and to draw them away from classical studies at those *pesantren* which still stressed learn-by-wrote methodologies. This policy coincided with the growing accommodation between the state and Islam, and Suharto and Munawir presented the course upgrades as evidence of the regime's deepening interest in Islam.[80]

However, the policy also reflected other considerations—namely, the upgrading of religious content at Islamic schools came from an awareness in government circles that secular campuses had become a breeding ground for 'radical' and 'fundamentalist' religious sentiment and goals, especially among students trained in the physical and technical sciences. Munawir explained that the 'fanatical' attachment of Muslim students to Islam's political goals arose from students (particularly those who had graduated from Islamic schools to secular institutions) not possessing sufficient comprehension of Islam.[81] Restrictions on campus activities, achieved through corporatist reordering of academic and student associations, had forced students underground and resulted in a proliferation of unregulated cells and study groups on campus. Many of these groups were committed to more fundamental and purist goals for the realisation of an Islamic society untainted by a secular state.[82] To a large degree, the groups managed to evade the state's security and surveillance apparatus, and thus greatly concerned Suharto.

By contrast, as a consequence of reorientation of Islamic education, understandably, graduates of Muslim tertiary institutes and state-run IAINs would develop a much broader understanding than their secular counterparts of the philosophical, theological and historical roots of religion. Relatively speaking, graduates of Muslim institutions, therefore, would tend to hold more moderate and tolerant views of Islam regarding other religions and the state, it was argued.[83] In short, the focus of state leaders had shifted from suspecting IAINs of being centres of Islamic political goals to suspecting secular campuses of becoming potential centres of Islamic fundamentalism and resistance.[84] This resulted in a rethinking of religious education policy insofar as it was seen as beneficial to increase religious content under the guidance of the state to help overcome unregulated religious ideology.

Thus, Munawir's reorientation of religious policy sought to re-take the initiative from student groups and Islamic organisations by increasing the state's involvement in the moral development and management of Islamic society and religious pedagogy. Among its initiatives, the government also tried to counter the proliferation of unmediated student groups by co-opting preachers who were known to conduct activities on campuses and sponsoring them to press the government's message at universities. It also established state-guided *pesantren kilat* (fast-track courses in Islamic morality for students) on campuses and organised children from their pre-school years onwards into *Qu'ran* recital clubs and other state approved social-religious activities. In an attempt to capture the unmediated activities of students and youth, these activities were organised through Golkar affiliates and other state corporatist groupings (discussed further in chapter five).[85]

In conclusion, the state's political strategy regarding Islamic education was determined by the same set of priorities that had led army leaders to pursue a strategy for the de-politicisation of the parties and de-Islamisation of politics. That is, the state's primary objective was to create stability for the sake of achieving economic take-off through growth-oriented development. New Order modernisers like Ali Murtopo decided that the best way to guarantee political stability was through restructuring the political system and institutions. This resulted in the re-channelling of mass memberships of organisations into professional and functional groups, thereby cutting them off from links to the political parties. The removal of NU party members from the Department of Religion and its education institutes was part of broader efforts to eliminate the dual loyalties of civil servants and bureaucrats to the government and the political parties. Compulsory membership of Korpri and the teachers' association, PGRI, and the mono-loyalty provisions were paramount to these efforts.

Murtopo, in particular, re-assigned the programs and activities of professional organisations to development-oriented tasks and away from political activism. Education was one crucial area that progressively came under political control—which, to some extent, was achieved through the incorporation of academics and teachers into corporatist organisations like

Golkar, Korpri and PGRI and through the formation of co-ordinating bodies as the intended sole mechanism for channelling student activities on campus. Campus restrictions, however, had forced Muslim students to establish numerous study groups and cells that by-passed the authorised co-ordinating bodies and university hierarchy and thereby remained unmediated by the state. Subsequent regime initiatives for the moral development of students and youth aimed to recapture, in state frameworks, unmediated activities. Like memberships of the political parties and organisations, students also were expected to undergo intensive ideological reorientation programs (P4). These programs had as their central goal the creation of academics, scholars, and students who would spearhead modernisation processes and remain disengaged from political parties and organisations.

MANAGING RELIGIOUS HARMONY

Similar to state initiatives regarding the political parties and Islamic educational institutions, Suharto's administration tried to increase its supervision over religious communities and to bring them into state-delineated parameters— especially as it sought conformity to *Pancasila* and to national goals for development and stability. Part of these efforts involved corporatist capture through state charter of national-level religious institutions. Thus, during the 1970s, the regime assigned religious associations as national peak bodies to channel the interests of Indonesia's five main religious communities—Islam, Catholicism, Protestantism, Hinduism, and Buddhism—religions that were accorded official recognition. There was the Indonesian Council of Ulama (MUI), the Communion of Indonesian Churches (PGI), the Indonesian Council of Bishops (MAWI), the Indonesian Association of Hindu Dharma, and the Representation of the Indonesian Buddhist Community (WALUBI). In 1980, the regime brought these five councils into a single Forum for Inter-religious Consultation (WMAB). WMAB was intended largely as a dialogue forum between religious communities and through which the regime could communicate official concerns and policy to selected spokespersons of the five religions.[86]

These organisations provided the regime with one formal means with which to regulate and inter-mediate relations between the state and religious communities. The regime sought to 'harmonise' state–religious relations, after a decade of sporadic inter-religious strife and growing antagonisms between the state and Islam (mid-1960s to late-1970s) had raised concerns about stability. As a culmination of these concerns, in 1978, the Minister of Religious Affairs, Alamsjah, issued a policy statement called 'three harmonies (*tri kerukunan*)', which was an attempt at reorientation and guidance of religious life, so that it would not disrupt social harmony and order.[87] The most important of the three harmonies was the attainment of harmony between the state and religion, especially Islam. The stated aim was to assist the government to establish national stability and security by reorienting religious life to the priority of national development. Good state–religious relations, it was stipulated, depended on the implementation of *Pancasila* (P4) indoctrination courses within society. In particular, the aim was to unify and harmonise the perceptions of Muslims concerning government policy. It sought to 'remove mutual suspicions between the state and Islam caused by sharp criticism of government policy' during the 1977 general election and at the MPR general session of 1978.[88]

Alamsjah identified as a second priority the attainment of internal harmony of each religious community, by removing 'internal contradictions', 'especially doctrinal ones.'[89] In practice, this meant that each religion was supposed to have a single interpretation of their creed, in conformity with *Pancasila* ideology. Thus, internal harmonising entailed defining and circumscribing what constituted mainstream religion, although efforts to define orthodoxy pre-dated the New Order. Suharto reinforced a decree, issued by Sukarno, that to obtain legal recognition in Indonesia, a religion must demonstrate belief in a transcendent almighty God, possess a prophet and have a holy scripture as a major point of reference and prayer.[90] In 1966, as an anti-communist measure, the Provisional MPR decided to ban atheism and make religious education compulsory.[91]

The objective of 'internal harmonising' was to bring religious groupings under the management of the state thereby eliminating unmediated religious tendencies. Suharto used the religious institutions to rubber stamp decisions to ban 'suspicious' religious movements. The main reason given for official prohibitions was that the group in question demonstrated unorthodox behaviour that deviated from mainstream religious practice and posed a threat to local and/or national order and security. The regime required religious splinter groups (*kelompok sempalan*) and spiritual movements that laid claim to being a religion, but fell outside of the official definitions, to merge with one of the five world religions that they most closely resembled. For instance, Religious Minister's Instruction No.8 of 1979 outlined the state's position regarding Islam. It clarified that, in joint cooperation, the Attorney General, the Department of Internal Affairs, Bakin intelligence, regional governments, MUI and Islamic institutions were to provide intensive 'reorientation, guidance and surveillance' of Islamic organisations and movements that were found to be in conflict with Islamic doctrine.[92] These nonconformist/'deviating' groups were to be guided back onto the 'correct path of Islamic teachings'.[93] If they failed to comply, their legal existence remained uncertain and they risked prohibition. In the name of religious guidance, between 1971 and 1987, the Attorney General's Department banned at least twenty-nine religious teachings, practices, movements, and/or books. Between 1988 and 1990, it prohibited twenty-one, eighteen of them related to Islam and three to Christianity.[94]

However, Suharto sponsored attempts by Javanese mystical orders (*kebatinan*) to attain separate legal status as a religion, later called *aliran kepercayaan* ('mystical belief systems'), as part of efforts by army leaders, who were themselves inclined to practise Javanese mysticism, to counter the influence of political Islam. In December 1970, Golkar incorporated *aliran* through establishing the Coordinating Secretariat of Belief Movements (SKK).[95] In 1978, as a concession to Muslim opposition, Suharto accorded to belief systems separate organisational recognition as a 'culture', not religion, under the jurisdiction of the Ministry of Education and Culture. In 1981, a sole national body named the Directorate for the Supervision of the Followers of Belief Systems was established.[96]

In this way, Javanese mystical sects and other religious orders could obtain legality outside of the five religions, but also had to adhere to strict parameters of belief and practice as defined by the state.[97] The state banned hundreds of mystical sects that failed to meet these requirements, especially in the aftermath of the 1965 coup attempt when it dissolved sects and outlawed forms of mysticism that state intelligence agencies had identified as being infiltrated by communists and as endangering social order and stability.[98] At first, the responsibility of monitoring and banning mystical movements resided with the watchdog authority, Supervision of the Belief Movements in Society (PAKEM), established by the Ministry of Religious Affairs in 1952.[99] By 1967, the Attorney General assumed control of PAKEM and responsibility for issuing formal bans after receiving instructions from President Suharto, who personally assessed the reports of Bakin intelligence concerning the activities of suspect religious movements. As part of the government's cultural assimilation policy, PAKEM also supervised restrictions on Chinese customs and rituals, which were to be practised within the confines of the family household and not in public.[100]

We have seen how the regime branded as 'deviant' religious tendencies that fell outside of mainstream religious belief and urged them to merge with authorised religion. The stigmatising of groups as religiously 'deviant' also became a weapon of state officials wishing to garner the support of religious authority behind its security operations against grassroots resistance and counter ideologies to the state. On one occasion, for example, in February 1989, the government mobilised Muslim opinion behind military actions against the alleged Islamic insurgency in and around the district of Way Jepara, Lampung (South Sumatra). The army reportedly killed at least twenty-seven 'militants' belonging to a group identified as 'warrior followers of Allah', led by Anwar (alias Warsidi). It denounced the group as a security disturbance movement (GPK—a derogatory label often employed by state officials against troublemakers). In an effort to discredit the local disturbance, government/ ABRI spokespersons accused Warsidi's group of spreading teachings that deviated from mainstream Islam and of trying to establish an Islamic state. Consequently, Muslim community leaders of Lampung chapters of the MUI, NU *pesantren*, the Muhammadiyah, IAINs, and Islamic *dakwah* organisations reiterated ABRI's calls for 'increased community vigilance against misleading religious interpretations and deviant sects'. The military commander in charge of operations, Hendropriyono, was at the forefront of a smear campaign against Warsidi. Before a specially convened meeting of 1,000 Muslim preachers, *pesantren* leaders and *dakwah* institutions, he declared that it was 'better to call' Warsidi's group 'dirty cats' as they had 'strayed from mainstream religious teachings and used the mask of religion for their own ends'.[101] The regional head of NU instructed his community to 'always hold fast' to government explanations of the incident, not to give outside preachers the chance to deliver sermons, and to report immediately such sermons to authorised agencies.[102]

Thus, after the security operations, government spokespersons announced the decision to establish tighter ideological control of the Way Jepara community with a regime of periodic religious guidance. The Minister of Internal Affairs sought to disassociate the disturbance from grassroots protest and instead declared that his department faced the challenge of raising 'village community national defense, especially in the fields of ideology and politics'.[103] The assistant rector of IAIN in Lampung proposed that the Departments of Religion, Education, and Social Affairs and IAIN and MUI should give religious guidance to the community 'so that those who once felt sympathy for [Warsidi's] movement know that they are wrong' and 'truly know the danger of misleading teachings'.[104] As part of the government's guidance of religion, the Lampung Attorney General banned twenty-four religious sects, and reportedly placed 11,596 adherents of sects under security surveillance.[105]

In the final analysis, the implementation of the state's 'internal' harmonising objectives had far-reaching implications for local communities. The idea of religious deviance was manipulated in order to legitimise state repression, which was then followed by intensive ideological guidance and reorientation programs. This constituted an extreme form of exclusionary policy, in which the government called on the state-chartered MUI and *dakwah* organisations (which had been corporatised—see chapter five), in conjunction with IAINs and local religious organisations to back the state's follow-up operations after crushing the localised dissent. Suharto resorted to repression in order to restrict the growth of independent religious movements and to stamp out religious insurgencies. These efforts reinforced corporatism in that they sought to eliminate unmediated religious tendencies and bring them under state guidance and control. Thus, as was the case with political parties, religious communities had to form corporatist mergers and were subject to ideological redefinition and exclusion.

The third harmony concerned inter-religious relations. Its purpose was to co-ordinate the activities of different religions, to unify and harmonise perceptions regarding sensitive issues of ritual belief and practice, and to remove 'contradictions' that might lead to conflict between religions. The inter-religious forum, WMAB, was established to mediate points of tension and to guide the behaviour of religious adherents so that one religious community did not disturb another (through proselytising or defamatory remarks) and cause social instability in the process.[106]

Thus, Alamsjah issued ministerial decisions for the regulation of religious life. For example, together with the Minister of Internal Affairs, he issued Joint Decision No.1 of 1979 concerning 'Methods of Implementation of Religious Propagation and Foreign Aid to Religious Institutes in Indonesia'. The crucial passages of this decision were clauses four and six. Clause four stated that 'implementation of religious propaganda directed at another group already embracing a faith was not permitted' if the following methods were used:

1) Offering enticements with or without giving goods, money, clothing, food and or water, medical treatment, medicines, and any other gifts aimed at converting adherents of one faith to the proselytising faith;
2) Distributing pamphlets, magazines, bulletins, books, etc., to those of another religion, or;
3) Conducting house-to-house calls to religious adherents (of another faith).[107]

Restrictions on proselytising sought to overcome points of tension and conflict that had erupted since the mid-1960s. Clause six aimed to monitor and control foreign aid and foreign missionary activities in Indonesia by placing them under the surveillance of the international co-ordinating work committee at the Department of Religion. Suharto was particularly sensitive to the potential challenge to Indonesia's sovereignty posed by unregulated influx of foreign aid through religious foundations.

WMAB was the formal mechanism for deliberating upon government regulation and control. However, inter-religious strife at provincial, regency and district levels was to be dealt with by the respective government authorities, including the Department of Internal Affairs, the Department of Religion and Kopkamtib in consultation with local religious leaders.[108] The Commander of security operations (Pangkopkamtib) explained local disturbances to the inter-religious forum and advised the religious councils therein of the public statements it was to issue nationally concerning particular incidents. For example, regarding inter-religious conflict in Solo (Central Java) in 1980, after clarifications from Pangkopkamtib, the five councils issued a statement typical of military propaganda. According to the statement, 'the whole community was to raise vigilance, awareness and national discipline', 'to increase implementation of *Pancasila*', and 'to increase understanding of religion'. The statement recognised the need to perfect a national system of education that trained and oriented Indonesian youth to nationalism, patriotism, greater intellectual and religious awareness and economic development.[109] Hence, the forum became an instrument of government propaganda and indoctrination.

Alamsjah also issued instructions regarding the tight monitoring of Islamic *dakwah*. For example, Minister of Religion Decision No.44 of 1978 established guidelines for the close guidance and surveillance of religious *dakwah*, including sermons given via radio broadcasts. This was followed by Minister of Religion Instruction No.9 of 1978 for the implementation of Decision No.44 and by Circular No.3 of 1978 to the heads of the office of religious affairs at provincial, regency and district levels. The instructions required that all sermons delivered before an audience of over three hundred people had to report their program itinerary, and names of organisers and preachers to the security forces/police. MUI was instructed to work in conjunction with the Department of Religion and other government agencies to streamline monitoring efforts. These efforts were to ensure that sermons did not carry any anti-government messages, did not stir up inter-religious strife, and were consonant with *Pancasila* ideology. The department was responsible for reporting violations to the police and offenders could receive a maximum sentence of five years gaol under criminal law.[110]

To sum up, as was the case with the other harmonising initiatives, in order to achieve harmony of inter-religious relations the state sought to regulate and reorient the religious communities, with the WMAB acting as a mediating institution between the state and religious communities, and as a channel for communicating the regime's concerns and messages to constituencies. Suharto was determined to ensure that inter-religious conflict and the potential of Islam becoming a source of local dissent (including through political-ideological goals for an Islamic state) did nor disrupt stability or undermine development.

CONCLUSION

The analysis has considered three different target areas of the state's policies of exclusion: the Islamic parties, Islamic education, and the religious harmonising program. The three target areas were interrelated as they were subject to the same set of policy objectives, political constraints and historical timeframe. In each case, state leaders sought to restructure the organisational existence of Islam and subject their memberships to ideological reorientation and guidance to conform with *Pancasila* and in fulfilment of development goals. National trends and struggles regarding de-politicisation of the Islamic parties (especially PPP) influenced government policy concerning education, which also was subject to de-politicisation efforts. In particular, the regime sought to rechannel the Muslim constituency away from Islamic political-ideological commitments (especially for the establishment of an Islamic state) and towards development priorities. Harmonising of religious relations reinforced these broader efforts to attain ideological and institutional conformity, through state guidance and regulation, in a de-politicised environment. To harmonise meant to unify both perceptions and institutions and to make them accord with overall political and ideological restructuring and/or reorientation. The regulation and control of religious life was partly achieved through exclusionary corporatist arrangements: the delimitation (through establishment of peak organisations) of what were permissible religious groups, conduct and activities and the prohibition of impermissible groups.

NOTES

1. The analysis does not consider the range of state interventions in the leadership choices and organisational operation of the five religious institutions, as this would move the discussion away from its specific focus on Muslim interests. Chapter four deals in detail with the corporatist organisations specifically created to channel the interests of Muslim *ulama* (religious scholars and leaders).

2. Moreover, as argued in footnote 27 of chapter three, 'organicist' thought commonly provided ideological support for corporatist systems of interest representation.

3. Noer, *The Modernist Muslim Movement*; Federspiel, *Persatuan Islam*.

4. Peacock, *Purifying the Faith*; Syamsuddin, 'The case of Muhammadiyah'; Federspiel, 'The Muhammadiyah'.

5. In particular, NU was established as a direct result of a decision to defend and represent the interests of traditionalists in the Hijaz after the Wahabbi leader, Abdul-Aziz ibn Saud had captured Mecca and restricted Syafi'i rituals and education there.

6. Barton and Fealy, *Nahdlatul Ulama*; van Bruinessen, *NU: Tradisi*.

7. Noer, *Partai Islam*; McVey, 'Faith as the Outsider'.

8. Barton, 'The Emergence of Neo-Modernism'.

9. Kamal, *Muslim Intellectual Responses*, pp.82–3; Crouch, 'The Indonesian Army', p.571.

10. Crouch, 'The Indonesian Army', pp.573–6; Salam, *Sedjarah Partai Muslimin*, p.29.

11. In one manoeuvre, Mintaredja enlisted a close colleague in Surabaya to dissolve the East Java executive of old guard leaders and form a new one under his own leadership. Ward, *The 1971 Election*, pp.115–20; Crouch, 'The Indonesian Army', pp.577–8.

12. Minteradja tried to persuade the Muslim youth that the modernists' struggle for implementation of Islamic prescriptions was misplaced and wasted Islam's energies that could be better spent on economic development goals. He promoted the young Muslims into executive positions within Parmusi as they replaced disaffected Masyumi leaders who were preoccupied with realising Islam's political objectives. Mintaredja's initiatives paralleled those of Murtopo, who used his OPSUS to craft Golkar's election strategy and growth-oriented development programs. Ward, *The 1971 Election*, p.128; Kamal, *Muslim Intellectual Responses*, pp.84–5.

13. van Bruinessen, *NU: Tradisi*, pp.93–103.

14. Ward, *The 1971 Election*, pp.42–3; Cahyono, *Peranan Ulama Dalam Golkar*, pp.87–115.

15. van Bruinessen, *NU: Tradisi*, pp.74–109; Imawan, 'The Evolution of Political Party', p.197.
16. Imawan, 'The Evolution of Political Party', p.198.
17. Jones, 'The Contraction and Expansion', p. 10.
18. As Imawan pointed out, the party fusion caused a 'bottle-neck' through which 'elements of the composite parties had to struggle to promote candidates' for a small number of seats in the regional and national legislatures. Imawan also observed that the security and intelligence operations of Bakin and Kopkamtib, including direct intervention in the choice of party leaders and 'spreading of controversial issues' 'were to keep conflict alive within political parties, so the parties could not consolidate power to challenge the government'. Imawan, 'The Evolution of Political Party', p.184.
19. Idham Chalid (the chairman of NU) became party president and Bisri Sjansuri (*rais aam* of NU's religous council) chairman of PPP's religious council (Majelis Syuro). van Bruinessen, *NU: Tradisi*, pp.103–4; Syamsuddin Haris, 'PPP and Politics', pp.11–12.
20. Suryadinata, *Political Parties*, pp.25–8; Liddle, 'The 1977 Indonesian Election', p.13.
21. Haris, *PPP Dan Politik*, p.1.
22. van Bruinessen, *NU: Tradisi*, pp.103–4; Imawan, 'The Evolution of Political Party', p.202.
23. Liddle, 'The 1977 Indonesian Election', pp.13–25; Ismail, 'Pancasila as the Sole Basis', pp.8–10.
24. van Bruinessen, *NU: Tradisi*, p.105; Liddle, 'The 1977 Indonesian Election', p.17.
25. The government required its citizens to profess one of five state-authorised religions. Official recognition of *aliran kepercayaan* would give Indonesians a fifth choice and would threaten to erode the claim of Muslim leaders that around 90 per cent of the population professed the faith of Islam; van Bruinessen, *NU: Tradisi*, pp.106–7; Adnan, 'Islamic Religion', pp.454–6.
26. Jones, 'The Contraction and Expansion', p.11.
27. Jones, 'The Contraction and Expansion', pp.10–11.
28. Jones, 'The Contraction and Expansion', pp.11–12; van Bruinessen, *NU: Tradisi*, p.111; Haris, *PPP dan Politik*, p.15.
29. Suryadinata, *Political Parties*, pp.44–8.
30. Suryadinata, *Political Parties*, p.56.
31. Haris, *PPP dan Politik*, pp.10–12; Suryadinata, *Political Parties*, p.31.
32. Morfit, 'Pancasila Orthodoxy', p.48.
33. Ismail, 'Pancasila as the Sole Basis', p.11.
34. Faisal, 'Pancasila as the Sole Basis', pp.11–12; Suryadinata, *Political Parties*, pp.49–50.

35. Faisal, 'Pancasila as the Sole Basis', p.14: Tamara, 'Islam under the New Order', p.17.
36. Tamara, 'Islam under the New Order', p.16.
37. 'Undang-Undang Republik Indonesia Nomor 8 Tahun 1985'; 'Penjelasan Atas Undang-Undang Republik Indonesia Nomor 8 Tahun 1985'; 'Pelaksanaan Undang-Undang Nomor 8 Tahun 1985'; 'Penjelasan Atas Peraturan Pemerintah Republik Indonesia Nomor 18 Tahun 1986', pp.1–28.
38. See previous footnote; Adnan, 'Islamic Religion', p.464.
39. Nakamura, 'NU's Leadership Crisis', pp.102–5; Haris, *PPP Dan Politik*, p.23.
40. Haris, *PPP Dan Politik*, p.1.
41. Tamara, 'Islam under the New Order', pp.17–18; Haris, *PPP Dan Politik*, p.21.
42. Tamara, 'Islam under the New Order', p.18; Imawan, 'The Evolution of Political Party', p.216; Haris, *PPP Dan Politik*, p.33.
43. Haris, *PPP Dan Politik*, pp.18–22; Tamara, 'Islam under the New Order', p.18.
44. Interview with Aisyah Hamid Baidlowi (Chairwoman of NU-Muslimat), 11 March 1997; Rasyid, 'Preparing for Post-Soeharto Rule', pp.155–6; *Forum Keadilan*, 10 February 1997; van Bruinessen, 'The 28th Congress of the Nahdlatul Ulama', p.146.
45. Meeting with GP Ansor leaders in Bangil, East Java, 10 August 1997; interview with Haji Ahmad Jaman (leader of GP Ansor Kotamadia Pasuruan), 10 August 1997; meeting in Situbondo of East Java chapters of NU, 5 August 1997; annual meeting of the leadership of Muslimat for the Greater Jakarta Region, 3 April 1997; meeting at P3M, entitled 'Menemukan "Jangkar" Politik Gus-Dur', 11 April 1997; 'Laporan Situasi Daerah', Pengurus Cabang NU, 7 May 1997.
46. Dhofier, *Tradition and Change*; Noer, *Administration of Islam*, pp.24–41.
47. The bill was first drafted in 1978 and was a continuing source of contention and debate.
48. Mudzhar, *Fatwas of the Council*, pp.58–9.
49. The removal of general subjects from the Islamic institutes sparked student protests on a number of the campuses. Aqsha et al., *Islam in Indonesia: A Survey of Events*, pp.385–441.
50. It is important to note that state-run Islamic education was not a dominant part of mainstream Islamic education, which was conducted by thousands of privately run Islamic boarding schools (*pesantren*) scattered throughout mainly rural Java. State-sponsored initiatives to incorporate education into a national system continually confronted the problem of how to deal with the independence of the *pesantren* universe. In seeking to overcome this problem, even before Education Act No.2/1989, the regime sought to turn the IAINs into a training centre for religious scholars (*ulama*), with the

intention of returning an increasing number of the state-trained, and especially western educated, *ulama* to teach at private *pesantren*. A survey conducted in 1986 by the *pesantren*-based NGO, P3M, found that graduates of state-run IAINs led around 10 per cent of *pesantren* in Indonesia. Since the Education Act, the regime has stepped up these efforts and, in the process, sought to increase the state's jurisdiction over Islamic education. Interview with Zamakhsyari Dhofier, 20 November 1997; Dhofier, *Tradition and Change*; 'Intellectual Engineering in IAIN', *Studia Islamika*; Aqsha et al., *Islam in Indonesia: A Survey of Events*, pp.385–441.

51. Information drawn from work done by Greg Fealy in April 1997 and May 1999.
52. Emmerson, 'The Bureaucracy in Political Context', pp.96–109; Ward, *The 1971 Election*, p.97.
53. Murtopo, *Strategi Politik Nasional*, p.80.
54. Feillard, 'Traditionalist Islam', p.64; Munhanif, 'Islam and the Struggle', pp.101–2.
55. Interview with Mulyanto Sumardi (former Director General of Islamic Tertiary Institutes), 27 March 1997; Munhanif, 'Religious Thought of Mukti Ali', pp.101–3.
56. Moertopo, *Strategi Politik Nasional*.
57. Interviews with Sumardi, 27 March 1997; Mukti Ali (former Minister of Religious Affairs and religious scholar educated at McGill University), 4 January 1994; Harun Nasution (former Rector of IAIN Jakarta), 12 June 1996; Daud Yusuf (Minister of Education, 1978–1982), 24 November 1997; Admiral (ret.) Sudomo, 30 October 1997.
58. At a practical level, Ali introduced subjects that gave instruction and training in economically productive skills that would aid community development. By the late 1980s, senior secondary madrasah were giving skills-training programs in electronics, dressmaking, computer skills, welding, automotive mechanics, business administration and agribusiness. Munhanif, 'Religious Thought of Mukti Ali'; Dhofier, *Tradition and Change*, p.56; Noer, *Administration of Islam*, p.41.
59. Before the New Order, in August 1960, the Department of Religion had appointed Mukti Ali to head the departments of comparative religion at IAIN campuses in Jakarta and Yogyakarta.
60. Sumardi explained that the government was initially forced to abort its program for the sending of graduates to western tertiary institutions because of strong protest by Muslim leaders, who viewed the initiative as an attempt to displace religion with secular education. Interview with Sumardi, 27 March 1997.
61. Munhanif, 'Religious Thought of Mukti Ali', pp.105–6.
62. Nasution, *Islam Ditinjau dari*.

63. Interview with Nasution, 13 June 1996; interview with Sumardi, 27 March 1997; Muzani, 'Intellectual Portrait of Harun Nasution'.
64. Interview with Nasution, 13 June 1996.
65. Interview with Azumardi Azra (former student activist at IAIN Jakarta and liberal scholar), 18 November 1996; Mackie MacIntyre, 'Politics', pp.13–14; Reeve, *Golkar of Indonesia*, p.348.
66. 'Sambutan Menteri Agama R.I. Pada Dies Natalis Ke XI IAIN', p.43; Southwood and Flanagan, *Indonesia: Law, Propaganda*, p.90.
67. Reeve, *Golkar of Indonesia*, p.348; Azis, 'Meraih Kesempatan Studi Kasus', p.6; Fuaduddin TM., 'Kelompok Keagamaan di IKIP', p.21; Haidlor, 'Kelompok-Kelompok Keagamaan', pp.40–1.
68. Azyumardi explained that student protests were over 'alleged government hostility to Islam', including its efforts to incorporate *aliran kepercayaan* into the GBHN, restrictions on student activities since the 'Malari' riots of 1974, and government manipulations of PPP during the 1977 election. For their part, state officials tried to discredit the protests by accusing Muslim students of seeking to establish an Islamic state. This was the view that Harun Nasution subscribed to, but Azumardi rejected the accusation as unrealistic. Interview with Azyumardi, 18 November 1996. (Azyumardi was among the student activists arrested and imprisoned for his role in the student unrest.) Two decades later the former Commander of Kopkamtib operations responsible for ordering the crackdown, Admiral (ret.) Sudomo, was firm in his view that 'there were political elements that entered the campuses from outside to try to bring the country to an Islamic state'. Interview with Sudomo, 30 October 1997.
69. Interview with Nasution, 13 June 1996; *Refleksi Pembaharuan Pemikiran Islam*, pp.44–9.
70. Interviews with Nasution, 13 June 1996 and Sudomo, 30 October 1997; Pour, *Laksamana Sudomo*, pp.234–8.
71. Interviews with Jusuf, 24 November 1997; Bambang Pranowo (an official at the BIMAS and Haji Affairs at the Department of Religion), 13 March 1997.
72. Parikesit and Sempurnadjaja, *H. Alamsjah Ratu Prawiranegara*, p.244; Sempurnadjaja, *H. Alamsjah Ratu Prawiranegara*.
73. Interview with Alamsjah Ratu Prawiranegara (Minister of Religious Affairs, 1978–1983), 22 September 1997.
74. 'Sambutan Menteri Agama R.I. Pada Dies Natalis Ke XII IAIN', pp.11–13; 'Sambutan Menteri Agama R.I. Pada Dies Natalis Ke XIV IAIN', pp.36–9.
75. As well as establishing greater control over student activities on campus, Suharto was determined to bring tighter discipline to the Department of Religion. According to Alamsjah, Suharto requested him to take control of, reorganise and bring military type administrative discipline to the Department of Religion and to bring it once and for all, loyally behind

Golkar. As Alamsjah noted, Suharto considered Mukti Ali had failed to remove satisfactorily NU's influence from the Department. 'New Order intelligence services (Murtopo's OPSUS and Bakin) remained suspicious of the Department, because only about 30 per cent of its staff had supported Golkar at the 1971 and 1977 elections'. Interview with Alamsjah, 22 September 1997.

76. Sjadzali, *Islam dan Tata Negara.*
77. Effendi, 'Munawir Sjadzali and the Development'; *H.Munawir Sjadzali, Bunga Rampai Wawasan Islam,* pp.42–8.
78. Interview with Munawir Sjadzali (Minster of Religious Affairs for two terms, 1983–1993), 4 April 1997.
79. Nafis et al., *70 Tahun Prof Dr H. Munawir Sjadzali,* p.85; Aqsha et al., *Islam in Indonesia: A Survey of Events,* p.385.
80. Aqsha et al., *Islam in Indonesia: A Survey of Events,* pp.386—404; interview with Munawir, 4 April 1997.
81. Interview with Munawir, 4 April 1997; Munawir, *Bunga Rampai Wawasan Islam,* p.14.
82. Two interviews with Imaduddin Abdulrahim (Islamic preacher, founder of the Salman Mosque student movement, and ICMI member), 15 February 1994, 2 September 1996; Rosyad, 'A Quest For True Islam'.
83. Interviews with Munawir, 4 April 1997; Komaruddin Hidayat (IAIN alumni), 16 October 1996; Harun Nasution, 13 June 1996; Nuryamin Aini (Faculty of Islamic Law, IAIN Jakarta), 16 October 1996.
84. Suharto was particularly concerned about the prospect of the Islamic revolution in Iran (1979) influencing developments in Indonesia, especially Indonesia's student population.
85. Established in 1976, the *Pesantren Kilat* movement began on campus with the aim of defending the faith of Muslim youth from 'secularisation movements and the Christian Mission'. Rifki, 'A Quest For True Islam', pp.71–5. By the mid-1980s, the original movement declined on campus after the state arrested some of its leaders for alleged subversive and terrorist activities. Since then, there has been a diversification of subsequent *pesantren kilat* activities in numerous Islamic organisations, mosques and government departments. However, it was not until June 1996, after meetings with the Department of Education and Culture, the Department of Religion and MUI, that Suharto launched nation-wide state-sponsored *pesantren kilat* courses for the 'development of students' religiosity', to 'build a better generation of Muslim youth'. "Pesantren Kilat": Building a Better Muslim Youth', *Studia Islamika*; Mimbar Ulama: Suara Majelis Ulama Indonesia, 1996; interviews with Ahmad Syafi'i (a senior researcher at the Department of Religion), 7 April 1997; Toto Tasmara (a founding member of the Indonesian Mosque Youth Communication Body, BKPRMI, which co-ordinates its activities nationally with state-sponsored al-Qur'an

recitals), 21 March 1997; 'Teaching Children to Read the Qur'an', *Studia Islamika*.

86. 'Keputusan Menteri Agama Nomor 35 Tahun 1980' and 'Keputusan Pertemuan Lengkap Wadah Musyawarah', pp.93–105.

87. Ideals of 'Rukun' (harmony) constituted an 'organicist' value—also outlined in Pancasila PMP and P4 courses—which prioritised hierarchical ordering of social relations, obiedience to authority, guidance by wise leadership and consensus. Interview with Alamsjah, 22 September 1997; Ludjito, 'Kenangan Bersama', p.263.

88. Djatiwijono, 'Kesan dan Kenagnan', pp.274–5; Hasyim, *Toleransi dan Kemerdekaan*, p.375.

89. Interviews with Sudomo, 30 October 1997; Alamsjah, 22 September 1997.

90. It was actually in 1961 that the Minister of Religion proposed this definition of religion as a means of denying legal status to Javanese mysticism. For reasons of social order, Sukarno issued presidential decree no.1/1965 giving official recognition to six religions (the sixth being Confucianism) and authorising the prohibition of religious orientations that threatened these religions and/or political stability. Under Suharto, in 1966, compulsory membership of an officially sanctioned religion was decreed and Confucianism was dropped as one of the acknowledged religions. Mulder, *Mysticism and Everyday Life*, p.6; Patty, 'Aliran Kepercayaan', p.97.

91. Feillard, 'Traditionalist Islam', p.61.

92. 'Instruksi Menteri Agama Nomor 8 Tahun 1979', pp.252–4.

93. 'Instruksi Menteri Agama Nomor 8'.

94. Presidential Stipulation No.1/1965, signed by Sukarno, and concerning the prevention of the misuse of and/or insult to religion, provided the initial legal basis for subsequent prohibitions of religious movements, publications and practices that the state considered as having 'deviated' from sanctioned religious conduct. This stipulation was incorporated into Presidential Stipulation No.5 of 1969, which enacted as law numerous of Sukarno's presidential instructions. 'Penetapan Presiden Republik Indonesia Nomor 1 Tahun 1965' and 'Undang-Undang No.5 Tahun 1969', pp.1–7; *Buku Peraturan Perundangan*; 'Daftar Aliran/Ajaran Kepercayaan Masyarakat Yang Telah Dilarang' (register of banned organisations supplied by MUI).

95. Mulder, *Mysticism and Everyday Life*, pp.7–9.

96. *Mimbar Penyuluhan Kepercayaan*, pp.12 13.

97. Efforts to define what constituted religion began at least in the early 1950s, well before the New Order period. As Mulder observed, 'In 1952, the Islam-dominated Ministry of Religion advanced a minimum definition of religion containing the following necessary elements: a prophet, a holy book, and international recognition. Such a definition would exclude mysticism as a valid religious expression and even outlaw its practice.' Mulder, *Mysticism and Everyday Life*, pp.4–5.

98. Interviews with Gen. (ret.) Benny Murdani (former Commander of Kopkamtib and former Commander of ABRI), 5 November 1997; Gen. (ret.) Sumitro (former Commander of Kopkamtib), 23 September 1997; Mulder, *Mysticism and Everyday Life*, p.6; Soerojo, *Siapa Menabur Angin*.
99. In 1955, the Ministry of Justice took control of Pakem, apparently in order to lessen the authority of the Ministry of Religion, but also to establish tighter supervision of mystical movements. Darmaputera, *Pancasila and the Search for Identity*, p.84.
100. Interview with Murdani, 5 November 199; 'Instruksi Presiden Republik Indonesia Nomor 14 Tahun 1967' and 'Keputusan Bersama Menteri Agama, Menteri Dalam Negeri Dan Jaksa Agung: No. 67 Tahun 1980', pp.11–14.
101. *Lampung Post*, 10–28 Febuary 1989.
102. One of the problems that greatly irked senior officials was that Warsidi had turned a cluster of hamlets into a separate, self-contained community rejecting outside authority. In particular, the issues of land dispute/evictions and government concern that Warsidi might influence discontented locals to refuse to pay taxes or cooperate with development programs appeared to be the main issues that were at stake. *Lampung Post*, 20 February 1989.
103. *Merdeka*, 20 February 1989.
104. *Lampung Post*, 28 February 1989.
105. *Lampung Post*, 24 February 1989.
106. 'Instruksi Menteri Agama Republik Indonesia Nomor 3 Tahun 1981', pp.106–10.
107. *Kompilasi: Peraturan*, pp.137–142.
108. *Kompilasi: Peraturan*.
109. 'Seruan Bersama Dihubungkan Dengan Kejadian Solo', pp.113–18.
110. 'Keputusan Menteri Agama Nomor 44 Tahun 1978', 'Instruksi Menteri Agama Nomor 8 Tahun 1978' and 'Surat Edaran Menteri Agama Nomor 3 Tahun 1978', pp.181–92.

Chapter 5

The Capture of Muslim Interests into Non-Party Entities

INTRODUCTION

Throughout the 1970s and most of the 1980s, Suharto's corporatist strategy reinforced his efforts to neutralise Muslim political opposition. In addition to establishing the Islamic-oriented political party, PPP, Suharto's regime developed a range of corporatist initiatives for the capture of target segments of the Muslim constituency, such as mosque, preachers', intellectuals', *ulama* (Muslim religious scholars/leaders), and women's associations into non-party organisations. Among the organisations to be examined in this chapter, are the peak organisation, the Indonesian Council of Ulama (MUI), and Golkar affiliates, the Indonesian Dakwah Council (MDI) and the Indonesian Mosque Council (DMI). These organisations were established during the 1970s when Suharto was trying to consolidate his corporatist control of organisations and when relations between the regime and Muslim political leaders were largely antagonistic. Through the incremental capture of Muslim interests, independent Islamic organisations like the NU and Muhammadiyah would run the risk of losing control over component member bodies which, in turn, would lose their distinctiveness and particularity. Additionally, enforced amalgams of this kind could engender internal contest between the constituent member organisations and cause a fragmentation of interests. The state therefore was engaged in a progressive capturing and simultaneous disorganising of the community's autonomous associational life.

The organisations were top heavy with state officials or Golkar functionaries in leadership positions and/or advisory councils. Like other corporatist associations (discussed in previous chapters), they were linked to bureaucratic centres, through *pembinaan* (guidance; supervision) sections—in this case to the Department of Religion—with the Department of Internal Affairs overseeing their operations. They were established at each level of government (national, provincial, and district) and their commissions or departments that handled their different organisational activities, and their programs and statutes, were kept strictly in line with government policy. These programs stressed the importance of giving paternalistic guidance to the Muslim community and its religiosity towards achieving harmonious state–society relations in fulfilment of stability and economic development goals. The management function was reflected in the programs and statutes of MUI, an institution for the incorporation of Islamic religious scholars/leaders. Outlined were the need for mosques to be used as centres of 'spiritual and ideological guidance' (*pembinaan mental spiritual*) aimed at 'securing the nation-state from the [latent] threats of communism, secularism, subversion and moral degradation'.[1] Accordingly, 'national vigilance' was required in order to safeguard inter-religious harmony, national security and stability.[2] Similar statements can be found in the publications of other corporatist organisations and government departments.[3]

Through the corporatist organisations the regime promoted an 'official Islam', that was consonant with the state ideology, Pancasila, fostered loyalty to the nation-state, and eschewed left-wing radical or Islamic fundamentalist ideologies. It was regarded as vital to nation-state building, modernisation and industrialisation that leaders of a secular state gain control of Islamic *ulama*, mosques and *dakwah* activities. These were the primary markers, locations and carriers of norms in society. Mosques constituted a major centre of *ummat* (Muslim community) activity, in which occurred most Islamic religious propagation and much political propaganda. *Kiai* (Muslim leaders, often attributed with possession of mystical powers who ran Indonesia's thousands of private Islamic boarding schools or *pesantren*) and *ulama* wielded enormous influence in local communities. By bringing mosques, preachers and *ulama* into state-supervised structures, which offered induction into officially-sanctioned religion through *pembinaan*, state leaders could hope to supplant community norms and the authority of independent *ulama* with its own religious norms, government-trained *ulama* and secular authority. Corporatist restructuring was one project for the achievement of these aims.

In the late-1980s to mid-1990s, there was a shift in Suharto's corporatist strategy from restrictive exclusion to greater incorporation of Muslim political interests as he cultivated a hitherto neglected but increasingly important Muslim middle-class sector as a new base of support. The founding in 1990 of the Indonesian Association of Muslim Intellectuals (ICMI), was the regime's most ambitious effort to absorb and channel Muslim middle-class aspirations. ICMI provided a new strategic function of support and legitimacy to Suharto's regime as it became one of Suharto's instruments of civilian elite recruitment into the state bureaucracy and political institutions (in the face of declining support from the mainstream military). In addition to ICMI, other initiatives were launched with the formerly independent Board of Indonesian Mosques (BKPMI) joining Golkar's DMI in 1990 as a subordinate member, and the Indonesian Co-ordinating Body of Muslim Preachers (BAKOMUBIN) being established in 1996. BKPRMI was brought, along with Indonesia's other independent mosque associations, into the national peak body, DMI. DMI, MDI, and GUPPI were among thirty-one Islamic peak bodies and independent organisations subsumed into the Golkar's Islamic Communication Forum for Mass Organisations

(FKOI-KK). Through Golkar channels, the regime also absorbed a plethora of small, sometimes radical, Islamic organisations into larger state-supervised amalgams.[4]

This chapter provides a detailed analysis of Suharto's corporatist initiatives from the 1970s to the 1990s. The chapter argues that, despite the state–Islamic accommodation and the founding of ICMI, Suharto's approach to organised Muslim politics in the 1990s represented a shift of emphasis rather than a major departure from the government's policy concerning Islam. Throughout the New Order period, Suharto's corporatist initiatives consistently had three broad objectives. In the service of the state's stability and economic development needs, the first was to co-opt, fragment and neutralise Islam as an autonomous political force. The second was to maintain close surveillance of Indonesia's associational life and ensure that it remained within state-circumscribed limits. The third was to effect a limited mobilisation of Muslim support for purposes such as obtaining clear Golkar victories at the five-yearly general elections and for assisting the government with its critical development projects. The discussion now turns to an elaboration of the functions and aims of the corporatist organisations.

MUI: STATE INCORPORATION OF MUSLIM *ULAMA*

Since 1970, in a political climate in which the regime was seeking to emasculate the parties, Muslim leaders had rejected government proposals to establish a nation-wide council of *ulama* suspecting that it was yet another attempt to restrict Islamic political activities. It was five years before the regime could gain the agreement of a sufficient number of Muslim leaders to proceed with its plans for the council. By May 1975, the Minister of Internal Affairs, Amir Machmud, had instructed governors to set up regional councils in nearly all of Indonesia's twenty-seven provinces. These councils, along with leaders of independent organisations including Muhammadiyah, NU, a few smaller entities, and the corporatist organisations, GUPPI and the Indonesian Mosque Council (DMI), were then brought in as members of the national MUI.[5]

Thus, in July 1975, the Council of Indonesian Ulama (MUI) was established at the instigation of the regime in a climate of mutual suspicion and distrust between itself and Muslim groups. The government-financed MUI was intended as an alternative channel of state–Islamic interest inter-mediation and communication to that of the political parties. Giving the address at MUI's founding conference, Suharto clarified that the council was neither permitted to engage in political activities, nor to carry out programs, but functioned in an advisory capacity to both the regime and the Muslim community. In line with the regime's 'floating mass' policy, MUI was not allowed to organise below the level of province and establish itself as a grassroots organisation. Nevertheless, at the lower administrative level, Muslim leaders were incorporated into *ulama* councils (MU) which were under the supervision of the office of religious affairs.[6]

In an apparent attempt to gain wider community approval for MUI, the regime persuaded the well-known and respected Muhammadiyah leader, Buya Hamka, to accept appointment as the council's first chairman. The independent-minded Hamka remained suspicious of the regime and, in 1981, chose to withdraw from the council rather than compromise his principles when the regime insisted that MUI rescind a *fatwa* (authoritative religious opinion) forbidding Muslim attendance at Christmas celebrations.[7] Since Hamka's resignation, the regime encouraged the appointment of compliant *ulama*, some of them bureaucrats, to the chairmanship and to leadership positions on the council's ten commissions.[8]

To keep a watchful eye on MUI's activities, the Minister of Religious Affairs, the Minister of Internal Affairs, and the Minister of Education and Culture sat on the council's advisory board. According to Mudzhar (an official at the Department of Religion), MUI gained access to President Suharto by appointment through the Minister of Religious Affairs. It liaised separately with the armed forces in a special joint committee, Social Communication (Kosmos), on religious issues related to national security.[9]

In broad terms, MUI's objectives were stated as strengthening national security, increasing religious harmony, and assisting the regime in making a success of its development programs.[10] One of MUI's main functions was to lend legitimacy to government policy initiatives and directives by explaining them in a religious idiom acceptable to, and understood by, the wider Muslim community. In effect, it was meant to deflect potential objections of Muslim groups that might choose to oppose government policy. MUI therefore remained under considerable pressure to justify government policy and in order to fulfil the requirement it set up a *fatwa* commission.

Its tendency to issue *fatwa* and pronouncements in support of government policy measures left MUI exposed to accusations by independent *ulama* and Muslim intellectuals that it furnished religious opinions and viewpoints primarily in order to satisfy the regime's wishes. For example, in 1988 the MUI made itself unpopular by siding with the regime during the controversy over rumoured pig-oil extract in canned foods and milk powders (Muslims are forbidden to eat pork). MUI leaders appeared with state officials on national television and dined on the allegedly contaminated products in an attempt to allay community fears.[11] A number of independent *ulama*, privately, also expressed their astonishment over the MUI's decision to back a government plan to market frogs as a nutritious cuisine, as frogs too were considered a forbidden meat by the *Syafi'i* school (the dominant school of Islam in Indonesia). The high profile role played by MUI on the food issue demonstrated the strategic legitimacy provided by the council as it gave an authoritative Islamic seal of approval to the regime's actions that sought to overcome public concerns. In return, MUI tried to establish itself as the prime authority on the labelling of food products.[12]

On another occasion, MUI was seen as siding too closely with the regime concerning the government-sponsored *Porkas*-lottery, established in December

1995. The Muslim mainstream, including student protestors, several Muslim organisations and regional councils of *ulama*, became upset when MUI refused to back public condemnations of the lottery and declined to issue a *fatwa* banning the lottery. Instead, the chairman of MUI's *fatwa* commission announced that the lottery did not constitute gambling (gambling is prohibited by Islam).[13]

MUI, however, did not always appear to give rulings—or withhold rulings— in support of the regime's position. A case in point was when the issue of the national lottery resurfaced into public view in late 1991 and again in late 1993, this time under the name of SDSB (Philanthropic Donation with Prizes).[14] Suharto's regime refused to heed calls to scrap SDSB, in which Suharto's family was thought to have a substantial investment, as Muslim students held impassioned nation-wide demonstrations against the lottery. MUI broke ranks with the regime and belatedly acceded to popular demand by announcing in 1991 that SDSB constituted gambling and therefore was forbidden by Islam. In 1993, the government banned the lottery.[15] However, the lottery continued under a new name and, in all probability, it suited Suharto to have MUI respond reassuringly to public pressure. By appearing responsive, it would enhance the credibility and viability of MUI as an instrument of communication between the state and the Muslim community.

Through its *fatwa* commission, MUI became an officially condoned religious authority that sought to monopolise orthodoxy, guiding the Muslim community and guarding it against heterodox doctrines.[16] In doing so, MUI fulfilled functions in the interests of the state's stability and security goals and functioned as an official instrument for countering autonomous Islamic organisation and political movements that could disturb stability and development. It closely liaised with the state's law-enforcement, security and intelligence agencies in providing surveillance of the Muslim community. For example, as part of this surveillance, it set up a commission for research, which investigated the literature and activities of Islamic sects and splinter groups that could cause local disturbances. After discussing research undertaken, the *fatwa* commission issued a ruling on whether a group should be banned. In cases related to security, it handed over its findings to state agencies such as its various intelligence units, the Department of Internal Affairs, the Department of Justice, the Attorney General, and the Department of Religion.[17] The Attorney General issued the formal bans.

Thus, MUI performed a complementary role to this intelligence collecting process and provided an 'Islamic' seal of approval to prohibitions of deviant religious tendencies and, in the process, acted as an indirect organ of the state's surveillance and control. Surveillance also was exercised through encouraging voluntary informing as a type of self-policing. That is, Muslim informants commonly reported to MUI suspicious mosque sermons and proselytising that were thought to constitute an insult against another religion or to carry anti-government content. The council then handed these reports to the local regent, the religious affairs office, or other authorities.[18] The fight against heterodoxy was related to the state's own domestic security concerns of ensuring that no religious ideas or activities broadened into a larger movement that might express anti-government sentiment or could erupt into religious conflict. For instance, MUI joined the Department of Religion in condemning Islamic insurgencies such as Warsidi's 'Islamic' rebellion in the province of Lampung in 1989 and, under the banner of Islam, continuing activities of the Aceh freedom movement.[19]

In general, the Muslim conservative mainstream represented by organisations like Muhammadiyah, Persis, Dewan Dakwah and NU tended to support the bans on deviant religious tendencies but this depended to some extent on the religious group being subject to the ban. For instance, regarding Darul Arqam (a sect banned by the Malaysian government), Ma'ruf Amin (a leader of NU's syuriah council and member of MUI's leadership board) said that the NU syuriah disagreed with the MUI that the sect be 'banned for religious reasons.'[20] However, he noted that the 'government banned the sect for security and order reasons but not nationally. The syuriah endorsed this ban'. Amin also noted that, on the whole, NU's syuriah endorsed *fatwas* issued by MUI on the matter of religious deviance and on other issues. The founder of the Salman Mosque movement (a forunner to Indonesian student mosque movements during Suharto's rule), Imaduddin Abdulrahim, expressed a common view held by many Muslim leaders and Muslims bureaucrats that 'MUI was doing its job well in protecting the purity of the religion'. However, he complained that the police and military 'did not enforce bans unless the group threatened security'.[21] A noted 'liberal' Muslim scholar, Harun Nasution, also insisted that if the religious practices of a group 'were in contradiction with Islamic teachings then the group' should be prohibited. 'MUI endorsed a ban on Darul Arqam. This was appropriate.'[22]

Finally, another function of MUI was to facilitate relations between the regime and *ulama* to assist in the limited mobilisation of Muslim support for development programs. The regime realised that *ulama* could obstruct its development programs in rural areas. A government study (September–October 1977) concerning 'guidance to town and village' noted that the role of religious figures was an integral part of village development. The study addressed the problem of how to get the participation of all levels of society in development. It concluded that the government ought to gain the participation of *ulama*, the carriers of norms and makers of public opinion, because the community regarded their religious advice or *fatwa* as 'the last word' on matters. The regime recognised that traditional/direct forms of communication such as the delivering of sermons at mosques and *pesantrens* were proving to be more effective than were electronic and printed media for carrying the regime's development message.[23]

Although MUI did not have an organisational presence in the countryside, it could still issue national and provincial *fatwa* and these rulings could be communicated through its *ulama* to the different levels of society. In particular, MUI was called upon to issue *fatwa* in the sensitive area of family planning.

Controversy over the use of IUDs (intra uterine devices) was one such example of regime mobilisation of Muslim support in aid of its family planning program. In 1971, a group of (eleven) prominent *ulama* issued a religious ruling declaring that Islamic law forbade the use of IUDs. The regime realised that the religious decision could seriously impair its free and aggressive contraception program. It therefore sought vigorously to persuade and pressure the *ulama* to lend their religious approval and justification to the use of IUDs. After years of resistance by religious conservatives, this approval finally came in 1983, when the Ministry of Religious Affairs and the National Family Co-ordinating Board convened a national conference of *ulama*. At the meeting, MUI reversed the earlier ruling with its own *fatwa* permitting IUD insertion.[24]

The regime also called on MUI to advance its development projects through the sending of *ulama* and *da'i* (preachers) to remote regions and transmigration sites. President Suharto launched the program in 1989, which was funded by his and his wife's private foundations (Yayasan Amal Bhakti Muslim Pancasila, YABMP, and Yayasan Dharmais).[25] The Departments of Religion and Transmigration were responsible for implementing the program, using the MUI as a vehicle for recruiting the preachers. Selected preachers were given the title of 'development preachers' and underwent a one-month preparatory training course. They were not only briefed in religious and pedagogical techniques, but were also trained in practical skills and community services like farming and plantation skills, marriage counselling, burial preparation and how to deal with the sick.[26]

Aspects of the regime's *pembinaan mental* (ideological guidance) curriculum for preachers included a strong dose of instructions on harmony, duties and rights to the nation, leadership discipline, and morals. It also included courses on national security, health and family planning and farm management. The regime sent them mostly to oil-palm plantation sites (PIR) and to areas for the mining of precious metals, fishing farms and forestry estates.[27]

Developing social harmony through religious guidance was central to the preachers' activities. Preachers were to assist migrants from different islands and ethnic groups to settle and assimilate. In particular, they gave *pembinaan mental* to the newcomers of Muslim faith (the majority of transmigrants) in order to avoid points of tension among the migrant settlers and between them and local communities.[28] The MUI supplied each preacher with a booklet of guidelines on maintaining inter-religious harmony. The booklet contained government regulations and decrees on religious propagation, constructing places of worship, mystical sects, foreign aid and violation of religious commemorations.[29]

The regime wished to ensure that each religious community maintained an interpretation of their religion consonant with government development policy. It therefore instructed preachers to monitor, in conjunction with state agencies, the unrestrained growth of deviant sects or alternative religious interpretations at sites. Preachers were charged with the task of bringing deviant religious movements or expressions back into the mainstream fold of government-sanctioned religious belief and practice and to guide the Muslim migrant community accordingly. The last scenario that the regime wanted to see develop was a Muslim leader arriving fresh from studies in the Middle East and trying to apply his own brand of 'intolerant' Islamic law to local communities. In short, MUI became an important vehicle through which the state tried to expand its supervision, regulation and control over Muslim community affairs. It did this in order to ensure that no unmediated religious tendencies threatened to disrupt stability and development in regions remote from the centralised control of Jakarta, thereby limiting associational pluralism and reinforcing corporatist reordering.[30]

As the above discussion has demonstrated, the regime engaged MUI primarily as an instrument of its own policy objectives, despite the fact that the council sometimes appeared to adopt positions contrary to the regime's wishes. Although its main role was outlined as mediating the relations of Muslim society and the state, in reality MUI largely served as a vehicle for the dissemination of state values and ideas and functioned as an instrument of social management. As will be discussed in the last part of the chapter, MUI performed an important role of organising pro-regime Muslim groups into public oaths of loyalty to President Suharto nearing the five-yearly general elections. Finally, MUI fulfilled three central functions performed by corporatist institutions in Indonesia. That is, first it sought to contain the interests of *ulama* in official structures as part of a broader effort to discourage the autonomous articulation of demands. Second, it provided the function of social control, in conjunction with military intelligence and other government agencies, through its supervision and monitoring of religious behaviour and activity. Third, it drew on the authority of the *ulama* (and preachers) in order to orient the Muslim community in a manner beneficial to official development goals by ensuring that religious values and/or fanaticism did not obstruct those goals and programs. The IUD program and the sending of preachers to transmigration sites were two examples of this last point.

DMI AND BKPRMI: STATE INCORPORATION OF MOSQUES

At the national level, the regime sought to regulate mosque activities through the Golkar's affiliate-organisation, the Indonesian Mosque Council (DMI), established in 1972 and situated in the Istiqlal mosque in Jakarta. By 1982, DMI represented mosque councils of the independent Islamic organisations. The chairman of MUI was vice-chairman (1972–1984) of DMI and then its senior advisor (1984–1994), suggesting—at least since 1975 when MUI was established—a close co-ordinating role between the two councils.[31]

The program of DMI was stated as co-ordinating, giving guidance, and behaving in the spirit of the (wider Golkar) family in its relations with the state and the Muslim community. A head of DMI, Z.H. Noeh, explained that the role of the DMI was to remind people of their 'collective duty to the state' by giving mosque associations supervision and instructions—*pembinaan*—regarding their tasks.[32] One of its main tasks was to train preachers and mosque *Imam*. Other tasks were to develop: (1) people's comprehension of *al-Qu'ran*; (2) formal and informal education and *dakwah*; (3) a program of health and welfare; and (4) the skills and role of women and youth. It also rehabilitated and built mosques at housing complexes in new settlements, transmigration sites, entertainment parks, and university campuses.[33] In short, DMI was one of the various corporatist institutions co-ordinated by the Department of Religion or Golkar, which was instrumental to the state's expanding jurisdiction over religious association through the propagation of an 'official Islam'.

Having said this, it appears that the tasks assigned to DMI were an indirect but nonetheless integral part of the unofficial political functions it performed. That is, it became a tool in the regime's strategy to co-opt and neutralise anti-regime Islamic organisations and activists by channelling them into social activities. One such target of state co-optation through the DMI channel was the Indonesian Mosque Communication Body (BKPMI), founded at the Istiqamah mosque in Bandung in 1977. Under the leadership of Muslim activists, BKPMI had remained locked in conflict with Suharto's regime. However, a growing rapprochement between Suharto and Muslim organisations in the late-1980s, especially after these organisations had accepted the government's sole foundation law of 1985, saw the BKPMI become part of the state's corporatist structure.[34]

In October 1990, BKPMI, upon the urging of the Minister of Internal Affairs, joined DMI as a subordinate member. The mosque body had to reorient its activities in line with government priorities and accordingly was assigned a new role in DMI. Reflecting the new role, the regime insisted that the mosque body include in its title the word 'youth (*remaja*)'. Thenceforth, BKPRMI focused its energies on assisting DMI with its program of teaching *al-Qur'an* literacy and recital to kindergarten children and youth groups.[35] To perform this task, BKPRMI was fused with another national level body, the *Al-Qur'an* Kindergarten Guidance and Development Institute (LPPTKA).

In August 1991, the director of LPPTKA–BKPRMI announced the government decision that Qur'an reading would become a central part of the national curriculum for religious education at government and private primary schools in the school year 1994/1995. In April 1992, Hutomo (Tommy) Mandala Suharto's (son of Indonesia's president) PT Humpuss group sponsored the National Contest of Qur'an Reading for Qur'anic Kindergarten Pupils and Festival of Pious Indonesian Children, organised by LPPTKA–BKPRMI. Indonesia's First Lady, Tien Suharto, opened the contest and the chairman of MUI gave the closing speech. The program priorities set out for the 1993–1996 period noted that the joint LPPTKA–BKPRMI had established 15,000 *al-Qur'an* reading units comprising 2.5 million children throughout the country. The aim of the LPPTKA–BKPRMI effort was to target children at an early age and give them *pembinaan mental* to inculcate a nationalistic religious piety, discipline, and understanding and thus make them future loyal subjects. One of BKPRMI's other main tasks was to keep loitering youth or juvenile delinquents off the streets and channel them into mosque-oriented social activities such as sports, art, morality lessons, and skills training.[36] The LPPTKA–BKPRMI initiatives were an integral part of the regime's overall effort to increase the state's jurisdiction over the Muslim community's religious affairs through religious instruction.

On BKPRMI's board of senior advisors were Suharto's protégé, the Minister of Research and Technology, Burhanuddin Jusuf Habibie, and Tommy Suharto. For his co-operation with the regime, BKPRMI's leader, Toto Tasmara, was appointed as the corporate secretary of Tommy Suharto's PT Humpuss Group.[37] Tommy's PT Humpuss group financed and assisted in some of LPPTKA–BKPRMI's activities.

BAKOMUBIN AND MDI: STATE INCORPORATION OF ISLAMIC PREACHERS' *DAKWAH* ACTIVITIES

Toto Tasmara also was behind a government/PT Humpuss–BKPRMI initiative to bring disaffected preachers from Islamic modernist organisations such as the ex-PII (Indonesian Muslim Secondary School Students), Persis (United Islam), and Dewan Dakwah Islamiyah Indonesia (the Indonesian Islamic Propagation Council)[38] into corporatist arrangements. The regime considered some of these preachers as holding extreme views. In June 1996, the Indonesian Co-ordinating Body of Muslim Preachers (BAKOMUBIN) representing twenty-six of Indonesia's twenty-seven provinces was established. Toto was chosen as chairman of the preachers' body.[39]

An official for the Department of Religion attending BAKOMUBIN's founding conference declared that 'Muslims must be fanatics [in adhering to religious belief] but they may not be [political] extremists'. He warned the preachers against using religion to create inter-community strife and asserted instead that they should apply themselves to the task of becoming 'problem solvers' in society.[40] He emphasised that they should no longer limit themselves exclusively to ritual concerns and instead become more socially oriented in outlook. He declared that he saw a new trend that was good: 'engineers were becoming preachers, doctors were becoming preachers, and even members of the armed forces were becoming preachers'.[41] Again, from the outset, BAKOMUBIN's *pembinaan* role was stressed. Toto announced that the preachers' body would aim to create quality cadre and not concern itself with building a mass membership. By acclamation, it was decided that the body would not involve itself in political activities, meaning that the body would not engage in autonomous forms of organisation as either an opposition party, or pressure group. In reality, Suharto's circle used BAKOMUBIN, as it did other corporatist institutions, for the attainment of political objectives, such as organising Muslim support for Suharto's renomination as Indonesia's president at the five-yearly elections (discussed below).

The regime was responsible for two other corporatist initiatives in the area of Islamic propagation: the Islamic Dakwah Council (MDI) and the

Communication Forum for Dakwah Institutes (FKLD).[43] MDI was created by Golkar's central executive board in mid-1978 and was given the task of overseeing Islamic missionary activities. The MDI initiative was apparently a response to the fact that Suharto's regime had faced fierce competition from PPP during the 1977 general election. This competition came especially from its NU contingent, which could effectively campaign and launch attacks against the regime through its religious-political activity (*dakwah*) at prayer meetings. Consequently, MDI became a political vehicle for the new chairman of Golkar, Amir Murtono, partly to combat the PPP-NU's *dakwah* campaign efforts.[44]

According to Hidayat (a head of MDI's Secretariat) one of MDI's main functions was to make overtures to 'extreme' Muslim organisations and bring them into the Golkar fold. To serve this purpose, MDI joined and oversaw the Islamic Forum of Communication (FKOI), which had thirty-one organisational members. Hidayat explained that FKOI was an amalgamation of 'moderate, conservative, and extreme elements' from the Muslim community and had the task of moderating, or 'softening', Islamic extremism.[45] What Hidayat omitted to mention was that the main function of MDI (FKOI) was to mobilise these Muslim groups at election time in support of the government election vehicle, Golkar.

Another part of MDI's program was to give guidance or *pembinaan* to Islamic organisations and sects to ensure that they did not deviate from state-sanctioned religious life, threaten religious harmony, or threaten to disrupt the government's development projects. To this end, MDI sponsored and trained mosque and community *Imam* in remote regions to promote the regime's development message and disseminate and help implement its official decisions concerning the regulation of religious life. Finally, Hidayat explained MDI screened reports and publications by the Department of Religion, and made corrections when it was felt necessary. It did this to ensure that the Department's language accorded with the regime's wishes and that no Islamic 'extremist' ideas 'crept into' the reports. As such, MDI appears to have performed an important supervision role over the affairs of Islam, with the task not entrusted solely to the Department of Religion.[46]

STATE INCORPORATION OF WOMEN

The regime developed an ideal model for the regulation of women's activities with the creation of the Dharma Wanita (Women's Service/Duty). Modelled on the military wives' association, the Dharma Wanita was established as an organisational adjunct to KORPRI for the wives of civil servants. The regime continually stressed women's dual role in public and domestic spheres as guarantor of harmonious social and family relations, as well as her supporting role to her husband. It expected the wives of public servants to maintain 'rukun' (harmony) with their husbands in support of their husband's important duties. It defined women's primary role as that of housewife, to educate the children, and to obey and serve the husband.[47] In its official ideology and programs, including the broad outlines of state policy (GBHN), the regime also assigned women a secondary and complementary role to men of participating in the workforce and home industries in advancement of the nation's economic development. Women's main public duties were an extension of their private household duties, as they were expected to work in areas such as child-care, teaching, family planning, and environmental sanitation.

The regime sought to apply this model and ideology in Muslim women's associations. It endeavoured to bring semi-autonomous women's sections of the independent Islamic organisations into corporatist arrangements. For example, the director of information at the Department of Religion supervised the Indonesian Islamic Women's Consultation Body (BMOIWI), which regulated the activities of Muslim women's groups. It did this in conjunction with the peak association, the Indonesian Women's National Congress (KOWANI), the Indonesian Women's Unified Action (KAWI) on family planning, and Golkar's Co-ordinating Body for Women. Corporatised Muslim women's organisations also carried out their activities in conjunction with the Department of Social Affairs, and MUI. Almost all women's organisations in Indonesia were co-ordinated nationally through their membership of KOWANI.[48]

In an attempt to capture at least one area of Muslim women's associational life, in the mid-1990s the regime tried to bring women's rural co-operatives into a nationally co-ordinated entity (the Women's Chief Co-operative). Prior to this, the regime had given a monopoly of representation to village unit co-operatives (KUDs), but the rural-based mass Muslim women's organisation, Muslimat-NU, resisted membership and maintained its own extralegal co-operatives. The regime eventually accepted the existence of these extralegal entities, largely because of shortcomings of its own co-operatives program.[49] However, from this moment on, all Muslim women's co-operatives had to accept the name '*Anisa*' (a Qu'ranic word for women).

The great risk existed, especially for Muslimat-NU, of confusing and alienating its mass supporters, as the supporters would no longer identify the new *Anisa* co-operatives with their parent organisations. The Secretary General of Muslimat expressed the apprehension that the separate identities of the different women's co-operatives would become one collective state-supervised corporate identity easily open to state manipulation.[50]

GOLKAR AND ICMI: WIDENING THE SCOPE OF STATE INCORPORATION

State–Islamic Rapprochement

With the installation of the New Order's fourth development cabinet (1983–1988), Suharto's regime began to focus much greater attention on recruiting Muslims into the ranks of Golkar. Incorporation of the burgeoning Muslim and non-Muslim middle-class, civilian politicians, and businesspeople into Golkar was part of Suharto's political strategy of expanding his power base beyond the armed forces and reducing his dependence on them. At Golkar's national congress of 1983, Suharto appointed his close confidant, the Secretary of State, Sudharmono, to Golkar's chairmanship. Suharto delegated to him the task of transforming Golkar from a 'co-ordinating and regulating executive for its myriad constituent organisations' into a party of 'active membership', which included Muslim leaders and followers.[51] Sudharmono became secretary of the president's personal foundation, YABMP, which was used as a principal channel of patronage with which to court the Muslim community by helping fund its religious activities.[52]

Under Sudharmono's leadership, Golkar became the arena of a power struggle between its chairman and the ABRI commander, Benny Murdani. However, with the appointment of the army general Wahono to the party's chairmanship in 1988, the military began to re-establish its dominant role in Golkar and, consequently, the Muslim and civilian membership of Golkar appeared to suffer a setback. We can view Suharto's subsequent initiatives to widen the scope of capture by bringing a growing educated Muslim middle class into corporatist arrangements as greatly informed by this deepening military–civilian rivalry.[53]

Beginning in the late 1980s, Suharto assiduously courted the Muslim political community. The regime made a series of conciliatory gestures and concessions to Muslim interests shortly after the political fallout that had witnessed a cooling of relations between the Benny-led armed forces and the president. For example, in 1989, Suharto's circle pursued an ambitious mosque building program funded by the YABMP, first conceived under Sudharmono's leadership.[54] Concessions also came in the form of a Religious Courts Law no.7/1989, reinforcing the authority of the Islamic courts over family law, and Law no.2/1989 on the national education system, which strengthened the compulsory nature of religious subjects. In 1990, after months of protest by Muslim leaders and students, Suharto's regime finally agreed that Muslim girls could wear the distinctive headscarf at school. The regime established Indonesia's first Islamic bank and the president embarked on a nationally televised pilgrimage to Mecca and returned as Haji Muhammad Suharto. Suharto's pilgrimage was an impressive piece of publicity. The president was accompanied by a coterie of family members (including his brother-in-law Maj. Gen. Wismoyo Arismunandar, and his son-in-law Colonel Prabowo Subianto), his close business associate Bob Hasan, Armed Forces Chief Try Sutrisno, and cabinet ministers.[55]

ICMI

Suharto's conciliation aimed to co-opt the Islamic sector and was followed, in December 1990, by the founding of ICMI, under the chairmanship of Suharto's protégé and trusted loyalist, the Minister of Research and Technology, Habibie. Suharto used Habibie in a similar manner to Sudharmono in that he had called upon his services as his new patronage dispenser to co-opt the Muslim community and counter Benny's formidable influence in the military.[56] ICMI became a new instrument for the recruitment of civilians into the state bureaucracy, the cabinet and the People's Consultative Assembly; a role previously performed by the State Secretariat, through Golkar, under Sudharmono's leadership (1983–1988).

ICMI not only became a tool in Suharto's strategy to diversify his power base before the 1992 general election and 1993 presidential election. It also served the political objective of absorbing and neutralising the growing political and populist demands of the educated middle classes. Muslims, in particular, for the previous two decades had undergone a tremendous cultural and religious efflorescence. The heavily circumscribed political structure and suppression of Islamic political activities together with the encouragement of religious and cultural aspects of Islam by the regime had added to a revival of Islamic consciousness. Mosques and prayer meetings, freer than other venues from police surveillance, became an alternative arena for the expression of political grievance.[57] The regime's initiatives covering mosque, *dakwah*, and intellectual activities (described above) were therefore defensive mechanisms to absorb and counter the growing Muslim restlessness and demands for greater political representation.

The breadth and diversity of membership in ICMI lent itself well to exclusionary corporatist strategy aimed at keeping the Muslim community politically disorganised and divided. ICMI began as a loose federation of Muslims representing a wide spectrum of moderate, reform-minded, conservative, and radical Muslim organisations and individual members with divergent views about the association's objectives. Its heterogeneous membership included Muslims from the Muhammadiyah and the Dewan Dakwah, some ex-Masyumi activists, a few NU leaders, NGO activists, theologians and scholars, politicians from the PPP, and dissenters highly critical of Suharto and government policy. We will henceforth refer to this diverse group of newly incorporated, non-bureaucratic members of the association as ICMI intelligentsia. It is best, perhaps, to think of the intelligentsia as existing somewhere on a continuum of least co-opted, partially co-opted, and fully co-opted. The least co-opted members, who remained highly critical of Suharto's regime despite their membership of ICMI, might approximate what Ding referred to as a 'counter-elite' within the state structures (see chapter two).

Despite their diversity of backgrounds and views, many of ICMI's intelligentsia shared at least one common goal. That is, they regarded ICMI as having provided them with a useful vehicle for gaining access to those in power, thereby enabling them in theory to pursue their own agendas and exert influence on state agencies, officials, and policy-making. ICMI also gave them protection from ABRI. Most of them were prepared publicly to support Suharto in return for Suharto's protection and the political opportunities (patronage) that they hoped such support would offer them. They argued that under Suharto's and Habibie's paternalistic protection, ICMI would enjoy the necessary hothouse conditions to establish itself as part of the New Order's institutional structure.

They held a long-term view that ICMI could outlive Suharto and Habibie's leadership and look forward to a more independent role in a post-Suharto political constellation. Much of the ICMI intelligentsia, like Ding's incorporated 'counter-elite', therefore, sought eventually to displace the official goals of ICMI with their own private agendas and goals.[58] Incorporation in ICMI had occurred during a period of limited political opening—itself, largely a product of the growing intra-elite rivalry between Suharto and ABRI (see chapter seven). Under these circumstances, there was the risk that Muslim interests would become re-politicised after Suharto, for the past two decades, had sought to demobilise and neutralise them through strategies of exclusion.

Suharto's regime was certainly not prepared to let this happen and was quick to establish tight control of ICMI and to surround its most independent and radical members, the main target of co-option, with government bureaucrats and pro-regime Muslim conservatives. By early 1991, Habibie had imposed an organisational command structure upon the association to constrain the various political agendas of the intelligentsia and provide close supervision over its programs and activities. He appointed to managerial positions his trusted staff of bureaucrats and 'technologists' from the Agency of Research, Technology and Application (BPPT) and from his ministry. In addition, he oversaw the establishment of a council of advisors (comprising pro-regime figures, retired state and military officials and respected Muslim elders) as a moderating and balancing mechanism to the council of experts (comprised largely of intelligentsia). In August 1993, in his capacity as a private citizen, Suharto became the chief patron of ICMI, with three former vice-presidents joining the *dewan pembina* (supervisor's council) to oversee the operations of ICMI.[59]

Thus, ICMI became a vehicle for the recruitment of elite members into the state bureaucracy and other centres of power. It became a repository of officialdom as membership of ICMI (and Golkar) was viewed as a ticket to career advancement within the bureaucracy and cabinet. From the point of view of aspirants to power, then, incorporation provided a conveyer-belt to higher positions of office. The corporatist organisations also acted as 'intermediate channels' of recruitment. As such, they behaved like sorting machines, letting through aspirants who could demonstrate their loyalty and amenability to Suharto's ruling circle, but shutting off channels of recruitment to critics whom incorporation had failed to co-opt.

Two community leaders who had their careers advanced through membership of ICMI and MUI, were Kiai Ilyas Ruchiyat and Kiai Ali Yafie, the president and the acting president of the Nahdlatul Ulama respectively. In September 1992, Ruchiyat and Ali were among nineteen pro-regime ICMI figures that gained appointment to the People's Consultative Assembly. Ali Yafie, who resigned his position as NU's acting president, eventually assumed the office in 1998 of chairman of MUI. Ali became a prominent preacher officiating at state-held religious ceremonies, particularly during the fasting month of *Ramadhan* at Istiqlal Mosque in Jakarta.[60] In return for moderating his critical voice and conforming to Habibie's policy line, the former NGO activist and regime critic (an engineer trained at the Bandung Institute of Technology), Adi Sasono, also gained rapid promotion. He rose to the position of Secretary General of ICMI in 1995.

The down side of incorporation was that the recruitment machine worked as a mechanism for sorting out and excluding the most unreliable elements from within the intelligentsia. As such, some members of the intelligentsia in ICMI had their various aspirations and ambitions for career advancement disappointed. For example, shortly after the association's founding in 1990, the outspoken intellectual, Dawam Rahardjo, had his sights on becoming ICMI's second-in-command. He had his hopes dashed when Habibie announced that he would not create the post of Secretary General, as ICMI's command structure did not necessitate this. Instead, he appointed his most trusted colleague from BPPT, Wardiman Djojonegoro as the assistant secretary.[61]

Dawam was very bitter at the time, even after a publicised mending-of-fences between himself and Habibie. Dawam also had his sights on the position of chief editor of the ICMI newspaper, *Republika*, but Habibie preferred his own candidate in the job, a long-time associate Parni Hadi.[62] In an interview in 1994, Dawam expressed some of his disappointment, saying 'if I had become the Secretary General, I would have been more prominent [in ICMI] than Habibie. I am critical of the regime. *Republika* is too much under the control and intervention of Habibie and Harmoko [the Minister of Information and the chairman of Golkar]. It would have been impossible for Harmoko to control me, had I become chief editor of *Republika*. I can understand why they did not choose me [for the job].'[63]

Members of the intelligentsia ostensibly co-opted in ICMI, who continued to level public criticism against Suharto and his regime, risked being disciplined, and sometimes faced heavy sanctions. A well-publicised case was that of Amien Rais. Amien had high profile as an outspoken leader of the Muhammadiyah. He appeared to take good advantage of his proximity to ICMI's chairman, becoming Habibie's foreign affairs advisor on the Middle East. He became vice-chairman of the ICMI think-tank, the Centre for Information and Development Studies (CIDES), and head of the association's council of experts. Indonesian observers inferred from Amien's public announcements in which he outlined five criteria for the office of vice-president, that he was supporting Habibie for the office.[64] However, Amien distinguished himself in the press as a vocal opponent of President Suharto. He regularly criticised Suharto's long period as president and called for the establishment of a reliable mechanism for presidential succession. In late 1996, he publicly criticised giant mining operations in Irian Jaya and Kalimantan, which were linked to the Suharto family's business interests. In February 1997, Habibie, acting on Suharto's instructions, removed Amien from his position as ICMI's head of the council of experts. Amien later reported how Suharto—through his Attorney General— investigated him, accused him of making subversive statements and requested that he apologise for his criticisms of the president. Following this, Suharto's circle undertook, unsuccessfully, a campaign to defeat Amien's candidacy for the leadership of Muhammadiyah.[65]

Suharto's reaction to Amien showed that the president had adopted an approach typical of military hardliners by stigmatising dissenters as subversives, thereby branding them as threats to national political stability. By doing so, he was indicating that dissenters like Amien were disobedient 'children', who had behaved outside the acceptable norms and behaviour of the '*Pancasila*' family (state), and therefore should be punished. Having misbehaved (by criticising Suharto's New Order), Amien was therefore excluded from participation in the formal system, which had sought to incorporate strategic middle-class interests.

Amien was not the only dissenter requiring disciplinary action. Another case was that of Sri Bintang Pamungkas, one of ICMI's council of experts, who refused full co-option into ICMI, preferring instead to maintain his critical distance. Bintang was a legislator for PPP, who made repeated calls for an overhaul of the political system to reflect people's democratic liberties and rights.[66] In 1994, the regime retaliated by bringing about Bintang's expulsion from the parliament. The regime accused him of challenging *Pancasila*, and charged him with helping organise an anti-Suharto demonstration during the president's April 1996 visit to Dresden. The court sentenced him to thirty-four months imprisonment for violating No.154 of Civil Law (KUHP) by insulting the head of state.

Bintang also established the Union of Indonesian Democracy Party (PUDI) before the 1997 general election and outside of the officially sanctioned three-party system. He daringly sent PUDI cards to government officials and members of parliament and advocated a boycott of the general election. He was struck from the civil service for violating discipline and, finally, faced subversion charges over distributing the PUDI cards. Bintang's decision to establish PUDI apparently crystallised President Suharto's objections against him.[67] Although Bintang was on ICMI's council of experts, he was regarded by other ICMI members as too outspoken in his opposition and could expect little support in his defence against subversion charges from the pro-regime Islamic association. He was removed from his membership of ICMI.

At ICMI's second national congress in December 1995, Suharto took steps in an apparent move to fragment ICMI's internal membership and to neutralise politically its intelligentsia. He appointed half the 1993 cabinet to the new 114-member board of ICMI. Several figures were regarded as rivals of Habibie (including the former Golkar chair, Lt Gen. Wahono, the Co-ordinating Minister for Politics and Security, Susilo Sudarman, and Suharto's daughter Siti Hardiyanti Rukmana).[68] In August 1997, after replacing Harmoko as Minister of Information, the former Army Chief of Staff Lt Gen. Hartono (a rival of Habibie) was appointed to a senior supervisory role within ICMI, apparently to bring its intelligentsia under tighter control. Admiral (ret.) Sudomo (former Commander of Kopkamtib) explained the reason for Hartono's entry into ICMI, as follows. 'We created ICMI as a strategy to bring Muslim radicals into "safe channels" rather than leave them outside the political system. Extremists like Adi Sasono and Amien Rais infiltrated ICMI. It was intended that Habibie would embrace the Muslim extremists and direct them into activities oriented to the development of science and technology. They were not supposed to raise religious issues. However, the extremists succeeded in infiltrating Habibie. They influenced him with their Islamic agendas. Habibie failed [to carry out his job, as anticipated].' This was why a military hardliner like Hartono was brought into ICMI, to offset the 'Muslim extremists'.[69]

The new Information minister was also responsible for tight control and surveillance of the press and became a member of MUI's supervisory board, highlighting his important supervision role within society, not just ICMI.[70] Coinciding with Hartono's entry into ICMI, the Indonesian press carried reports of four prominent members of ICMI's intelligentsia (Adi Sasono, Watik Pratiknya, Jimly Asshidiqie, and Dawam Rahardjo) being struck from the MPR list of candidates. Parni Hardi (an ICMI intellectual) was sacked from ICMI's newspaper, *Republika*. It was deemed that Parni, the editor of the *Republika* and close colleague of Habibie, pursued a policy line that was too critical of the regime.[71] The ICMI intelligentsia, including its Secretary General Adi Sasono, expressed open disaffection over their failure to translate Habibie's patronage into cabinet appointments in March 1998.[72] Suharto ensured that ICMI was an effective instrument with which to neutralise Muslim political activities.

Another important function performed by ICMI was that it served as a vehicle through which Habibie, a German-trained aeronautical engineer lacking any constituency at home could promote his costly projects in the field of high-end scientific and technological (Iptek) development among the Muslim constituency.[73] In line with the regime's strategy for the de-politicisation of Muslim interests, Habibie established program guidelines to rechannel the activities of its intelligentsia away from overtly political activities and towards his vision for a scientific and technological great leap forward in Indonesia. His promotion of Iptek dominated the organisation's pronouncements and programs outlined at its national work meetings and congresses. He stressed that ICMI had an important role to perform in support of Iptek—namely, that of developing Indonesia's potential in human resources with his so-called 5K, or 'five qualities', program: quality of faith, quality of work, quality of thought, quality of expertise and quality of life. A department of human resources and culture was created to promote and supervise this main area of ICMI's activities. Habibie also issued occasional warnings against ICMI becoming a vehicle for the fulfilment of Islamic political aspirations, although these warnings were partly directed towards assuaging the concerns of ABRI commanders that ICMI represented a re-politicisation of Islam.[74] Thus, Habibie wrote, 'honestly, ICMI never intended to place its members in the government structure. We always stressed ICMI's 5K [program].'[75]

ICMI had financial backing from the highest political and business centres to channel or divert its energies, as outlined at its first national congress, into the increased 'participation of Muslim intellectuals in the elaboration of the strategy for national development'.[76] For example, in August 1992 forty-five prominent

Indonesians, who also became its board members and senior advisors, inaugurated a funding entity for ICMI's operations, the Yayasan Abdi Bangsa (the Foundation of Devotion to the Nation).[77] The foundation launched ICMI's think-tank, the CIDES, and its mouthpiece, *Republika*, which provided two important channels for the dissemination of Habibie's Iptek message to Muslims. In addition, earlier in May, Suharto's half-brother and Indonesian tycoon Probosutedjo donated a princely sum of money from his Mercu Buana Group to support ICMI's program to help small-scale Muslim enterprises in the name of combating poverty and raising general living standards.[78] Probosutedjo's donation was part of Suharto's efforts to absorb and thereby deflect the business aspirations and agendas of the intelligentsia by implementing programs aimed at giving equity, loans, management, and technical assistance to Muslim entrepreneurs who belonged to the 'poorest section' of society.[79]

In addition to deflecting Muslim aspirations, some of ICMI's program activities became a means through which the state sought to increase its jurisdiction over Muslim community affairs in support of New Order development goals. For example, ICMI launched a project in co-operation with YABMP, and the Islamic Bank (BMI), as well as with the corporatist organisations—the Indonesian Chamber of Commerce (KADIN) and MUI—for the promotion of the education of science and technology in fifty of the 8,000 *pesantren* in Indonesia. State officials sought to bring an increasing number of *pesantren* under ICMI's, and therefore the state's, supervision.[80]

MOBILISING MUSLIMS FOR SUHARTO'S RE-ELECTION

The above analysis has touched briefly on the idea that the state's corporatist initiatives were employed to mobilise Muslim support behind the regime at election times. This, at least, was the case since the state–Islamic rapprochement in the 1990s when the state leadership was behind efforts to co-ordinate corporatised and semi-autonomous Islamic sectors for the achievement of such political ends. A striking case in point was the mobilisation of support for President Suharto's re-nomination before the five-yearly MPR sessions. For example, the former Minister of Religion (1978–1983), Alamsjah Ratu Prawiranegara (in an effort to revive his political career perhaps) organised incorporated groups into public endorsements of Suharto's re-nomination to the presidency at the 1993 MPR session. Beginning in 1990, he arranged for twenty-one leaders of Muslim organisations to issue a resolution entitled 'the Joint Standpoint of the Indonesian Muslim Community' urging the People's Consultative Assembly to re-elect Suharto. At least half of the signatories to the resolution were members of corporatist organisations such as MUI, MDI, DMI, and the Council of Development of Mathla'ul Anwar chaired by Alamsjah.[81]

In April 1992, he led a mass prayer meeting reaffirming the 1990 resolution. The approximately 3,000 people who attended the mass prayer belonged to thirty-seven Muslim and general mass organisations co-ordinated by Alamsjah in the 'Collective Prayer Group–37'. The Prayer Group–37 included conservative leaders from the independent Islamic organisations. The leaders of 'independent' organisations invariably belonged to corporatist organisations. Twenty-four organisational affiliates of Golkar, including MDI, GUPPI, and the Satuan Karya Ulama (the Ulama Functional Union), as well as the MUI chairman and four ministers and former ministers signed a statement supporting the mass prayer.[82]

The endorsements by *ulama* in support of Suharto's 1993 re-nomination appeared to coincide neatly with the disbursement of Golkar campaign funds to privately owned *pesantren* of influential *ulama*. By one account, Kiai Badri Masduki of the Badridduja *pesantren* in Probolingo, East Java, collected over 1,000 signatures in support of Suharto's re-nomination. Shortly before this, the former armed forces commander for East Java, Lt Gen. Hartono, had delivered Rp. 70 million to Badri's *pesantren*. Suharto's daughter, Siti Hardiyanti Rukmana, whilst campaigning for Golkar in East and Central Java, offered a large sum of money to the Denanyar *pesantren* in Jombang.[83] Ultimately, Suharto's growing reliance upon engineered endorsements of Muslim support reflected the deepening rift between the president and the military.

From 1994, in the context of the approaching general and presidential elections of 1997–1998, there occurred a series of similar orchestrated 'unanimous endorsements' and political prayers for Suharto's re-nomination. For example, in March 1994, Suharto held a meeting with the general chairmen of the main Islamic organisations—with MUI playing a leading role—in order to assure them that, despite rumours that he might stand down mid-term, he would run again for the presidency. The Secretary of State, Murdiono, then arranged a delegation of sixty *ulama* to meet with Suharto at the state palace.[84]

In September 1995, a delegation of dozens of *ulama* from the provinces of Aceh, North Sumatra, and East and West Java met Suharto at the state palace and offered a prayer for his well being. Again MUI played a prominent role and probably co-ordinated the meeting. The chairman of the Aceh branch of MUI led the sixty-eight strong delegation from Aceh. In addition, the most senior leader of NU, Rais Aam Ilyas Ruhiyat, who was also an active member of MUI's managing board, led the West Java delegation.[85]

In June 1996, the Golkar amalgam of thirty-one Islamic groups, FKOI, co-ordinated by MDI, arranged a signed political statement recording a unanimous endorsement and prayer of support by thousands of Muslims for Suharto's re-nomination. The Chairman of Golkar, Harmoko, and the Chairman of MUI, Hasan Basri, delivered speeches and witnessed the endorsement. Again, in March 1997, 150 Muslim leaders represented in MUI prayed at the state palace for Suharto's good health and next term in office.[86] ICMI did not join the other corporatist organisations in declaring public support for Suharto, possibly because of its eagerness to deny earlier allegations that the association was established as a support base for Suharto before the 1993 presidential election. However, this did not detract from the fact that ICMI still was a major pillar of support for the Suharto regime.

CONCLUSION

Although the New Order state's corporatist initiatives spanned two to three decades that witnessed state–Islamic relations shift from antagonism to closer collaboration, there emerged a common pattern. Throughout much of the New Order period, the regime sought to compartmentalise and fragment Muslim interests by capturing components (mosque, preachers', *ulama*, *dakwah*, women's, and intellectuals' associations) of independent organisations (such as NU, Muhammadiyah, Dewan Dakwah, Persis) in state-chartered entities. The amalgams were linked to government agencies and to Golkar so that the potential for autonomous political organisation was subdued, deflected and under close supervision. The regime re-channelled organisational activities into state-guided development oriented tasks and in support of Suharto's presidency.

ICMI shared similarities with the other corporatist initiatives. A broad spectrum of Islamic organisations and interests were brought into a peak organisation for Muslim intellectuals. The grouping together of diverse political interests within ICMI appeared to serve further Suharto's strategy of stimulating fragmentation, by bringing rival interests into the organisation. ICMI also sought to absorb and re-channel the activities of the Muslim intelligentsia into development-oriented projects, in accordance with Habibie's 'iptek' vision.

However, ICMI was a product of state–Islamic accommodation. It was established to co-opt strategic middle-strata elite into the existing power arrangements, without providing them with sufficient means to endanger the status quo. If co-option failed to silence the dissension of individual members, they were excluded from incorporating arrangements and punished. More importantly, ICMI was an example of the tactical deployment of incorporated Muslim interests as a support base with which to counter-balance rival networks of power, such as influential segments of the military. This carried implications beyond earlier corporatist initiatives—namely, there was a risk that incorporated Muslim interests would become re-politicised. This was after Suharto had gone to great pains to de-politicise Islam and de-mobilise Islam's autonomous organisational base.

NOTES

1. *15 Tahun Majelis Ulama*, p.183.
2. *15 Tahun Majelis Ulama*, pp.191–223.
3. Documents and official statements relating to ICMI place great stress on the role of Muslim intellectuals in promoting projects of technological development, and the role of Islam in upholding national unity, defence and security. 'Anggaran Dasar dan Anggaran Rumah Tangga (ICMI)'; *Suara Karya*, 27 August 1993; *Merdeka*, 26 August 1993.

4. Interviews with S.M. Hidayat (head of MDI Secretariat), 12 November 1997; Toto Tasmara (leader of BKRMI), 21 March 1997; 'Daftar Anggota Forum Komunikasi Ormas Islam Karya-Kekaryaan'.
5. Mardjoned, *KH. Hasan Basri*, p.154.
6. Anlov and Cederroth, 'Introduction', p.9.
7. *Tempo*, 30 May 1981.
8. Mostly pro-government figures have held senior posts in MUI, including Hasan Basri (a former Masyumi party leader) as chairman, the fomer vice-president of NU's syuriah council Ali Yafie, the Rector of the state-run Islamic Tertiary Institute (IAIN), Quraish Shihab, and the President of NU's syuriah council, KH. Ilyas Ruchiyat. 'MUI Commission membership lists, Kep-180/MUI/IV/1996', Jakarta.
9. *Jawa Pos*, 12 August 1997; interview with Nasri Adlani (Secretary General of MUI), 4 November 1997; Mudzhar, *Fatwas of the Council*, p.60.
10. *15 Tahun Majelis Ulama*, p.102.
11. See Mudzhar, *Fatwas of the Council*, concerning the issuance of *fatwa* on the subject of the mechanised slaughter of cattle (pp.96–7), the breeding and consumption of rabbits (p.98), and the breeding and consumption of frogs (pp.99–100). In each case, the MUI *fatwa* served the purpose of assisting the government to overcome points of confusion that might cause controversy surrounding the establishment and/or success of commercial projects. *Ummat*, 20 January 1997.
12. *Ummat*, 20 January 1997; *Gatra*, 28 December 1996, 1 March 1997; *Forum Keadilan*, 23 December 1996.
13. Mudzhar, *Fatwas of the Council*, pp.63–4; Vatikiotis, *Indonesian Politics under Suharto*, p.133.
14. The lottery, with its first prize of one billion rupiah, held out the chance to millions of Indonesia's poorest section of society of obtaining luxury items otherwise out of their reach. The lottery also carried the high social cost of plunging addicts deeply into debt. The deleterious effects of the SDSB, and the fact of a disclosure that Muslim organisations were receiving substantial funds from the lottery, aroused Muslim community anger and moral outrage. Muslim leaders called on the state to scrap the lottery claiming that it constituted gambling and threatened to boycott the general election of 1992.
15. Lowry, *The Armed Forces*, p.198.
16. It must be noted, however, that the Ministry of Religious Affairs acted as the principal official organ of state approved religious orthodoxy.
17. Gen. (ret.) Benny Murdani (the former Commander-in-Chief of ABRI and former head of military intelligence agencies) explains that ABRI worked together in field operations with Bakin and compiled reports about Islamic sects and movements that might threaten stability. Once Bakin confirmed the reports, it would take the list of groups slated for prohibition to

President Suharto. Interviews with Murdani, 5 November 1997; Admiral (ret.) Sudomo (head of the Supreme Advisory Council, former Minister of Politics and Security and former Kopkamtib commander), 30 October 1997; Nasri Adlani, 4 November 1997; *15 Tahun Majelis Ulama*, p.135.

18. Interview with Isa Anshari (Secretary to the MUI chairman), 15 December 1996.
19. See chapter four; *Waspada*, 4 March 1997; *Lampung Post*, 10–28 February 1989.
20. Interview with Ma'ruf Amin, 18 and 25 July 1996.
21. Interview with Imaduddin Abdulrahim, 2 September 1996. In order to arrive at this conclusion the author canvassed a range of opinions of Muslim leaders of independent Islamic organisations, Muslim bureaucrats at the Department of Religion, and academics at the IAIN in Jakarta. It appears that Muslim liberal thinkers who opposed bans were in the minority.
22. Interview with Harun Nasution, 13 June 1996.
23. 'Laporan Loka Karya, Bimbingan Beragama Masyarakat Kota Dan Desa', pp.2–23.
24. The *ulama* had originally opposed IUD insertion because Islamic law did not permit a man, other than her husband, to see a woman's 'aurah'. They gave their approval twelve years later with the understanding that female medical doctors or paramedical officers would carry out the insertions. The MUI *fatwa* listed twenty-one verses of *al-Qu'ran* and *Hadiths*, followed by ten paragraphs explaining the significance of the government's family planning program, and those parts that did not violate Islamic law. Munawir Sjadzali explained that 'Relying precisely on the words of the Al-Quran and Al-Hadiththey...[the *ulama* now] endorse and lend their support to all government programmes on population, and using the "religious language" they take an active part, both collectively and individually, in the propagation and popularisation of the programmes, through both traditional and modern channels'. Mudzhar, *Fatwas of the Council*, pp.61, 113; Sjadzali, *Islam: Realitas Baru*, pp.72–3; *Himpunan Keputusan dan Fatwa*, pp.103–12.
25. In the first phase of the program (1990/1991), the government settled 973 preachers with their families at sites. In the second phase (1992/1993 and 1995/1996), 900 placements were made. In the third phase (1996/1997), the government succeeded in settling only 208 preachers. 'Pelatihan, Penempatan dan Pembinaan Transmigran Da'i', p.2.
26. Interviews with the Director of Sociocultural Guidance (Department of Transmigration), 10 November 1997; Drs. Muslim (advisory staff to the Director of Sociocultural Guidance), 10 November 1997; Subagio (Director of Information at the Department of Religion), 13 November 1997; interview with Anshary, 15 December 1996.

27. Transmigrants worked on plantations as part of the government's 'partnership' policy contained in its sixth five-year development plan (Repelita VI), wherein private investors supplied finance and technology and transmigrants the manpower to work on estates. In aid of development goals, one of the preachers' briefs was to assist the government to open areas of production and to establish new villages. Because preachers had a basic education (transmigrants were usually uneducated farmers), they naturally began to fill new leadership and government positions such as village chief created at the sites. *Da'i dan Petani Membangun Daerah Baru*, pp.7–96; interview with the Director of Sociocultural Guidance, 10 November 1997.

28. The main emphasis of transmigration was assimilation and acculturation as part of the nation-building project of establishing more even development. Anecdotal accounts and reports have indicated that transmigration and migration created increased competition for resources, which also resulted in land alienation of indigenous 'minority' communities. Moreover, it appears that estates jointly owned by the Suharto family's commercial interests, local conglomerates and multinational companies were greatly responsible for land displacement of indigenous farming communities. The project of state-guided harmony appears to have been integrally related to an attempt by the powerholders to subdue communal tensions that had been spawned by modernisation and land alienation. Interviews with H. Zaini Ahmad Noeh (head of the DMI and former advisor to Alamsjah), 8 October 1997; Hidayat, 12 November 1997; Drs. Muslim, 10 November 1997; the Director of Sociocultural Guidance, 10 November 1997.

29. (Nos. 1/1965, 1/1969, 4/1978, 14/1978, 70 and 77/1978, 8/1979, 1/1979, and MA/432/1981), 'Petunjuk Bagi Umat Islam', Majelis Ulama Indonesia.

30. Interview with Hidayat, 12 November 1997; *Da'i dan Petani Membagun Daerah Baru*, pp.7–96; interview with the Director of Sociocultural Guidance, 10 November 1997.

31. The Istiqlal mosque in Jakarta houses the MUI central office and several other corporatist organisations; Mardjoned, *KH. Hasan Basri*, p.201.

32. Interview with Noeh, 8 October 1997; Mardjoned, *KH. Hasan Basri*, p.200.

33. University campuses in particular have been a continuing focus of concern as unauthorised Islamic organisations (*usroh* groups) have proliferated, using campus mosques as centres for organisation. The government was determined to neutralise the popular growth of *usroh* groups among youths, and government-built mosques were no doubt one effort in this direction. Mardjoned, *KH.Hasan Basri*, p.203.

34. According to Toto, members of the mosque body were youthful idealists—the government branded them as 'Masyumi'—who delivered strident anti-government sermons in the late 1970s. Its anti-government cast was encouraged by the fact that the Indonesian Islamic Secondary School Students (Pelajar Islam Indonesia, PII), known for its radical polemics

against a host of rivals had a large contingent of members in the BKPMI. Toto spent a seven-month term in jail in 1978 because the BKPMI joined the chorus of Muslim voices opposing the inclusion of Javanese mysticism in the broad outlines of state policy (GBHN). In 1981, the government suspected them of involvement in the Imron group's hijacking of a Garuda flight to Bangkok. It implicated them in other anti-state activities related to the Komando Jihad, the Tanjung Priok anti-government riots, and Warsidi's alleged attempts to found an Islamic state in Lampung. Interview with Toto, 21 March 1997.

35. Aqsha et al., *Islam in Indonesia: A Survey of Events*, p.283; 'Teaching Children to Read the Qur'an', *Studia Islamika*, pp.1–5.
36. Aqsha et al., *Islam in Indonesia: A Survey of Events*, pp.135, 401; 'Hasil Keputusan Muktamar III Dewan Masjid Indonesia', pp.56–7.
37. Tasmara, *Etos Kerja Pribadi* and *Menjawab Tantangan Zaman*.
38. Disaffected ex-Masyumi party leaders establised the Dewan Dakwah Islamiyah Indonesia (Indonesian Islamic Dakwah Council) in 1967, under the chairmanship of Muhammad Natsir (former Prime Minister and Masyumi leader). Through the Dewan, they sought to advance their political-religious agendas. Dewan leaders remained highly critical of Suharto and the military until the advent of the state–Islamic accommodation in the late-1980s.
39. At the conference, attendees set up three makeshift commissions. One commission had the task of drawing up the BAKOMUBIN's new program. The main reason expressed at the commission for establishing the nationally co-ordinated body was to improve the welfare and income of its preachers. Members discussed the need for life insurance, proper medical care, and good and regular sources of funding, which depended on gaining access to influential government personnel. 'The Silaturahmi Mubaligh SeIndonesia' was held at Asrama Haji Jakarta (Pondok Gede) on 6 June 1996.
40. Herbert Feith applied the term 'problem solvers' in the 1950s for technocratic-minded administrators.
41. A speech by an official from the Department of Religion at the Silaturahmi Mubaligh SeIndonesia, 6 June 1996.
42. A speech by Toto Tasmara at the Silaturahmi Mubaligh SeIndonesia, 6 June 1996.
43. FKLD was established in February 1993 as a national co-ordinating institute for all Islamic missionary organisations. It was placed under supervision of the Director of Information at the Department of Religion. Several corporatist organisations participated in its founding including MDI, DMI, and ICMI. FKLD was to fulfil a purpose similar to the corporatist institutions (discussed above) of regulating relations between the different Islamic propagation institutes and between those institutes and the regime. Interview with Subagio, 13 November 1997; *Islam in Indonesia: A Survey of Events*, p.302.

44. Suryadinata, *Military Ascendancy*, p.79; Reeve, 'The Corporatist State', p.155.
45. Interview with Hidayat, 12 November 1997. The co-option by Golkar of 'extreme' Muslim groups is not a development resulting from Suharto's recent post-1988 courtship of Islam. Such efforts date back to the pre-1971 election campaign period (e.g., the amalgamation of the Muslim sect Darul Hadiths into Golkar just prior to the general election).
46. Interview with Hidayat, 12 November 1997; the former Minister of Religion, Gen. (ret.) Alamsjah Ratu Prawiranegara admitted that, during the early New Order period, state intelligence services did not wholly trust the Department of Religion. Continued monitoring of the Department appears to have remained a task of intelligence services through to the late-1990s.
47. Women's role as housewife in the family, as depicted in government publications, is exemplary of the New Order state's official ideology, which designates the family as the smallest unit in ever widening concentric circles to the nation-state. The family is seen as the pillar of society and of the nation. Women are seen as the pillar of the family. The harmony of the nation is viewed as dependent upon women's maintenance of harmony in the family.
48. Interviews with Aisyah Hamid Baidlowi (Chairperson of the NU-Muslimat), 11 March 1997; Subagio, 13 November 1997; Ma'shum and Zawawi, *50 Tahun Muslimat NU*, pp.25–6; Soewondo, *Kedudukan Wanita Indonesia*, pp.233–8.
49. Interview with Susy Machsusoh Tosari Witiajar (the Secretary General of Muslimat and the wife of the Secretary General of PPP), 4 April 1997; Eldridge, *Non-Government Organisations*, p.68.
50. Interview with Susy Witiajar, 4 April 1997.
51. Reeve, 'The Corporatist State', pp.152–5; Liddle, 'Politics 1992–1993', p.31; Robison, 'Organising the Transition', pp.53–7; Pangaribuan, *The Indonesian State Secretariat*, pp.59–60.
52. President Suharto established several foundations, including YABMP, which served as enormous slush funds for investment projects of Suharto, his children and business associates, as well as for the ruling party Golkar. Colmey and Liebhold, 'The Family Firm', *Time*, 24 May 1999; Pangaribuan, *The Indonesian State Secretariat*, pp.60–1.
53. At the March 1988 MPR session, Benny Murdani led the armed forces fraction in opposition to Suharto's successful nomination of Sudharmono as vice-president. A deepening personal hostility between Suharto and Benny resulted in the latter being kicked-upstairs to Minister of Defence. At the March 1993 MPR session, the armed forces appeared to momentarily out-manoeuvre Suharto by having their nomination of Armed Forces' Commander-in-Chief, Try Sutrisno, for vice-president pushed through in preference to the president's choice of his close friend and protégé

B.J. Habibie. Ramage, *Politics in Indonesia*, p.85; Liddle, 'Politics 1992–93', pp.31–2; Robison, 'Organising the Transition', p.56; Reeve, 'The Corporatist State', pp.168–72; Lowry, *The Armed Forces*, pp.189–90.

54. According to government figures, in 1969 there were about 36,000 places of worship throughout Indonesia. In 1995, the number of mosques and Islamic places of worship alone had phenomenally increased to 589,454. Yet the figure in 1998 for mosques built and funded by the YABMP was estimated only at 800, with most construction coming from community initiatives. Indonesian national television news (TVRI), 6 February 1998.

55. Vatikiotis, *Indonesian Politics under Suharto*, pp.135–6; Hefner, 'Islam, State, and Civil Society', p.32; Schwarz, *A Nation in Waiting*, p.191; Ramage, *Politics in Indonesia*, p.86.

56. Liddle, 'Politics 1992–1993', p.33; Pangaribuan, *The Indonesian State Secretariat*, pp.59–77.

57. Robison, 'Organising the Transition', p.53; Schwarz, *A Nation in Waiting*, p.174; Ramage, *Politics in Indonesia*, pp.79–83.

58. Interviews with Adi Sasono (NGO leader who rose to the position of Secretary General of ICMI in 1995 and chairman in 2000), 21 January and 16 February 1994; Sri Bintang Pamungkas, (parliamentary legislator from PPP and member of ICMI and CIDES), 8 February 1994; Amien Rais (Muhammadiyah leader, head of ICMI's council of experts), 4 January 1994; Nurcholish Madjid, (liberal theologian/scholar, founder of the Islamic educational foundation, Paramadina, and ICMI member), 12 January and 16 February 1994.

59. Golkar leaders, cabinet ministers, businessmen and professionals also joined the association. The Minister of Religion and his staff, officials from MUI, the Minister of Internal Affairs, and the Minister of Information participated in ICMI's first steering committee meetings; Aqsha et al., *Islam in Indonesia: A Survey of Events*, p.275; Hefner, 'Islam, State, and Civil Society', pp.18–28; Schwarz, *A Nation in Waiting*, p.177.

60. Aqsha et al., *Islam in Indonesia: A Survey of Events*, p.24; *Forum Keadilan*, 6 April 1998; *Kompas Online*, 11 February 1997; *Panji Masyarakat*, 11–20 May 1992.

61. Habibie later caved in to pressure by creating the post of Secretary General.

62. Interviews with Haidar Bagir (an editor and senior board member on Republika), 11 February 1994; Dawam Rahardjo (ICMI intellectual and NGO leader), 27 January 1994.

63. Interview with Dawam, 27 January 1994; *Tempo*, 9 February 1991, 23 February 1991.

64. Interview with Amien, 4 January 1994.

65. Amien's popularity as an opponent of Suharto had soared since his ouster from ICMI. Dissension against Suharto had grown significantly between the mid-1990s and early 1997, with new, independent organisations appearing

on the political landscape to challenge corporatist arrangements. In this context, state intervention in the leadership choices of the main political and social organisations increasingly had failed to prevent the rise of independent figures to the top leadership of these organisations. Despite state interventions, Megawati was elected as PDI chair in 1993—although she was cast aside in July 1996—and Abdurrahman Wahid narrowly defeated the state-backed candidate in 1994. It appears that Amien can be counted among the independent leaders that successfully defeated state interventions of this kind. *Tempo*, 11 January 1999; *Harian Terbit*, 24 February 1997; John McBeth, 'Line in the Sand', *Far Eastern Economic Review*, 27 March 1997; interview with Marzuki Darusman (leader of Komnas HAM), 6 July 1997.

66. Interview with Sri Bintang, 8 February 1994.

67. *The Jakarta Post*, 22 February 1997; *Poskota*, 8 March 1997; interview with Marzuki, 6 July 1997.

68. *Republika Online*, 10 December 1995; Fealy, 'Indonesian Politics, 1995–96', pp.25–6.

69. Interviews with Sudomo, 30 October 1997; Murdani , 5 November 1997.

70. *Jawa Pos*, 12 August 1997. Honna highlighted the important role performed by Hartono when he was in charge of the National Resilience Institute (Lemhamnas) of routinising ABRI's vigilance discourse as part of the military's social surveillance, intelligence and security operations. Honna, 'The Military and Democratisation', pp.156–64.

71. *Jawa Pos*, 12 August 1997; *Gatra*, 16 August 1997; *Kompas Online*, 7 August 1997.

72. See chapter eight.

73. Ultimately, Habibie's projects such as the state-owned aircraft manufacturing plant (IPTN), a shipyard, the controversial purchase and refurbishment of thirty-nine warships from the former East German navy, and the promotion of nuclear power plants have required extensive protection and massive government subsidies, dependent mostly on the good will of President Suharto. Mackie and MacIntyre, 'Politics', p.36.

74. For example, at the ICMI's national work meeting in December 1992, B.J. Habibie and the Minister of Internal Affairs both confirmed that the association could not become a political party in the style of the old Masyumi, as it had been 'established to contribute to the development of human resources of all Indonesians'. Aqsha et al., *Islam in Indonesia: A Survey of Events*, pp.266–73; Ramage, *Politics in Indonesia*, p.101.

75. *Panji Masyarakat*, 21–30 July 1994.

76. Aqsha et al., *Islam in Indonesia: A Survey of Events*, p.263.

77. Included among the Foundation's members and advisers were Tien Suharto, Vice-President Sudharmono, Armed Forces' Commander Tri Sutrisno, the Chairman of Golkar, the Chairman of MUI, several cabinet ministers, and

national tycoons such as Suharto's son Bambang Trihatmodjo, Probosutedjo, and Bob Hasan. *The Jakarta Post*, 19 August 1992; *Angkatan Bersenjata*, 18 August 1992; *Media Indonesia*, 18 August 1992; *Antara*, 18 August 1992.

78. More importantly, perhaps, was that the donation of funds was aimed at garnering the support of Muslims for Suharto's presidency and for Golkar's election campaign. Probosutejo's personal donation, in fact, coincided with his efforts to rally Muslim support behind his own campaign for Golkar. ICMI and Golkar together frequented Islamic rural *pesantren* to drum up support for Habibie and Golkar before general and presidential elections. *Antara*, 22 May 1992; *The Jakarta Post*, 31 January 1994, 1 February 1994; *Merdeka*, 1 February 1994; *Republika*, 3 November 1996–24 February 1997; *Harian Umum Pikiran Rakyat*, 6 May 1997; *Kompas Online*, 4 November 1996.

79. One of the major demands of the intelligentsia had been for the implementation of policies, along the lines of Malaysia's New Economic Policy of positive discrimination in favour of Bumiputra, that would provide a fairer distribution of Indonesia's economic goods between wealthy Chinese capitalists and struggling indigenous traders. Porter, 'Accommodation or Islamisation'; Aqsha et al., *Islam in Indonesia: A Survey of Events*, p.265; interviews with Sudomo, 30 October 1997; Sucipto Wirosarjono (former government statistician and ICMI member), 11 January 1994; Sasono, 21 January and 16 February 1994; Dawam, 27 January 1994; Haidar, 11 February 1994; Sri Bintang, 8 February 1994; Lukman Harun (Muhammadiyah leader and ICMI member), 23 January 1994; Dewi Fortuna Anwar, 7 February 1994; Muslimin Nasution (Secretary to Chairman of Bappenas and ICMI leader), 10 February 1994; Amien, 4 January 1994 and Bambang Sudibyo, 4 January 1994.

80. The following sources are a sample of the newspapers and editions consulted. *Merdeka*, 21 February 1992; *Antara*, 13 April 1992; *Pelita*, 2 January–13 February 1993; *Republika*, 3 November 1996–24 February 1997; *The Jakarta Post*, 1 February 1994.

81. Aqsha et al., *Islam in Indonesia: A Survey of Events*, pp.7–8.

82. Other community leaders strongly criticised Alamsjah's initiatives. Alamsjah responded by declaring that 'political engineering' was sometimes necessary. According to him, the idea of holding the mass prayer originated with Golkar's affiliate organisations as it was felt that some Golkar members were 'reluctant to make a pledge' in support of Suharto 'as they had done during [previous] presidential elections'. His statement expressed the regime's concern over the growing rivalry in Golkar, especially between the senior military and junior civilian members, since the organisation had opted to draw in a wider range of individual and mass

membership. Aqsha et al., *Islam in Indonesia: A Survey of Events*, pp. 19–60.

83. *Media Indonesia*, 17 September 1995.
84. *Media Indonesia*, 17 September 1995; *Republika Online*, 8 June 1996; *Tiras*, 27 July 1995; *Poskota*, 22 March 1997.
85. Ibid.
86. Op. cit.

Chapter 6

Nahdlatul Ulama: Between Incorporation and Independence

INTRODUCTION

The voluntary organisation, Nahdlatul Ulama (Revival of Religious Scholars), is the most problematic of the Islamic associations to analyse in terms of Suharto's corporatist strategies. The reasons for this are not only because of NU's large, sprawling organisational structure and mass membership, much of which was based in rural Java and only loosely tied to the organisation, but also because NU had remained largely outside of state structures for much of Suharto's New Order period, had resisted state interference in its internal affairs, and thus had remained a fairly independent but marginalised political and economic force. Nonetheless, Suharto did seek to capture, channel, and politically exclude the interests of NU, and marshall NU support behind his presidency at elections. The argument can be made that NU's peripheral position in the political system indeed highlighted the success of Suharto's strategy of corporatist exclusion, of shutting interests out of power and denying effective channels of participation to group, and especially Muslim group, interests. This chapter considers how Suharto's corporatist strategy both exacerbated and created divisions in NU. An examination also is made of how Golkar and ICMI became organisational channels through which Suharto sought to consolidate more informal types of clientelistic co-optation of leaders of NU's *pesantren* (Islamic boarding schools).

Much of the study concerns Abdurrahman's chairmanship of NU (1984–1999), because he was representative of, and influenced different trends in, the organisation and had a major voice in national politics. He was an outspoken critic of Suharto, vocal advocate of democracy, and an opponent of Habibie and ICMI. He was later to become Indonesia's fourth president and the first to be democratically elected. He strongly disagreed with the state–Islamic accommodation through ICMI. He claimed that the accommodation, among other things, was an unacceptable attempt to build formal links between the state and Islamic politics. He defended NU's independence from state

106

encroachments. Significant segments of the NU membership (including many leaders of the *pesantren*) also were determined to remain independent from state frameworks. His leadership of NU, nonetheless, was often controversial and contested. There were pressures within the organisation for him to reconcile with Suharto. Other elements discussed in this chapter were unimpressed with, or openly opposed to, Abdurrahman's leadership.

Suharto's strategies concerning NU were complicated by the changing political context of the 1990s. This was a period of intensifying intra-elite conflict and growing succession crisis, and Abdurrahman was among those who competed for political advantage before an anticipated post-Suharto era. Suharto in turn was trying to preserve his power and ensure his own unanimous endorsement as president. Consequently, Suharto sought to replace the NU chairman with a more compliant, pro-regime figure. He recruited ICMI, Golkar, and other state interests into his campaign to topple Abdurrahman. The analysis, therefore, looks at how NU was caught up in power struggles, as well as considers how corporatist organisations became embroiled in the power struggles.

THE NAHDLATUL ULAMA

NU was an organisation of immense diversity, complexity and size, claiming a membership of over 30 million people, located mainly in rural Java. The organisation had a heterogeneous membership in terms of social origins, political affiliation, and religious outlook. Its membership included politicians, businessmen, NGO activists, youth and women's groups, liberal *ulama*, conservative *ulama* and a mass rural following of townsfolk, peasant farmers, and *santri* (devout Muslim students). Much of NU's membership was only loosely affiliated with the organisation, holding emotional attachments rather than membership cards. Arguably, NU was more easily able to elude government authority and frameworks—because of the organisation's loose affiliation and amorphous nature—than the centralised and bureaucratic structures of Islamic modernist organisations and the political parties. As McVey notes, 'adopting modern organisational forms means confronting the modern state on its own grounds'.[1]

However, NU did not completely neglect modern organisation and established its own general schools (*madrasah*), orphanages, social and education institutes, *dakwah* and mosque bodies, women's and youth associations, with a decentralised branch structure that, nonetheless, was subject to many of the edicts and decisions of NU's Central Board in Jakarta. The organisational affiliates had a degree of autonomy from NU. For example, women's affiliates, Muslimat, Fatayat and IPPNU (Association of Daughters of NU) could conduct their own programs and affairs but in a manner consonant with the basic outlines of NU.[2] Through corporatist organisations, the Muslimat and Fatayat established links and working relations (in areas of education, health, welfare, rural development and family planning) with government departments independently of NU's central board.[3]

NU's relative decentralisation largely derived from the personalistic and informal networks and authority of individual *kiai* and *ulama*. The main social base of NU was its system of Islamic boarding schools (*pesantren*) run privately by *kiai* and *ulama* (religious leaders and scholars) for the spiritual, moral and religious development of *santri*. Many *kiai* had a reputation of being fiercely independent, especially from larger political structures of the state, and customarily drew livelihood from minor trade, small landholdings, school fees, and community support and donations to *pesantren* coffers.[4]

Suharto's Incorporation of NU

The relative autonomy of NU's affiliate organisations appeared to facilitate the capture of the organisations into corporatist arrangements. Thus, as outlined in chapter five, Suharto brought NU's affiliates, including women's organisations, *dakwah*, mosque, and *ulama* bodies—and/or members of these organisations—into peak corporatist organisations like BMOIWI, Golkar, MDI, DMI, BAKOMUBIN and MUI. There was also a state-charted *pesantren* organisation, the Pondok Pesantren Co-operative Body (BKSPP). The capture in stages of NU's affiliates was partly a response to the fact that NU had resisted capture in state frameworks as it had refused to become a compliant member of PPP. Instead, NU had opposed certain government decisions deemed harmful to the organisation's interests, and vigorously contested the general elections in 1971 (before the party merger), 1977 and 1982.[5] Heavy state interventions in PPP led to NU's withdrawal from PPP in 1984 and to acceptance of *Pancasila* as NU's sole ideological foundation.

NU's departure from PPP facilitated Suharto's co-optation of many NU members and *pesantren* leaders. Although NU officials could no longer remain in PPP, other NU members were permitted to join any of the three parties (Golkar, PPP or PDI). This freed up leaders of NU's affiliate organisations and *pesantren* to join Golkar and to bring their rural support bases with them. After the state–Islamic rapprochement in the late-1980s, Suharto intensified efforts to draw NU's *pesantren* into state frameworks and to co-opt individual *kiai* and *ulama* with disbursements of patronage through Golkar and state channels. *Kiai* and *pesantren* were becoming increasingly dependent upon state funding. For example, NU's official *pesantren* organisation, Rabithalul Mai'ahidil Islamiyah (RMI, an association of around 4,000 *pesantren*, half of Indonesia's approximately 8,000 *pesantren*) became reliant upon state funding for the holding of its national meetings. More significantly, by 1997, more than 75 per cent of *pesantren* were penetrated by the state education curriculum, with uniformed government teachers supplying much of the school staff.[6]

Suharto also used corporatist organisations such as Golkar, MDI, ICMI, and MUI to penetrate NU's *pesantren*. He did this to open a breach in the NU constituency through which Golkar could enter and win over Muslims to its campaign banner. The previous chapter considered how Golkar and other state leaders distributed funds to *pesantren* before general and presidential elections. Habibie and ICMI were among the multiple state interests that frequented *pesantren* in attempts to drum up political support for Golkar and their own political careers before the holding of elections.

For example, at NU's fourth national meeting of RMI in Jakarta (January 1994), ICMI, Golkar, and other state interests made concerted efforts to win political influence. Several ministers and senior government officials attended the meeting, which was formally opened by President Suharto and closed by Vice-President Try Sutrisno. There was a hive of activity in the month before the national meeting, as senior government, Golkar, and military officials did their rounds of *pesantren*. Habibie held a dialogue with 1,200 NU *ulama* in Madura (an island off East Java), and was later made 'honorary chairman' of the *pesantren* body, BKSPP, in Bogor (West Java). The visit to Madura appeared to be part of an attempt to build an ICMI presence in the island's *pesantren*, and to win support for his own ambitions to become the next vice-president.[7]

Two prominent *kiai*, who became targets of co-optation were KH Ilyas Ruchiyat (NU's acting *rais aam*, *katib* of NU's syuriah council) and KH Yusuf Hasyim (a member of NU's syuriah council). Both leaders ran their own *pesantren* and still had respect and authority within their respective communities, but had benefited from their co-optation and joined corporatist organisations. Their *pesantren* received considerable state funding. Ruchiyat became deputy-chair of MUI and an ICMI member. Yusuf was once a fierce critic of the regime and PPP leader in the 1970s and early 1980s. He was one of the PPP leaders whom Naro had punished with the re-drafting of party lists in 1982. By the 1990s, however, Yusuf appeared to change allegiances, as he opposed a return to PPP, joined ICMI and supported Suharto.[8]

Both Yusuf and Ruchiyat—and the former deputy chairman of NU's syuriah, Ali Yafie (ICMI and MUI member)—gave public pledges of support for Suharto's renomination to the presidency at election times.[9] Along with several other ICMI figures, the three leaders were rewarded for their loyalties with appointment to the MPR in 1992, but they were not given access to the real decisional structures of government. Most of these ICMI figures entered the MPR on a Golkar ticket in support of Habibie's ambitions to become vice-president.[10] In this case, ICMI and Golkar acted as conduits to broader state structures, in a manner that sought to contain interests and channel them as a form of regime support.

ABDURRAHMAN'S LEADERSHIP OF NU

KH Abdurrahman Wahid was the grandson of two of the NU's founding fathers, Kiai Hasjim Asjiari and Kiai Bisri Syansuri. As such, he embodied the moral authority of great *kiai* and the legitimacy derived from belonging to NU's revered lineage. He became NU chairman when NU was seeking conciliation with Suharto and withdrew from PPP. He was one of the architects of NU's conciliation with Suharto and supplied some of the main arguments for NU's departure from PPP. The incorporation of NU in PPP, he contended, had placed the organisation in a tight corner with no political room of manoeuvre. He insisted that NU would be better positioned to play politics outside of 'the formal structure of New Order politics'. Withdrawal from PPP gave NU enhanced 'freedom of "political' movement", as it was no longer subject to direct state control and interventions.[11]

By the early 1990s, after an apparent thaw of relations between Suharto and NU, Abdurrahman–Suharto relations rapidly declined. Abdurrahman did a number of things that upset Suharto. He became an outspoken advocate of democracy and criticised aspects of Suharto's rule. He helped establish and led a discussion group called the Democracy Forum in March 1991 to promote democratisation.[12] He saw NU's vast constituency as a starting point for a pluralistic, civil society; one based on a tolerant society, democracy and respect for human rights. He stressed the strategic role NU could play as an independent social force, a countervailing power to the state that would gain a better bargaining position in relation to state power. Other liberal-minded intellectuals in NU shared similar views to Abdurrahman regarding the potential of NU becoming a democratising force or civil society.[13] In line with his views, Abdurrahman refused to join the state-sponsored ICMI, thereby resisting state corporatist strategies and sending a clear rebuff to Suharto. In March 1992, he called together a mass rally (*Rapat Akbar*) of NU supporters to demonstrate to Suharto and ICMI that his organisation was still a force to contend with. At the rally, he pledged NU's loyalty to *Pancasila* rather than endorsing Suharto for a fifth term as president, despite the indirect pressure on NU to give the endorsement.[14] During the 1990s, he attacked cosy state–Islamic relations represented by ICMI.

However, the NU chairman had not always resisted incorporation into state arrangements. For example, before the decline in relations with Suharto, in 1988 he joined the MPR as a Golkar candidate.[15] As such, one could question whether Abdurrahman's attitude regarding state incorporation of Muslim interests depended, to some extent, on what concessions he could obtain from Suharto in rivalry with other interests in the political system.

Opposition to ICMI

Abdurrahman's opposition to ICMI was greatly informed by his perceptions of his own position within emerging power-struggles. He considered that NU was locked in competition with ICMI—which largely represented modernist organisations like Muhammadiyah and HMI—as both organisations competed for political predominance. In particular, he was highly critical of what he saw as B.J. Habibie's 'core group at BPPT' becoming a 'new power centre in the fifth development cabinet (1993)', and using ICMI as a support base. Abdurrahman disagreed with Islam being used to advance Habibie's political ambitions, especially as the latter had his sights on becoming Indonesia's next vice-president. Habibie was Suharto's favoured candidate for the vice-presidency at the 1993 and 1998 MPR elections, and he became vice-president in 1998.[16] From 1993 onwards, Abdurrahman was irreconcilably opposed to the prospect of Habibie becoming Indonesia's future vice-president. 'It was inappropriate that he [Habibie] become vice-president', he said.[17]

The NU chairman was acutely aware of NU's marginal position in the political structure relative to Muslims from the modernist organisations. He wanted to bring NU in from the cold and back into the political mainstream (albeit on his terms), after years of NU–government antagonisms that had greatly hurt the organisation's economic and political activities. He had support from NU's business people, *kiai*, and other NU members who wished to improve the economic conditions of NU's constituency through improved relations with Suharto. Abdurrahman expressed his disappointment at being excluded from the political mainstream. 'Look at how [the regime] tries to block NU people from entering the key positions in ICMI. Influential mass organisations [NU] are neglected and given peripheral positions in ICMI.'[18] He confided that it was dangerous for him and NU to remain at the political margins, as he was exposed to attacks from state–ICMI interests.[19]

Abdurrahman also was opposed to a certain kind of mutual co-optation occurring between modernist Islam and the state. He argued that not only were Muslims being co-opted by Suharto and Habibie, members of ICMI's intelligentsia were trying to enlist the state in aid of their Islamising agendas. He claimed that those who desired an Islamic society, mostly Muslim modernists attached to the Muhammadiyah, really dreamt of establishing an Islamic state. He was opposed to what he considered to be a resurgence of universal-cum-formal-legalistic Islam, which sought to provide a complete set of rules and laws that required the state to regulate the conduct of people's lives. At the very least, he argued, Islamic society was offered as an alternative system to the current one underwritten by nationalistic commitments. He considered ICMI an unwelcome move towards the 're-confessionalisation' of politics, after the New Order government had successfully 'de-confessionalised' or 'de-Islamised' Indonesian politics.[20]

'De-Islamisation' of politics had been achieved largely through strategies of corporatist containment. Abdurrahman, however, was concerned that Suharto's more recent incorporation of Muslim interests through ICMI had the effect of not containing but re-politicising Islamic agendas. (See chapter seven for a discussion on ICMI's Islamic agendas.)

Guarding NU's Independence: Responses to State Encroachment

Abdurrahman extended his attacks against cosy state–ICMI relations to criticism of the government's tendency to increase its jurisdiction over the community's religious affairs. He accused the government, and its Department of Religion, of 'over institutionalising' Islam on such diverse issues as the state's increasing control of the collection of Islamic alms tax, of the pilgrimage to Mecca, the determining of the beginning of fasting month, religious education, the labelling of food items as 'permitted' (*halal*) or 'prohibited' (*haram*), and Islamisation of the state's laws. He regarded the role of the Department of Religion and MUI in regulating the religious affairs of the nation as unnecessary. He made numerous other attacks against cosy state–Islamic relations by directing much of his criticisms against corporatist organisations like MUI and ICMI.[21]

Abdurrahman's criticism of the state's 'unnecessary interference' in the internal affairs of the Muslim community reflected an underlying concern of many *kiai* to guard NU's independence from the state. Abdurrahman expressed the concern that Suharto was using the state, including corporatist organisations like ICMI and MUI, in order to encroach upon the NU constituency.[22] ICMI and MUI threatened to win the allegiances of his NU constituency. For example, Abdurrahman objected to the *Rais Aam* of NU, Ilyas Ruchiyat, being appointed as a deputy-chair of MUI. NU's former Secretary General, Ichwan Syam, and its former chairman, Idham Chalid, were also appointed to MUI's board at its Fifth National Consultation in July 1995. He complained that

> With the most senior NU leader becoming an MUI leader, serious questions are raised about the ability of NU to maintain an attitude of independence from MUI. MUI cannot claim itself as a representative of the entire Muslim community's aspirations. This is because a great deal of policy products of MUI led by KH Hasan Basri is determined unilaterally, without consultation with leaders of other Islamic organisations...[including] NU.[23]

Abdurrahman was also highly critical of the state's encroachment on the NU's grassroots support, its rural network of *pesantren*. The various state-backed incursions into *pesantren*, at least potentially, presaged gradual erosion of Abdurrahman's hold on his constituency. Addressing the Buntet *pesantren*, in Cirebon (1996), the NU chairman repeated one of his common themes by warning that *pesantren* were losing their independence because of an inability to finance their own existence, thereby making them dependent on outsiders. Just before his address, the Minister of Defence and the Minister of Religion had donated 50 million *rupiah* to the Buntet *pesantren*.[24]

Beyond Abdurrahman's leadership, NU's membership gave mixed responses to Suharto's attempts to woo the *pesantren*. This was especially the case before the 1997 and 1998 elections. For example, Ilyas Ruchiyat cautiously rejected speculation that the presence of so many high-powered state officials in NU *pesantren* was related to attempts to win influence before the elections. Ruchiyat's *pesantren* in Tasikmalaya was widely known to be in receipt of substantial state patronage. Ruchiyat already had been drawn into the state–Islamic accommodation. The Deputy Chair of the NU's religious council, KH Sahal Mahfudz, declared that ICMI and Golkar would 'definitely be received openly at the NU *pesantren*'.[25]

Others were less sanguine. One NU leader asserted that those who adopted the 'Masyumi approach [a clear reference to ICMI]' needed 'to be reminded not to become disappointed when they failed to influence the *pesantren*'.[26] Another *pesantren* leader, Kiai Yusuf Muhammad, explained that if Suharto, Habibie, or ICMI wished to interfere in NU's *pesantren* 'this will be resisted'.

> The mistake that Suharto and Habibie make is that they enter NU's first door and think that all the warmth and smiles attended to them means that they have successfully won over the religious leaders of the *pesantren*. However, this [friendliness] is only protocol afforded to all guests. The other doors in the NU's *pesantren* universe remain closed. In short, Suharto and Habibie cannot hope to win over the *pesantren* constituency.[27]

A Muhammadiyah intellectual, Mansour Fakih (a man who sympathised with Abdurrahman's leadership of NU), criticised the state and ICMI's encroachments. He warned, 'it appears they [the ICMI members] offer their ideas and interests to the *pesantren* community in a manner that will cause a reaction from those groups that feel it [the *pesantren*] is their jurisdiction'.[28] He accused ICMI of siding with the power holders against the interests of 'other groups', creating the impression that the state-backed ICMI was trying to win influence in rivalry with the NU constituency. A group of thirty-seven NU supporters, calling themselves the Communication Forum of Nahdlatul Ulama's Youth Generation, also lodged their protest against such political campaigning in a signed petition entitled 'the *Pesantren* Must Remain Independent'.[29]

The language of these NU figures (and Mansour) reflected their desire to resist Suharto's encroachments made through Golkar and ICMI. Resistance to Golkar also originated from supporters of PPP within NU (discussed further below). As such, there were clearly different categories of 'incorporated' interests, with PPP becoming a source of opposition at election times. Another factor is that many NU *kiai* perhaps resented the terms and conditions attached to their incorporation. Although they might have been keen to receive state funding for their struggling *pesantren*, they were much less likely to accept conditions attached to that funding through their absorption into the state-run education system. Another cause of likely grievance was that the state leadership often did not follow through with pre-election promises of patronage to *pesantren*. For example, KH Hasyim Muzadi (head of NU's East Java branch), told of how the government promised 10 billion *rupiah* of funds to KH Kholil As'ad's *pesantren* in Situbondo (East Java) in return for the *pesantren*'s support for Golkar at the 1997 election. Situbondo was a PPP stronghold, and Kholil supported PPP. Fearful that large funds would simply strengthen Kholil's *pesantren* as a PPP support base, according to Hasyim, the government only delivered on 5 million *rupiah* of its promise.[30]

CREATING DIVISIONS

After NU's exit from PPP, new rivalries arose from the fact that NU leaders and their followers had their loyalties increasingly divided along party lines (Golkar, PPP, and PDI). Political and business interests keen to improve their access to state patronage joined Golkar, while PPP loyalists remained with the Islamic-oriented party, and a small number joined PDI. Golkar sought to entice and bully NU members into joining Golkar and, according to different accounts, this caused a major reaction from PPP supporters.[31] Leaders of NU's Ansor Youth Movement (from branches in Bangil and Pasuruan, East Java), for example, pointed out that the freedom to join any party after 1984 'created an unhealthy climate of mutual suspicion and contest between Golkar and PPP supporters in Ansor. Golkar claimed that Ansor had joined the ruling party.'[32]

According to KH Nurcholis Musytari (the deputy rais syuriah of NU's branch in Bangil), after 1984, there also was continued competition between NU leaders and the MI faction in PPP. The government ensured that MI candidates gained the lion's share of seats—and denied them to NU's PPP candidates—in most of the district parliaments of East Java.[33] The denial of political representation to NU's PPP candidates shows that Suharto was still seeking to fragment and exclude opposition from NU, despite NU's formal withdrawal from PPP. Party-based divisions in NU were especially evident at the 1992 and 1997 elections, which witnessed PPP supporters in NU clash with NU's Golkar supporters in many of the towns of Java.[34] NU's exit from PPP and resultant rivalries seemed to be an outcome (if not objective) of Suharto's corporatist strategy.

The establishment of ICMI also exacerbated divisions in NU. Most of the NU leaders who joined ICMI were opponents of the NU chairman. The deterioration of Suharto–Abdurrahman relations during the 1990s strengthened the hand of rival factions within NU that wished to see Abdurrahman replaced as NU's chairman. Prominent among his adversaries in NU, who joined ICMI, were Ali Yafie, Fahmi Saifuddin (assistant to the Minister of Public Health), Slamet Effendi Yusuf (former leader of the NU's Ansor Youth Movement), Yusuf Hasyim (Abdurrahman's uncle), and Chalid Mawardi (also Chairman of MDI-Golkar). Ali Yafie and Chalid Mawardi were members of the so-called 'Cipete' group, which was defeated by the 'Situbondo' group and the government in determining NU's central leadership. NU's 1984 Congress in Situbondo (East Java) elected Abdurrahman to the chairmanship of the organisation.[35] The Cipete group was prominent among rival contenders for NU's leadership mantle at the NU's 28th Congress at Krapyak, Yogyakarta in November 1989.

One example of rifts in NU was the growing antagonism between Abdurrahman and Ali Yafie. At the Krapyak congress, Ali was elected to the post of deputy *rais aam* and had his sights on becoming NU's next *rais aam*.[36] After the incumbent, Achmad Siddiq, had passed away in 1990, Abdurrahman thwarted Ali's efforts to become *rais aam*. Abdurrahman thought that Suharto was behind Ali's bid for the senior post. The national magazine, *Tempo*, reported that (it was said) Ali spent too much time in MUI to be able to assume NU's top post.[37] After having his career path blocked in NU, Ali channelled much of his activities through MUI and ICMI. He resigned from NU in January 1992 in protest over the alleged involvement of Abdurrahman and NU's Secretary General in a national lottery scandal.[38] Ali was clearly dissatisfied with Abdurrahman's leadership of NU and was a pro-Suharto figure, who had become co-opted into the system. In the mid-1990s, he campaigned for the idea that NU's and Muhammadiyah's constituencies should be unified under the umbrella of ICMI and MUI. Ali's proposal stood in direct contrast to Abdurrahman's view that the NU constituency should remain entirely independent from state interference or from membership of corporatist organisations. We could take Ali's campaign on behalf of MUI and ICMI as one of his, perhaps state-backed, attempts to erode Abdurrahman's hold of the NU constituency as well as promotion of his own leadership ambitions.[39] Ali became head of ICMI's council of advisers in 1995 and chairman of MUI in 1998.

Cipasung Congress and Post-congress Developments

Suharto was determined to remove Abdurrahman from the leadership of NU and replace him with a more pliable figure. He did this to secure his own unanimous endorsement for re-election as president in 1998, and Abdurrahman had refused to give this endorsement. Suharto responded by bringing ICMI, Golkar, and other state interests behind his campaign to unseat Abdurrahman and replace him with a state-backed candidate. These efforts coincided with initiatives by ICMI, MUI, and Golkar to penetrate *pesantren* and mobilise support (discussed above).

The campaign to upset Abdurrahman's chairmanship was underway at the NU's 29th Congress in Cipasung, West Java, in December 1994. The Army Chief-of-Staff for Social-Political Affairs, Gen. Hartono (a Golkar and ICMI partisan), the ICMI Chairman Habibie, the Chairman of Golkar Harmoko, the Minister of Religious Affairs, and Suharto's daughter Siti Rukmana (deputy chair of the Golkar board) were some of the senior state officials who backed Abdurrahman's rivals for the chairmanship. Fahmi Saifuddin, Chalid Mawardi and the wealthy businessman, Abu Hasan (the latter two being former members of the Cipete faction), were the most credible pro-government candidates put forward against Abdurrahman's re-nomination in a race that deeply polarised the NU constituency.[40]

In a determined campaign to unseat Abdurrahman, state officials and segments of the armed forces combined the offer of inducements to, and intimidation against, NU members at the congress in order to garner a vote against the incumbent. Despite the concerted efforts to unseat him, Abdurrahman survived the attempt by winning re-election to the NU chairmanship by a slim margin (174 votes to 142) against Abu Hasan, the strongest alternative candidate. A rival NU board was set up under Abu Hasan's leadership, but the board failed to gain sufficient grassroots support within NU to enable it to present a serious challenge to Abdurrahman's chairmanship.[41]

Throughout much of 1995, Abdurrahman's other major rivals, his two uncles Yusuf Hasyim and Shohib Bisri, led an anti-Abdurrahman campaign. Meanwhile, pro-Suharto forces—Gen. Feisal Tanjung, Gen. Hartono, Habibie, and Siti Rukmana—regularly visited NU's *pesantren* constituency and dispensed patronage in the form of financial and material rewards to Abdurrahman's main rivals. Greg Fealy accurately depicted the congress and post-congress events as 'an internal battle for control of the NU'.[42] It was in the post-congress fallout of the mid-1990s that Abdurrahman and his supporters, as discussed above, levelled much of their attacks against ICMI-linked state interference in the affairs of NU's *pesantren* and in the affairs of the greater Muslim community. It is clear, from the various state-backed manoeuvres, that ICMI and Golkar interests were drawn into this intra-elite contest in support of efforts by Suharto's circle to topple one of Suharto's, and ICMI's, most outspoken critics, Abdurrahman.

Icy relations continued between Abdurrahman and Suharto throughout most of 1996. The NU chairman had fostered close relations with the opposition leader Megawati Sukarnoputri (the daughter of the erstwhile President Sukarno who had been ousted from power by Suharto). He indicated that NU might throw its support behind PDI at the 1997 general election, and this prospect greatly threatened the usual orchestrated endorsement of Suharto for the presidency.[43] After Megawati's government-backed ouster as PDI chairperson on 27 July, which sparked a riot in Jakarta, Abdurrahman, together with two retired generals and outspoken critics of Suharto, signed a 'petition of concern' about the direction of Indonesian politics.[44]

During the year, there occurred a series of incidents in Java, in which Muslim rioters went on a destructive rampage looting and burning churches in Surabaya (June) and Situbondo (October), in East Java, and Tasikmalaya (December) in West Java. Many NU leaders, and Christian leaders, suspected that the church burning was part of Suharto's attempts to undermine Abdurrahman's leadership of NU.[45] The regions where the destruction occurred were major areas of NU and PPP support, and therefore at risk of giving the public impression that the NU constituency was an organisation of religiously intolerant fanatics. Abdurrahman had hitherto based much of his reputation on his image as a man of moderation that led a community of measured tolerance. Proving that he was unable to control his own community would potentially undermine his credibility as both a national leader and as the NU's chairman. Several local *pesantren* leaders and PPP supporters in East Java districts also believed that Suharto was instigating a campaign to discredit PPP before the general election.[46] Placed in a tight spot, Abdurrahman eventually pointed the finger of blame at a regime-backed plot that (to the incredulity of many observers) he claimed was orchestrated by ICMI to destabilise and discredit NU.

Escalation of Abdurrahman–ICMI conflict

The analysis next considers that a besieged Abdurrahman continued to perceive ICMI as NU's main rival organisation, as he sought to secure his leadership of NU from Suharto's heavy-handed interventions. He moved from a position of open opposition to Suharto, to a position of conciliation with the regime—all the time seeking to place himself and NU in a stronger bargaining position relative to ICMI in intra-elite power struggles. Abdurrahman's perception of ICMI as a political threat was largely in response to Suharto's divide-and-rule tactics, whereby the president had harnessed incorporated Muslim interests (in Golkar and ICMI) to his own partisan interests before elections. NU under Abdurrahman's leadership had been greatly disadvantaged by the state–Islamic accommodation, and Habibie, the pro-Golkar/pro-ICMI generals, and Suharto's daughter had joined efforts to topple the NU chairman.

Thus, a culmination of episodes in 1996 spilled over into conflict between Abdurrahman and ICMI. In particular, the NU chairman and ICMI's Secretary General, Adi Sasono, exchanged harsh words as the former tried to implicate the later in Suharto's (alleged) plot to discredit NU. Abdurrahman startled the Indonesian public by announcing that two state-backed operations had been mounted, a 'red dragon' operation to undermine Megawati Sukarnoputri's leadership of PDI (discussed in chapter eight) and a 'green dragon' operation to discredit his own chairmanship of NU. The following discussion is concerned with the so-called 'green dragon' operation, inasmuch as it throws light on the Abdurrahman–ICMI conflict.

Abdurrahman raised the spectre of a green dragon operation in response to the spate of church burning. He sought to convince his NU members and Christian groups that the burning had been orchestrated in order to undermine his chairmanship of NU before the elections. In January 1997, he went further and accused a foundation called Humanika (the Community Association for Humanity and Justice), the ICMI think-tank CIDES, and Adi Sasono of being the main actors behind the green dragon operation to destabilise and discredit NU. He left open to speculation the possibility that green dragon also referred to the so-called 'green' or Muslim generals (Feisal Tanjung and Hartono).[47]

He claimed that Humanika had funded the Tasikmalaya riot. He identified Bursyah Zarnubi (a Humanika leader) and Eggy Sudjana (a staff member of the ICMI think-tank CIDES chaired by Adi Sasono) as two key figures behind the riot.[48] The NU's Ansor Youth Movement produced a 'white book', which claimed that Hadi Mustofa (a member of the *Republika* staff), accompanied by four ICMI figures had also financed the activities of NU members to organise the riot in Situbondo.[49] Abdurrahman's statements and the findings of the 'white book' were received with widespread disbelief. The significance of

117

Abdurrahman's allegations, however, was not so much the accuracy of his version of events. It was more to do with the reality that, between 1994 and 1996, Suharto's attempts to undermine his leadership of NU had pushed him into a threatened position. With his political survival endangered, Abdurrahman and his supporters identified their main rival, ICMI, as the culprit behind anti-NU actions.[50]

An angered Adi Sasono immediately refuted the allegations. He insisted that Abdurrahman had wrongly accused him of being a founder of the *Humanika*.[51] He then launched an attack against his accuser by counter-claiming that

> Abdurrahman is the only source of accusation...It is comical that anyone would want to discredit Gus Dur through unrest. If his objective was to discredit me or ICMI in Suharto's eyes, we know that he did not succeed. Meanwhile, he wants to get close to Suharto [but] he cannot...He still remains [locked] outside the mainstream.[52]

Probolinggo: Reconciliation Between NU and Suharto?

Before making allegations against ICMI, the NU chairman had begun in late 1996 to make conciliatory gestures to Suharto's regime and tried to distance himself from Megawati. The convening of the NU-RMI's fifth national meeting in Probolinggo, East Java, on 13 November 1996 was the first public indication that reconciliation between Suharto and Abdurrahman was under way. The front covers of the national press were plastered with pictures of the Indonesian president and the NU chairman shaking hands as they attended the national meeting in Probolinggo, East Java. Shortly afterwards in Situbondo, Abdurrahman met and warmly shook hands with his sworn rival, Gen. Hartono, who had earlier tried to topple him at the 1994 congress. NU members expressed a mixture of jubilation and relief at the prospect of better NU–Suharto relations in the future. Some of Abdurrahman's rivals in NU and ICMI responded with scepticism, contending that the Probolinggo handshake was, in itself, a meaningless piece of publicity that did not mean Abdurrahman would gain greater access to power.[53]

At the national meeting, Abdurrahman declared that NU did not object to Suharto being re-nominated as president in 1998. His announcement was an about-face on his earlier position adopted since the NU's mass rally in 1992, when he had refused to endorse the president's re-nomination at the 1993 election. The fact is that the State Secretary, Murdiono, together with the president and secretary general of the RMI, Aziz Masyhuri and Ali Haidar, prevailed upon Abdurrahman to attend the RMI against the NU chairman's wishes.[54] Abdurrahman was not a willing participant in the reconciliation between Suharto and NU. Nonetheless, Abdurrahman offered his own explanation of what the rapprochement meant. He insisted that Suharto had finally realised that politics could no longer be dominated by ICMI, especially by a 'militant group' (the Muslim intelligentsia) within ICMI, which had 'falsely claimed' to represent the Muslim majority. By excluding the largest Muslim group (NU) and minority groups from political life, he continued, Suharto had become aware that he risked alienating a major support base for his own power. Suharto therefore made 'a correction' by recognising that 'the NU could also represent Islam'.[55] There was an element of truth to Abdurrahman's statement insofar as Suharto realised he needed NU's support if he was to receive unanimous endorsement at the MPR. The fact is that Abdurrahman had also identified the central role played by Suharto of alternately incorporating (ICMI) and excluding (mostly NU) Muslim interests.

As was the case with the RMI held in Jakarta in 1994, Habibie and the ICMI intelligentsia saw the 1996 national meeting of *pesantren* at Probolinggo as a chance to promote their own interests amidst speculation that Habibie was being groomed for the vice-presidency. Habibie introduced Adi Sasono, the Chief Editor of the *Republika*, Parni Hadi, and Slamet Effendi Yusuf to a packed crowd. He asked the *kiai* and *ulama* to open the door of *pesantren* 'as wide as possible for the ICMI so that it could help bring in appropriate technology to assist the surrounding community'.[56] Habibie donated 50 million *rupiah* to the RMI's activities. The ICMI members from the NU, Salaluddin Wahid (Abdurrahman's younger brother), Mohammad Thohir, and Slamet Effendi Yusuf regarded the Probolinggo meeting as an opportunity to bring about a reconciliation between Habibie and the NU chairman, and they formed a 'small team' to pursue their objective.[57]

Mohammad Tohir was behind an initiative to convene a meeting between the ICMI chairman and the NU chairman. Abdurrahman replied to the initiative, suggesting that he had no objections to the idea, providing that Habibie promised to announce at the meeting's close that ICMI would 'no longer dominate political power'. Later that month, at ICMI's national work meeting, Habibie reacted to Abdurrahman's comments by declaring that he could see no reason to meet with the NU chairman.[58]

It appeared, after all, that fences could not be mended between ICMI and Abdurrahman. His bad relations with Habibie, however, did not prevent him from trying to win Suharto's approval. The NU chairman escorted Suharto's daughter, Siti Rukmana (the leader of Golkar's campaign in East and Central Java), on a tour of *pesantren* and made public statements endorsing her credentials as a national leader. On 20 January 1997, he declared that it was all right if Siti Rukmana won NU over to Golkar.[59] It appears that Suharto had tried to establish his daughter's strong presence in the PDI and NU/PPP strongholds. The Suharto government, keen to gain substantial rural votes for its Golkar campaign, promised to funnel large funds into the NU's traditional support base—the *pesantren*. In this context, the Minister of Religion arranged a meeting between Abdurrahman's sister, the Chairperson of NU-Muslimat and Golkar member, Aisyah Baidlowi, and Siti Rukmana at which Suharto's daughter contributed funds for the construction of the Muslimat's new headquarters.[60]

In other signs of rapprochement, in mid-February it was reported that Abdurrahman would escort the Minister of Transmigration and Golkar campaigner, Siswono Yudohusodo, on a tour of *pesantren* in West Nusa Tenggara. And later that month, he visited his political rival within NU, Abu Hasan, who invited him on a trip to honour the graves of the NU's founders in Surabaya and Jombang, and eased (momentarily) the greatest split that NU had experienced in decades.[61] By early 1997, Abdurrahman appeared to have overcome Suharto-backed attempts during and after the NU's 1994 congress to unseat him—attempts that had also involved Hartono, Habibie and Siti Rukmana. By the same token, he had kept Habibie off-side, and had made attempts to manoeuvre himself and his NU constituency into a stronger bargaining position with Suharto's circle whilst seeking to diminish the influence of the Muslim interests in ICMI.

Before the Suharto–Abdurrahman rapprochement the NU chairman had mostly defended NU's independence from state encroachments involving Golkar and ICMI. However, as Abdurrahman reconciled with Suharto, he correspondingly changed his attitude to Golkar's and ICMI's forays into *pesantren*. He said that

> There is no resistance by the *pesantren* to government efforts to develop the *pesantren*. ICMI expects us to participate [in these efforts]—it need not cause a reaction from NU. Also, the local *pesantren* leaders should not be confined to following the policy of PBNU [NU's central board]. If they choose to join Golkar and work with the government, that is their business.[62]

The NU chairman had obviously overstated things when he claimed that there was no resistance by *pesantren* to government incursions. However, he was careful to explain that NU was not a monolithic organisation and 'there was no fixed pattern of relations between NU and the government'.[63]

Colleagues of Abdurrahman and NU's membership responded to his apparent reconciliation with Suharto and support for Siti Rukmana's Golkar campaign with a mixture of concern, bewilderment and betrayal. There were sympathisers and supporters who defended his actions. For example, at a meeting of P3M (an NU-linked NGO), one speaker maintained that Abdurrahman

> has only got close to the government and Suharto to protect NU [from state interventions]. Besides, NU must have access to the centre of power. You cannot achieve anything for your community if you do not have access to the power brokers.

However, the speaker also noted

> NU already has its long established pockets of political culture and will not be greatly affected by what Abdurrahman does or who he invites to NU, or who he takes around the *pesantren* circuit.[65]

Not surprisingly, NU's PPP supporters were outraged. The Secretary General of Muslimat and PPP supporter, Susy Witiajar, claimed that Abdurrahman had lost a lot of credibility at the grassroots. 'The Muslimat members [from PPP], in particular, are highly critical of his accommodation with Siti Rukmana and Golkar. It is very clear that Abdurrahman moved close to Golkar in order to protect his own leadership position.'[66] The leader of P3M and liberal scholar, Masdar Mas'udi said, 'the youthful supporters of Abdurrahman feel betrayed by his accommodation with the state. They were brought up on his ideas of democracy and democratic struggle, then they witness his actions that contradict the kind of democratic behaviour that they were taught by Abdurrahman to believe in.'[67]

In summary, in the context of intra-elite power struggles, the NU chairman manoeuvred himself and NU between a difficult position of opposition to Suharto, maintaining NU's independence from state arrangements, and securing NU from heavy state interventions. He was faced with the problem of how to respond to threats and pressures from the state to support Suharto and Golkar, whilst trying to maintain the integrity of NU's independence. However, Abdurrahman did not always act alone in negotiating a narrow gorge between the available choices. He also responded to pressures within NU. On the one hand, we considered how NU's RMI leaders and Murdiono pressured Abdurrahman into conciliation with Suharto. For a period, Abdurrahman even seemed to embrace accommodation with Suharto by taking Golkar leaders on a political tour of the *pesantren*.

On the other hand, there were counter-pressures in NU to remain independent from Suharto and to oppose Golkar's and ICMI's incursions into *pesantren*. NU was such a large and heterogeneous organisation with different, sometimes opposing, political orientations. Under these conditions, it would have been difficult for Abdurrahman to maintain a consistent standpoint and still represent all of the concerns of the organisation. When he caved in to pressure to reconcile with Suharto he faced the reprobation of pro-democracy elements in NU and defenders of NU's independence.

CONCLUSION

The conflicts in NU were partly a product of Suharto's corporatist strategies, which affected the different issues and pressures in NU and influenced the standpoints adopted by Abdurrahman. Suharto tried to bring as much as possible of Muslim interests behind Golkar so that he could achieve unanimous endorsement at the presidential election. He attempted this through strategies of corporatist capture, using organisations like ICMI, MUI, and Golkar to penetrate *pesantren* and garner support. Corporatist capture served to fragment interests, to reinforce pre-existing cleavages, and to create new ones, in NU. Suharto's initiatives to neutralise NU's influence in PPP after 1984 had a similar outcome of reinforcing and creating divisions between members in NU who backed PPP and those who supported Golkar. One purpose of the fragmentation strategy appeared to be to weaken oppositional tendencies so that interests could be marshalled more easily behind Golkar and Suharto.

Abdurrahman represented significant segments of NU, who were committed to guard NU's independence from state interference and thus opposed Golkar's and ICMI's incursions into rural *pesantren*. Suharto harnessed state actors, including Golkar and ICMI leaders, to his efforts to remove Abdurrahman from the chairmanship of NU. However, these efforts failed to displace the NU chairman, and constituted a significant defeat for state interventions in the leadership choices of major social and political organisations. State interventions also had failed to prevent Megawati from becoming general chairperson of PDI (see chapter eight for more on this topic).

The regime then changed tactics and began to court Abdurrahman for Suharto's renomination to the presidency. Suharto successfully distanced the NU chairman from Megawati and brought him behind Siti Rukmana's campaign for Golkar. Despite this success, attempts to bring about reconciliation between Abdurrahman and Habibie (ICMI) failed. Abdurrahman continued to see ICMI as a main rival organisation. His rivalry with ICMI was based, partly, on his determination to defend NU's independence from state interventions. The rift was also due to Suharto's corporatist strategy. At the very least, the founding of ICMI served to drive a deeper wedge between rival interests and communities, especially as Abdurrahman's opponents in NU moved over to membership of ICMI and joined the modernists in support of Suharto. The divide-and-rule tactics pursued by Suharto seem to have provided much of the framework of Abdurrahman's retaliations and reconciliation, as the NU chairman sought to bring NU into a better bargaining position with state power and to displace the political influence of Habibie's ICMI.

NOTES

1. McVey, 'Faith as the Outsider', p.216.
2. At an annual general meeting of Muslimat on 3 April 1997, the NU leader, Abdul Latif Rahman, gave the opening address and reminded his audience that Muslimat 'may not deviate or exit from the basic outlines of the NU based on its faith of 'ahlusunnah wal jema'ah (Sunnism)'. However, this was a multi-interpretable statement as he stressed that NU's outline meant

Muslimat may not join PPP—although its individual members were free to do so, but not in the name of Muslimat.

3. Interviews with Aisyah Hamid Baidlowi (head of Muslimat NU), 11 March 1997; Susy Machsusoh Tosari Witiajar (Secretary General of Muslimat), 4 April 1997; Ermalena (head of Fatayat), 1 June 1996. IPPNU had not joined any state corporatist organisations according to the head of the organisation. Interview with Dra Hj. Safira Machrusah (head of IPPNU), 5 April 1997. Ma'shum and Zawawi, *50 Tahun Muslimat*.

4. The social geography of many *pesantren* was cemented through participation of *kiai* and *santri* in Sufi brotherhoods or *tarekat*. These *pesantren* had association with at least one brotherhood, which, through genealogies (*silsilah*), linked *kiai* and students in a master-disciple relationship within an unbroken spiritual chain to the Prophet. One outcome of genealogies has been the great reverence accorded to deceased teachers, saints, and living *kiai*, especially those *kiai* thought to possess supernatural powers. Much of the authority of *kiai* also has been hereditary; McVey, 'Faith as the Outsider', pp.206–10.

5. See analysis in chapter four.

6. Interview with Dr Ali Haidar (Secretary General of NU's RMI), 14 August 1997; *Republika*, 11 November 1996; information drawn from work done by Greg Fealy in April 1997 and May 1999.

7. Habibie's trip to Madura was motivated by the desire to turn the island into an industrial zone in much the same manner that Batam Island was a planned industrial zone under his supervision; Editor, 10 February 1994; *The Jakarta Post*, 31 January–1 February 1994; *Merdeka*, 1 February 1994.

8. See chapter four regarding Naro's intervention; van Bruinessen, 'The 28th Congress of the Nahdlatul Ulama', p.145; Aqsha et al., *Islam in Indonesia: A Survey of Events*, pp.24,118.

9. Ruchiyat, however, refused on one occasion to support a unanimous pledge for Suharto's re-nomination. See the previous chapter for an account of Ruchiyat's role in supporting Suharto. For an account of Hasyim's public support of Suharto see Aqsha et al., *Islam in Indonesia: A Survey of Events*, pp. 20,118.

10. Aqsha et al., *Islam in Indonesia: A Survey of Events*, pp.24–5.

11. Two interviews with Abdurrahman Wahid (chairman of NU), 13 January 1994 and 15 July 1996; Closed Discussion entitled 'NU and Empowerment of "Civil Society"' at Gedung PKBI (Perkumpulan Keluarga Berencana Indonesia), 15 June 1996; *Ummat*, 25 November 1996.

12. The Forum's members included NGO advocates, nationalists, democracy activists and representatives of religious minorities. Although a number of state officials denounced the Forum, the regime mostly tolerated its existence, as it had been established during a period of regime-initiated political opening. Moreover, the Forum was established as a discussion

group and therefore did not pose a structural or grassroots threat to established power relations.

13. These include Mohammad A.S. Hikam (a former researcher at LIPI and member of Abdurrahman's current cabinet), Dr Ali Haidar, Sa'id 'Aqiel Siraj (member of NU's syuriah council), Gaffar Rahman (former Secretary General of NU), Masdar Mas'udi (head of P3M), and intellectuals belonging to NU's student organisation PMII, among others. Interviews with Masdar Mas'udi, 29 May 1996; Sa'id 'Aqiel Siraj, 30 October 1996; Gaffar Rahman (several discussions), July 1996; Mohammad Hikam, 10 October 1996; Hikam, 'Menelusuri Pemikiran Politik Gus Dur: Berangkat dari Paradigma Civil Society', *Jawa Pos*, 3 January 1996.

14. Finally, he upset Suharto when his tactless criticism of the president, quoted in Schwarz's book, 'A Nation in Waiting', found their way back to the palace. In 1994, in an open political rebuff, the president refused to recognise or meet with NU's new leadership under Abdurrahman's command. Fealy, 'The 1994 NU Congress', pp.274–5.

15. van Bruinessen, 'The 28th Congress of the Nahdlatul Ulama', p.146.

16. Abdurrahman, 'Gerakan Islam Dan Kaum Teknolog', *Suara Pembaruan*, 5 April 1993.

17. Instead, the NU chairman indicated on different occasions in early 1994 and early 1998 (before the convening of the MPR session), his preference of Habibie's rival, Try Sutrisno, for re-nomination to the vice-presidency. Editor reported in 1994 that Abdurrahman had announced that Try was acceptable to the *pesantren* and to the lower classes (the NU grassroots). The central NU leaders cultivated close relations with the incumbent vice-president, and Try was enthusiastically received on his regular circuits of the *pesantren*. In early February 1994, in an apparent display of support for Try's renomination as vice-president in 1998, Abdurrahman led a group of prominent NU leaders to Try's residence to request financial aid. *Editor*, February 1994; *Tempo*, 12 February 1994. Alternatively, he said that it was better for older generation generals like Edi Sudrajat, Benny Murdani and M. Jusuf to become Indonesia's future vice-president in preference to Habibie. *D&R*, 29 November 1996.

18. When Abdurrahman was first elected to the chairmanship of the NU in 1984, he had sought to forge an accommodation with Suharto's circle and was able, over the years, to have some NU leaders well placed in the government and political parties. Fahmi Saifuddin became an adviser to the Coordinating Minister of Public Health, Rozy Munir was given a post of the board that helps draft the broad outlines of state policy (GBHN), and others became active in Golkar, the PPP, and the PDI; interview with Abdurrahman, 13 January 1994.

19. Interview with Abdurrahman, 30 July 1997.

20. Several of the ICMI intelligentsia did aspire to establishing an Islamic society in Indonesia and some hoped to achieve this objective by first

making state officials more deeply committed to Islam in their public lives (see chapter seven). According to Abdurrahman, the goal for an Islamic society had worrying implications for the rights of religious minorities, as minority groups that refused to comply with Islamic laws would fall outside of the law. They would become discriminated second class citizens with reduced rights. Abdurrahman was disappointed by the actions of ICMI intellectuals, Amien Rais and Nurcholish Madjid who, in October 1990, joined the chorus of Muslim voices demanding that the editor of the Catholic-owned magazine, Monitor, be punished for blasphemy and the magazine's license be revoked. Interviews with Abdurrahman, 13 January 1994 and 5 June 1996; *Tempo*, 29 December 1991; *Kompas*, 19 November 1991; Abdurrahman, 'Demokrasi, Agama, dan Perilaku Politik Bangsa', *Jawa Pos*, 7 December 1993; Abdurrahman, 'Dialog Kepemimpinan Umat Islam (2): Mencari Legitimasi Sendiri-Sendiri', *Jawa Pos*, 6 April 1993.

21. Interview with Abdurrahman, 5 June 1996; Abdurrahman, 'Islam dan Birokrasi', *Jawa Pos*, 13 Febuary 1993; *Tempo*, 29 December 1991; Abdurrahman, 'Gerakan Islam Dan Kaum Teknolog', *Suara Pembaruan*, 5 April 1993.
22. *Merdeka*, 20 February 1993; *Jawa Pos*, 1 March 1993.
23. *Media Indonesia*, 28 July 1995.
24. In an interview in 1996, Ali Haidar complained that even the NU's *pesantren* association (RMI) relied on the government to fund its activities at national meetings, and that the NU was under immense pressure to build links of patronage with the power holders. *Republika*, 11 November 1996.
25. *The Jakarta Post*, 31 January 1994.
26. Abdurrahman had actually developed and made popular the idea that ICMI was a neo-Masyumi and, like a 'Trojan Horse', it sought to infiltrate the state and Islamise politics from within. *Republika*, 1 November 1996.
27. Interview with Kiai Yusuf Muhammad (*pesantren* leader), 3 February 1994 at the NU's RMI national meeting beginning on 31 January in Jakarta.
28. *Media Indonesia*, 5 February 1994.
29. *The Jakarta Post*, 1 February 1994.
30. Interview with Hasyim Muzadi (head of East Java Provincial office of NU), 5 August 1997.
31. Interviews with GP Ansor, 10 August 1997; KH Nurcholis Musytari (deputy rais syuriah NU, Bangil Branch), 10 August 1997; Hj. Ahmad Jaman (Pembina Ansor Kotamadya Pasuruan), 10 August 1997; KH Choiron Syakur (Leader of Pesantren Wahit Hasyim in Pasuruan), 10 August 1997; Fathor Rasjid (NU leader, Situbondo branch), 4 August 1997; an observer of conflict in Situbondo during the 1997 general election (he wished to remain anonymous), 4 August 1997. A civil servant (Golkar member from NU, who wished to remain anonymous) told of the conflict between Golkar and PPP in the pre-election climate (late-1996), 6 August 1997.

32. Interview with leaders of GP Ansor (H. Nur Cholish: Rais syuriah NU, Bangil branch; Drs. Subari, Ketua PP Ansor Bangil and others), 10 August 1997.

33. Interview with Musytari, 10 August 1997. Chapter four showed that the MI faction dominated PPP after 1984.

34. At the Annual Meeting of Muslimat on 3 April 1997, there were palpable tensions between PPP leaders and Abdul Latif Rahman (an NU leader and Golkar campaigner) as they vigorously debated various issues. In an open rebuff, several elder PPP leaders walked out of the session in protest over NU's continued commitment to remaining outside of PPP. During my travels in East Java, after the 1997 general election campaign, the hostility between PPP/PDI supporters within NU, on the one hand, and Golkar supporters within NU, on the other, was obvious. NU had become deeply divided by this campaign. I conducted a series of interviews and meetings (referred to elsewhere in the book) during my travels in East Java, 4 August 1997 to 13 August 1997.

35. van Bruinessen, *NU: Tradisi*, pp.115–40.

36. Idham Chalid's Cipete faction competed for NU's top posts. Idham was put forward as a counter-candidate to Siddiq, Ali became the deputy president, and Chalid Mawardi, after contesting the chairmanship, was made one of the five deputy chairmen of NU. Abdurrahman shrugged off the challenge by managing to have his favoured candidates maintain control of NU. van Bruinessen, 'The 28th Congress of the Nahdlatul Ulama', pp.140–54.

37. Information based on interview of Abdurrahman Wahid by Greg Fealy, early December 1991; *Tempo*, 16 November 1991.

38. It was alleged that Abdurrahman and the Secretary General had signed a letter requesting 50 million *rupiah* of funding from the managing board of the state-run national lottery, SDSB. SDSB was already embroiled in a nationwide controversy, as Muslim student demonstrators were demanding that the national lottery be discontinued for reasons that it constituted gambling and Islam prohibited gambling. Yafie assumed the moral high-ground on the issue by announcing his own resignation from NU hinting that he would only return to the NU after those responsible for requesting SDSB funding resign their offices. Amidst calls from several NU branches for the persons responsible to be removed from their posts, NU's Secretary General took the rap for Abdurrahman and tendered his resignation. *Tempo*, 16 November 1991.

39. Ali was among the NU *kiai* who had his allegiances split between his home constituency and state interests represented by Suharto's regime, as he became associated with pro-Suharto standpoints and was duly rewarded for it. Through his membership of ICMI and MUI, he provided religious legitimacy to Suharto's regime on public ceremonial occasions, as did the NU President Ilyas Ruchiyat, especially at prayer meetings held at Istiqlal

Mosque. Interview with Ali Yafie, 5 February 1994; *Panji Masyarakat*, 1–10 January 1994, p.12; *Republika Online*, 10 December 1995.

40. Meanwhile, the Minister of Defence Edi Sudrajat (who Suharto replaced as Commander-in-Chief of ABRI in 1993 with Feisal Tanjung), Murdiono, and other Habibie rivals within the military, backed Abdurrahman's renomination to the NU chairmanship. Fealy, 'The 1994 NU Congress', pp.261–4; Gaffar, 'Indonesia 1995', p.57.

41. During the congress, Abdurrahman's camp complained of biased reporting in the media, particularly by the ICMI-funded newspaper, the *Republika*, which they claimed had misquoted statements about the chairman's chances of re-election and then refused to publish a correction whilst the congress was still in train. Fealy, 'The 1994 Congress', pp.264–73.

42. Fealy, 'The 1994 Congress', pp.274–6.

43. From 1992 onwards, Suharto had become increasingly concerned about the growing popularity of PDI and the potential electoral threat it posed. Since then, he had intensified his efforts to expand Golkar's support base and create a Muslim counter to the nationalist-oriented PDI.

44. Meanwhile, the ICMI intelligentsia joined the chorus of voices that praised the Suharto government's handling of events and condemned the 'forces of anarchy' as it cracked down on pro-Megawati forces.

45. Victims of the church burning—pastors, priests and their families—and eyewitnesses pointed to the organised manner in which militant and tatooed thugs systematically tore down churches. Some of the mobs were brought in by trucks from outlying regions. Many suspected that the military had a hand in organising the mobs for attacks on churches. Both NU and Christian leaders in Surabaya accused Lt Gen. Hartono of orchestrating the violence. According to the anecdotal accounts, then, these were not simply spontaneous outbursts of outraged Muslim mobs seeking revenge on a rival religious community. Interviews with Fathor Rasjid (NU member, Situbondo Branch), 4 August 1997; Hasyim Muzadi, 5 August 1997; K.H. Cholil As'ad (a *pesantren* leader in Situbondo), 4 August 1997; Hanafi Maslim (civil servant and NU member), 6 August 1997; Musytari, 10 August 1997; Pendeta Ismai Sinlay (Bethel Church of Indonesia, Sidutopo, Surabaya), 13 August 1997; Pendeta Hendrik Tulangow (Alfa Omega Pentecostal Church), 13 August 1997; Prof Dr J.E. Sahetapy (Spokesperson for the Indonesian Council of Churches, PGI), 14 August 1997; Thomas Santoso (Sociologist and Christian spokesperson, Surabaya), 11 August 1997; Dr Paul Tahelele (heart surgeon, personal physician to Abdurrahman Wahid, and Christian spokesperson), 22 July 1997.

46. A number of NU leaders and sympathisers in Situbondo (East Java) told of how the Regent and ABRI, on various occasions, used heavy-handed tactics against PPP supporters before the spate of church burning and then tried to blame PPP supporters for the destruction. Interviews with Cholil As'ad,

4 August 1997; Fathor Rasjid, 4 August 1997; a lawyer representing clients who were accused by ABRI of instigating the church burnings in Situbondo (he wishes to remain anonymous), 4 August 1997; several self-confessed rioters (who wished to remain anonymous), 4 August 1997.

47. The following interviews were held in Surabaya, the industrial capital of East Java, unless otherwise stated. Abdurrahman, 24 October 1996 (in Jakarta) and 1 August 1997; Dr J.E. Sahetapy, 14 August 1997; Romo Beny (a prominent Catholic leader from Situbondo), 3 August 1997; Dr Paul Tahalele, 27 July and 3 August 1997; Santoso, 11 August 1997; *Forum Keadilan*, 10 February 1997; *Adil*, 19–25 February 1997; *Forum Keadilan*, 10 February 1997.

48. Bursyah and Eggi were underlings of Adi, and Abdurrahman accused Adi of being a founding member of the Humanika.

49. The white book alleged that 'AR', 'AS' and 'LH' (people widely interpreted the initials as standing for Amien Rais, Adi Sasono and Lukman Harun), and other ICMI leaders were involved in a conspiracy to undermine NU.

50. *Paron*, 8 February 1997; *Ummat*, 17 February 1997; *Sinar*, 22 February 1997; *Forum Keadilan*, 10 February 1997.

51. He was instead, he insisted, a founding member of the Humaika (the Community Association for Humanity), which was responsible for the rehabilitation of imprisoned communists, had ceased its activities in the late-1980s, and had no connection with the Humanika. Abdurrahman, it appears, had confused Humanika with Humaika, which had the effect of discrediting his own allegations. *Ummat*, 17 February 1997.

52. *Forum Keadilan*, 10 February 1997.

53. *Swadesi*, 18–24 February 1997; Hikam, 'Jabat Tangan dari Probolinggo', *Ummat*, 25 November 1996–23 December 1996; *Gatra*, 23 November 1996.

54. Abdurrahman first refused to attend the RMI meeting and insisted he was travelling to Germany, but Moerdiono warned him not to go. Information drawn from confidential interviews with RMI leaders done by Greg Fealy, April 1997.

55. *D&R* 29 November 1996.

56. *Kompas*, 4 November 1996; *Ummat*, 25 November 1996; *Republika*, 3 November 1996; *Suara Pembaruan*, 5 November 1996.

57. *Ummat*, 25 November 1996.

58. *Ummat*, 23 December 1996.

59. *Forum Keadilan*, 10 Febuary 1997.

60. Aisyah pointed out that 'at election times, Golkar had immense funding to dispense. Muslimat saw the general elections as an opportunity to get funding.' Interview with Aisyah Hamid Baidlowi, 11 March 1997. The Secretary General of Muslimat, Susy Witiajar, held a quite different attitude to the latest events. She said, 'the Muslimat members were angry over Siti

Rukmana's sponsorship of the organisation. The price of receiving funding for the building was greater than the actual benefit. I wrote to the Muslimat branches that Siti's funding did not tie NU's constituency to choosing Golkar at the election'. Interview with Susy Witiajar, 4 April 1997; *Sinar*, 22 February 1997; *Forum Keadilan*, 10 March 1997; *Ummat*, 17 February 1997.

61. *Poskota*, 22–24 February 1997; *Harian Terbit*, 12 February 1997.
62. Interview with Abdurrahman, 24 October 1996.
63. Interview with Abdurrahman, 24 October 1996.
64. Long-term loyal supporters of Abdurrahman expressed their ambivalence over his accommodation with Suharto. They said, to paraphrase, we do not really understand what you are doing, but we trust that there is some logic to it and that it will be in the best interests of NU. Informal discussion called 'Menemukan Jangkar Mutakhir Gus-Dur', at the office of P3M, 11 April 1997.
65. Discussion at P3M, 11 April 1997. The speaker's name was Ismed Natsir. Ismed was neither a formal P3M nor NU member, but he expressed a viewpoint held by others at the discussion.
66. Interview with Susy Witiajar, 4 April 1997.
67. Discussion at P3M, 11 April 1997. It is important to note that Masdar had been one of Abdurrahman's close supporters and disciples.

Chapter 7

Intra-Elite Rivalry
Incorporated Islam in Conflict with the Military

INTRODUCTION

Newly incorporated interests in ICMI and Golkar came into conflict with rival segments of the military and the government bureaucracy that had been antagonised by the rise of new groups and the state–Islamic accommodation. An outcome of this conflict was a re-politicisation of state–Islamic relations, after Suharto had made concerted efforts to de-politicise state–group relations for the past two-decades.

In exploring this proposition, there are important contexts and considerations to take into account. First, the state–Islamic accommodation was the outcome of an intra-elite conflict during a deepening succession crisis, as competing interests (both state and non-state) positioned themselves to take best advantage of an anticipated post-Suharto period. In context of the rivalry, Suharto drew on the support of civilian leaders and Muslim middle-class interests to offset his reliance on the military in order to remain firmly in control of the succession process—assuming he intended one to take place. ICMI/anti-ICMI conflict, it is argued, therefore was part of larger intra-elite power struggles.

Second, the rapprochement coincided with a period of limited political opening, brought about by the intra-elite conflict. The political opening raised people's expectations for further political freedoms and political participation and stimulated independent organisational activity within society (as discussed in chapters eight and nine). Under these circumstances, the state–Islamic rapprochement raised expectations among members of the newly incorporated Muslim intelligentsia that they would have greater room for manoeuvre to pursue their political agendas and influence government policy. In other words, they sought increased political participation, through their incorporation, in competition with other group interests.

Finally, the circumstances surrounding the incorporation of Muslim interests raise a number of theoretical questions concerning the nature of Suharto's corporatist strategies. For at least two decades political exclusion had been a significant feature of corporatist structuring. However, chapter two argued that regimes seeking renewal alternate between different policy instruments, with inclusionary mechanisms sometimes being employed when exclusionary ones lose efficacy and ruling elites decide to incorporate new social groups in support of the regime. Did Suharto's sponsorship of ICMI, then, signify a shift in corporatist strategy from an exclusionary approach to a selective inclusionary one, as he drew on Muslims as a new support base? After all, Suharto was trying to co-opt (and counter) growing aspirations of middle-class Muslims at a time of mounting societal demands for participation. A shift to inclusionary strategies would have been one way for the regime to maintain corporatist containment of interests whilst being more responsive to societal demands (of at least one important constituency). Chapter three, in fact, considered how Suharto reorganised Golkar to broaden its base of support by appealing to young voters, who were increasingly disaffected with the political system. ICMI appears to have been part of this corporatist reorganisation aimed at regime renewal through broadening support.

Before we turn to the chapter analyses, another theoretical issue requiring attention is the proposition that adoption of inclusionary strategies carries inherent risks and problems for the regime. Stepan, Bianchi, and Ding have identified these risks (see chapter two). One risk is that once corporatism becomes too inclusionary, competing interests tend to use their acquired positions in the state structure to increase their demands on the state. The interests can extend their influence and veto powers over state policy, as well as hijack the policy goals of their intended incorporation and supplant them with their own 'private' objectives. In this way, the growing intrusion and penetration of 'external' interests threaten the autonomy of the state and its leaders. Incorporated, but by no means co-opted, actors can behave like a 'counter-elite', in Ding's terminology, and can attack the policy goals, power relations, and institutional apparatus of the state from within.[1]

We have seen (chapter five) that some members of ICMI's intelligentsia behaved like a 'counter-elite' and levelled criticism at Suharto and the institutions of authoritarianism. It appears that ICMI might have represented a partial shift to inclusionary corporatist strategy but Suharto was determined to neutralise the political aspirations of the Muslim intelligentsia within the association. Much of the intent of the strategy was therefore exclusionary, as it still sought to suppress independent political activity and keep Muslim aspirants outside of power sharing arrangements.

Another means by which regimes can deal with over-incorporation is to maintain a shifting power 'asymmetry' of competing interests by periodically readjusting which groups the regimes choose to incorporate and exclude. By offering an adjustable range of incentives and disincentives to different groups, regimes can play these groups off against one another in divide-and-rule fashion. The significance of corporatist interests in a political system, therefore, is how they interact, or are made to interact, with other types of represented (or underrepresented) interest groups.

Taking into account the above-mentioned points, the chapter examines the interactions between corporatised and other state interests. The analysis considers the idea that, in order to preserve his power, Suharto periodically readjusted the balance between corporatised civilian interests in Golkar and ICMI and rival interests in the state. In short, corporatist organisations served Suharto's strategy of divide-and-rule, especially as both ICMI and Golkar were drawn into intra-elite rivalries.

ARMED FORCES–ICMI RIVALRY

The military was becoming the clear loser in the contest over the future succession of an ageing president, as Suharto surrounded himself with loyalists and family members in what was becoming an increasingly personalist regime. Suharto progressively promoted to the country's political institutions civilian alternatives to military men, as he and the military leadership competed over the choice of candidate for the vice-presidency in 1988, 1993, and 1998. The chapter will look at how political interests of the president and ABRI diverged, as Suharto's support base contracted with the rise of a civilian oligarchy (i.e., privileged families). Suharto loyalists and family members were promoted up the military hierarchy and were strictly subordinated to Suharto's rule, thereby greatly reducing ABRI's autonomy.

Before proceeding further, the analysis distinguishes between those elements in ABRI, who had been hurt by the rise of civilian/Muslim interests and were opposed to ICMI, and Suharto loyalists and beneficiaries within ABRI, who did not openly object to ICMI. Among the military officers most antagonistic towards ICMI were those associated with Gen. Benny Murdani (discussed below). Under Benny's command the military had established a considerable degree of institutional autonomy from the president and now this autonomy was being compromised by the reconfiguration of civilian-Muslim interests behind Suharto. Benny, and two successive commanders of ABRI, Gen. Try Sutrisno and Gen. Edi Sudrajat, belonged to the so-called 'nationalist' officers, who were opposed to the establishment of formal linkages between political Islam and the state. ABRI elements that did not openly oppose ICMI included the so-called 'green' or 'Muslim' officers, Suharto loyalists, and family members, who were the new beneficiaries of power arrangements but had become very subordinate to Suharto's authority.

The first group of disgruntled military officers particularly disliked civilian leaders like the Minister of Technology B.J. Habibie and Golkar chairmen, Sudharmono and Harmoko, because of the role they played in assisting Suharto to reduce his reliance on support from the armed forces. First, under Sudharmono's leadership, the State Secretariat and Golkar became Suharto's main instrument of civilian elite recruitment into the country's political institutions and government bureaucracy. Then ICMI, under Habibie's chairmanship, assumed the role as one of Suharto's chief instruments of civilian recruitment to offset ABRI. It appears that both ICMI and Golkar served as instruments for Suharto's wider divide-and-rule strategies, as he readjusted a shifting balance of forces in his favour. Consequently, significant elements of the military leadership, who had initially opposed Sudharmono's leadership of Golkar were hostile to cosy state–Islamic relations and Habibie–ICMI interests.

The chapter also considers that aggravating these tensions was the noticeable congruence between the ICMI discourse on de-militarisation of society and Suharto's measures to create an acquiescent military leadership subordinate to his authority. Reinforcing this hostility towards ICMI was the military's historical prejudice against Islamic political agendas, and the tendency of leading members of the ICMI intelligentsia to consider the goal of demilitarisation as enhancing the objective of Islamising society. Perceptions that Habibie was drawing on Muslim support in ICMI in order to advance his political career and interests at the expense of ABRI greatly contributed to animosities. The analysis now turns to a fuller treatment of the points just raised.

Purging Benny's Men

Beginning as one of Suharto's inner-circle, Gen. Benny Murdani emerged as a serious threat to Suharto's hold on power. Benny reached the zenith of his power in the years after 1983, when concurrently holding positions of commander-in-chief of the armed forces, chief of the Command for the Restoration of Security and Order (Kopkamtib), with its extensive extra-judicial powers of arrest and detainment, and head of the Strategic Intelligence Agency (BAIS). However, signs of conflict between Benny and the president had appeared by 1988, especially after Suharto appointed Sudharmono as vice-president against the military leadership's wishes.[2]

A number of active-duty leaders (associates of Benny) began to withdraw their support from Suharto, following which Suharto courted the Muslim constituency to offset their support. The military under Benny's command opposed Sudharmono's nomination to the vice-presidency, and Kopkamtib embarked on a campaign to discredit Sudharmono's chairmanship of Golkar, by claiming that the ruling party had been infiltrated by communists. Suharto retaliated and, in September 1988, liquidated Kopkamtib and replaced it with the institutionally less independent and more 'civilianised' Bakorstanas. With Sudharmono becoming vice-president, Suharto kicked Benny up-stairs to what was then the less powerful position of Minister of Defence and Security. However, Benny turned the Ministry into a major power base for himself, retained control over BAIS, and remained an intolerable threat to Suharto. Suharto moved to emasculate further the intelligence network loyal to Benny. In January 1994, BAIS was renamed the ABRI Intelligence Agency (BIA) and its 'previous operational independence' under Benny 'was curtailed'.[3]

Between 1988 and 1993, Suharto took measures to purge his rivals within the military from the government's political institutions, including Golkar and cabinet posts (see discussion below), and thereby weaken ABRI's *dwi-fungsi* role. Political posts were a major source of military career advancement and patronage and any reduction of these threatened ABRI's access to benefits and power. In the face of rising public criticism over ABRI's *dwi-fungsi*, Suharto placed the military's extensive role in Indonesia's political institutions squarely on the public agenda. At an ABRI leadership meeting in 1990, in the spirit of 'political openness', Suharto had announced that ABRI should take a backseat role in the nation's affairs and 'lead people from behind' (*tut wuri handayani*).[4] Although *tut wuri handayani* had long been part of ABRI's doctrine, Suharto's statement had definite political overtones, as it coincided with the president's initiatives to give civilians a greater role in the nation's political institutions.[5] His pronouncement sparked a broadening public debate on the issue, as NGO activists, intellectuals, politicians, and elite dissidents intensified their criticisms of ABRI's official doctrine. It appears that Suharto was attempting to turn 'openness' to his advantage by using it as a weapon against ABRI, and the public controversy stimulated by his statement fitted in well with such a scenario.[6] Suharto's objective was to subordinate ABRI fully to presidential authority, so that he could establish his own firm control over the vice-presidential race and the terms of future succession.

ICMI's Agendas

The purge of Benny's network, the Suharto–military rift, and growing concern about the succession issue provided the backdrop to ICMI's rise to prominence in the early-to-mid-1990s. These factors, and the prevailing climate of political openness, encouraged members of ICMI's intelligentsia to pursue, or at least aspire to, agendas for the demilitarisation, democratisation, and Islamisation of society which, in turn, provided likely points of tension between the organisation and ABRI. Some members of the intelligentsia viewed ICMI as a vehicle for gaining access to the power holders and decisional structures so that they might influence the direction of national politics in support of their agendas. For example, two ICMI intellectuals, Aswab Mahasin (a liberal scholar and NGO leader) and Sucipto Wirosarjono (a former bureaucrat at the Bureau of Statistics), thought that ICMI gave Muslims 'leverage within the government' by building networks of contacts with government officials. Sucipto averred 'using their networks [they can] influence the way the system behaves…ICMI's role can be observed from how they influence the changing balance of power, but in accordance with what is best for the interests of the Muslim community'.[7]

Thus, it appears that members of ICMI's intelligentsia might have acted like a 'counter-elite', in Ding's sense of the term, in that they sought to displace (or at least modify) the official goals of ICMI with their own, alternative goals. ICMI's 'unofficial' agendas not only placed the intelligentsia in tension with ABRI but potentially brought them into conflict with Suharto. For example, two outspoken critics of Suharto, Amien Rais and Sri Bintang Pamungkas—before their removal from ICMI—tried to bring the succession issue into ICMI's discourse and into national discourse. Both figures anticipated that Suharto would be out of office in 1998.[8] However, in line with the regime's stance that

ICMI should not make political statements of any kind, Habibie ensured that the succession issue remained outside of ICMI's formal pronouncements.[9] Despite such caution, ICMI members were concerned to gain influence over the terms of future succession, as political competition between elite groups was much more in the open than had hitherto been the case. Consequently, Adi Sasono, Amien Rais, and Dawam Rahardjo were among the ICMI interests backing Habibie in opposition to the military's choice of Try Sutrisno for the vice-presidency in anticipation of a future presidential race. Support for Habibie's vice-presidential ambitions at a time of intensifying intra-elite competition provided an inevitable point of conflict between ABRI leaders and ICMI. However, ICMI did not have any public political platform that reflected the aspirations of the intelligentsia, and their informal goals consequently lacked clear articulation or action programs.

The following analysis first considers ICMI's 'unofficial' agendas and then looks at points of ABRI–ICMI tension, including ABRI's objections to the agendas.

Demilitarisation

Suharto's retaliation against Gen. Benny Murdani's network corresponded with an anti-Benny predisposition among ICMI's intelligentsia and their desire for demilitarisation of society. As defenders of the interests of a rising, educated middle class, the ICMI intelligentsia were committed to the removal of military influence in the country's political institutions. Members of this group also expressed their discomfort with the kinds of security-intelligence rationales used by ABRI in its suppression of dissent. In particular, they regarded the Catholic general as being responsible for much of the New Order state's anti-Islamic political and military repression, and they blamed him for ordering the killing of hundreds of Muslim demonstrators at Tanjung Priok in 1984. Since 1974, Benny had maintained close contact with the Centre for Strategic and International Studies (CSIS), a largely Chinese-Catholic run think-tank long associated with anti-Islamic measures when the Centre was part of Ali Murtopo's empire. Their attacks against Benny Murdani for what they regarded was his anti-Islamic security measures, in particular, suited Suharto's need to purge the armed forces of Benny's security network and loyalists.[10]

This congruence of interests, perhaps, was demonstrated by the appointment, in 1993, of the former Deputy Chief-of-Staff of the Army, Sayidiman Suryohadiprojo, as senior ICMI adviser to Habibie on the military defence industry. In an interview with the national magazine, *Editor*, in his capacity as Habibie's advisor, Sayidiman insisted that the intelligence role of the armed forces must be curtailed. Sayidiman mentioned the oversized role of intelligence, which he attributed to Ali Murtopo's Special Operations and military intelligence officers (Murdani's men) who 'still wished to maintain' their dominant role.

Prominent members of ICMI's intelligentsia promoted this line. For example, Sucipto Wirosarjono reiterated Sayidiman's statement that 'the role of military intelligence had to be reduced to its correct proportions'.[12] The ICMI leader, Adi Sasono also insisted that the military's role had to be reduced. He grasped the portent of *tut wuri handayani*. He pointed out that 'ABRI's' new, 'official' policy would result in a significantly smaller and more professional military, with civilian politicians assuming a greater share of Indonesia's leadership burden.[13]

> We should condemn militarisation. The military is everywhere [represented in the political institutions, government, and its territorial structure]. It is too much! We do not need a large and extensive intelligence network [with which to] maintain stability. We have to widen the basis of political recruitment beyond the military. Civilian professionals should replace [the military in politics].

It seems, then, that criticism by ICMI of the military (intelligence) network under Benny's command was permitted by Suharto as part of his strategy to restrain military influence.

Despite the apparent concurrence of interests, however, Suharto still depended on the military and its doctrine to underpin his own power. At the end of the day, he sought to attenuate, rather than eliminate, military influence. Public exposure of the issue also resulted in a backlash by the armed forces' leadership in defence of their *dwi-fungsi* doctrine. Apparently, the ICMI leadership was worried that the organisation might face reprisals from an angered military should they push too openly against the latter's political interests.[15] Thus, the sensitivity of the *dwi-fungsi* issue prevented the Muslim intelligentsia from bringing it, or discourses on demilitarisation, into official ICMI discussions. For example, at a meeting with ICMI's council of advisors, according to one of its members, Habibie had broached the subject of the need for a demilitarisation of Indonesian politics. The council of advisors (some of them military veterans) cautioned their chairman against raising the subject of demilitarisation in ICMI, as, they said, it was 'a very sensitive word'.[16] Thus, ICMI's council of advisors exercised their supervisory role over the organisation by helping ensure that ICMI's critical voice stayed within acceptable limits, as they even moderated Habibie's stance on the issue.

Despite ICMI's caution, as discussed below, the congruence of Suharto–Habibie–ICMI interests nonetheless caused tensions that led to rivalry with elements of the armed forces, particularly with those who had been sidelined by the new power configurations.

Democratisation

Members of ICMI's intelligentsia were hopeful that the purging of Benny's men during the climate of political openness had provided them with an opportunity to influence the political system and gain greater representation of Muslims in government. They appealed for the re-allocation of political representation (seats in the MPR, cabinet posts, and senior government appointments) to Muslims and away from what many Muslim leaders regarded as the coalition of Christian and secular army modernisers in proportion to their respective per centages in Indonesia's population. Muslims were estimated as comprising 87 per cent of the population. The call for proportional access was a retaliation against a perceived and actual domination of the political power structures by a coalition of individuals, whom Muslim leaders regarded as hostile to Islam because of the state's security approach towards Islamic movements and the regime's efforts to de-politicise Islam.[17]

A broad spectrum of Muslims, not only the ICMI intelligentsia, shared the desire for Muslims to gain proportional access to political representation. Many maintained that during the first two decades of New Order rule (1970s–1980s), when Ali Murtopo and then Benny Murdani were at the peak of their power, Christian and secular army interests had gained preponderant control of the political system. Murtopo had disproportionately favoured the Christian (Catholic) minority, bringing them into the power structure to reinforce a coalition of army 'abangan' and civilian modernisers who viewed political Islam with great suspicion.[18] The ICMI intelligentsia argued that this Christian–secular–army coalition deliberately locked Muslim politicians out of the power structure. The founding of ICMI had given them an unparalleled opportunity to redress the imbalances, especially after the emasculation by Suharto of Benny's intelligence apparatus. A common sentiment expressed was that the removal of Benny's network marked the end of the military's security approach and 'spying on Islam'.[19]

As part of the effort to 'redress imbalances', members of ICMI's intelligentsia established their own think-tank, the Centre for Information and Development Studies (CIDES), to rival the intellectual influence wielded by CSIS.[20] The ICMI newspaper, *Republika*, also gave organisational form and 'Muslim' voice to this rivalry, as it was established as a competitor to the *Kompas* newspaper published by the Catholic-owned Gramedia group. ICMI members argued that for too long, because of their superior financial resources, Chinese-Catholic interests had preponderant control of the national printed media. *Republika* was the first newspaper that could effectively represent the Muslim constituencies on a national scale. Later, Muslim-oriented newsweeklies, *Ummat* and *Gatra*, were also established. *Republika*, on various occasions, ran articles and editorials that revealed an anti-Benny attitude and sometimes reported political events in a manner that reflected hostility towards Christian leaders.[21] Thus, the argument can be made that, within the framework of state–Islamic accommodation, corporatisation of Muslim interests had provided Muslim leaders with an organisational means of countering their main rival community. They sometimes perceived this rival community, which included influential elements in ABRI, in terms of religious difference.

However, several ICMI members claimed that they stood for democracy and sought more than just proportional representation for Muslims. Adi Sasono was among a number of Muslim reformers who regarded ICMI, CIDES, and *Republika* as contributing to capacity building aimed at strengthening 'civilian institutions to offset military power'.[22] Sasono insisted that CIDES, in particular, provided a forum for opening dialogue on reform with the government. 'Reform from within the state was instrumental to change [and this was] achievable through working with the government [not against it].' Sasono considered that internal reforms were necessary in order to bring about 'peaceful transformation' to democracy and prevent a process of 'social radicalisation' that could lead to 'revolution'.[23] Dewi Fortuna Anwar (a close advisor to Habibie and CIDES member) agreed with Sasono's assessment that CIDES had an important role to play in opening dialogue on the democratic reform process.[24] CIDES gave regular seminars, which were attended by government officials, retired military officers, government critics and spokespersons of the different political and religious communities. One of the aims of the seminars was to raise sensitive issues such as presidential succession, human rights, and ABRI's political role and to prepare public officials to think about these issues.[25]

For Suharto CIDES must have seemed like a mild and safe forum for discussion on democracy and human rights compared to other groups agitating against the regime. For example, during the 1990s, a proliferating number of NGOs, student groups, publications, and informal seminars became centrally concerned with issues of democracy and human rights and were highly critical of Suharto's rule. Despite the relative moderation of Muslim intellectuals, in May 1992 (before the founding of CIDES), the police closed down an ICMI seminar discussion on human rights that was attended by outspoken human rights advocates and Suharto critics. In December, CIDES successfully re-held a one-day seminar on human rights, which was critical of the regime's track record in this area. Habibie was initially alarmed when CIDES published in its journal, *Afkar* (February 1993 issue), the papers given by seminar panelists. He apparently exclaimed, 'Oh my God, how am I going to show this to Suharto!'[27]

Islamisation

Another agenda of ICMI's intelligentsia was for the Islamisation of Indonesia's way of life. Islamisation meant different things for different people. In general, there were two orientations—namely, those who aspired to establishing an Islamic society and those who advocated, at least partial, Islamisation of the state's laws.

The first orientation was the most intangible among the different agendas aspired to by ICMI members. ICMI did not have theorists who were defining or systematically expounding upon what was actually an Islamic society. Rather, some of them at least had an image of an Islamic society that appealed to ideals of economic equity, social justice, democracy, clean government and an enlarged role for Muslims in, if not preponderant control of, the political institutions of the nation (as considered above). On the whole, these individuals presented themselves as purveyors of a 'moderate'[28] brand of Islam and claimed to aspire to establishing an Islamic society in which the values of Islam's religious morality would become a dominant social good within an expanding middle-class, cosmopolitan culture. They hoped that the projection of ICMI as a moderate force would overcome objections against organised Islam and improve the chances of Muslims becoming a trusted partner in government.[29] Aspirations for an Islamic society, therefore, dovetailed with democratisation agendas. However, Ramage argues that 'it seems clear that democratisation is not the primary goal of many in ICMI. The main objective, in varying degrees, is to encourage the development of an Islamic society.'[30] Although there were advocates of an Islamic society who were not committed to democratic values, a number of ICMI's intelligentsia saw nothing inconsistent with trying to achieve democracy and to establish Islamic morality.[31]

The more liberal-minded intellectuals and reformers in ICMI argued that Islam should be a source of political morality. Adi Sasono expressed this view, stating that 'Islamic tradition has respect for pluralism, for rights. If we link democracy with Islam's teachings then society will understand democracy. Democracy must be acculturated in Indonesia—Islam is the key to that process.'[32] Dawam Rahardjo maintained that 'Islamic morality should be reflected in the attitude [and behaviour] of the state [actors]. The state should function for the betterment of all people, not to control and dominate society.'[33] Dewi Fortuna Anwar reinforced this standpoint by pointing to the lack of morality in the New Order regime.

> Islam would be an important element to influence morality within the power [structure]. The government should be imbued with some of Islam's morality, in the way it operates and rules. I am in favour of Islamisation in our way of life, in the sense that we will have…less of this corruption, less of these abuses of power, less of these human rights abuses—because Islam as a religion does not allow you to do [these things].[34]

The second orientation included Muslim radicals and moral conservatives who advocated the implementation of Islamic *shari'ah* (law) in areas of the family and criminal law. Among the Muslim conservatives were functionaries and law scholars at MUI, the Department of Religion, and the Faculty of Shar'iah at the IAINs, as well as leaders of the voluntary associations, Muhammadiyah and NU, who embraced the desire to have an increased role for Islamic *shar'iah* in the life of the state and nation. These conservative scholars and bureaucrats desired to see a greater proportion of Islamic laws incorporated in national laws. They claimed that they did not seek a dominance of Islamic law and therefore rejected goals for the establishment of an Islamic state.

Muslim radicals, many of them associated with the organisation, Dewan Dakwah, were more firmly committed to the implementation of state Islamic laws, although a range of alternative views also existed within this organisation. The '*shar'iah*-minded' scholars did not necessarily consider ICMI as the principal vehicle through which they could achieve their objectives. Nonetheless, they belonged to pro-establishment forces that viewed their collaboration with Suharto's circle as an opportunity to influence the state to enact Islamic laws. They viewed the state's enactment of Islamic family and court laws and the founding of an Islamic bank, and other concessions to Muslim interests as a step in the right direction to establishing a more Islam-oriented government and society.[35]

There was a possible convergence between the two orientations, as some advocates of an Islamic society envisaged that ICMI could be at the vanguard of efforts to turn state officials into more pious, practising Muslims. They considered that a deepening of religious belief within the state would then radiate out to wider society, as it too became more Islamised. ICMI member, Masdar Mas'udi (a liberal scholar and NGO leader), argues that there was a growing tendency of Muslim 'modernists' to 'Islamise the state' both by placing more and more Muslims in the government bureaucracy and by implementing Islamic laws.[36]

In summary, agendas within ICMI for demilitarisation, democratisation and Islamisation were evidence of a re-politicisation of Muslim middle-class interests. State sponsorship of Islam had kindled hopes among its intelligentsia that they might be able to advance their political agendas through ICMI. ABRI leaders were unlikely to view too kindly any attempts by ICMI's intelligentsia to formulate openly, or to realise, their goals.

ABRI's Objections to ICMI's Agendas

Objections within ABRI to ICMI's different agendas arose from ABRI's perceived role as guardian of national stability against the forces of disintegration. ABRI leaders perceived themselves as defenders of an Indonesian unitary state based on *Pancasila*—an integralist ideology of a dominant state and subordinate society constituting an indivisible organic union. The state ideology precluded establishment of an Islamic theocracy or liberal democracy from constitutional possibilities. Military leaders regarded Islamic political and ideological movements, communism, and liberal democracy as the three principal threats to the *Pancasila* state. In particular, they were concerned about Islam's potential as an agent of independent political organisation, especially because Muslim leaders could mobilise the masses against other religious communities or in opposition to state authority. Military leaders had an historical distrust of partisan political parties and religious groups that might assert their own 'sectarian' interests above and beyond those of the national interest which, the leaders argued, could lead to national disintegration.[37]

Thus, ICMI's agendas for democratisation (demilitarisation), Islamisation, and the prospect of Islam becoming a force for democracy, were all good reasons for an entrenched military state to deeply suspect ICMI. Islam was a latent political force that had immense potential for mobilising Indonesians for various causes and ICMI represented an organised block. As Aswab Mahasin observed, 'ICMI was a bigger threat [to power holders] than unorganised dissenting communities, and ABRI was worried about ICMI'.[38] Ramage argues that significant segments of the ABRI leadership opposed ICMI on the grounds that it acted like a party. ABRI leaders pointed out that ICMI had established a nationwide organisational structure, with provincial, district (and overseas) branches and was trying to build grassroots support. Ramage notes, there was 'a generalised concern that ICMI could be a potential manifestation of newly politicised Islam'.[39] However, it is possible also that ABRI leaders were concerned that ICMI provided a means for 'civilians' to bypass ABRI-dominated Golkar branches in the provinces and districts and would compete for people's allegiances at election times.[40] A number of ABRI officers also claimed that ICMI constituted a sectarian religious threat to the multi-religious nation, and that the organisation 'surreptitiously' supported an Islamic state in contravention of *Pancasila*.[41]

Suharto shared ABRI's allergy to political Islam, inherited from earlier periods in Indonesia's pre-and-post-independence history. Indonesia's recent history included Islamic rebellions in Aceh and West Java, and constitutional debates over the final form of the post-independence nation-state (Islamic, secular or *Pancasila*). Accordingly, the perception of Islamic threat was imbedded in the psyche of commanders who had inherited a deep apprehension about the growth of Islamic militancy in Indonesia.[42] In order not to give extra ammunition to ABRI against ICMI, members of the Muslim intelligentsia were careful to distance themselves from the Islamic state ideal. Of course, many ICMI members also opposed the ideal of an Islamic state. They rejected the idea of Islamic clerics gaining control of the state apparatus and proclaiming a theocratic state as had occurred in (Shi'ite) Iran.[43] In addition, although Suharto ensured that ICMI's Muslim intelligentsia did not pose such a threat by keeping them outside of key political institutions and the public-policy arena, his efforts apparently failed to mollify entirely ABRI's concerns.

Concerns about ICMI's democratising and Islamising agendas, perhaps, were not the main motivation behind ABRI's apprehension of ICMI. The military leadership might well have raised the spectre of ICMI as an 'Islamic threat', as a means of discrediting their political rival, Habibie.[44] By associating his chairmanship of ICMI with the potential spread of Islamic political ideology, they could hope to ruin Habibie's prospects of ascending to the vice-presidency. Habibie was Suharto's favoured candidate for the post against the military's candidates. Nurcholish Madjid (a liberal scholar and ICMI member) acknowledged this conflict, pointing to the fact that 'nationalist' officers 'were the ones who felt threatened by ICMI because they saw ICMI as [synonymous with] Habibie. Everything that Habibie does at the bureaucratic level in regard to jobs and money…in their [the nationalists'] thinking they will attack ICMI.'[45]

Perhaps in cognisance of the potential for destabilising conflicts, the Suharto regime fostered a conciliatory approach to Muslim interests providing they did not manifest themselves as organised political demands. At the same time, once he had successfully established his control over an acquiescent ABRI leadership, he sought to placate ABRI's concerns about the re-politicisation of Islam. As such, Suharto and his ministers made numerous announcements to try to assuage ABRI's suspicions of Islamisation, and as firm warnings to the ICMI intelligentsia. They declared that ICMI's activities were neither directed towards Islamisation or to the establishment of a political organisation or pressure group. They also vociferously denied claims that ICMI constituted a pro-Golkar/pro-Suharto power block before the 1992 general elections and Golkar's 1993 national congress. The public denials failed to mollify deep-seated suspicions of Habibie, driven, as they were, by the awareness that Suharto was using Habibie and Islam in order to diminish the political influence and institutional autonomy of the armed forces.

Which Military Opposes ICMI?

ICMI–military antagonisms partly reflected the psychology of winners and losers, in an eminently excluding and including power game of divide-and-rule. Military officers most inclined to attack ICMI and its chairman were those who were associated with Benny's declining influence, or had been ousted from strategic and political posts by Habibie's increasing power. Conversely, other *santri* (orthodox Muslim) generals who had gained promotions, either as a result of the ouster of Benny's forces, or because of association with Habibie, tended to endorse the ICMI chairman and praise ICMI publicly. Ultimately, President Suharto promoted the new generation of Muslim generals as part of his divide-and-rule tactics to increase his own autonomy vis-à-vis ABRI.

The promotion of younger military officers caused a long-standing debate in the media and among Indonesian analysts, about a rift in ABRI between the so-called 'green (Muslim)' officers and 'red-and-white (nationalist)' officers. The new Commander-in-Chief of the Armed Forces, Feisal Tanjung (appointed in May 1993)—who, according to one view may have gained his promotion because of his links with the technology minister—was one of the rising generation of Muslim officers. As ABRI commander, Feisal oversaw the purging of Benny's intelligence network.[48] Shortly after assuming office in May 1993, Feisal ingratiated himself to Habibie and ICMI by praising the organisation for what he said was its dynamic role in assisting the military with its stability and development goals.[49] Feisal was responsible for promoting Muslim officers up the military hierarchy, one prominent example being the appointment in March 1996 of Syarwan Hamid (the military's Chief of Social-Political Affairs, Kassospol after Lt Gen. Hartono).

Another prominent example was Lt Gen. Hartono—a Muslim officer who, in January 1994, became the chief of the military's social-political affairs (Kassospol) before being promoted to army chief of staff, replacing Wismoyo Arismunandar (the brother-in-law of Ibu Tien Suharto) in January 1995. Lowry notes that Wismoyo 'had been trying to distance the Army from the president, the new Golkar leader (Harmoko), Dr Habibie, and the C-in-C ABRI [Commander in Chief, Feisal] who was believed to be under their influence'.[50] Upon his accession to Kassospol, Hartono promptly indicated his support for ICMI by announcing that the association was a positive development that unified Muslims and therefore contributed to national integration.[51] Hartono, in particular, was responsible for promoting Muslim officers up the military hierarchy to replace Benny's men.[52] There was speculation at the time that Hartono had received his new post because of Habibie. Nonetheless, he later came into tension with Habibie when he decided to back openly the political ambitions of Suharto's daughter, Siti Rukmana, against the vice-presidential ambitions of the technology minister. Lt Gen. Yunus Yosfiah assumed the position of Kassospol in December 1996 shortly after publicly praising Habibie's credentials as a leader of technology. (He was later to become the Minister of Information on President Habibie's cabinet in May 1998.)[53]

The new generation of officers rejected arguments employed by Benny, Admiral Sudomo (another Christian officer), and other older generation officers (who regularly cautioned the public of impending Islamic extremist threats to national stability). They considered that Indonesian Muslims unfairly had been branded as extremists.[54] If the newly ascendant generals were happy to deliver some praise to ICMI, the Muslim intelligentsia was relieved to witness a generation of officers who were more sympathetically inclined to Muslim aspirations.[55] Its members sought to cultivate close relations with the military leadership under Feisal's command, and some insisted they trusted his military to run Indonesia. *Republika* published an article in 1993 proclaiming Feisal as the Muslim community's choice of man-of-the-year.[56] The attitude of ICMI's intelligentsia to the new generation of officers may have been in contradiction with commitments to demilitarisation and democratisation. However, it is important to understand that members of ICMI's intelligentsia were keen to cultivate better ties with ABRI because of the recent history of the military's repressive security approach against Islamic political activities.

The promotion of Muslim generals helped polarise Indonesian politics into ICMI/Golkar interests and anti-ICMI officers, who were strongly nationalist in orientation and despaired of the alignment of state and Islam. The anti-ICMI officers were sidelined as the direct result of a change of guard when Suharto reshuffled the upper echelons of the armed forces, with five reshuffles taking place from August 1992 to August 1994.[57] The reshuffling of senior military officers was a common ploy that Suharto used in order to keep ambitious generals from becoming too powerful and posing a threat to his presidency.

Consequently, Suharto left Benny Murdani out of the 1993 cabinet. Benny's social and political affairs chief, Harsudiono Hartas, who had earlier successfully pushed through the vice-presidential nomination of Try Sutrisno (Commander-in-Chief of ABRI) against Suharto's choice of Habibie, also seemingly was punished. Upon retiring from his post, Harsudiono failed to become Minister of Internal Affairs, as he had hoped, and had to settle for a position in the largely uninfluential Supreme Advisory Council. In a meeting with Suharto, the Chairman of Golkar, Wahono, also put forward Try as Golkar's choice for vice-president. At Golkar's mid-year congress, Suharto had Wahono replaced as the ruling party's chair.[58]

In an interview conducted at the Supreme Advisory Council in 1994, a disgruntled Harsudiono bluntly criticised Habibie, Habibie's bureaucrats, and ICMI. He claimed that ICMI 'radical fundamentalists', as he called its intelligentsia, were using Suharto's and Habibie's protection in order to infiltrate the ranks of the armed forces, the government bureaucracy, the political parties, Golkar and the new cabinet. They were seeking to change or replace the state's 'integralistic' ideology of *Pancasila* with an Islamic state and/ or with liberal democratic ideals of individualism—anathema, Harsudiono insisted, to the military's 'integralistic' and collectivist ideals of organic unity between the military state and society. According to Harsudiono, ICMI radicals 'must be brainwashed until their minds are empty and clean so that "we" can all be of one mind'. Finally, he claimed that the decision of ICMI members to support Gen. Feisal Tanjung was part of a tactical ploy to gain legitimacy and political freedom so that they could 'confront the military and weaken it from within. These people are too naive, too stupid! If the strategy of infiltration continues, conflict will break out [between the ICMI "radicals" and the military].'[59]

Harsudiono's remark about Feisal was an allusion to the power reshuffle that witnessed Feisal's men replace Benny's network (including Harsudiono), and the fact that the ICMI intelligentsia had pinned its hopes and fortunes on this change of guard. Harsudiono perceived that the new coalition of ICMI–Habibie–military interests was responsible for his own ouster. In return, the intelligentsia clearly perceived Benny and Harsudiono as two major obstructions to the advancement of their own political careers. They strongly opposed Try Sutrisno's election (backed by Benny's men) to the vice-presidency. One ICMI intellectual warned that if the armed forces commander became vice-president, it would create the public impression that Indonesia was a military state.[60]

Golkar's National Congress of 1993

The tensions between Suharto–Habibie–civilian interests and the nationalist-oriented military leadership centred on Golkar as preparations were made for the ruling party's national congress in May 1993. Competition for the post of Golkar chairperson reflected an ongoing rivalry and mistrust between the military and civilian bureaucracy. ABRI leaders were determined to retain a military man in the ruling party's top job, as well as to maintain military control over regional and branch levels of Golkar. Of greater significance, it was an important staging post in the growing power struggle over succession.

The ABRI leaders fought to have a military man retain chairmanship of the government party. The military put forward three senior officers as candidates for Golkar's Chair—Lt Gen. Harsudiono Hartas, Gen. Susilo Sudarman (the Coordinating Minister of Politics and Defence), and Gen. Try Sutrisno (the new vice-president). Appointed in February, the Commander-in-Chief of the Armed Forces, Edi Sudrajat, publicly declared that a military figure was best qualified for the post of chairman. As head of the committee of formateurs responsible for selecting the new Golkar chairman, Habibie ignored the wishes of the military top brass, and pushed through the civilian Minister of Information and Suharto loyalist, Harmoko, as the new chair.[61]

Harmoko was the first civilian to lead Golkar. In his capacity as head of Golkar's board of patrons, Suharto clearly backed the choice of Harmoko to replace the military general Wahono. Analysts interpreted Suharto's choice of Harmoko as retribution against the ABRI leadership after they had successfully pushed through the candidature of Try Sutrisno for vice-president. In a further move, in late 1995, Golkar's Chairman Harmoko arranged the removal of Wahono's team of supporters from their positions in Golkar.[62]

After Golkar's congress, the Deputy Chairman of the armed forces faction in parliament, Maj. Gen. Sembiring Meliala, was unable to contain his bitterness in a public outburst against the election of Harmoko. He warned that Harmoko and Habibie depended entirely on Suharto for their political survival and that 'Golkar without military support will be nothing. If in the next election the military decides to support the PDI, this party will surely be the winner, not Golkar.'[63] The military leadership under Edi Sudrajat's command was clearly displeased with the latest turn of events.

It was in this context that Suharto appointed Feisal Tanjung as commander-in-chief of ABRI, with Edi Sudrajat retaining his position of Minister of Defence. The editors of the journal *Indonesia* note that 'Gen. Edy Sudradjat in his brief days of "record" glory as simultaneously Minister of Defence, armed forces commander, and army chief-of-staff, made strategic appointments to assure colonels and brigadier generals that "army institutional rationality" would not be interfered with by the president. Since then, however, palace countermeasures have been going on in waves of reshuffles.'[64] Edi subsequently became a major critic of Habibie, Golkar and ICMI, as he backed various initiatives to establish organisations, under the banner of nationalism, with which to combat cosy state–Islamic relations and to oppose Habibie's camp.[65]

The military mainstream, therefore, resented Habibie for his central role in assisting Suharto to have a civilian bureaucrat assume control of Golkar. Resentment of Habibie spilled over into hostility towards ICMI. Suharto tried to manage the rivalry in an apparent effort to defuse the potential for open conflict against Habibie and ICMI. He became the chief patron of ICMI and endorsed the appointment of the new vice-president, (ret.) Gen. Try Sutrisno, and two former vice-presidents to ICMI's council of patrons, which took place in August 1993 at the Presidential Palace. Try (a man long considered to be in Benny's camp) hitherto was viewed as Habibie's adversary and was known to be critical of ICMI.[66]

In a sign of rapprochement, after the August meeting, the press carried pictures of a gathering of state officials, the military top brass, and sixty ICMI members who witnessed Try warmly shaking hands with Habibie. In his public address, reading from an official text of platitudes, Try outlined ICMI's role in the field of technological development, and as a promoter of nationalism and national unity. He nonetheless indicated that he was not entirely satisfied with ICMI by warning the organisation against becoming 'trapped in narrow communalistic-sectarian behaviour'.[67] Highlighting his intended supervisory role in ICMI, he warned its members to demonstrate vigilance (*kewaspadaan*) in order that they did not 'stray' from agreed organisational channels and goals. Speaking off-the-cuff, he also hinted that much still had to be done to mend fences between ICMI and the military, as he cautioned ICMI against creating the public impression that 'generational' divisions existed within the armed forces.[68] Try's warning was a reference to the inclination of ICMI's intelligentsia to view the armed forces as split between pro-Feisal/pro-Islamic officers and those anti-Islamic officers aligned against ICMI.

The appointment of Try to ICMI can be considered as one of several attempts by Suharto to maintain a shifting balance of competing interests within and outside of ICMI (and Golkar) in order to preserve his own autonomy and power. On the surface, at least, relations between Habibie and ICMI on the one hand, and the armed forces' leadership on the other seemed to have improved. Despite surface appearances, there remained a strong undercurrent of dislike for Habibie's leadership position as technology minister and Suharto's close confidant.

Defence Purchases

One year later, in mid-1994, a controversy erupted over Habibie's purchase of warships from the former East German navy, as antagonisms between the technology minister and his military adversaries became public. Mainstream military officers resented Habibie for taking over lucrative state contracts, and making foreign deals over their heads, in military hardware purchases. Habibie, like Sudharmono before him, was unpopular for commandeering military hardware purchases from the defence department. Habibie not only undermined the military's budgetary control of defence purchases, but he also deprived them of non-budgetary kickbacks.

For example, in 1993 he arranged the purchase of twenty-four Hawk fighter jets from Britain. In addition, to their chagrin, the armed forces leadership was forced to buy aircraft, which were considered inferior to planes available overseas, from Habibie's IPTN plant. Creating the greatest controversy, however, was his purchase of thirty-nine dilapidated warships from the former East German navy. Habibie bought the warships at bargain-basement prices but his plans to refurbish them at an estimated cost of US$1.1 billion (about three quarters of the official defence budget) drew sharp criticism. He had made the latest purchase, debiting it to the defence department's budget.[69]

Consequently, in retaliation, military officers and the economic technocrats—who did not share Habibie's vision for a high-tech, high-cost economic take off—forged an open alliance against Habibie's purchase of the ships. The Minister of Finance, Mar'ie Muhammad, and the Minister of Defence and Security, Gen. Edi Sudrajat, publicly criticised Habibie's purchase and severely slashed his projected refurbishment budget to US$320 million.[70] Suharto had appointed Mar'ie Muhammad, an economic conservative, to the position of Minister of Finance in 1993 partly to maintain a check on Habibie's over-zealous projects.

Comprehensive press coverage of the intra-elite dispute was one of the factors that prompted Suharto's information minister to revoke the licenses in June 1994 of two national magazines, the *Tempo* and the *Editor*, and of the popular tabloid *DeTik*. Habibie was thought to have been behind the decision to ban the publications, as Habibie's military antagonists were apparently behind the press campaign to expose the ICMI chairman's bad management of defence purchases.[71] The ICMI intelligentsia closed ranks to defend their beleaguered chairman, insisting that he was not responsible for banning the publications. Instead, they accused *Tempo* of conspiring with 'non-Muslims and the military to destroy Habibie's reputation over the ship purchase. The issue was portrayed not in terms of press or other democratic freedoms, but one of Muslims versus non-Muslims.'[72] The partiality of ICMI against *Tempo* was not entirely unwarranted, as the news weekly regularly had adopted a critical and partisan editorial stance against the Muslim association.

The public exposure of intra-elite rivalry between Suharto's civilian supporters and ABRI had led Suharto to curtail the period of political openness with a clampdown on the press.

Rivalry within ICMI

Suharto's sponsorship of ICMI had not only created a political divide between pro-ICMI and anti-ICMI interests. It had also stimulated rivalry within ICMI between competing patrons seeking to use ICMI as a potential client base for the advancement of their own future power aspirations. That is, at ICMI's congress in 1995, several of Habibie's adversaries joined the Muslim intellectuals association, including Suharto's daughter Siti Rukmana (see chapter five). Measures to offset Habibie's influence within ICMI also included the appointment in August 1997 of Siti's close ally Lt Gen. (ret.) Hartono, the new Minister of Information, to a senior advisory role within ICMI. At the time, Siti gave strong public endorsement to Hartono's entry into ICMI.[73] There also was speculation at the time that Suharto might be grooming his elder daughter for a dynastic succession. Thus, Hartono might have had his sights on the ICMI chairmanship to harness Muslim support behind Siti for the vice-presidency.[74]

The contest for vice-presidential stakes highlights the fact that ICMI and Golkar had become arenas in which rival patron-client networks competed for political advantage. Both ICMI and Golkar provided strategic access to high office for senior state officials. In March 1998, however, the armed forces' leadership acquiesced to the president's choice of Habibie as Indonesia's new vice-president replacing Try Sutrisno. Nevertheless, many of them were not happy with the prospect of the former technology minister becoming Indonesia's future president. New ABRI commander, Wiranto, was regarded as a likely threat both to Habibie's personal ambitions and to ICMI interests.[75]

The discussion to this point has demonstrated that state incorporation of Islam had outcomes beyond the immediate stated and implicit objectives of neutralising political Islam. One of the broader implications of incorporation was that Muslim interests were drawn into partisan struggles that facilitated Suharto's tactics of sowing division and circumventing potential threats to his power. ICMI and Golkar also became important nerve centres for the negotiation of patron-client struggles. That is, patrons like Suharto, Habibie, Siti Rukmana and Hartono sought to use the organisations as client support-bases in advancement of their own careers and survival interests against rivals. The biggest cleavage occurred between disgruntled military leaders and the newly ascendant pro-ICMI groups. Intra-elite contest, however, remained within the predictable limits of New Order politics and therefore did not disrupt a carefully maintained power balance underpinning Suharto's presidency. Corporatised Muslim and civilian (ICMI/Golkar) interests became important arenas, if not instruments, for mediating these contests and reinforcing Suharto's role as the final arbiter of dispute.

RIVALRY BETWEEN ICMI AND ANTI-HABIBIE BUREAUCRATS

The kinds of tensions and lines of conflict between pro-Habibie (ICMI) interests and their military antagonists found an echo in the state bureaucracy. Bureaucratic infighting particularly centred on competition for cabinet positions as the succession crisis deepened. As part of divide-and-rule, Suharto had maintained a shifting balance of competing interests in consecutive cabinets. The following case study illustrates how, after the appointment of the sixth development cabinet in March 1993, ICMI interests were drawn into the contest in defence of their patron against other state interests.

Bureaucratic Competition in Development Cabinets

The sixth development cabinet comprised an uneasy balance of competing interests, especially between the economic conservatives/technocrats and, roughly speaking, the economic nationalists (and the respective constituencies they served). That is, after a sustained period of economic liberalisation, the economic technocrats and the burgeoning interests of private capital were coming up against the entrenched rent-seeking practices of privileged family interests. Suharto's children and Habibie's family were among those who had built their own economic empires through state protection and rent seeking.[76]

On the side of state protectionism, Habibie retained his portfolio as Minister of Research and Technology. Three of his bureaucratic colleagues from the Agency of Applied Technology Research (BPPT), the Minister of Education and Culture Wardiman Djojonegoro, the Minister of Transport Haryanto Dhanutirto and the Minister of Trade Satrio Budiharjo Judono also gained ministerial rank in the cabinet. They belonged to one stream of economic nationalism (that promoted investment in high-end technology) which adhered to a policy of investment in import-substitution industries requiring government protection of domestic, particularly indigenous, capital. Other economic nationalists were the Minister of Transmigration Siswono Juhohusodo (a business client of the State Secretariat), and the State Minister/Chairman of the National Planning Board (Bappenas, formerly a preserve of the technocrats), Ginanjar Kartasasmita. Ginanjar's career was in the State Secretariat. The Co-ordinating Minister of Industry and Trade, Hartarto, ideologically was positioned somewhere between the economic nationalists and the technocrats.

From the conservative/technocrats' camp, some ministers were retained from the previous cabinet. One important addition was the new Minister of Finance, Mar'ie Muhammad, who was appointed to maintain economic austerity and to keep a check on Habibie's sometimes run-away budgetary expenditures. Meanwhile, three influential economic technocrats (of Christian faith), and long-time cabinet members, Radius Prawiro, Adrianus Mooy and J.B. Sumarlin were dropped from the cabinet. These technocrats, under the early strong influence of Suharto's economics advisor, Widjojo Nitisastro, adhered to free-market policies that emphasised non-oil/gas exports. The competing economic visions between Habibie and the technocrats has been disparagingly termed 'Widjojonomics' and 'Habibienomics'.[77]

The departure of the technocrats from the cabinet, at the same time that Benny Murdani was dropped, was seen as serving two main purposes. One was to placate Muslim demands for greater, proportional representation in Indonesia's political institutions, as Muslim political interests associated with ICMI claimed that Christians had, for too long, dominated political institutions disproportionate to their community numbers. Consequently, only four ministers (or 10 per cent) of the sixth development cabinet were non-Muslims. The second purpose was Suharto's effort to readjust the balance of influence away from the economic technocrats and towards economic nationalists after the preceding (fifth) development cabinet had accorded enhanced influence to the technocrats. The competing interests brought into the cabinet reflected earlier struggles and cabinet compositions, as the pendulum of economic influence swung between the technocrats and nationalists and each school of thought sought to gain Suharto's 'preferential' ear.[78]

A rival of Habibie's, the State Secretary, Murdiono (a military general who had spent most of his career in civil administration), was appointed for a second term. Both officials were close advisors to Suharto, no doubt competing for influence with the president. There existed potential points of tension between the two ministers. Hadiz identified one point of tension, noting that 'ICMI's new-found prominence has…encroached on Sekneg's [the State Secretariat's] role of controlling access to the president'.[79] In addition, Murdiono had leaned in favour of policies promoted by the economic technocrats, anathema to Habibie's brand of economic nationalism. Gaffar also identified an alliance between Murdiono and Gen. Edi Sudrajat, one of Habibie's major opponents in the mainstream military.[80] Murdiono–Habibie tensions stemmed from Suharto's cultivation of rival networks, particularly between economics ministers and departments, and allowing disputes to build before mediating in favour of one side.

Corruption Allegations Against an ICMI Bureaucrat

Thus, the entry of Habibie's team of bureaucrats and loyalists at BPPT into the 1993 cabinet, at the expense of other state interests, stimulated continuing intra-elite/intra-cabinet conflict. These tensions came to a head in 1995. The political storm began on 10 October, when the Inspector General of Development, Maj. Gen. (ret.) Kentot Harseno (a former military adjutant to the president, and a confidant of Benny Murdani's), sent the first of three reports marked 'top secret' to Suharto of corruption allegations against the ICMI bureaucrat, the Minister of Transport Haryanto Dhanutirto. Harseno's office was loosely within the orbit of the State Secretariat. His report, written on State Secretariat letterhead, accused Haryanto of diverting 9 billion *rupiah* of funding, in the form of 392 non-budgetary levies, for his own personal enrichment from eighteen of twenty-seven State-Owned Companies (BUMN) under his supervision at the Department of Transport.[81]

The report was leaked to the press, by an unknown source, and was distributed widely to government departments and community leaders. One photocopied report landed on the desk of Amien Rais, then the head of ICMI's council of experts (before his ouster). A controversy was soon sparked by detailed coverage of the corruption allegations, which indicated that Habibie's rivals in the state bureaucracy, associated with Murdiono's State Secretariat, were behind efforts to undermine the technology minister's reputation. Murdiono promptly gave his public support to Harseno's report and called for an internal investigation of Haryanto. The report caused a furore as Muslim interests associated with ICMI closed ranks to defend the ICMI bureaucrat against corruption allegations, in an open rift with Habibie's antagonists at the State Secretariat.[82]

After the corruption allegations against Haryanto became public, the ABRI fraction and the PDI fraction of parliamentary commission II quickly backed Harseno's report and demanded Haryanto's immediate resignation. The two parliamentary fractions stressed that the source of the leak was not at issue, but the contents of Harseno's document were of upmost importance because it centred on the damaging problem of corruption.[83] Meanwhile, Muslim interests centring on ICMI considered Harseno to have falsified the report, and viewed the vital issue to be the source of the leak, which they believed led to the offices of Murdiono's State Secretariat and to Harseno's office.[84]

Suharto assigned to Vice-President Try Sutrisno the task of investigating the allegations. After a meeting with Suharto and meetings with Try, Haryanto announced that he had been reprimanded and requested to undergo a period of introspection and to make procedural corrections to the administrative conduct of his transport department. After the investigation by the vice-president's office, Murdiono announced the president's decision on 26 December that 'there was no valid proof' that Haryanto had 'used state money...for his own needs or gain'.[85]

Other Muslim members of parliament, Muslim student groups, the radical organisation Solidarity Committee for the Islamic World (KISDI) and the ICMI intelligentsia were far from persuaded by Murdiono's assurances that he had not leaked 'state secrets'. They were upset by what appeared to be a government whitewash of the case, and what some perceived as Murdiono's backhanded swipe against the transport minister. They were convinced that Suharto's investigation was not motivated by the desire to establish 'clean government', and therefore that it had not sought to investigate those responsible for leaking Harseno's report to the press. Amien Rais was among the ICMI leaders who accused Harseno of falsifying the report, and added his voice to demands for the government to bring to trial whomsoever was found to have leaked the report containing 'state secrets'. Amien claimed that the offices of Harseno and Murdiono were responsible for the leak aimed at discrediting Habibie's ministers and ICMI interests.[86]

Muslim student organisations (including the Muslim University Student's Communication Forum, the Islamic University Student's Association, HMI and the University Students Solidarity Forum for Anti-Deviationism) held several demonstrations outside of parliament and the Attorney General's office. They called for the Attorney General to investigate the leaking of state secrets and to rehabilitate Haryanto's name. Protests also occurred in Bandung, Surabaya and other cities. The CIDES leader, Eggi Sugjana (an underling of ICMI's Secretary General Adi Sasono), organised a student demonstration at Murdiono's offices at the State Secretariat in Jakarta, demanding a clarification of earlier accusations against Haryanto.

One of the largest protests was co-ordinated by KISDI and held at the Al-Furqon Mosque on the grounds of the Dewan Dakwah organisation. KISDI's leader, Ahmad Sumargono, asserted that the leaking of Harseno's report was clearly an 'illegal act' that must face 'heavy sanctions'. In Manado, North Sulawesi, fifteen Islamic organisations representing a broad spectrum of organisational interests, including NU, Muhammadiyah and HMI, urged the government to investigate the circumstances surrounding the leak of Harseno's report. The ICMI leader, Amien Rais, went further than most by calling the leak 'an act of subversion'.[87]

Concluding Comments

ICMI was part of Suharto's corporatist strategy aimed at neutralising Muslim political aspirations. Yet, ICMI, and the general Muslim backlash against Haryanto's accusers created a highly politicised and potentially embarrassing climate for the government. Attempts by Harseno and Murdiono to discredit Haryanto had backfired. That is, the ICMI intelligentsia redirected the focus of debate from one of corruption allegations against Haryanto to one of demands to punish the official who leaked the state secrets. Members of ICMI's intelligentsia perceived that the attack against Haryanto was part of a planned strategy by ABRI-linked forces hostile to ICMI and Habibie to reduce Muslim influence in the future MPR and cabinet. They tried to deflect the allegations against the ICMI bureaucrat by accusing other senior government officials— Murdiono and Harseno—of collusion against Muslim interests. They claimed the collusion was part of a broader systemic corruption afflicting the New Order political system.[88]

One interpretation of the corruption controversy is that Suharto's circle did not look kindly upon ICMI's role in arousing political opposition to Murdiono, in exposing the intra-elite rivalry, or in claiming that the government was systemically corrupt. This would have reflected badly on the president's own rule. A corporatist organisation, top-heavy in government bureaucrats who were positioned there by Suharto in order to subdue the potential for anti-government dissent, in this instance, had the contrary effect. It became embroiled in conflict in a manner presumably undesired by Suharto's power-holding elite. Had state supervision of ICMI therefore failed to suppress political agitations of its intelligentsia?

An alternative interpretation is that the intra-elite rivalries were simply a consequence of strategies pursued by Suharto of cultivating competing patronage networks. That is, the president was happy to witness contestations between Murdiono and Habibie, as the two state leaders offset each other's power and, in doing so, ensured that Suharto retained his role as ultimate goal-keeper and arbiter of dispute. Suharto's attempt to resolve the controversy, by delegating an investigation to Vice-President Try Sutrisno's office, did not detract from the fact that the intra-bureaucratic conflict arose in the first place from pro-Habibie/anti-Habibie cleavages in the cabinet. And Suharto had consistently compiled cabinets to reflect, and exacerbate, competing interests, visions and trends in national politics.

The ICMI intelligentsia became embroiled in political controversy by siding with Habibie against the minister's detractors. This outcome was contrary to one of the main stated aims of ICMI (see chapter five) to remain outside of politics. In the final analysis, contests between different patron-client interests— Habibie (ICMI) and Murdiono/Harseno (State Secretariat)—had caused a client-base, the ICMI membership, to be drawn into that conflict. The defence of Habibie and of other ICMI interests was tied integrally to perceptions about

ICMI's own position within future power constellations as the 1997 general election and the 1998 MPR election approached.[89]

The Seventh Development Cabinet: Continuing Cleavages

The swearing in of the seventh development cabinet in 1998 further exacerbated the divisions and contest. Some of Vice-President B.J. Habibie's allies were re-appointed to a cabinet that was widely recognised as a 'crony cabinet' of the president's loyalists, business associates and family members. Despite earlier corruption allegations, Haryanto Dhanutirto (the new Minister of Food, Horticulture and Medicine), was among three of Habibie's associates who were appointed as ministers.[90] At the end of the day, Haryanto was regarded as a Suharto loyalist. Meanwhile, Murdiono was replaced after two stints as State Secretary.[91]

Along with the appointment of former presidential military adjutant, Wiranto, and Suharto's son-in-law, Prabowo, to the military leadership, the cabinet was meant to bolster Suharto's authority at a time of deepening economic and political crisis when he was experiencing narrowing support for his presidency. Suharto's children, Siti Rukmana and Bambang Trihatmodjo, reportedly had a decisive say in the cabinet's formation, which saw Habibie's influence diminish. Economic technocrats and conservatives, including Mar'ie Muhammad, were displaced by economic nationalists under the new Minister of Finance, Ginandjar Kartasismata's leadership.[92]

Despite enormous hopes that Habibie's ascension to the vice-presidency would result in cabinet appointments for the ICMI intelligentsia, Suharto ensured that they did not gain a single seat. They were disappointed sorely by their exclusion from the 1998 cabinet and from power configurations and began to criticise openly Suharto's crony cabinet. Amien Rais and other members of ICMI identified Haryanto as one of Suharto's most corrupt ministers.[93] They no longer identified with Habibie's minister against other state interests, as their stance regarding Haryanto and corruption seemed greatly determined by their perception of their own position within the power configurations and contests. This time they opposed a cabinet in which Haryanto had become a minister and they had become clear losers.

CONCLUSION

Muslim interests were brought into state structures that served as mechanisms for the regulation of relations between intermediate elite groups and the upper-reaches of power; specifically President Suharto's regime. One of the main functions of incorporation, as discussed in this chapter, was to regulate the access of these groups to patronage and power opportunities, which resulted not only in winners and losers but supplied one of the arenas in which struggles for position and power took place. This study has shown how corporatist organisations (Golkar and ICMI) can serve authoritarian strategies of divide-and-rule with the aim of maintaining an imbalance of competing interests.

Thus, the analysis considered how the corporatist organisations were subject to the interplay of patron-client networks and to intra-elite competition, in which Suharto was the senior patron and final arbiter of dispute. Consequently, conflict occurred between newly incorporated interests (in ICMI), which were seeking access to political power and career advancement, and rival interests (military leaders and state bureaucrats). Some of the rivals had been sidelined or excluded from power arrangements by the rise of the new groups.

However, incorporation in ICMI also failed to translate into real positions of power for its intelligentsia. Suharto had continued to maintain a balance of competing interests in the political institutions as a means of preserving regime integrity and personal power. The president's reliance on tactics of divide-and-rule, to date, had continued to serve him well by keeping possible rival centres of power, or patron-client networks, in a constant state of mutual struggle. It was not necessary for Suharto to orchestrate the contests for power; it was sufficient that he presided over them and cultivated competing interests in a manner that would reinforce his own role as supreme leader of Indonesian politics. In conclusion, incorporated Muslim interests helped Suharto maintain a shifting disequilibrium of forces as they contended for political predominance at the time of growing public perceptions of an impending succession crisis.

Insofar as conflict reinforced Suharto's dominance over Indonesian politics, and remained within predictable limits by not threatening to spark society-wide conflagrations, it can be assumed that intra-elite rivalry was not an undesired consequence of state management strategies. However, the state–Islamic accommodation, coinciding as it did with a period of political openness, had stimulated rising political aspirations on the part of the Muslim intelligentsia. Consequently, Muslim interests in ICMI were showing early signs of moving beyond their corporatist containment by formulating their own private agendas. Chapter eight examines the expansion of organised societal interests that, as a result of intra-elite conflict and the changing composition of Indonesian society, were unleashed by a period of political openness.

NOTES

1. Ding, *The Decline of Communism*.
2. *Indonesia*: 58 (October 1994), p.85; Bourchier, 'Crime, Law and State', pp.177–201; Kingsbury, *The Politics of Indonesia*, pp.112–19.
3. Honna, 'The Military and Democratisation', pp.148–9; Lowry, *The Armed Forces*, pp.61–74; *Indonesia*: 58 (October 1994), p.85.
4. Honna, 'The Military and Democratisation', pp.14–15.
5. Telephone discussion with Robert Lowry, 10 May 2000.

6. Responding to pressures from Suharto and to public criticism, the military leadership announced in 1992 that it would thenceforth pursue a policy of 'back to basics'. The announcement sparked rumours that the armed forces might return to the barracks and withdraw from its dominant role in politics. Reinforcing public speculation was a public statement in April 1994 by the Commander-in-Chief of the Armed Forces, Feisal Tanjung, that he would conduct a review of the military's social-political role. The armed forces leadership, however, made it clear that they would review the formulation but not the substance of the military's social-political role. Lowry, *The Armed Forces*, p.195.

7. Interview with Sucipto Wirosarjono (former government statistician and ICMI member), 11 January 1994; Aswab Mahasin (ICMI intellectual and NGO activist), 4 February 1994.

8. Interviews with Amien Rais (Muhammadiyah leader, head of ICMI's council of experts), 4 January 1994; Sri Bintang Pamungkas (parliamentary legislator from PPP and member of ICMI and CIDES), 8 February 1994.

9. Adi Sasono pointed out that ICMI's think-tank, CIDES, 'officially launched discussion on the succession issue...[we] want Suharto out...If Suharto does not go, we [the nation] will be in a difficult position'. Interview with Adi Sasono (NGO leader who rose to the position of Secretary General of ICMI in 1995 and chairman in 2000), 16 February 1994.

10. This viewpoint was prevalent among Muslim leaders that I interviewed. However, I have supplied only a sample of the interviews held. Interviews with Gen. (ret.) Benny Murdani, 5 November 1997; Toto Tasmara (leader of Bakomubin and BKPRMI), 21 March 1997; Hartono Mardjono (a Dewan Dakwah figure, member of parliament and lawyer by profession), 26 September 1996; A.M. Fatwa (a Dewan Dakwah figure who was incarcerated for his alleged involvement in the Tanjung Priok riots), 26 June 1996; Dawam Rahardjo (ICMI intellectual and NGO leader), 27 January 1994.

11. *Editor*, 10 July 1993.

12. Interviews with Sucipto, 11 January 1994; Dawam, 27 January 1994; Nurcholish Madjid (liberal theologian/scholar and ICMI member), 12 January 1994; Sri Bintang, 8 February 1994; Sasono, 16 February 1994.

13. Interview with Sasono, 16 February 1994.

14. Interviews with Sasono, 21 January and 16 February 1994.

15. Lowry, *The Armed Forces*, p.195; interview with Sucipto, 11 January 1994.

16. Interview with Sucipto, 11 January 1994; interview with Lukman Harun (Muhammadiyah leader and ICMI member), 23 January 1994. In an interview by the *Tempo* newsweekly, Lt Gen. Harsudiono Hartas (the former Kassospol serving under Benny's command) also retold how, in 1993, after he had pushed through the nomination of Gen. Try Sutrisno as ABRI's vice-presidential candidate, Habibie exclaimed that this constituted 'militarism'. *Tempo*, 3 May 1999.

17. Ramage, *Politics in Indonesia*, pp.98–9.
18. Kamal, *Muslim Intellectual Responses*, p.6; Hasyim, *Toleransi dan Kemerdekaan*, p.291; Pangaribuan, *The Indonesian State Secretariat*, pp.22–37; Ward, *The 1971 Election*, pp.35–6; Polomka, *Indonesia Since Sukarno*, p.188; Brian May, *The Indonesian Tragedy*, p.238; interviews with Harry Tjan (a founder of CSIS), 29 October 1997; Murdani, 5 November 1997; Toto, 21 March 1997; Hartono Mardjono, 26 September 1996; A.M. Fatwa, 26 June 1996.
19. The following interviews support statements in the whole paragraph. Interviews with Nurcholis, 12 January and 16 February 1994; Sasono, 20 and 21 January and 16 February 1994; Dawam, 27 January 1994; Sucipto, 11 January 1994; Haidar Bagir (a member of the editorial board of the *Republika* newspaper), 11 February 1994; Amien, 4 January 1994; Sri Bintang, 8 February 1994; Imaduddin Abdulrahim (Islamic preacher and ICMI member), 15 February 1994; Dewi Fortuna Anwar (close advisor to Habibie and CIDES member), 7 February 1994; Mahasin, 4 February 1994; Muslimin Nasution (Secretary to Chairman of Bappenas and ICMI leader), 10 February 1994; Lukman Harun (Muhammadiyah leader), 23 January 1994; Jalaluddin Rakhmat (a Muslim intellectual of pro-Shi'ite leanings, and ICMI critic), 6 January 1994.
20. Interviews with Murdani, 5 November 1997; Sasono, 21 January and 16 February 1994; Sucipto, 11 January 1994; Dewi, 7 February 1994; Nasution, 10 February 1994; Mahasin, 4 February 1994; Amien, 4 January 1994; Dawam, 27 January 1994; Nurcholish, 12 January and 16 February 1994; Lukman, 23 January 1994; and Sri Bintang, 8 February 1994.
21. For example, *Republika* and ICMI adopted a pro-government line against Bishop Belo when, in 1995, Muslims were forced to evacuate East Timor after a spate of ethnically motivated attacks by indigenous Catholic mobs against the Muslim migrant community. In the post-27 July 1996 crackdown against pro-democracy groups, the newspaper adopted a pro-government line against Catholic priests who had harboured the leader of the left-wing radical Democratic People's Party. In early 1998, coinciding with a propaganda campaign against Chinese conglomerates, in which state officials held ethnic Chinese businessmen responsible for the economic crisis, *Republika* ran anti-Benny, anti-CSIS editorials and stories.
22. Dawam Rahardjo also maintained that, through ICMI, the Muslim intelligentsia at least had 'political space to maneouvre. We try to strengthen the middle class. We have a newspaper, Republika', to give voice to middle-class aspirations. Interview with Dawam, 27 January 1994.
23. Interview with Sasono, 16 February 1994.
24. Interview with Dewi, 7 February 1994.
25. A number of ICMI members were sceptical about the usefulness of organisations like ICMI, CIDES, and *Republika* for the cause of democracy and viewed them as too co-opted and controlled by Habibie and Suharto.

For example, Sri Bintang Pamungkas bemoaned how Suharto had 'crushed Islam's political identity' through decades of the New Order's security approach and now Suharto had 'lulled Muslims to sleep' with a few small concessions, such as giving them the *Republika* newspaper and an Islamic bank. Masdar Mas'udi (head of P3M, an NU-affiliated NGO, and liberal scholar) regarded ICMI as an 'instrument of the ruling political elite that lacked any real links with the grassroots'. Interviews with Sri Bintang, 8 February 1994; Masdar, 25 January 1994.

26. Uhlin, *Indonesia and the 'Third Wave of Democratisation'*, pp. 98–150; *The Limits of Openness*, pp.1–17.
27. Hefner, 'Islam, State, and Civil Society', pp.29–30; interview with Dewi, 7 February 1994.
28. This is not to suggest that advocates of Islamic law did not view themselves as moderates.
29. Interviews with Nurcholish, 12 January and 16 February 1994; Sasono, 20 and 21 January and 16 February 1994; Dawam, 27 January 1994; Sucipto, 11 January 1994; Haidar, 11 February 1994; Amien, 4 January 1994; Sri Bintang, 8 February 1994; Imaduddin, 15 February 1994.
30. Ramage, *Politics in Indonesia*, p.110.
31. The Muhammadiyah leader, Lukman Harun, and the Muslim preacher, Imaduddin Abdulrahim, are two ICMI members that come to mind, who advocated the establishment of an Islamic society but seemed to have little commitment to principles of democracy. Interviews with Lukman, 23 January 1994; Imaduddin, 15 February 1994.
32. Interview with Sasono, 21 January 1994.
33. Interview with Dawam, 27 January 1994.
34. Interview with Dewi, 7 February 1994.
35. Interviews with Z. Abidin Abu Bakar (Director of Religious Courts at the Department of Religion), 28 June 1996; Busthanul Arifin (Department of Religion), 15 May 1996; H. Ichijanto (legal advisor at the Department of Religion), 28 June 1996; Daud Ali SH (University of Indonesia law graduate and Dewan Dakwah sympathiser), 14 June 1996; Ibrahim Hosen (head of MUI's *fatwa* commission), 10 June 1996; Hussein Umar (Secretary General of Dewan Dakwah), 2 July and 24 September 1996; Ramlan Marjoned (Dewan Dakwah preacher and BAKOMUBIN leader), 23 August 1996; Hartono Mardjono, 26 September 1996; Misbach Malim (Dewan Dakwah leader), 15 July and 23 August 1996; Badruzzaman Busyairi (Dewan Dakwah leader), 16 July 1996; A.M. Fatwa, 26 June 1996; Muhammad Quraish Shihab (Rector of IAIN Ciputat campus), 16 August 1996; Nuryamin Aini (law scholar at IAIN Ciputat campus), 16 October 1996; HA Chaeruddin (Chairperson and Dean of the Faculty of Islamic Law at IAIN Ciputat campus in an interview-discussion with faculty staff), 27 June 1996; H. Moeslim Aboud Ma'ani (general-secretary at Al-Azhar Pesantren Foundation and Dewan Dakwah activist), 18 October 1996;

Imaduddin, 2 September 1996; Syukron Makmun (former chair of NU's Dakwah Institute), 22 October 1996; Ma'aruf Amin (leader of NU's syuriah council), 25 July 1996; KH Dawam Anwar (leader of NU's syuriah council), 18 July 1996; and Abdurrahman, 5 June 1996.

36. Interviews with Masdar, 29 May 1996; Imaduddin, 15 February 1994; Dawam, 27 January 1994; Lukman, 21 January 1994.
37. Ramage, *Politics in Indonesia*, pp.128–40.
38. Interview with Mahasin, 4 February 1994.
39. Ramage, *Politics in Indonesia*, p.139.
40. Interviews with Mahasin, 4 February 1994; Mukti Ali (former Minister of Religious Affairs and liberal scholar), 4 January 1994.
41. Ramage, *Politics in Indonesia*, p.138.
42. Ramage, *Politics in Indonesia*, pp.122–54; van Dijk, *Rebellion Under The Banner*; Anshari, *The Jakarta Charter 1945*; Nasution, *The Aspiration for Constitutional Government:* Boland, *The Struggle of Islam.*
43. Interviews with Dawam, 27 January 1994; Dewi, 7 February 1994; Mahasin, 4 February 1994; Nurcholish, 12 January 1994; Sri Bintang, 8 February 1994.
44. Military intelligence—especially during the periods of Ali Murtopo's special operations and Benny Murdani's command—commonly invoked threats to national stability from the 'extreme left' (communism) and the 'extreme right (Islam)'. This was done as a means of discrediting rivals within state and society, particularly as it targeted NGO activists and pro-democracy groups during the 1990s. Military intelligence also regularly uncovered 'plots' by Muslims seeking to found an Islamic state, allegedly in an effort to topple the legitimate New Order government. But state officials and military leaders used the label of 'Islamic insurgency' or 'Islamic sedition,' in cases such as the Komando Jihad, the Tanjung Priok riots and Lampung, to discredit localised dissent, land disputes and grassroots protest movements and once branded as such the affected communities risked the full weight of New Order state repression. *Forum Keadilan*, 23 October and 6 November 1995; Burns, 'The Post Priok Trials'; 'The Farmers Of Badega Mountain: They Face Forcible Eviction From Their Land And Process of Poverty' and 'The Torching Of The People's Homes And The Destruction of Their Fields In Subdistrict Pulau Panggung, Lampung Selatan, Sumatra Indonesia', *Laporan Kasus*, Cimerak, Badega, Pulau Panggung, YLBHI dan Jarim: 1/1990; *Lampung Post*, 10 February– 28 February 1989; Jenkins, *Suharto and His Generals.*
45. Interview with Nurcholish, 16 February 1994. Haidar Bagir made a similar comment that ABRI is upset with Habibie over his interference in the military industry, which then affects 'ABRI's perceptions of ICMI'. Interview with Haidar, 11 February 1994.

46. *Suara Karya*, 11 May and 3 June 1992; *Antara*, 1 March 1992; *The Jakarta Post*, 6 May 1992; *Bisnis Indonesia*, 23 May 1992; *Angkatan Bersenjata*, 23 November 1992; *Merdeka*, 30 November 1992; *Media Indonesia*, 8 December 1992; *Panji Masyarakat*, 21–30 July 1994; *Kompas*, 1 February 1994.

47. Ramage, *Politics in Indonesia*, pp.139–54; Lowry, *The Armed Forces*, p.197.

48. Murdani commented on Feisal Tanjung's rise to power as follows: 'When Feisal was Military Chief of General Staff, Habibie was already assembling recruits from the German school. Habibie promised Feisal that he would become Commander of ABRI. Feisal believed Habibie, because he [Feisal] did not have a relationship with Suharto himself. When I was close to Pak Harto, I would have lunch with him 2–3 times a week. During my time, ABRI—we were senior to the bureaucrats. Feisal's generation has come in much later after the bureaucrats have established themselves. Ministers like Habibie are now senior, and ABRI officers (including Feisal) look up to them.' Benny's statement reflected an ongoing rivalry between ABRI and the civilian bureaucracy and, as such, he was expressing his distaste for the fact that senior military officers clearly had become subordinate to Suharto and senior civilian bureaucrats like Habibie. Interview with Murdani, 5 November 1997; Malley, 'The 7th Development Cabinet', p.163.

49. *Merdeka*, 26 August 1993; *Republika*, 26 August 1993.

50. Lowry, *The Armed Forces*, p.65.

51. Rasyid, 'Indonesia: Preparing for Post-Soeharto'.

52. Malley, 'The 7th Development Cabinet', 163.

53. *Editor*, for example, reported that people believed Habibie had promoted the new Kassospol in order to strengthen his own position with the military. *Editor*, 10 February 1994. Hartono was brought in to replace Lt Gen. Hariyoto, a figure critical of Habibie and the ICMI. Rasyid, 'Indonesia: Preparing for Post-Soeharto', p.151; Jenkins, 'Islam's generals', *Sydney Morning Herald*, 10 January 1998; Gaffar, 'Indonesia 1995', p.55; Lowry, *The Armed Forces*, pp.190–9; Ramage, *Politics in Indonesia*, p.113. *Indonesia*: 58 (October 1994), p.181; *Indonesia* 65 (April 1998), pp.181–3; *Merdeka*, 26 August 1993; *Republika*, 26 August 1993.

54. However, Gen. Feisal Tanjung still highlighted ICMI's vital role in 'actualising national defence'. He said that the Muslim association would serve to 'mediate national ideology' and 'reinforce national unity and integrity'. In the end, Feisal's statement did not diverge significantly from ABRI's overriding concern for domestic stability, and ICMI was seen as complementing this role. Hence, caution needs to be exercised in order not to over-state the extent to which differences of opinion among ABRI leaders influenced the military leadership's approach regarding Islam. *Republika Online*, 9 December 1995; *Editor*, 13 February 1993.

55. Interviews with Nurcholish, 16 February 1994; Sasono, 16 February 1994; Dawam, 27 January 1994; Mahasin, 4 February 1994; Imaduddin, 15 February 1994; Dewi, 7 February 1994.
56. Sucipto said that the ICMI members did not make Feisal man-of-the-year without political calculation. Interview with Sucipto, 11 January 1994; *Jawa Pos*, 28 December 1993.
57. *Indonesia* 58 (October 1994), p.84.
58. *Indonesia* 58 (October 1994), p.84; *Editor*, 4 September 1993; *DeTik*, 10 March 1993; Liddle, 'Politics 1992–1993', pp.33–6.
59. Interview with Hartas, 15 February 1994.
60. Interviews with Sasono, 16 February 1994; Hartas, 15 February 1994; *DeTik*, 10 March 1993; *DeTik*, 10 March 1993; *Editor*, 27 March 1993; *Tempo*, 27 March 1993.
61. *DeTik*, 5–13 May 1993; Lowry, *The Armed Forces*, pp.189–90; Liddle, 'Politics 1992–1993', pp.33–9; Rasyid, 'Indonesia: Preparing for Post-Soeharto', p.152; *Indonesia*: 58 (October 1994), p.84.
62. Suharto-backed attempts to wrest control of Golkar from the military leadership had begun in the early 1980s. *Gatra*, 23 December 1995; *Indonesia*: 58 (October 1994); Kingsbury, *The Politics of Indonesia*, pp.121–2; Liddle, 'Politics 1992–1993,' pp.31–4.
63. Rasyid, 'Indonesia: Preparing for Post-Soeharto', p.152; Robison, 'Organising the Transition', p.58.
64. *Indonesia*: 58 (October 1994), p.84 and 65 (April 1998), p.180.
65. See chapter eight.
66. Ramage, *Politics in Indonesia*, p.114.
67. *Republika*, 26 August 1993; *Suara Karya*, 26 August 1993; Rasyid, 'Indonesia: Preparing for Post-Soeharto', p.151; *Editor*, 4 September 1993.
68. *Republika*, 26 August 1993; *Suara Karya*, 26 August 1993.
69. John Land, 'The Indonesian warship fiasco', *Green Left*, 22 June 1994; Harold Crouch, 'Big Ideas or Big Ambition?', *The Independent Monthly*, August 1994, pp.44–5; John Owen-Davies, 'Indonesia Slashes Funds for Controversial Warships Priority', *Reuter World Service*, 8 June 1994; Rajiv Chandra, 'Indonesia: Habibie, in the Eye of the Storm', *Inter Press Third World News Agency (IPS)*, 5 July 1994; *Tempo*, 4–18 June 1994.
70. See above footnote.
71. Although increasing scrutiny by the press of government corruption, particularly of the Bapindo scandal involving Eddy Tansil's Golden Key Group and senior state officials, appears to have contributed significantly to the closures. Robison, 'Organising the Transition', pp.69–70; Crouch, 'Big Ideas or Big Ambition?', pp.44–5; Kingsbury, *The Politics of Indonesia*, p.158.
72. Ramage, *Politics in Indonesia*, pp.96–142.

73. *Republika Online*, 10 December 1995. Chapter five mentioned Suharto's daughter, Siti Rukmana, as one of Habibie's rivals, who joined ICMI at the organisation's national congress. Other new additions to ICMI were the Minister of Industry and Trade, who had replaced Habibie's colleague, Satrio Judono, as trade minister under a new rationalisation of departments, and economic technocrats, who were opposed to Habibie's vision for a high-end technological take-off, Saleh Afif and Sumitro Djoyohadikusumo.
74. *Kompas Online*, 7 August 1997; *Gatra*, 16 August 1997; *Ummat*, 4 May 1998.
75. John McBeth, 'Suharto's Way', *Far Eastern Economic Review*, 26 March 1998, p.20.
76. John McBeth, 'Family and Friends: Suharto unveils an inner-circle cabinet', *Far Eastern Economic Review*, 26 March 1998, p.22.
77. *Tempo*, 27 March 1993; *Editor*, 27 March 1993.
78. *Indonesia*: 65 (April 1998), p.159; Pangaribuan, *The Indonesian State Secretariat*, pp.58–80.
79. Hadiz, 'The Sekneg Experience', p.86.
80. Gaffar, 'Indonesia 1995?', p.56.
81. *Strait Times*, 19 December 1995; *Ummat*, 22 January 1996; *Kompas Online*, 3 January 1996; *Tiras*, 28 December 1995.
82. Matthew Fletcher and Keith Loveard, 'Suharto Strikes Again This Time, Censure for a Minister in Graft Inquiry', *Asiaweek*, (apakabar@access.digex.net), 2 January 1996; *Ummat*, 25 December 1995 and 22 January 1996; *Tempo Online*, 29 August 1997; *Tiras*, 28 December 1995.
83. *Surabaya Post*, 16 December 1995; *Republika Online*, 26 December 1995.
84. *Tiras*, 28 December 1995, p.25; *Gatra*, 6 January 1996; Fletcher and Loveard, 'Suharto Strikes Again'.
85. *Gatra*, 6 January 1996.
86. *Tiras*, 28 December 1995; *Gatra*, 13 January 1996; *Ummat*, 22 January 1996; *Republika Online*, 28 December 1995.
87. *Republika Online*, 2 January 1996; Hadi, 'Resonansi: Jurnalistic Investigatif', *Republika Online*, 23 December 1995; Hardi, 'Resonansi: Introspeksi'; *Republika Online*, 30 December 1995; *Ummat*, 22 January 1996.
88. *Ummat*, 22 January 1996.
89. Interview with Amien, 26 September 1998 in Canberra; *Ummat*, 22 January 1996.
90. The other two were Rahardi Ramelan (replacing Habibie as Minister of Technology) and Giri Suseno Hadi Hardjono—in a cabinet in which all but one minister were Muslim.
91. ICMI interests attributed Murdiono's removal to the minister's embroilment in the corruption controversy. *Indonesia* 65 (April 1998), pp.159–62.

92. See chapter nine for details of the cabinet reshuffle and supporting citations.
93. *Forum Keadilan*, 6 April 1998; Abu Kamil (ICMI Komisariat Eropa), 'ICMI Tolak Susunan Kabinet,' abukamil@yahoo.com, apakabar@ clark.net.

Chapter 8

Mobilisations and Counter-Mobilisations of State and Society

INTRODUCTION

By the mid-to-late-1990s, there were growing signs that society could no longer be constrained by the corporatist framework or by the politics of exclusion. Intra-elite conflict began to move beyond the predictable boundaries of the New Order's exclusionary framework and began to re-connect with grassroots politics. Disgruntled members of the elite (including sidelined ABRI generals, disaffected politicians, and unincorporated interests)[1] and grassroots activists started identifying with, and/or organising, the grievances and causes of some of Indonesia's politically excluded classes against Suharto's regime. In particular, elite-level contest stimulated society-wide conflagrations, and resulted in a series of anti-regime mobilisations of pro-democracy groups and state-orchestrated counter-mobilisations of pro-regime groups against the mounting opposition.

Bianchi explains this phenomenon of escalating conflict between contending interests. He argues that state offers of special treatment and concessions to one associational constituency generates resentment among the neglected groups, which then organises to demand greater participation (inclusion) in the public decision-making processes and power-sharing arrangements. There is a consequent tendency for contending interests to vie for political predominance which, in turn, can trigger a 'chain reaction' of mobilisation and counter-mobilisation of differentially affected group interests. In particular, disaffected members of the elite begin to cooperate with excluded groups in fashioning an alternative pluralist arena with which to counter the power of the state. Developments in Indonesia also confirm some of the general findings of scholarship on regime transitions. Suharto's New Order regime appeared to follow a pre-transition sequence, in which deepening intra-elite rivalry during a crisis of succession sparked escalating levels of societal mobilisation. The mobilisation of opposition elicited a hardline response from the regime, a response which (in the long run) proved unable to stifle dissent.

This chapter looks at how sidelined members of the elite, dissidents, the intelligentsia, and student-led NGOs began to organise against Suharto's regime and the state(Islamic collaboration, as isolated islands of pluralism gradually formed into co-ordinated group actions. The PDI and PPP also showed signs of exiting from their corporatist containment as the party leaderships began to identify with grassroots opposition to Suharto. Meanwhile, societal activation met with a policy reversal in the form of hardline reaction, which brought to an end the period of political openness. As part of this hardline policy, Suharto sought to 'counter-organise' against grassroots opposition by drawing incorporated Muslims and other pro-regime groups to the defence of 'legitimate government order'. However, the institutions of authoritarianism were showing signs of decay, because they no longer were able to contain, channel, neutralise, or co-opt effectively the diversifying demands and challenges of society. It is to the broader trends that the analysis now turns.

ORGANISATION OF INTERESTS AGAINST ICMI, HABIBIE, AND SUHARTO

Initial signs of challenge to the status quo came from disaffected members of the elite who, in the years after ICMI's founding in December 1990, made several efforts to organise against the Suharto–Muslim rapprochement. A cross-section of interests coalesced in the new organisations under the ideological banner of nationalism in opposition to what was perceived as an attempt by Muslim interests in ICMI to build formal links between the Islamic religion and the polity. The range of interests arrayed in the new organisations against ICMI included retired army generals, representatives of minority religions (mainly Christians), unincorporated Muslim leaders, and pro-democracy advocates and human rights activists. They claimed to be making a principled stand in defence of national unity against the danger posed to that unity by the mixing of religion and politics at the level of the state.

The fundamental view that these varied interests promoted was that religious tolerance and therefore national unity depended on all citizens being treated equally by the government. The state ideology of *Pancasila* and the Indonesian constitution were the accepted common platforms and standards that guaranteed religious tolerance, equality of citizenship, and national integrity. The spectre of Muslim interests in ICMI using their 'primordial' or religious affiliation as a basis for channelling their political demands and aspirations was thought to greatly threaten the *Pancasila* and the constitution. The groups couched their arguments variously, but most concluded the Indonesian nation currently was threatened by the virulent rise of sectarianism, with ICMI being the prime example of that threat. In order to ward off the imminent threat of sectarianism, they argued, organisations were needed that incorporated a wide variety of religious, ethnic, political and other groups that were willing to work together in the national cause.[2]

Despite the nationalistic sentiments, sceptics observed that the new coalitions of anti-ICMI forces mainly consisted of retired military figures, pensioned state officials, and defeated politicians. The Habibie–Harmoko team had ousted many of them from their positions in Golkar, the MPR, and the DPR, or they were the losers in recent reshuffles of the armed forces and cabinet. Active armed forces leaders and cabinet ministers who were opposed to Habibie and ICMI also gave their sometimes strong endorsement to the organisations, usually under the auspices of their commitment to the protection of Indonesia's national integrity.[3]

The first attempt to organise against the ICMI phenomenon occurred before the 1993 political reshuffles (discussed in chapter seven) with the establishment of the Democracy Forum in March 1991 under Abdurrahman Wahid's leadership. Christians, secular-nationalists, anti-ICMI Muslim intellectuals and pro-democracy figures joined the Forum. Its members established the Democracy Forum in reaction to what they saw as disturbing signs of religious and ethnic intolerance and sectarianism such as the Monitor Affair in October 1990 and the creation of ICMI in December.[4] Forum members were apprehensive about the government's highly restrictive brand of authoritarianism which, they believed, left people with few channels to mobilise politically and forced them instead to mobilise on the basis of volatile ethnic and religious issues. Suharto's government easily manipulated these issues for its own short-term gains, they claimed, and was therefore complicit in the rise of sectarianism.[5]

By the mid-1990s, a plethora of new organisations had been created both in reaction to ICMI, and encouraged by the period of political openness, although not all with nationalism as their ideological platform. In 1991, two separate intellectuals' associations for Hindus and Buddhists had been formed. In April 1993, Vice-President Try Sutrisno gave his approval to the founding of the Nusantara Intellectuals' Association (ICNU) as a nationalistic vehicle aimed at the bridging of divergent constituencies in order to counter sectarian tendencies. In November, the New Parkindo (the Indonesian Christian Participation)—an apparent resurrection of the old Parkindo (the Indonesian Christian Party)—was established.[6]

It was efforts to build a broad coalition of national forces, beginning in 1994 and gathering momentum in 1995, however, which represented the most concerted attempt both to combat ICMI and to open new political space for dissenting groups. The banning of *Tempo*, *Editor*, and *DeTik* in June 1994 was a major context of new organisational activity of pro-democracy groups,[7] as the Suharto–military rift widened. Suharto tried to curtail the period of political openness and press freedoms, especially because detailed reporting in the three weeklies had exposed a rift between ABRI and Habibie. Elements in ABRI sympathised with the protesters and the military 'publicly distanced itself' from the closures,[8] while ICMI in defence of Habibie had backed the banning of *Tempo*.[9] Attempts to found nationalist organisations largely occurred after the press closures, if not in direct response to them.

Initiatives in 1994 to create a nationalist entity under various acronyms foundered before an agreement was reached to form the Association of Pancasila Development Intellectuals (PCPP) in mid-1995. Retired military officers, the Indonesian Christian University Student Movement (GMKI), the Catholic University Student Association of the Republic of Indonesia (PMKRI), and the Indonesian Nationalist University Student Movement (GMNI), the students' wing of the former Indonesian Nationalist Party (PNI), were prominent supporters of the new PCPP. The Minister of Transmigration, Siswono Yudohusodo (a former GMNI activist), the Environment Minister, Sarwono Kusumaatnadja, the Minister of Defence, Edi Sudrajat, and the Secretary of State, Murdiono—four ardent Habibie and ICMI adversaries— reportedly attended the opening session of PCPP. Edi and Siswono were among the state officials who gave strong endorsements to PCPP, and similar nationalistic organisational initiatives, which they hoped would foster national reconciliation and promote peaceful coexistence of Indonesia's heterogeneous society.[10]

It proved difficult for new organisations to escape the interference and divisive tactics of Suharto's regime. A fissure quickly developed within PCPP between a group led by Muhono (a former military secretary to Suharto) and one led by Sambas Wirakusumah (the elder brother of Edi Sudrajat). Muhono was considered to be too close to Suharto. As well, he had earlier tried to set up the Indonesian Nationalist Intellectuals Association (ICKI) together with Gen. (ret.) Alamsjah Ratu Prawiranegara—a pro-Suharto figure who was one of the figures behind the initiative to found ICMI. However, these two figures also clashed over leadership of ICKI. The ICKI initiative, lacking Suharto's approval, was stillborn, while PCPP came quickly under Suharto's control. Thus, disaffected members of PCPP left to join another more independent vehicle founded in October, the National Brotherhood Reconciliation Foundation (YKPK).[12]

YKPK was soon branded the 'rainbow group' because of its diverse membership. Most of the YKPK's members were retired state officials, bureaucrats, military officers, and politicians who had been sidelined by Habibie's rise to power. For example, the YKPK was led by two disaffected retired generals, Kharis Suhud (also the former chair of the MPR) and Bambang Triantoro (the former armed forces chief-of-staff of social-political affairs under Benny Murdani's command of ABRI). Maj. Gen. (ret.) Sunarso Djajusman (the former ambassador to Malaysia) and Maj. Gen. Samsuddin (a former MP from the armed forces' parliamentary faction) were heads of the YKPK's executive board. There were figures like Jacob Tobing, Marzuki Darusman, and Anton Prijatno, who had served in Golkar under Gen. (ret.) Wahono's chairmanship before Habibie ousted his team. Since their removal, Wahono and his supporters had become some of the government's most outspoken critics.

A group of NU members close to Abdurrahman Wahid, such as its former Secretary General Gaffar Rahman and the former Secretary General of PPP, Matori Abdul Djalil, joined YKPK. Matori helped found the YKPK after his failed bid to become the new chairman of PPP at the party's 1994 national congress, having been defeated by the government-backed candidate, Ismail Hasan Metareum. Matori and his supporters were then purged from PPP, reportedly for their membership of YKPK. Indonesia's media carried reports of a so-called 'de-Wahono-isation' of Golkar and 'di-YKPK-isation' of PPP.[13]

One of the main objectives of the 'rainbow group' was to prevent Habibie from becoming Indonesia's next vice-president in 1998. Gen. Edi Sudrajat was one of the military top brass who had, in 1993, supported Try Sutrisno's nomination for vice-president against Suharto's choice of Habibie, and had since decided to back those forces allied with the rainbow group. As Minister of Defence, Edi had opposed openly Habibie over the latter's appropriation of defence contracts. The former Minister of Environment and YKPK leader, Sarwono, had strongly criticised the sixth development cabinet of 1993, calling it unco-ordinated and of low-calibre, and had been castigated by Suharto for his criticism. Gen. (ret.) Harsudiono Hartas who, together with his mentor Gen. (ret.) Benny Murdani, had been sidelined after the appointment of the new cabinet in 1993, also apparently backed YKPK. Thus, the sharp rivalry in the old cabinet had subsequently spilled over into support for organisations like YKPK, as the politically marginal forces prepared to retaliate against Habibie in the approaching presidential election of 1998.[14]

It was hoped that the mushrooming organisations would provide the marginal figures with political vehicles with which they could gain access to power and have better bargaining positions vis-à-vis Habibie and ICMI in an anticipated post-Suharto era. People of all political shades speculated that the 1998 election would bring about a period of transition triggered by presidential succession. The organisations were also a response to the inability of the established political system to channel people's aspirations. As such, there was a strong tendency of politicians to hark back to a pre-Suharto period by trying to resurrect old political affiliations of the 1950s as a means of re-channelling people's aspirations. We have already mentioned the New Parkindo. On 26 October, a New PNI was created under the leadership of Nyonya Supeni, a former PNI leader and ambassador under President Sukarno. Following this, a New Masyumi was established but few old Masyumi sympathisers were willing to identify with the party, partly out of fear of a military reprisal, but also because they had made accommodations with Suharto through ICMI.[15]

An independent elections watch-dog (Komite Independent Pemantau Pemilu, KIPP) was also set up on 15 March 1996 to monitor the approaching general election and make sure that no ballot-box or other election irregularities occurred. To the government's consternation, the formation of KIPP spawned a number of other initiatives to establish independent election monitoring bodies in April. In March, the former Minister of Internal Affairs, Gen. (ret.) Rudini, made a public appeal to Suharto's regime not to suppress new organisations like PCPP, YKPK, the New PNI, and the KIPP. He insisted that these organisations reflected a widespread desire of the people to participate in the life of the nation. In addition to these organisations, quasi-political parties, including the People's

Democratic Party (PRD), and the Indonesian Democratic Union Party (PUDI) were founded. The decision to found new quasi-parties was encouraged, no doubt, by the regime's lifting of restrictions on freedom of assembly (December 1995) and its introduction, in January 1996, of regulations enabling people to hold social, cultural and political gatherings without official permits.[16] Overall, the proliferating 'rainbow' groups constituted initiatives by opponents of the regime to open up democratic space and establish alternative channels of interest representation and political participation outside the restrictive corporatist structure.

Although PRD was viewed as a potentially significant threat to Suharto's regime because of its grassroots following (discussed below), the other 'rainbow' organisations did not constitute a direct threat to power arrangements. As elite-centred initiatives with no real grassroots membership, these organisations were limited in their ability to represent people's unfulfilled and rising expectations. They were, at the end of the day, set up as vehicles with which to promote the ambitions and interests of one set of (sidelined) elite figures, who wanted to gain inclusion in the power structure, against another set of elite interests that were more closely allied to the state.

Having said this, the power holders still perceived the 'rainbow' organisations as a threat because they operated outside of the authorised political rules, which prohibited the formation of new political organisations. Moreover, the highly paternalistic state normally regarded open dissent as an intolerable act of insubordination or subversion. Although Suharto tolerated a certain level of dissent in order, among other things, to allow people to let off steam, he was not accustomed to the extent of criticism that leaders of the new organisations directed against the New Order establishment. An example of this criticism was, at a two-day national meeting of YKPK in Surabaya (8–9 January 1996), when speakers highlighted the Suharto government's failure to provide democratic, accountable and transparent government that would permit people's genuine participation. Included among the dignitaries present at the national meeting opened by Wahono, were Marzuki Darusman of the National Human Rights Commission, the NU Chairman Abdurrahman Wahid and several prominent former PPP and Golkar leaders. The 'de-Wahono-isation' and the 'de-YKPK-isation' of the parties had hurt a number of these figures.[17]

The Suharto government, no doubt, also was worried about the prospect of a domino effect should the new organisations provide an example for others to follow. Despite the government's apprehensions, it was not until the 'rainbow' organisations lent their support to broader dissent in society coalescing round a faction of PDI led by the popularly-elected Chairperson Megawati Sukarnoputri, that Suharto's circle of power holders decided to take decisive action against them.

GROWING DISSENT OF THE 'RAINBOW' OPPOSITION AND STATE RETALIATION

This section of the chapter shifts to an analysis of grassroots agitation, much of it led by student, NGO and pro-democracy leaders seeking to harness popular dissent. It considers how the newly established quasi-parties and rainbow groups joined coalition-building efforts, centred round Megawati Sukarnoputri's PDI faction, against the political status quo. The analysis also deals with the retaliation by Suharto's regime, as it engaged state instruments of coercion and repression and its propaganda machine in a systematic campaign to eradicate opposition. Suharto's regime resorted to policies of more direct coercion once existing political arrangements had clearly failed to ensure the continued exclusion of autonomously organised interests that could mobilise mass society. In addition, Suharto's circle sought to mobilise pro-government forces, including incorporated Muslim interests, against the opposition. Finally, this section considers how societal interests retaliated against harsh state repression, reprisals and manipulations, as these interests sought to create new space for their own—long denied—participation in the political life of the nation.

Increasing challenges to, and confrontation with, the established order came from elements both within and outside of the state's corporatist structure. In particular, the PDI faction led by Megawati became a rallying point for mass dissent and a catalyst for coalition building against Suharto's regime. This was despite the fact that PDI, until then, had been a largely subordinate and compliant part of the corporatised party system. Megawati was the first popularly elected party leader since the beginning of the New Order and she came to represent a symbol of opposition. Some scholars argue that disgruntled segments of ABRI backed Megawati's nomination to PDI leader (December 1993) in possible rebuke to Suharto for reducing the military's political role in Golkar and as a counter to Habibie and Muslim political interests.[18] Megawati's election was an historic defeat for Suharto, as it was the first time that heavy state interventions had failed to impose a pro-regime leader on a political organisation. Subsequently, a diverse array of pro-democracy groups, new 'rainbow' organisations, NGO activists, disaffected government opponents, and millions of supporters rallied to her political banner in reaction to efforts by Suharto's regime to derail her from leadership of the party.[19]

Megawati was perceived as a threat to the political status quo largely because Suharto's regime did not tolerate any form of organised opposition to its rule, and because it constituted a challenge mounted from within the authorised political arrangements. It appeared as if PDI might break loose from its corporatist containment, as it became a crucial rallying point for the forces of opposition. The attraction of grassroots movements to Megawati's banner was diametrically opposed to the established party system, which sought to prevent the autonomous mobilisation of social-political forces and the institutionalisation of opposition. Megawati was highly critical of the government's record of corruption and cronyism, and had her name put forward as a presidential candidate. Suharto was unwilling to tolerate anything less than his own unanimous endorsement as Indonesia's next president at the MPR session of 1998, and Megawati threatened his chances of being elected unopposed. Suharto was also backing his daughter Siti Rukmana's campaign to bring about a Golkar victory in the PDI stronghold of East Java, which necessitated the defeat of the new chairwoman. Megawati's popularity as the eldest daughter of late President Sukarno—deposed by Suharto—her image as an incorruptible democrat and motherly figure, and her symbolisation of Sukarno's comeback against Suharto's corrupt and arbitrary regime, attracted millions of new followers to PDI.[20]

Suharto's battle against Megawati began in earnest after her assumption of the PDI leadership since 1993. Since then, constant attempts were instigated by officers loyal to Suharto to unseat Megawati, including the setting up of government-backed rival boards of PDI. For instance, Gen. Hartono (then the army chief-of-staff) supported a rival board led by Yusuf Merukh against the PDI chief. At the provincial level, similar splits also were created in 1994 as the government was behind the setting up of rival boards. The manipulations were just one recent example of a common practice of Suharto's circle to interfere in the selection of party leaders, with the aim of cultivating rival factions in order to weaken the internal cohesion of parties. It was a classic example of Suharto's exclusionary politics and tactical use of divide-and-rule based on fragmenting and neutralising opposition and preventing grassroots mobilisation.

In 1996, the situation heated up considerably as the Commander-in-Chief of the Armed Forces, Feisal Tanjung, the Chief-of-Staff of Social-Political Affairs, Lt Gen. Syarwan Hamid, and the Minister of Internal Affairs, Lt Gen. (ret.) Yogie S. Memet, were behind efforts to establish a rival PDI congress in Medan. They recruited a former Chairperson of PDI, Soerjadi, and the leader of PDI's parliamentary faction, Fatimah Achmad, to lead the campaign against Megawati. In East Java, the provincial government refused to allow Megawati to attend a PDI meeting to be held in January. The government-backed faction engaged in a number of meetings and actions to support Fatimah's and Soerjadi's leadership of PDI.[22]

The state-sponsored measures to cow and drive into retreat opponents met with initial stiff resistance. Indonesia's 'floating mass' of political and economic under classes retaliated against their political exclusion as they sought re-entry into politics, not through existing channels, but through acts of civil and mass protest. In June, hundreds of thousands of Megawati supporters demonstrated against the planned Medan congress in cities and towns throughout Indonesia.[23] On 20 June, security forces violently broke up about 12,000 pro-Megawati and pro-democracy supporters as they were conducting a peaceful long-march to the national monument in central Jakarta. Megawati rejected the results of the Medan congress, held between 20–23 June, which elected Soerjadi as the new party leader. Megawati supporters defiantly occupied the PDI headquarters in Jakarta, holding a series of 'mimbar bebas' (free speech forums), at which they publicly aired their views and condemnation of Suharto's rule. Feisal Tanjung declared that the free speech forums had to be halted, as they constituted a 'plot' (*makar*) to destroy or topple the legitimate government.[24]

By mid-1996, therefore, Megawati's PDI began to represent the re-entry of the masses into politics after thirty years of de-politicisation, thereby constituting a direct challenge to the Suharto circle's ruling formula that relied on a heavily circumscribed political system. At this point, newly established organisations and hitherto unorganised, illegal and unrepresented social and political forces began to gravitate to PDI, forming a loose pro-Mega alliance. The Council of Indonesian People (MARI), founded in June, became an umbrella organisation in support of Megawati's PDI. MARI included among its affiliate members the New Masyumi, the new PNI, the unrecognised political parties PRD and PUDI, the Indonesian Legal Aid Institute (YLBHI), the independent trade union (SBSI), the Alliance of Independent Journalists (AJI), NGOs, and Muslim and Christian students' groups. Suharto's circle regarded this new 'rainbow coalition' as an intolerable threat to the regime's survival interests.[25]

YKPK leaders gave their support to the pro-Megawati opposition forces. They issued a petition of concern on 1 July, entitled 'Return to the Nation's Noble Ideals', about the direction of Indonesian politics. The petition, signed by leaders of YKPK, the NU chairman, and leaders of Muslim, Catholic, and nationalist university students' organisations (PMII, HMI, PMKRI and GMNI), was widely seen as criticising the government's interference in PDI's internal affairs.[26]

One of the rainbow coalition's members, the People's Democratic Party (PRD), established under a different name in 1994, but declared a party in April 1996, was a worry to Suharto's coalition because it successfully organised its activities at the grassroots. Any hint of organised grassroots activity threatened the state's exclusionary political arrangements designated by the 'floating mass' policy. PRD had spread its activities to struggles on behalf of industrial workers, and worked together with student activists and artists on its various social and political agendas. Its members were radical and leftwing student and labour activists who, among their demands, regularly called for a lifting of restrictive political laws, a higher minimum wage, a new president and new parties, and the scrapping of the armed force's *dwi-fungsi* doctrine. PRD leaders expressed much of their political protest in Marxist language, which was anathema to the anti-communist military establishment.[27]

By 1996, a new phenomenon had clearly entered New Order politics as PRD, together with its student wing (Solidarity of Indonesian University Students for Democracy, SMID), and its affiliate organisation, PPBI (Indonesian Centre for Labour Struggle), organised several large-scale workers' strikes and student demonstrations, which carried political demands against the government. Gradually students, workers, NGO activists and other 'pro-democracy' forces came to identify with each other's grievances and causes and to build anti-government alliances. SMID launched several mass actions in Surabaya, Yogyakarta, Jakarta, Medan, Lampung and Menadao on 14 May.

Pro-democracy activists organised one of the largest strikes on 23 May. An estimated ten thousand workers from eleven factories in Tanjungsari, East Java demonstrated, during which at least one factory was damaged, and security police arrested the suspected organisers.[28] Coinciding with this, fifteen university students from SMID held a three-day hunger strike (20–23 May) on the grounds of East Java's provincial parliament in Surabaya. They protested the military's brutal crackdown on demonstrators at a university campus in Ujung Pandang, South Sulawesi, which had left several students dead.[29]

The mass protests of 1996 indicated a change in public mood. A growing number of people no longer were prepared to tolerate, as a foregone conclusion, that Golkar would dominate general elections and that the elections offered no prospect of altering power configurations. Many had grown tired of the reality that the elections and parties served the main purpose of endorsing President Suharto's unopposed dominance of the political system. More than on any previous occasion during the New Order period, Indonesians were beginning to agitate against restrictive political rules and coercive measures that kept them cordoned off from political participation. Hence, PRD members, student activists, and disaffected members of the New Order elite alike called for the revocation of restrictive political laws, a reduction of presidential power, the elimination of corruption and the removal of the military from its privileged position in the nation's political institutions. This represented a new and, to Suharto, threatening democracy discourse, which rejected the ideological rationales and structures of authoritarianism.

Policy Reversal: Suharto Retaliates

In retrospect, the period of political openness, which Suharto had initially tried to stem in June 1994 with the press closures, had stimulated a substantial level of societal activation in the following years. By 1996, however, the level and diversification of opposition activity became intolerable to Suharto's regime and, accordingly, began to elicit more stringent responses. One of the means by which Suharto responded to Megawati supporters and pro-democracy activists was to instigate a sophisticated public opinion-building campaign aimed at stigmatising and discrediting the opposition forces in preparation for a planned harsh crackdown. ABRI hardliners who were loyal to Suharto branded dissenters as enemies of the state who were seeking to overthrow Suharto's government. They reintroduced ABRI's discourse on vigilance ('kewaspadaan'), and claimed that the PRD, pro-Megawati groups, student agitators, labour strikers and government opponents were agents of instability who were adopting organisational methods and ideology reminiscent of the Indonesian Communist Party (PKI).[30]

Among the generals acting under Suharto's instructions, who stigmatised opponents with the PKI label, were the Commander of ABRI, Feisal Tanjung, the Army Chief of Staff, Hartono, and the ABRI Chief of Staff of Social and Political Affairs, Syarwan Hamid. There was the ABRI Chief of Staff for

General Affairs, Suyono, the former Governor of the National Resilience Institute (Lemhanas) and Habibie's advisor, Sayidiman Suryohadiprojo and the three regional commanders of East, West and Central Java.[31] Feisal, Hartono, and Syarwan also were responsible for rallying the interests of incorporated Muslims behind the state's anti-Megawati campaign.

The East Java commander, Lt Gen. Imam Utomo, offered a typical example of the military's anti-PRD campaign, which was implemented throughout the country. In early July, he ordered his troops to break-up student and workers' demonstrations. He claimed that the protest actions were not genuine and that organisations like PRD wished to bring about a communist-type resurgent socialist movement. On 9 July, the day of a mass demonstration, he held a press conference, with East Java's Chief Prosecutor, the Vice-Chief of Police, and other military officers at his side, at which he condemned the PRD actions.[32] Finally, on 26 July (one day before a military crackdown on the PDI headquarters), Suharto announced that there were 'bald devils riding on the back of PDI'.[33] A week later, he convened a full cabinet meeting and made it clear who the 'bald devils' were, by identifying PRD as the prime culprit responsible for masterminding the Jakarta riots on 27 July.[34]

Jun Honna identifies how ABRI leaders deployed the *kewaspadaan* ideology in order to protect ABRI's 'role perception' and corporate interests— exemplified by its *dwi-fungsi* doctrine—against mounting popular criticism and to serve Suharto's political objective of discrediting the pro-democracy movement, and its liberal and left-wing ideas, with a 'counter-democracy' discourse. Honna writes that *kewaspadaan*, 'which was first intended to standardise the military's threat perception regarding national stability was transformed into ABRI's security-intelligence project aiming to discipline political ideas in society'.[35] The military had returned to its reliance on identifying shared threats to national aspirations, in order to justify a more active policy of discrediting and eliminating opponents.

The Crackdown

The full extent of the state's repression was engaged to remove the opposition forces coalescing around Megawati's PDI. In a blatant show of force, supporters of the government-installed PDI leader, Soerjadi, and police mobile brigade (Brimob)[36] stormed the PDI headquarters on 27 July, brutally ousting Megawati stalwarts defiantly occupying the premises. The military clearly backed the operation and there were indications that they recruited thugs dressed as Soerjadi supporters for the attack against the PDI headquarters.[37] Violence spilled out onto the streets of Jakarta in two days of destructive rampage, as Megawati supporters and thousands of Jakarta's urban classes clashed with anti-riot military units.[38]

It was in the aftermath of the riots, however, that Suharto's coalition launched its most systematic witch-hunt against the opposition forces, driving them over the next few months into temporary retreat.[39] State security forces conducted sweeping investigations and extra-judicial arrests of thousands of PRD radicals, MARI activists, and PDI leaders. The Attorney General conducted an investigation into Megawati's alleged involvement in the riots. Investigated were figures like Ridwan Saidi (chair of the New Masyumi), Nyonya Supeni (chair of the new PNI), Goenawan Mohammad (the chief editor of the banned *Tempo* magazine and KIPP member), and Berar Fathia (of MARI). Retired generals, such as Rudini, Wahono, and Bambang Triantoro (leader of YKPK)—who appeared to support the rainbow coalition and publicly criticised Suharto—reportedly were investigated. The PRD leader, Budiman Sudjatmiko, and three other party leaders who had gone into hiding were arrested in late September and placed on charges of subversion. The leader of the independent workers' union SBSI, Muchtar Pakpahan, a man already facing jail terms for his alleged involvement in a worker's demonstration in Medan in 1994, was arrested on subversion charges. The 'paranormal' and vocal anti-government critic, Permadi Satrio Wiwoho, was held for questioning after the riot.[40] The fact that PDI became a major source of opposition to the regime demonstrated the recent failure of the corporatised party arrangements to contain and neutralise political dissent. The systematic use of state coercion against the opposition was itself a clear indication of the failure of corporatism to maintain peaceful state–society interest relations.

STATE ORCHESTRATED COUNTER-DEMONSTRATIONS

The argument can be made that, faced with the societal challenges, Suharto abandoned the strategy of corporatist containment and came to rely on direct repression of dissent. He began to use corporatist organisations for purposes that were at variance with the original purposes of establishing and maintaining a de-politicised environment. That is, he contributed to a politicisation of state–society relations by mobilising state-backed Muslim groups against the opposition. He did this as part of a propaganda campaign, both before and after the crackdown, with his loyalist generals organising pro-government militant youth groups, paid ruffians and Muslim organisations into a series of counter-demonstrations against the 'rainbow' alliance. The organisation of counter-demonstrations serves the purpose giving the appearance of furnishing the government with the legitimacy or credibility of popular support, as pro-regime forces can be mobilised behind various causes against detractors.

The period after the July riot provided the setting for large-scale and sustained government-arranged oaths of loyalty, as Suharto's circle mobilised Muslims and other groups in wholesale condemnation of PRD and forces coalescing round Megawati's PDI. In particular, Suharto's circle drew on the support of corporatised Muslim organisations like MUI, ICMI, the Pondok Pesantren Co-operation Body (BKSPP), BAKOMUBIN, mosque organisations—and pro-regime Muslim leaders from the NU, the Muhammadiyah, and the Dewan Dakwah—to denounce PRD and the 'rainbow' alliance. The orchestration of counter-demonstrations involved the deployment of incorporated Muslim interests as an instrument of the state's policy of exclusion by seeking to isolate and discredit dissent. In particular, at a time of growing middle-class hostility to Suharto, the bringing of a substantial portion of the Muslim middle classes behind the regime could hope to divide and dissipate anti-regime energies. The regime could combat the opposition's value-orientation of democracy and human rights with an anti-democratic discourse, which gave priority to political legitimacy and stability of the established order.

There was an indication that Suharto's circle had anticipated the need for Muslim approval of its pre-planned attack against Megawati's supporters at the PDI headquarters. For instance, Gen. Hartono met with Toto Tasmara and other BAKOMUBIN leaders at Tommy Suharto's corporate headquarters (the PT Humpus building) a few days before the 27 July incident. Hartono advised the organisation's leaders that shortly a movement, 'PDI anarchy', would take place and result in destruction that would hinder national development. He said that there needed to be a moral invitation in order that the nation would behave in accordance with the Islamic culture of harmony.[41] This meeting demonstrates that ABRI was gauging Muslim responses and seeking community support for its attack on the PDI headquarters. It was also a grand manipulation of the idea of harmony, encouraging Muslim leaders to co-operate with ABRI against social 'disorder', in this case against Suharto's adversaries associated with Megawati's PDI faction.

After the riot, on 28 July leaders of BAKOMUBIN organised Muslim leaders to appear at the DPR. They spoke before the Golkar, ABRI, and PPP factions at the DPR calling for introspection and denouncing the PDI riots, pro-democracy groups and government critics. In an interview, Toto explained that ABRI leaders felt they had the support of Muslim leaders. The BAKOMUBIN hung posters in the DPR's lobby declaring 'Vigilance against Neo-Communists using the mask of Human Rights and Democracy, False Fighters For Democracy; Beware of Anarchism, Communism, Secularism, Vandalism'.[42]

On the 29th, MUI grabbed the initiative from BAKOMUBIN by gathering Muslim leaders at the national monument in central Jakarta. The collaborating Muslim leaders issued a joint statement supporting the armed force's version of events surrounding the PDI riots. They readily parroted the language of the armed force of threats from communist party elements in PDI, and treacherous 'formless organisation' and third party activities threatening national stability.[43] Members of ICMI's intelligentsia, and other Muslim leaders, contributed to the anti-opposition rhetoric. For example, the Chairman of Muhammadiyah (and Head of ICMI's council of experts), Amien Rais, alluded to the fact that 'people power', as he called it, was unacceptable to Indonesia's cultural traditions and that Muhammadiyah's masses could be brought in to counteract the anti-regime forces. He likened the 27 July riots to the 'trauma of communism'.[44] Another prominent Muhammadiyah and ICMI leader, Lukman Harun, announced that the 'PKI is our country's and nation's enemy, and the Muslim community has a huge responsibility [to counter the enemy]. It is appropriate that the Muslim community respond harshly to the [27 July] incident.'[45] The chairman of NU's

175

Ansor Youth insisted that his supporters were 'ready to help ABRI to eliminate the new communist movement'.[46] A few Muslim leaders supported the government's decision to charge PRD and pro-democracy activists under the state's harsh anti-subversion laws.[47]

The right-wing Dewan Dakwah, having itself fostered warm relations with 'Muslim' generals and with Habibie's ICMI, was particularly vociferous in denouncing a host of pro-democracy, labour and farmers' rights groups. Dewan Dakwah's various media denounced the MARI, PRD, 'paranormals' (Permadi), and retired officers critical of the regime (an allusion to the YKPK). Responding to the 1 July statement of concern, one article referred to the YKPK leaders and the NU chairman as politically sidelined interests who espoused democratic ideals but were really seeking to undermine Islam and topple the legitimate government. Relying on its propensity for conspiracy theory, the Dewan Dakwah linked to the riots a variety of 'PKI penetrated' groups, including 'socialists, Christians/Jews, upholders of human rights, and NGO western agents'.[48] The Dewan Dakwah's strong reaction against the 'rainbow coalition' was partly provoked by the burning by rioters of the Al-Irsyad's (a small radical Islamic organisation) headquarters just down the street from the council's own central office.[49] However, the council was probably most inspired by its need to demonstrate its loyalty to the armed forces as it joined regime-arranged condemnations of the pro-democracy forces.

Over the next few months, whilst the security apparatus conducted sweeping arrests of opponents, the government sponsored similar mass ritual oaths in which pro-government leaders continued to condemn PRD, MARI and pro-Mega PDI activists and liken them to communist party agitators of a by-gone era.[50] These efforts culminated on 29 September–1 October, with a state-sponsored mass rally, a five-kilometre parade, and an exhibition of photos and documents in Jakarta. MUI and ICMI had leading roles in organising the two-day event, which was held to commemorate Pancasila Day and to re-live the so-called 'tragic events' of the 'Communist Party coup' of 1965. The Secretary of MUI and ICMI Vice-Secretary, Jimly Asshidiqie, chaired the implementation council for the event. The NU's Ansor Youth played an organising role on the council. This event was arranged to coincide with a mass gathering of Muslim students from Tebuireng Pesantren held at Blitar, East Java. Government dignitaries and military and police chiefs were in force at all of the mass gatherings, which were brought together at the behest of military leaders. Government officials and rally organisers insisted, however, that the mass rallies were spontaneous demonstrations of popular support for the government against its 'enemies'.[51]

The degree to which pro-government Muslim leaders adopted ABRI's language of vigilance in identifying 'the common enemy' again indicates the success of hardline military leaders to inculcate parts of society with its security-intelligence mentality. The fact that corporatist institutions contained program outlines which reflected this mentality, and that the main emphasis of these organisations was on their *pembinaan* (guidance) function, probably goes some way to explaining how ABRI had so successfully inculcated its ideas of national threat. Admittedly, the PKI was a shared historical threat deeply imbedded in the psyche of ABRI officers and Muslim leaders alike. Nonetheless, as will be discussed below, the 'rainbow' alliance presented a real threat to the political ambitions of incorporated Muslim interests.

The support of these collaborating Muslims for Suharto's regime was informed by the fear of placing at risk closer relations between Islam and the state, which had gradually been fostered since the late 1980s. This 'honeymoon' period of state–Islamic relations since the creation of ICMI led to the belief and hope that if Muslims patiently stood in the wings, they would eventually inherit a significant share of political influence and power.[52] Megawati's rising star, and the coalition of anti-ICMI forces, threatened to upset this aspiration and, therefore, it was in the interest of incorporated Muslim groups to side with Suharto's regime and have PDI removed from the political contest. In line with this thinking, an article by Media Dakwah affirmed that PPP could become an Islamic party to once again prevent a resurgence of nationalism and communism. The Chairman of Dewan Dakwah, Anwar Harjono, expressed the political aspiration that PPP could work in partnership with Golkar, and could position itself as the people's representative to form the next government.[53] Anwar's political vision was one that excluded PDI from future power configurations.

Collaborating Muslim interests expressed the anti-'rainbow' rhetoric. Not all Muslim leaders were willing to join Suharto's regime in its condemnation of Megawati's forces. A sworn rival of ICMI, Abdurrahman Wahid, counselled his constituency not to follow suit with other Islamic organisations and to refrain from giving a ritual oath of loyalty to Suharto's government.[54]

Assessment

Suharto's crackdown had driven the opposition into retreat and left it divided and in disarray, yet its anti-PRD rhetoric and propaganda campaigns appeared to lack credibility among broad sections of society, as well as among segments of the state elite. Fealy notes that the post-27 July events 'seriously undermined confidence in the regime's competence and harmed the prospects for a smooth transition to a post-Suharto era'.[55] Megawati's forced ouster caused an immense loss of legitimacy for Suharto's rule and opened the way for future and even more serious challenges to the survival chances of the Suharto regime.[56]

Hitherto, PDI had been an integral component of the New Order's corporatised party system based, among other things, on heavily circumscribed politics in which a loyal opposition was not tolerated. Megawati's faction of PDI threatened the ruling formula, as opposition forces rallying to her banner mounted a challenge to the political status quo. Chapter six considered the idea that unequal access to political resources had caused autonomous interests associated with NU to compete for political predominance with state-sponsored Islam. This chapter has demonstrated the actual pitting of corporatist (Muslim and Golkar-affiliate) groups against pro-democracy forces (including disaffected NU interests, sidelined ABRI officers, the minority Christian community, student, NGO and labour activists). Suharto, in fact, regularly created divisions across the political spectrum, between different constituencies, parties and organisations and fostered splits within the different organisations, including Golkar, PDI and PPP. In his attack on Megawati's faction, his regime had mobilised incorporated Muslim groups against another part of its corporatist system (PDI). It had done this specifically because PDI under Megawati's leadership threatened to move beyond the established rules of the game by seeking to represent grassroots interests. However, in its exuberance to remove Megawati as a political force, Suharto's coalition had unintentionally emasculated PDI to the point of electoral impotency. The corporatist design of two parties plus Golkar was reduced thereby to a direct pre-election race between Golkar and PPP.[57]

ELECTION FEVER: PPP ASSUMES THE MANTLE OF OPPOSITION

If Suharto had sought to remove dissenters in order to facilitate his unopposed re-election at the 1998 MPR, the government's reliance on repression coupled with Golkar's no-holds-barred campaign strategy, may have had some other unintended repercussions for the power holders. One such repercussion was the steady increase in conflict between the government's election machine Golkar and the Islamic-oriented PPP, which was well evident by early 1996. In short, the state's continued exclusion and repression of opposition, instead of containing political forces within predictable and acceptable boundaries, unleashed further mass resistance. That is, the other corporatised party, PPP, assumed the mantle from the decimated PDI, of opposition party against Suharto. State deployment of incorporated Muslim interests against the 'rainbow' opposition had not prevented Islam, itself, from becoming a major banner of social-political protest. The chapter, therefore, next considers the rising conflict between PPP and Golkar within the context of election contests.

The provinces of East, West and Central Java, which contained most of Indonesia's voting-age population (69.7 million or 56 per cent of voters from a registered 124 million voters by one count),[58] were of strategic importance to Golkar's campaign. Suharto's daughter Siti Hardiyanti Rukmana, in her capacity as head of Golkar's central committee, was placed in charge of Golkar's crucial campaigns in East and Central Java. The Army Chief of Staff, Gen. Hartono, accompanied Siti on her regular rounds of rural *pesantren* in the two provinces to drum up support for Golkar. He caused a controversy when, on 13 March 1996, he announced before a gathering of Golkar supporters in Central Java that members of the armed forces were Golkar cadres. Wearing a grey Safari suit and yellow Golkar jacket, he stood beside Siti and declared that, 'as a Golkar cadre', he 'took his orders from the head of the Central Committee'.[59] The next day, at Sabilil Muttaqin Pesantren in Magetan, East Java, he repeated his comments. In another publicity stunt, Siti Rukmana gave her strong endorsement to Gen. Hartono, the new Minister of Information, when he joined ICMI's and MUI's senior advisory boards. This manoeuvre was undoubtedly aimed at consolidating the support of Muslims behind Golkar, at a time when some of that support may have been in doubt.[60]

Hartono's statements outraged leaders of PPP and PDI, and the ABRI leadership, which was supposed to maintain a non-partisan stance toward the three parties, sought to distance itself from his comments. Nonetheless, his strident assertions highlighted the intensity of competition that was mounting in the pre-campaign months in which Golkar, with ABRI's backing, was launching an early and aggressive foray into Muslim and PDI constituencies. In January 1996, Harmoko and Siti Rukmana appeared before tens of thousands of Golkar supporters at Sri Wedari Stadium in Solo, Central Java. In a symbolic gesture, Harmoko embraced a *becak* driver and promised to improve the working hours for labourers.[61] In doing so, Harmoko was attempting to appeal to the grassroots in an effort to counter the popular appeal of Megawati's PDI, in a like manner that Golkar sought to win the traditional Muslim vote from PPP.

As mentioned in chapter six, Suharto pulled off a major coup by winning over the NU Chairman, Abdurrahman Wahid's support to Golkar's campaign, who then facilitated Siti Rukmana's visits to rural *pesantrens* to gain access to NU's Muslim masses. In doing so, the government had shrewdly eliminated the possibility of Abdurrahman bringing his NU constituency firmly behind Megawati's PDI, as he had earlier intimated. With Abdurrahman's support, the government also could continue to exploit divisions within Islam, as the NU chairman was a rival of PPP's Chairman, Metareum, and was staunchly opposed to the rise of modernist Islam in ICMI.[62] This was at a time that PPP's chairman had become increasingly critical of the government's aggressive election campaigning, and Abdurrahman's apparent support for Golkar could bring a significant portion of NU's masses behind Golkar and act as an effective foil to PPP recalcitrance. Moreover, the support of NU's constituency and of incorporated Muslim (mainly) modernists behind Golkar, could significantly reduce what limited influence PDI and PPP had in determining the outcome of the election campaign.

Golkar's early campaign-related activities stimulated reactions and counter-activities from PPP and PDI, as neither party wished to be totally sidelined by the government's powerful electioneering machine. In particular, PPP leaders complained about government-Golkar interference and intimidation aimed at driving their party supporters into retreat. For example, the Islamic magazine, Panji Masyarakat, aired opinions that sympathised with the plight of Megawati's PDI faction and criticised Suharto's government for interfering with the internal affairs of both PDI and PPP.[63]

The usually cautious Chairman of PPP, Ismail Hasan Metareum, a figure acceptable to the government, who generally endorsed major government decisions, began on this occasion to level caustic criticism against Golkar. He expressed his upset over the defection of around 3,000 PPP supporters who declared their allegiance to Golkar at a meeting in Sukabumi, West Java on

11 March. Ismail accused Golkar of practising 'political thuggery' and claimed it had rallied together disaffected PPP leaders and their supporters, bringing them to the gathering by bus at which PPP leaders were given Golkar jackets and party cards. On another occasion, Ismail called on the government to change Indonesia's election laws of 1985 so that they would be more open, honest and fair to all three parties. The Minister of Internal Affairs responded to some of Ismail's criticisms by insisting that PPP's chairman was ill and, by implication, not fully in charge of his mental faculties, when he made his comments.[65]

The PPP chairman issued his complaints in response to what PPP leaders considered to be Golkar's unfair practices, election fraud and intimidation at the 1992 general elections and in anticipation of future unfair practices, which seriously hurt PPP's election chances, they claimed. Leaders of five PPP branches declared that if Golkar's unfair practices were repeated in 1997, they would stage a walkout of parliament in rejection of the election results.[66] Reports of Golkar's unfair practices soon entered the media in 1996. For example, in January, as PPP commemorated its anniversary, the party's flags and banners were banned in Kendal, Sragen and Batang regencies, East Java. Written on the banners were messages such as 'It Is Not a Matter of Win-Lose, the General Election Must be Honest and Fair', 'The Matter Is to Uphold Justice', and 'PPP Must Always Be with the Muslims'.[67] The prohibition may have been reasonable had Golkar not planned to hoist its own party flags and banners. In June, for instance, leaders of the PPP-affiliated Development Youth Organisation in Surakarta, Central Java, lodged a complaint against a plan by Golkar's youth affiliate AMPI to hoist Golkar flags in 8,500 villages, one year before the official campaign date.[68]

By the commencement of the official campaign in April, PPP had assumed much of the mantle of opposition to Suharto's government and to Golkar's election campaign. Party leaders and campaigners of PPP saw clearly the historic opportunity handed to them with the decimation of Megawati's PDI. As Jusuf Syakir, leader of the party council explained

> with the still chaotic situation in PDI, PPP sees the opportunity to recruit as many as possible of Megawati's PDI masses...PPP's image as the party that can defend as well as struggle for their interests must be upheld before them...we have a 'golden opportunity'...[it] only comes once...we are convinced that our votes will increase.[69]

He spoke of the need to present PPP as a viable alternative that promoted necessary change in order to address the community concerns of the Democracy Party supporters.

Metareum made a surprisingly frontal attack on government corruption, collusion, dishonesty and misuse of power. He appealed to the higher moral fibre of Muslim *ulama*, suggesting the party was the *ulama*'s inheritance, the *ulama* were the source of its inspiration determining the party's political morality and ethics.[70] In a broadside against Golkar's 'immorality', he asserted that

> We still witness the growth of immoral politics, the politics of achieving objectives by any means, along with deceitful political communication...shamelessly...Golkar claims to be the most meritorious group in this Republic. It is the most New Order, the most Pancasilaist—in short, it is everything. In fact, Golkar's marketing method tends to force...we witness an old style of politics—namely, the political style of 'preman' [paid thugs]...Golkar entices people to change party [affiliation] with promises of a picnic...by giving pocket money...so that people will vote for the party. Golkar also threatens civil servants with dimissal if they do not vote for the party.[71]

Identifying PPP as synonymous with Islam and morality (by enforcing the 'sole foundation' law in 1985 the government had sought to discourage parties from identifying themselves with distinct constituencies), Metareum directly appealed to the grass roots. In his effort to open a breach in Golkar's campaign, he dug up local issues of simmering social discontent, linking them to Islam's/ the PPP's ability or promise to construct honest, open and just government. He appealed to the *ulama* not to break ranks with the PPP in order to join Golkar.[72] He claimed that the party stood for weak economic classes, such as small business people and traders, 'becak' (tricycle passenger service), 'ojek' (motorcycle), and bus drivers, farmers and youth. He raised the highly sensitive issue of forced land eviction and the inalienable right to ownership, as well as the right to political freedoms and personal security from law enforcement officers. In this all-out campaign effort, he also targeted economic monopoly (of the Chinese) in collusion with state officials, 'greasing the wheels with money', and sending indigenous business people bankrupt. He discussed government credit discrimination that favoured large malls and privately-owned shop complexes at the expense of *wong cilik* (the little people).[73]

In particular, Metareum's public criticism of the state's deployment of paid ruffians and security forces behind Golkar's election campaign suggests that even New Order elite members were becoming fed up with the state's coercive politics of exclusion. That is, once Muslim interests allied to PPP were on the receiving end of state-sponsored intimidation they began to bluntly reject such tactics and instead protested against state directed violence. Moreover, a New Order stalwart like Metareum, in order to defend the interests of PPP against Golkar's heavy-handedness, also had begun to appropriate the democracy discourse of regime opponents.

The PPP's campaign strategy and language touched a raw nerve among Indonesia's Muslim masses in an already volatile situation, sharpening social discontent, as PPP supporters were willing to defend their party at almost any cost it seemed. PPP campaigners from NU, which included among their ranks revered *ulama* and *kyai* of the traditional *pesantren* system, called upon the loyalty of their millions of rural followers, in their determination to arouse the emotions and allegiances of their devout followers against Golkar. Metareum's campaign language had set the tenor of more radical statements by less constrained local Muslim leaders. Several sources agree that certain NU leaders affiliated with the PPP proclaimed that to struggle for the 'star party' was to fight an Islamic *Jihad* (holy struggle or war), to oppose injustice and the like.[74] At a campaign sermon, the charismatic *kyai* and NU leader, Kholil As'ad of Situbondo (East Java) proclaimed that 'if the PPP had not defended the religion of God, I certainly would not have gone to such pains to attend this meeting. I do all this only in order to struggle in the path of God.'[75] The call to *Jihad* can be viewed as the Muslim-oriented PPP's counter-discourse to the state's propaganda of vigilance and intelligence-security approach. That is, local Muslim leaders who campaigned for PPP no longer adopted the language of *kewaspadaan* towards pro-democracy forces, but replaced it with religious symbolism of resistance.

In what became a remarkably new phenomenon in Indonesian politics, displaced PDI supporters joined PPP campaigns in an anti-regime 'people movement', calling themselves Mega–Bintang. (Bintang or Star is the emblem of the PPP and the name of the popular, jailed PPP leader.) PPP's campaign strategy of attracting disaffected Megawati supporters to the 'star party's' ranks seemed to have worked. However, scenes of brutality marred the election campaign, as Golkar supporters and anti-riot troops and police clashed with Mega–Bintang crowds in the streets of numerous towns, in hotly contested electorates inside and outside of Java.

Sparking PPP indignation was the over-zealous methods, unfair practices and campaign restrictions against the Islamic-oriented party, with Golkar seeking to monopolise the pre-election atmosphere. For example, the government issued a ban on Mega–Bintang placards and symbols being displayed at rallies, and ordered PPP to stop holding rallies before the official campaign period commenced, although Golkar continued to conduct rallies. Subsequently, citing the level of campaign-related violence, the government banned public rallies and restricted campaigning to indoor meetings, media broadcasts and printed materials. After a three-day meeting in Jakarta, PPP announced that the campaign restrictions were undemocratic and that the party would disregard the rules. PPP also approved a boycott of the elections by seven branches in Central Java in response to the refusal by the police to permit public campaigning in that province.[76]

In addition to the government's campaign restrictions, one of the main factors that reportedly sparked PPP reactions was Golkar's crusade to turn towns and streets yellow as it painted public facilities, buildings, vehicles and roadsides in its party colour. Consequently, street battles were commonly provoked by tit-for-tat exchanges that typically began either with one party removing the street banners, posters and flags of another, or with exchanges of taunts followed by rock throwing and clashes, with sometimes serious casualties.[77]

Central Java was the scene of the earliest and initially worst campaign violence. Central Java's northern coastal town of Pekalongan, one of the few towns in Indonesia held by PPP, recorded the first major instance of campaign-related violence in late March 1997, one month before the official campaign period. Angry PPP supporters, joined by locals (and Megawati sympathisers), burnt down a stage that was to host a Golkar rally by Suharto's daughter, Siti Rukmana. Local Muslims expressed outrage over the fact that the stage was erected in an Islamic boarding schoolyard next to a mosque, and that Golkar used Islam 'superficially' in its campaign to attract supporters. They were incensed by the fact that the popular Muslim musician, Rhoma Irama, and the equally popular preacher, Zainuddin MZ—previously PPP campaigners—had moved over to Golkar, and that Golkar had the temerity to campaign in this PPP bailiwick. The East Java police later arrested a Muslim preacher for his alleged use of prayer meetings to stir up anti-government sentiment in which he apparently criticised both Suharto's daughter and the Golkar Chair Harmoko, and called Rhoma and Zainuddin traitors to Islam.[78]

The burning of the stage was provoked initially by a dispute over the removal of PPP flags by Golkar rally organisers. The incident spilled over into massive anti-government riots, which deteriorated into attacks against the commercial and residential properties of Indonesia's ethnic-Chinese minority, the usual scapegoat of political and social tensions in Indonesia.[79]

Pekalongan, and surrounding districts and towns, remained flashpoints of violent clashes between PPP supporters and Golkar supporters from March to the end of the campaign in late May. In early May, outside of Pekalongan town, PPP mobs attacked a housing complex for civil servants and Chinese. They reportedly threw molotov cocktail bombs into the houses, burnt the contents and yelled 'Hang Suharto!'[80] Among the districts in Central Java that continued to experience unrest were Kudus, Jepara, Demak, Rembang, Magelang, Kendal, Semarang, Wonosobo, Banjarnegara, Solo, Surakarta and Yogyakarta—all containing significant PPP pockets and therefore constituting major targets of Golkar's aggressive campaign. On numerous occasions, PPP crowds confronted heavily-armed anti-riot troops, who sometimes unleashed volleys of rubber bullets, tear gas and water canons to break up rallies. On one occasion in Kudus, PPP supporters clashed with anti-riot police when holding a campaign boycott over the regent's issuance of a regulation banning PPP's vehicle and motorcycle cavalcades.[81]

In some of these districts and towns, PPP leaders complained about the use, especially by Golkar-affiliate youth organisations, of thugs against PPP rallies. The Yogyakarta chapter of PPP decided to withdraw from the campaign after Golkar's militant youths attacked PPP supporters returning home from a rally in Kotagede and damaged the PPP branch office in Yogyakarta. There were some reports of thugs wearing Ninja outfits attacking PPP's branch offices. The PPP also gave accounts of 'preman'-type activities in Wonosobo, Banjarnegara and other districts, in which knife-wielding and rock-throwing youths incited pay-back raids on villages and PPP convoys. Blaming paid thugs for instigating what otherwise would appear to have been PPP-directed violence was sometimes possibly motivated by the desire to clear PPP's image of brutality. The New Order state was, nevertheless, known for its deployment of 'preman' to achieve certain political ends, and PPP leaders claimed that it was to tarnish the opposition party's image and reduce its appeal for electorates.[82]

Similar riots and street clashes occurred in PPP strongholds in East Java province, in the districts and towns of Bangkalan (Madura), Surabaya, Pasuruan, Gresik, Jombang, Bondowoso, Malang, Jember and Banyuwangi. A report by the Pasuruan branch of the NU on 7 May 1997 captured the campaign-related conflict by the opposing Golkar and PPP supporters in that district. The report noted that on PPP rally days, its supporters displayed total disrespect for religious leaders who supported Golkar, throwing insults at them. PPP supporters tore down Golkar banners, and damaged parked vehicles, while at Golkar rallies, PPP supporters carrying sharp weapons clashed with Golkar campaigners and security police.[83]

The closing days of the official campaign recorded the greatest amount of violence and bloodshed. In Jakarta, PPP supporters eclipsed Golkar rallies with Jakarta's traffic heavily congested or brought to a standstill. In PPP pockets in Jakarta's poorer suburbs, such as Cawang, Kampung Melayu, Depok and Ciputat rioting and street battles broke out between convoys of PPP sympathisers and anti-riot forces and Golkar supporters. On 23 May, the last day of the campaign, PPP supporters in a retaliatory raid against Golkar sacked the trading city of Banjarmasin. Reportedly, Golkar campaigners on motorcycles, who were creating a din outside of a mosque during mid-day prayer, incited the PPP supporters into violence. Jakarta had to send in crack troops to bring peace to the city, after a day of carnage, which left over 100 people dead. The election period left an estimated 300 people dead and hundreds wounded, although a large number of campaign-related deaths were due to traffic accidents. By any account, this was an historical calamity.[84]

One of the outstanding points about the campaign rallies, was that PPP supporters continued to enter the streets by their thousands to vent their frustrations against the regime, even after the more moderate national and regional party leaders had called off rallies in order to avert further bloodshed. PPP supporters and sympathisers had become a mass dynamic in their own right, without the need for leadership in order to take action. Like the PDI masses before the post-July crackdown, PPP and Mega–Bintang masses had little choice but to participate directly through demonstration and protest. These were the only remaining outlets for the bottled-up frustration of economically and politically marginalised electorates. Previous elections had served as opportunities for Indonesians to let off steam, but in a fairly controlled and manageable environment. This time, however, violence appeared to escalate out of control and move beyond predictable or acceptable limits for the regime.

However, it was easy for the state's security apparatus to disperse such leaderless actions, which often resulted in rioting and were open to manipulation by security forces.[85] Immediately after the campaign, Suharto's government placed a strict ban on all street rallies and brought 20,000 troop reinforcements into Jakarta to re-establish order before the scheduled poll of 29 May. The armed forces announced that it would shoot rioters on sight, and a steady calm soon returned to Indonesia. The MUI chairman outraged Indonesia's educated elite when he reinforced the military threat by proclaiming that to shoot rioters and looters was permitted ('halal') by Islam. Again, a leader of a corporatist organisation sought to provide Islamic legitimacy to the regime's repressive actions.

CONCLUSION

The chapter has considered how different members of the elite, who were disaffected with the conduct of New Order politics, began to identify with growing resentment in society against Suharto's corrupt and arbitrary rule. Suharto's rule was underpinned by a political system that was weighted heavily in favour of the regime and fortified by Golkar's landslide victories at the five-yearly general elections. The unleashing of public resentment and social protest, and the organisation of sidelined elite against Suharto's regime, became increasingly apparent as the 1997 general and the 1998 presidential elections drew near, and as anticipation of a presidential succession increased. Contending elite interests aligned to and against Suharto's regime jostled for advantage before a succession took place. This was why the 'rainbow' forces in organisations like YKPK had as one of their central objectives, the prevention of Habibie from becoming Indonesia's next vice-president. Constitutionally, the vice-president would automatically inherit the presidency if Suharto stepped down mid-term, as many speculated he would. Should Habibie become Indonesia's next president, then it would be Habibie's main supporters in ICMI, Golkar and the military that would ascend to power. Meanwhile, those civilian and military figures who had lost out in power contests to Habibie since the 1993 reshuffles would stand to be further marginalised from power.

The 'rainbow' groups identified with mounting grassroots opposition to Suharto's rule. Meanwhile, members of the intelligentsia, opposition politicians, and pro-democracy activists played important roles in organising societal protest. There even were significant efforts to build an opposition coalition, which transcended class and group interests, round Megawati's PDI. After the removal of Megawati as party leader, more spontaneous attempts were made to form a loose coalitional grouping of Mega–Bintang supporters with which to combat the strength of Golkar. This was a phenomenon never before observed in Indonesian politics. Nevertheless, the coalition-building initiatives were tactical rather than enduring. The frailty of coalition building, and the lack of co-ordinated planning between opposition groups, contributed significantly to the failure of societal interests to combat the state's much superior resources.

One reason for this failure was that disaffected members of the political elite (reformers and dissidents both within and outside of the state) generally did not attempt to build grassroots support for their organisations. This was notwithstanding efforts by PDI and PPP party leaders to organise grassroots following for the purpose of contesting the election. Disaffected members of the elite were more interested in gaining concessions from the regime, in terms of their own participation in the political system, in competition with Muslim interests backing Habibie, than with creating societal movements that one day might bring down Suharto's regime. Largely, this elite-centred approach was a product of decades of Suharto's patronage games, divide-and-rule tactics, and the 'floating mass' policy, which still effectively severed links between elite level politics and the masses.

As one of his divide-and-rule tactics, Suharto sought to draw on Muslim support, including his mobilisation of incorporated Muslim interests, in order to discredit the rival forces. The recruitment of incorporated and collaborating Muslims behind his anti-Megawati/PDI campaign, nonetheless, did not prevent the Muslim community from becoming a source of opposition to Golkar during the election campaign. Instead, Muslim interests associated with PPP became alienated by the government's over-zealous Golkar campaign, and began to support grassroots causes against key aspects of Suharto's corrupt and arbitrary rule. The 'Mega–Bintang' phenomenon was the peak of this trend of opposition. Opposition to the regime from within PDI and PPP demonstrates the increasing ineffectiveness of exclusionary, or for that matter inclusionary, corporatism in trying to contain societal interests. The systematic use of repression against the opposition was further evidence of this failure.

Despite the growing opposition to Suharto's rule in the pre-election period, Golkar won 74.5 per cent of the votes cast (its largest victory yet at the polls), with PPP coming second (22.43 per cent), and PDI trailing with only 3.07 per cent.[86] In the subsequent months until the holding of the March 1998 session of the MPR, Suharto once again demonstrated his mastery at establishing his control over Indonesia's political system. In March, he was re-elected unopposed for a seventh term as president, with his largest mandate yet ensuring that the 1,000-member MPR would be filled with compliant politicians, Suharto stalwarts and family members. Given his commanding control of Indonesian politics, an analyst at the time might have been forgiven for concluding that the mounting pre-election opposition and violence was fairly inconsequential to the overall political process.[87]

The PPP chairman and leaders did complain about vote rigging after the poll, with several branches threatening to boycott the election results. In some parts of the country, PPP supporters rioted in protest over the election result with at least one rioter being shot dead. In the district of Sampan, Madura (East Java) the government even conducted an unprecedented re-count of dozens of polling booths in an effort to assuage PPP tensions. At the end of the day, however, PPP, under Metareum's leadership, assumed its more characteristically accommodating stance and signed the official election results, which still saw the Islamic-oriented party increase its share of the vote from 1992. In an interview, Metareum admitted that neither a boycott nor protest would measurably alter the established political arrangements.[88]

Was it the case, then, that Golkar's over-zealous campaign strategy had been an outstanding success, as it did garner a robust result for Golkar in the face of rising opposition? To the contrary, analysts had quite correctly perceived at the time that the Suharto government still had a price to pay for the underlying resentment to its rule, harboured by Indonesia's politically excluded and disadvantaged classes. Seismic shifts were destined to occur in the Tectonic plates of Indonesian politics, as long suppressed resentments of Suharto's rule and intra-elite machinations were eventually to erupt into the open and bring about the demise of President Suharto and his New Order. The 1997 election contest had set in motion a new dynamic, providing an early example of agitation by Indonesia's excluded lower classes. By identifying with the concerns of Indonesia's hitherto disenfranchised 'floating mass', Indonesia's elite thereby had shifted political competition beyond the predictable boundaries of the New Order political system. The ramifications of this shift in politics were soon to be felt.

NOTES

1. By 'the elite' I mean the 'political elite', which includes the ruling elite (the president and his immediate circle) and supporting elite (ministers, bureaucrats, legislators, politicians, economics advisers and the like) within the state. It also includes leaders of non-government organisations and high-profile intellectuals, government opponents, and dissidents, who interact with the state elite, are recognised for their contribution to national discourse, or are involved in elite-level political negotiation and contest.

2. *Tiras*, 2 November 1995; *Ummat*, 27 November and 11 December 1995; *Gatra*, 11 November 1995; *Tempo*, 4 June 1994.

3. *Tiras*, 2 November 1995; *Gatra*, 31 October–25 November 1995; Tirtosudarmo, 'Indonesia 1991: Quest for Democracy', p.131.

4. See footnote 20, chapter six.

5. Ramage, *Politics in Indonesia*, pp.156–65; Tirtosudarmo, 'Indonesia 1991: Quest for Democracy', p.128.

6. *Gatra*, 18 November 1995; *Editor*, 1 May 1993.

7. Uhlin argues that 'the banning of Tempo, Editor, and DeTik in 1994 was a hard blow against the Indonesian press, but it also led to the creation of new groups fighting for press freedom and democracy in general'. Uhlin, *Indonesia and the 'Third Wave'*, p.115. For example, in June protesters established an organisation called Indonesian Solidarity for Press Freedom (SIUPP—these initials were a deliberate play on the acronym for the press publishing license, also called SIUPP). In August, a group of journalists and

editors established the Alliance of Independent Journalists (AJI) as an alternative to the government-sanctioned Indonesian Journalists Association (PWI). From June to August, journalists, students, NGO groups and other pro-democracy forces held a series of demonstrations against the closures. Although the demonstrations met with police repression, ABRI permitted a student protest to reach the gates of the Presidential Palace.

8. *The Limits of Openness*, p.11.
9. *The Limits of Openness*, pp.5–20; Ramage, *Politics of Indonesia*, pp.111–51.
10. *Tiras*, 2 November 1995; *Kompas*, 8–10 November 1995; *Tempo*, 4 June 1994; *Suara Independen*, October–November 1995.
11. Imaduddin Abdulrahim told of how Alamsjah facilitated Imaduddin's first meeting with Habibie in order to persuade the technology minister to establish ICMI. Interview with Imaduddin, 15 February 1994; Hefner, 'Islam, State, and Civil Society', p.17.
12. *Tempo*, 4 and 18 June 1994; *Forum Keadilan*, 23 October 1995; *Gatra*, 2 September 1995.
13. *Gatra*, 28 September 1996; *Tiras*, 1 August 1996; *Kompas*, 9 January 1996.
14. *Gatra*, 28 September 1996; *Kompas*, 26 October 1995; *Suara Independen*, December 1995.
15. The New Masyumi no longer served the political interests of ex-Masyumi figures who had joined ICMI and hoped for greater access to power through the new arrangements. *Surabaya Post*, 24 November 1995; *Tiras*, 23 November 1995; *Kompas*, 5 November 1995; *Ummat*, 27 November 1995.
16. Greg Fealy, 'Indonesian Politics, 1995–96', pp.27–9; Heryanto, 'Indonesia: Towards the Final Countdown?', pp.117–19.
17. *Kompas*, 9–10 January 1996; *Tiras*, 1 August 1996; *Gatra*, 28 September 1996.
18. Lowry only went so far as to say 'it is clear that some elements of ABRI saw a strong PDI as a potential counter to the lure of Islam and a reaction to tensions within Golkar'. Lowry, *The Armed Forces*, p.204; McIntyre, 'In Search of Megawati Sukarnoputri', p.13; Kingsbury, *The Politics of Indonesia*, pp.230–32.
19. McIntyre, 'In Search of Megawati', pp.12–13; Kingsbury, *The Politics of Indonesia*, pp.230–32; Heryanto, 'Indonesia: Towards the Final Countdown?', pp.113–21; Rasyid, 'Indonesia: Preparing for Post-Soeharto', p.154.
20. McIntyre, 'In Search of Megawati', pp.17–19; Fealy, 'Indonesian Politics, 1995–96', p.30; interviews with Marzuki Darusman (leader of Komnas HAM), 16 July 1997; Bondan Gunawan (member of Forum Demokrasi and Nur Kebajikan Foundation—he later became the State Secretary in President Abdurrahman Wahid's cabinet), 25 July 1997.

21. In East Java, for instance, a government-sponsored candidate Latif Pujosakti was chosen as PDI leader for the province. PDI's central council under Megawati's leadership refused to acknowledge his election and nominated its own candidate. In West Java, two wings were formed and Megawati's wing accused the government of being behind the split. In Central Java, the government embarked on a campaign to discredit the pro-Mega provincial chair with the local branch of the military intelligence body Bakorstanasda employing its discourse on vigilance ('kewaspadaan'), by declaring that the chair had Communist Party links. Megawati was forced to replace the chair but the provincial government nonetheless refused to acknowledge Megawati's new candidate for the job. *Gatra*, 8 June 1996; *1996: Tahun Kekerasan*, p.8; Fealy, 'Indonesian Politics, 1995–96', p.31.

22. For example, in mid May and early June, PDI representatives from the province visited the Department of Internal Affairs in Jakarta to call for a congress to replace Megawati as chair. In addition, in early June, Latif's faction held a work meeting to prepare for the Medan congress. East Java's Governor financed Latif's faction to attend the congress. On 17 June, 34 PDI branches from East Java and 35 branches from Central Java asked Suryadi to be the new PDI chair. On 20 June, pro-Fatimah factions in East, Central and West Java pushed for the Medan congress whilst pro-Mega factions roundly rejected it. Security police ousted Megawati's supporters from Central Java's provincial PDI headquarters and had the office plastered yellow with Golkar's party colour. This action, although perhaps an isolated incident, highlighted the extent to which PDI was really only intended as a supporting component of the authorised party system that furnished Golkar's one-party dominance of the political system. *Jawa Pos*, 15–18 May and 10–19 June 1996; *Tiras*, 10–20 June 1996; *Gatra*, 8 June 1996.

23. This included Megawati supporters holding protests in East and Central Java, on 4 June, to protest against the anti-Mega factions and Suryadi's challenge. In East Java, the supporters stabbed their hands and signed their support for Megawati in their own blood. Sucipto's faction established a Command Post on 6 June in Surabaya to rally support against the congress. On 17 and 18 June, it formed a 'Mega Support Front' together with pro-democracy student activists and PRD members and marched down the main streets of Surabaya to make a last ditch protest against the Medan congress.

24. *1996: Tahun Kekerasan*, pp.8–11; Heryanto, 'Indonesia: Towards the Final Countdown?', p.114; author's own eyewitness accounts outside the PDI headquarters in Jl. Diponegoro, Central Jakarta, during the days of Free Podiums.

25. McIntyre, 'In Search of Megawati', pp.17–19; Heryanto, 'Indonesia: Towards the Final Countdown?', pp.115–19; Fealy, 'Indonesian Politics, 1995–96', p.31.

26. *Kembali ke Cita-Cita Luhur Bangsa*, signed by Bambang Triantoro, Abdurrahman Wahid, and A. Dahlan Ranuwiharjo on 1 July 1996, Jakarta; *Gatra*, 13 July 1996.

27. Fealy, 'Indonesian Politics, 1995–96', p.27; Heryanto, 'Indonesia: Towards the Final Countdown', pp.117–18.

28. *Surabaya Post*, 27 March and 15 December 1996; *Tiras*, 23 May 1996; *Jawa Pos*, 24 May 1996; Nezar Patria, 'Rangkaian Aksi Nasional SMID Untuk Makassar Berdarah: Insiden Surabaya', *Secretary General SMID Press Release* (apakabar@clark.net), 20 May 1996.

29. State-sponsored attacks against the hunger strikers in an attempt to evict them from the steps of parliament created a strong reaction. East Java chapters of GMNI and the Indonesian Legal Aid Foundation YLBHI, themselves members of PDI's support organisation MARI, protested the incident. YLBHI called the attack a violation of people's freedom of speech and human rights. SMID activists demonstrated outside of the Brawijaya Military Command calling on the military to arrest the thugs. Their protest was in reaction to a statement by the East Java Military Commander, Lt Gen. Imam Utomo, who sought to discredit the SMID by accusing it of orchestrating the brutal attack on students in order to boost its own popular appeal. On 24 May, students at 11th March University in Surakarta, Central Java, demonstrated against the incident. A week later, on 4 June in Jakarta, hundreds of students, NGO activists and supporters of PUDI held a protest action called 'Prayer of Concern over the 40 Day Makassar (Ujung Pandang) Tragedy'. Demonstrating youths marched to the YLBHI office, the Ismail Marzuki Park and marched on the office of the Co-ordinating Minister for Politics and Security in Central Jakarta. They unfurled banners which read 'New President, New Party! Smash Military Dominance!' Demonstrators clashed violently with security forces that were guarding the front yard of the legal aid office. (See citations in the previous footnote.)

30. Since at least late-1995, in fact, government officials and army generals referred to the 'rainbow groups' supporting Megawati's PDI as 'formless organisations (OTB's)' that had been infiltrated by PKI. The generals insisted that PKI-infiltrated OTB's were seeking to pit communities against one another, to stir up ethnic and religious strife, and to destabilise the government through instigating social unrest and 'spreading slander' through the distribution of 'illegal' leaflets. *Forum Keadilan*, 6 November 1995.

31. *Forum Keadilan*, 6 November 1995.

32. Utomo announced that the dissemination of propaganda and pamphlets by PRD, which launched piercing criticisms against the military and state, had

become intolerable. In particular, he intimated insult over PRD pamphlets that allegedly had called the armed forces the 'dogs of industry', accused the New Order regime of 'murdering millions of communists', and demanded the revocation of restrictive political laws and the removal of ABRI's *dwi-fungsi* role. *Surya*, 9 July 1996; *Memorandum*, 9 July 1996; *Jawa Pos*, 9 July 1996.

33. *Far Eastern Economic Review*, 8 August 1996 quoted in Greg Fealy, 'Indonesian Politics, 1995–96', p.33.
34. *Jawa Pos*, 8 August 1996 and *Republika*, 9 August 1996 quoted in Greg Fealy, 'Indonesian Politics, 1995–96', p.33.
35. Honna, 'The Military and Democratisation'.
36. *1996: Tahun Kekerasan*, p.49. A report by the National Commission of Human Rights (KomnasHAM) mentioned that the security forces were complicit in the 27 July incident. Munawir Sjadzali and Baharuddin Lopa, *Keterangan Pers Tentang Laporan Komnas HAM Mengenai Peristiwa 27 July 1996 di Jakarta*, 10 October 1996; McIntyre, 'In search of Megawati', p.18.
37. Ryter, 'Pemuda Pancasila', p.68.
38. The author was a participant-observer to the unfolding events and riots of the 27th and 28th, insofar as he was caught in the middle of the riots and clashes between police-military units and protestors.
39. Sjadzali and Lopa, *Keterangan Pers*, pp.17–18; author's own eyewitness accounts of incidents on 27 and 28 July 1997 in Menteng-Central Jakarta locations.
40. The government had already brought blasphemy charges (for insulting the Prophet Muhammad) against Permadi, with the trial opening on 6 July 1995, after he had publicly contradicted a statement made by the military commander of Central Java that Megawati was unfit to lead the PDI. Earlier in the year, in March, and in retaliation against Permadi, the government sought to mobilise Muslim outrage against the Permadi for having, in April 1994, called the Prophet a dictator at a gathering of students at Gadjah Mada University. At the gathering Permadi had been highly critical of Golkar, Harmoko and Habibie and had focused on the issue of the presidential succession. *1996: Tahun Kekerasan*, pp.34–5; Fealy, 'Indonesian Politics, 1995–96', pp.32–4.
41. See chapter five for an account of BAKOMUBIN and other corporatist initiatives; interview with Toto Tasmara (leader of BAKOMUBIN and BKPRMI), 13 November 1997.
42. Interview with Toto, 13 November 1997; *Ummat*, 2 September 1996; *Serial Kutbah Ju'mat*, September 1996; *Media Dakwah*, September 1996; *Serial Khotbah Ju'mat*, September 1996.
43. The head of the women's wing of NU (Muslimat), Aisyah Hamid Baidlowi, attended the meeting at which the joint statement was made.

According to Aisyah, 'Representatives of all Islamic organisations attended. At the meeting the MUI condemned the riots. Without avail, I tried to suggest a softening of MUI's language. Not long after this gathering at the MUI headquarters the social political wing of ABRI invited all Islamic groups to attend the armed forces' clarification of events surrounding the riots.' Interview with Aisyah Hamid Baidlowi, 11 March 1997; *Gatra*, 10 August 1996; *Tiras*, 25 July 1996; *Media Dakwah*, August 1996.

44. *Gatra*, 14 September and 5 October 1996.
45. *Gatra*, 10 August 1996.
46. *Gatra*, 10 August 1996.
47. *Gatra*, 17 August 1996.
48. *Tekad*, 5 August 1996.
49. Interview with Hussein Umar, 24 September 1996; *Media Dakwah*, September 1996.
50. For example, on 9 August, Yusuf Hasyim (the NU leader of Tebuireng Pesantren, Jombang, Central Java, and the uncle and adversary of the NU chairman) helped organise a meeting of 200 *ulama* at the Shangri-la Hotel in Surabaya. At the meeting, attended by East Java's Brawijaya Military Commander and its Governor, the *ulama* publicly denounced the 27 July riots. Two days later, Suharto's generals marshalled together a crowd of between 30–50,000 people in Jakarta to declare their oath of allegiance to the government and to denounce PRD as the architect of the riot. Chief of ABRI's Social and Political Affairs, Lt Gen. Syarwan Hamid, the Jakarta regional military commander, Sjafrie Sjamsuddin, the Jakarta regional police chief and the Jakarta governor were among the state officials who attended the public gathering. On 31 August and 1 October, two separate mass gatherings of Indonesia's main Islamic youth organisations were held in East Java. Clad in distinct military-style uniforms, the Barisan Ansor (the paramilitary wing of GP Ansor) organised the first gathering of approximately 40,000 of its supporters at the Brawijaya Stadium, Kediri. The Muhammadiyah Youth Preparedness Command arranged a gathering of around 70,000 of its supporters at the Tenth of November Gelora Stadium in Surabaya. As on other such occasions, East Java's Governor and top-military brass attended the mass meetings. *Indonesian Times*, 12 August 1996; *Straits Times*, 12 August 1996; *Media Dakwah*, September 1996; *Gatra*, 5 October 1996.
51. *Gatra*, 5 October 1996.
52. *Republika*, 12 March 1997.
53. 'Wawancara Anwar Harjono', *Humas Manajmen Kampanye Pemilu*.
54. Abdurrahman's usually critical voice became somewhat muted in late-1996, once he had made his rapprochement with Suharto, Siti Rukmana and Gen. Hartono. Heryanto, 'Indonesia: Towards the Final Countdown?', p.111.
55. Fealy, 'Indonesian Politics 1995–96', p.34.

56. See chapter nine.
57. Louise Williams, 'Victory at a cost', *Asia OnLine*, 31 May 1997.
58. *Forum Keadilan*, 2 June 1997.
59. *Tiras*, 28 March 1996; Lowry, *The Armed Forces*, pp.211–12.
60. Kingsbury, *The Politics of Indonesia*, p.143.
61. *Tiras*, 11 April 1996.
62. Rasyid, 'Indonesia: Preparing for Post-Soeharto Rule', pp.155–6.
63. *Panji Masyarakat*, 15–31 January 1996.
64. Other accounts reported incidents of growing dissent within PPP, as disaffected leaders at branch and provincial level (West Java, West Sumatra, South Sulawesi, Riau, and West Nusa Tenggara) protested the selection of leaders by PPP's Central Leadership Council. *Tiras*, 28 March and 25 April 1996.
65. *Panji Masyarakat*, 15–31 January 1996.
66. *Panji Masyarakat*, 15–31 January 1996.
67. *Republika*, 13 January 1996.
68. *Jawa Pos*, 4 June 1996; *Tiras*, 4 April and 2 May 1996; *Jawa Pos*, 21 May 1996.
69. 'Wawancara: Drs H Jusuf Syakir', *Humas Manajemen Kampanye Pemilu*.
70. 'Kolom Buya: Ulama dan Pemilu', *Humas Manajemen Kampanye Pemilu*.
71. 'Kolom Buya: Mewaspadai Politik', *Humas Manajemen Kampanye Pemilu*.
72. *Suara Pembaruan*, 23 February 1997; *The Jakarta Post*, 24 February 1997.
73. 'Kolom Buya: Pilihan Partai Persatuan', *Humas Manajemen Kampanye Pemilu*.
74. Interviews with leaders of GP Ansor (Bangil, East Java), 10 August 1997; KH. Choiron Syakur (Chairman of the Pesantren Wahid Hasyim in Bangil), 10 August 1997; Hj. Ahmad Jaman (leader of Ansor, Pasuruan), 10 August 1997; KH. Hafid Hasyim (leader of Pesantren Darul Ulum in Pasuruan), 10 August 1997.
75. *Jawa Pos*, 12 May 1997.
76. 'PPP Minta Aparat Tidak Bertindak' and 'DPC Se-Jateng Sepakat', *Humas Managemen Kampanye Pemilu: Tempo Online*, 5–19 May 1997; *Forum Keadilan*, 2 June 1997; Aspinall, 'What price victory?', *Inside Indonesia*, July–September 1997; Louise Williams, 'Jakarta acts against alliance', *Asia OnLine*, 14 May 1997; Louise Williams, 'Jakarta poll riots flare', *Asia OnLine*, 22 May 1997; Louise Williams, 'Growing violence a sign of Indonesian regime's legitimacy is leaking away', *Asia OnLine*, 21 May 1997; Forrester, 'Towards March 1998', p.60.
77. See citations in previous footnote.
78. *Suara Pembaruan*, 26 March 1997; 'Rhoma Irama: "Saya Pilih",' *Humas Managemen Kampanye Pemilu*; Forrester, 'Towards March 1998', p.60; Louise Williams, 'Protests count for nothing at poll', *Asia OnLine*; Louise

Williams, 'Growing violence a sign', *AsiaOnLine*; 'Campaign Violence in Indonesia: "Suppressed Rage" and Calls for Reform', *USIS Foreign Media Reaction Report*, 28 May 1997.

79. *Dow Jones News Service*, 29 March 1997; Louise Williams, 'Poll tension: police fire rubber bullets at crowd', *Sydney Morning Herald*, 28 March 1997; Louise Williams, 'Poll march shuts down Java town', *Asia OnLine*, 30 April 1997; Louise Williams, 'Indon police fire on Muslim riot mob', *Asia OnLine*, 28 March 1997.
80. *Straits Times*, 14 May 1997.
81. Forrester, 'Towards March 1998', p.60; *Forum Keadilan*, 2 June and 16 June 1997; *Surabaya Post*, 3 May 1997; *Suara Merdeka*, 26 April 1997.
82. See previous footnote.
83. *Laporan Situasi Daerah Kodia*, 7 May 1997; *Forum Keadilan*, 2 June 1997.
84. *Jakarta Post*, 27 May 1997; *Republika*, 27 May 1997; Louise Williams, 'Fire kills 130 in Indonesian election riots', *Asia OnLine*, 26 May 1997; Louise Williams, 'Jakarta poll riots flare', *Asia OnLine*.
85. Aspinall, 'What price victory'.
86. Forrester, 'Towards March 1998', p.62.
87. Aspinall, 'What price victory'; Forrester, 'Towards March 1998', p.67.
88. Forrester, 'Towards March 1998', pp.63–4; *Jakarta Post*, 16 June 1997; Louise Williams, 'US pressures Jakarta as poll anger mounts', *Asia OnLine*, 2 June 1997.

Chapter 9

The Unravelling of Suharto's Regime: Muslims Join Call for Change

INTRODUCTION

By early 1998, major cracks were appearing in the established political arrangements underpinning Suharto's rule. A nascent university student movement mobilised against Suharto and by May spearheaded a popular challenge to the New Order. As the deepening political crisis converged with a debilitating economic crisis, the reliance of Suharto's regime on old tactics and patterns of survival politics was no longer able to cope with the nature of the growing pressures for change. These pressures emanated from broad sections of society as well as from key elements of the New Order elite. The legitimacy of Suharto's continued right to rule rested on the twin claims that his New Order could deliver the benefits of economic development and political stability to its people. Indonesia's economic collapse of 1997–1998, which witnessed most businesses go into insolvency, placed millions of Indonesians out of work and threatened to have almost 50 per cent of Indonesians living below the poverty line by 1999, undermined Suharto's first claim to power. Political signs of instability evident in 1996, and spiralling out-of-control by mid-1998, undermined his second claim to power.[1] The Suharto regime's inability to cope with the Asian economic meltdown of the late-1990s exacerbated the ongoing political crisis of presidential succession and resulted in Suharto's resignation on 21 May.

The analysis focuses on two aspects of the popular challenge to Suharto. First, the student movement is examined, with attention given to the role of Muslim student organisations in opposing Suharto. Second, a study is made of incorporated Muslim interests as they withdrew their support from Suharto. There are two interrelated parts of the argument presented. The first part of the argument reinforces discussion (in chapter eight) that managing state–society relations through policies of exclusion could no longer contain social interests or deter them from organising against the political status quo. In Huntington's terms (1968), people's demands for political participation were outstripping the poorly institutionalised structures of authoritarian rule, which were unable to absorb the multiplying demands. The establishment since the early-1990s of a growing number of independent organisations and coalitions unrecognised by the state, and intensification of protest actions and unrest were strong indications of mounting societal pressures for participation. These organisations and activities both by-passed and, thus, fundamentally challenged the corporatist framework.

The second part of the argument is that Muslim interests associated with ICMI turned against their patron when their expectations of finding a role in the 1998 cabinet remained unfulfilled. Suharto's corporatist strategy through ICMI, until this point, had succeeded in dampening the political dissent of Muslims to his rule. However, by denying significant inclusion of these interests in political institutions at a time that support for Suharto was crumbling, Suharto effectively scuttled what remained of Muslim support for his presidency. Instead, Muslims joined opposition voices in the call for Suharto to resign and threw their support behind Habibie's presidency. After having been sidelined from the seventh development cabinet announced in March, ICMI members were among 'strategic insiders' who defected from Suharto because of his failure to overcome the political and economic crises. In the past, exclusion of the majority of Indonesians from political participation had relied on a consensus of strategic (middle and elite) classes that had a stake in the maintenance of Suharto's rule. Suharto had managed challenges to his presidency by maintaining shifting alliances of supporting elite groups and by isolating opponents. However, the cabinet line-up (consisting of his most trusted loyalists, family members, business associates, and corrupt bureaucrats) disrupted the managed consensus of supporting elite for his regime. This time the sidelining of elite interests from power had the effect of tilting the otherwise careful balance of forces against the status quo. Fewer and fewer elite and middle-class groups had a stake in Suharto's narrowly based, coercive and repressive rule and hence supported the student-led impetus for political change. The brief convergence of elite disaffection and societal pressures for Suharto to resign contributed to a volatile and politicised environment. A detailed analysis of the elite defections is not given, as the analysis focuses primarily on the defection of corporatised Muslim interests.[2]

THE UNIVERSITY STUDENT MOVEMENT

Early in 1998, students supported by Indonesia's educated classes were the first to call for major reform of the political system and for Suharto to step down. It is common for students to spearhead protest movements, however—in the case of Indonesia—university students represented a section of society affected by the state's corporatist controls since the Minister of Education's Campus Normalisation Act of 1978.[3] Under the normalisation policy, which prohibited independent student councils and political activities on campus, students were effectively excluded from participation in Indonesia's formal political processes.[4] However, the recent student agitations were largely the result of a new period of relative openness, beginning in the late-1980s, when the government offered some respite to its controls by replacing the student co-ordinating bodies with less restrictive student senates.[5] By the mid-1990s, students had already begun to engage in organisational activities and agitation to test the boundaries of New Order tolerance, as the case of SMID in 1996 attested (see chapter eight). Although, in reaction, Suharto's government clamped down on student-led labour strikes, hunger strikes and demonstrations, it had, in retrospect, failed to silence the call for political change.

In the final analysis, the period of openness, followed by a repressive clampdown on political activism in the 1990s, had the unintended outcome of raising people's expectations for change. It was therefore, perhaps, no coincidence that students were at the forefront of a movement, in which its most activist members called for the lifting of political controls and the return to full participation of Indonesia's otherwise 'floating mass' in a totally reformed and 'democratic' political system.

Starting in February 1998, the student demonstrations were triggered by rising prices of basic commodities, as the value of the *rupiah* all but collapsed and millions of average Indonesians were left with little or no purchasing power for staple foods and sundry items. From late-February to mid-March, thousands of students held protest actions and hunger strikes throughout the country in Java (Jakarta, Bogor, Bandung Yogyakarta, Surabaya and Solo), Sulawesi (Ujung Pandang), Kalimantan (Banjarmasin), and Sumatra (Medan, Palembang and Bengkulu). To their key demands for price reductions on, and distribution of, basic commodities, students added calls for far-reaching economic and political reforms, including a change of national leadership and clean government.[6]

In a demonstration of their open rejection of Suharto's New Order, on 25 February, at the University of Indonesia's Salemba campus in central Jakarta, students and alumni covered over with a white cloth the large campus sign, which read 'Welcome to the Campus of the New Order Struggle'. The following day, students at the university's Depok campus in South Jakarta erected a huge banner on which was written 'Campus of People's Struggle', as they vigorously denounced the New Order. At the different campuses, assistant rectors, former rectors, deans, academic staff and alumni joined the protests and sometimes lent strongly worded support to the students' actions, although they were not so forthright in condemning the New Order. Rather, they stressed the need for reform through constitutional channels, in preference to the certain alternative of unrest.[7]

The demonstrations in the different Indonesian towns and centres remained orderly and peaceful and ABRI ensured that they were kept within the confines of campuses by maintaining tight security at the perimeters of universities. But organised student protests grew in size and intensity after the March sitting of the MPR's general session which re-elected Suharto as president but failed to address adequately people's major concerns. The announcement of the seventh development cabinet (consisting mainly of Suharto loyalists) demonstrated the government's lack of resolve to implement genuine economic or political reforms, causing the *rupiah* to plummet from 2,500 in July 1997 to below 10,000 to the US dollar.

Thereafter, demonstrations began to spill out onto the streets, and the first major clashes between students and the security forces occurred, as anti-riot troops resorted to tear gas, batons and rubber bullets. Student demands began to focus on calls for 'total reform', in rejection of official pleas for gradual reform. To the slogan of 'reduce prices' protesters added, 'we reject the seventh development cabinet'.[8] The new Minister of Education and Culture, Wiranto Arismunandar, came under particularly sharp rebuke because of his reputation as one of the New Order's most hard-line officials, when he was rector of the Bandung Institute of Technology, and because, as minister, he uncompromisingly continued to enforce the government's policy of campus normalisation.[9]

The Role of Muslim Students

One of the features of the student movement was the forging of cross-campus communication networks with student leaders organising joint protests with students from several campuses at a time. Islamic student organisations performed an important role in the co-ordination of demonstrations. For example, on 29 March representatives of Campus Dakwah Institutes (LDK) from sixty tertiary institutes established the Muslim University Students Action Front (KAMMI) in Malang, and organised several cross-campus actions of students from both secular and Islamic tertiary institutes. The Yogyakarta League of Muslim University Students (LMMY)—a front for the Islamic University Students Association (HMI)—was responsible for holding similar joint demonstrations. State-run and private Islamic universities and tertiary institutes, such as IAINs, the Islamic University of Indonesia and the Muhammadiyah University played prominent roles in nationwide demonstrations.[10]

Mosques served as one of the main centres for organising the student operations. For example, in March the Islamic student organisations, including HMI and the Islamic Youth Movement (GPI), held protests at the Al-Azhar Mosque in Jakarta (a centre of student activities), which resulted in the issuance of an 'Al-Azhar Declaration'. The declaration was part of countrywide demonstrations over an interim list of proposed cabinet members in circulation in early March. Students rejected the list because it included too many corrupt bureaucrats and Suharto loyalists and did not give representation to Muslim or students' aspirations.[11]

The fact that mosques became important centres of student activities was rooted in the de-politicisation of campuses in 1979, after which they served as alternative venues for the organisation and expression of political grievance.

Mosques had allowed students to organise their activities outside the purview of the state and its university administration. Since the normalisation policy, throughout the country's universities, students had begun to organise themselves into numerous, tiny and difficult-to-monitor Islamic *usroh* and *haraqoh* groups, cells and clubs, unmediated by the state.[12] Over the next two decades, although students were prohibited from conducting overtly political activities on campus, Muslim students were able to operate autonomously from the university hierarchy through their religious activities. Madrid argues that, by 1998, Muslim students (or *Islami* students in his terminology) functioned with a high degree of autonomy, were 'experienced in organising campus activities and mosque-related social activities', 'were part of various Indonesia-wide student networks', and 'were used to engaging in political analysis'.[13]

Fragmented Student Movement

Despite some co-ordination of cross-campus protest activities, in many respects, the student movement was a fractured one that lacked nationwide cohesion. Aspinall observes that the heterogeneous movement was divided roughly into those students who evinced a moderate and cautious stance and more radically inclined and militant student activists. State authorised student senates and Muslim organisations represented the first tendency and the outlawed, but underground, PRD and its front organisation, the People's Struggle Committee for Change (KPRP), were representatives of the second, militant tendency. In outlook, tactics, and demands these two tendencies differed markedly. The moderates saw themselves as a moral force guarding the 'purity' of their movement from contamination of other political forces and interests. Therefore, they rejected collaboration with the ruling elite and opposition politicians and were wary of making any links with Indonesia's lower classes (labour, peasants, and the urban dispossessed). At first, they rejected pleas and taunts by radical groups to leave the campuses and take to the streets. They heeded the warnings of ABRI not to risk confrontation with the security forces or the potential for rioting that might result from non-students joining their cause. In their demands, they also avoided controversial issues such as calling for an end to ABRI's *dwi-fungsi* doctrine, as taken up by the radicals.[14]

In particular, before May, Muslim student organisations were constrained in their criticisms of Suharto and the New Order, and kept their protests within the confines of campus. KAMMI was among those organisations that joined street protests only in the last days of Suharto's rule, when opposition against him was overwhelming. The reason for this, explains Madrid, was because the Islamic students saw themselves as a movement for moral regeneration that eschewed violence and rejected the Marxist language and confrontational tactics of more left-wing radical student organisations. It is also probable that much of the Muslim student movement initially subdued its criticisms of Suharto because Muslims were beneficiaries of the state–Islamic rapprochement of the 1990s and feared state reprisals against Islam reminiscent of the pre-accommodation period.[16]After the appointment of the cabinet in March, however, Muslim students became openly critical of Suharto but KAMMI only joined street protests on 20 May when Suharto's downfall was imminent.

By contrast, the most radical groups considered that building alliances with the urban lower classes and taking to the streets, against ABRI's firm warnings, was critical to their anti-regime struggle. The more militant among them deliberately sought confrontation with the security forces as a means of drawing public attention to their struggle. Rather than the non-violent and gradualist stance of moderate student reformers, many of the radicals called for 'total reform' or revolutionary overthrow of the regime.[17]

Another problem facing the student movement was that it failed to gain the support of national political leaders. For students to have a chance of bringing about a fundamental change of regime, they needed the combined support of national opposition leaders. However, a number of students expressed their disappointment with the failure of the most prominent opposition leaders—Abdurrahman Wahid, Amien Rais and Megawati—to reach a shared understanding about the goals and direction of the reform movement. Historical and personal mistrust still ran deep between Amien Rais and his Muhammadiyah organisation (Islamic modernism) on the one hand, and Abdurrahman and his supporters in the Nahdlatul Ulama organisation (Islamic traditionalism), on the other.[18] More fundamentally, although students engaged in collective group actions against the regime, students and opposition members of the political elite were largely distrustful of one another. This mistrust militated against the building of lasting opposition coalitions that could bridge differences and form into a strong movement with which to seize power.

The fractured nature of opposition, partly, was the result of Suharto's divisive politics that sought to play off these historical divisions by offering organisational interests unequal access to patronage and power opportunities. Also reinforcing antagonisms was decades of state suppression of autonomous political organisation, through corporatist containment. This severely stunted the development of open political competition, which otherwise might—if given the chance to become institutionalised—have led to a normative consensus about the rules of the political system within which contest would occur.[19]

Military Responses to the Student Movement

Rival factions of the military adopted two different approaches in their handling of student demonstrations. On the one hand, the stated position of ABRI, under Gen. Wiranto's leadership, was that of conciliation with students and tolerance of protests providing they remained within the perimeters of university campuses. On the other, the Special Forces (Kopassus) under the indirect command of Lt Gen. Prabowo Subianto (the Commander of Army Strategic Forces) instigated military terror, kidnappings and repression of students in an attempt, many believed, to undermine Wiranto's strategy of moderation and to discredit his command of the armed forces.

Reformists within ABRI, who were keen to protect the military's institutional interests and professionalism in an increasingly destabilised political climate, influenced Wiranto. They saw the need for peaceful presidential succession, and recognised the necessity for gradual and negotiated reforms as a means of reconsolidating their power within established institutional arrangements. They also felt strong loyalties to their patron, Suharto, and knew the risks to their own political careers if they opposed the president. They, therefore, were unprepared to take direct action against him. From the reformist camp was Wiranto's social and political affairs chief, Lt Gen. Bambang Yudhoyono. Bambang initiated a series of dialogues and meetings with moderate community leaders, intellectuals, university hierarchy and students in order to sound out their views on political reformation, including presidential succession.[20]

Wiranto also was possibly acting on Suharto's instructions as a tactical ploy to divide the student movement. It appears, to some extent, that Wiranto's lenient approach had as its purpose to drive a wedge between the student-led opposition. This could be achieved by offering student moderates the choice of negotiated settlement, whilst promising harsh action against radical students who chose to take their demands to the streets. In all likelihood, the holding of dialogues with ABRI would dissipate the students' resolve and energy to continue their struggle.[21] Meanwhile, dialogues with ABRI would quarantine the problem by restricting it to the military's security and order concerns.

Thus, many student activists remained deeply suspicious of the military's motives and feared that dialogue was simply a tactic to keep them off the streets. They mostly rejected Wiranto's offer for dialogue, and Gen. Feisal Tanjung refused the students' requests for dialogue with the president. Feisal announced that the appropriate channel for them to express their wishes was through established hierarchy (the university administration) and by conducting themselves according to the protocol of polite observance (*tata krama*).[22] Suharto's rebuff demonstrated that the regime still would not countenance the participation of students outside of the formal mechanisms of New Order hierarchy, which, in fact, ensured their exclusion from political participation.

An outcome of the military's restrained response to the student movement, however, was that student leaders and academics became emboldened vocally to press their demands on the state, as they tested the limits of New Order tolerance. The approach by Prabowo's Special Forces of direct repression against student demonstrators, was in stark contradiction to ABRI's public position of moderation, and further served to crystallise indignation against Suharto's New Order. In particular, the deployment of troops with live ammunition against students at the prestigious private Trisakti University on 12 May, and the consequent killing of four students, sent the situation spiralling out of control. Speculation at the time was that Prabowo's tactic was to create instability and thereby prove that Wiranto's lenient approach had failed to quell the student opposition or to calm down political tensions. Officers serving under Prabowo later faced military tribunal for their alleged role in the kidnappings of radical activists, for which eleven soldiers, including several junior officers, were found guilty in a trial that lasted from December 1998 to April 1999.[23] By 14 May, in Jakarta's central business district, menacing black plumes of smoke bellowed out of ransacked buildings as fires claimed an estimated one thousand or more lives—and the public mood swung more assuredly against Suharto's rule.[24]

Concluding Remarks

Despite its fragmented nature, the student movement had articulated a broadly shared desire for change, thus inspiring support from the middle- and lower-class sections of society. One of the demands aired by students had been the lifting of corporatist curbs on campus life and the return to independent student councils. More broadly, they called for the revocation of political laws and political arrangements that had excluded the vast majority of Indonesians from participation in the formal structures of politics.[25] They declared that the political parties and the parliament had failed to channel the aspirations of the people and, therefore, students were filling the representational void by direct forms of participation. By early April, more cautious reformers and public intellectuals (all with civil-servant status) at the Indonesian Institute of Sciences (LIPI), some of whom had criticised Suharto in the past, identified with the students and made scathing criticisms of the New Order political system.[26]

In the end, the escalation of anti-Suharto student demonstrations from late-1997 to mid-1998 was indicative of the failure of the New Order corporatist structure to contain and exclude the political activism and participation of students. Student demonstrations that had begun peacefully ended up by pitting a cross-section of society against the most repressive arm of the state, its security forces. The desire for change could not be extinguished. Finally, internal division within ABRI made impossible a co-ordinated response to mass demonstrations and the contradictory responses of reformists and hard-liners within ABRI only intensified opposition to the regime.[27]

FORMER ICMI LEADER IN THE VANGUARD OF PROTESTS

The Muhammadiyah Chairman, Amien Rais, was the most prominent national leader to express sustained support for student demands in favour of political and economic reform. As an outspoken academic at Gajah Mada University he already had a considerable student following. After his forced resignation as the head of ICMI's council of experts, he became one of the most visible symbols of opposition against Suharto's corrupt and authoritarian government and his popularity soared among students.[28] Overall, ICMI had failed to co-opt Amien or silence his dissenting voice over presidential succession, Suharto's family wealth and other controversial issues. He could not channel his aspirations through the ICMI and, once he was forced outside of the organisation, he appealed to the idea of building a coalition of opposition groups against Suharto's power in order to resolve Indonesia's crisis.

Between January and May, Amien identified with students holding nationwide vigils and demonstrations calling for political reformation and for Suharto to step down as president. He denounced Suharto's government for engendering 'corruption, collusion, nepotism, greed and moral denigration' and alluded to the self-serving nature of Suharto's family business empires. He drew on his growing popularity by threatening to bring the Muslim masses onto the streets as a 'people power' against Suharto's rule.[30] This contrasted dramatically to his statement in mid-1996 against pro-democracy forces allied to Megawati, in which he had condemned 'people power' and backed state repression.[31]

The student movement offered Amien an ideal opportunity to demonstrate his credentials as a national leader of moral standing. At the Indonesian Legal Aid Institute in September 1997, he declared his preparedness to be nominated as an alternative presidential candidate to Suharto. Later, on 15 January, at the Yogyakarta residence of the chairperson of the New PNI, Nyonya Supeni, he met with the opposition PDI leader, Megawati Sukarnoputri. In front of the small gathering, Nyonya Supeni read out a statement of concern about the monetary crisis and announced that both Amien and Megawati were putting themselves forward as presidential candidates.[32]

The meeting at Nyonya Supeni's house represented a phenomenon of emerging tactical alliances against Suharto, which revealed a growing disaffection with established arrangements under Suharto's control, as it aimed to bring together leaders of different political camps—nationalist, Islamic traditionalist and Islamic modernist. However, it also represented the failure to build an enduring or viable alliance against Suharto, as the NU Chairman, Abdurrahman Wahid, failed to appear at the meeting. After the meeting, Megawati also tried to play down the significance of the meeting by rejecting suggestions that she was seeking an alliance with the Muhammadiyah chairman.[33]

Two factors contributed to the failure of alliance building. One, according to Mietzner, was that Suharto shrewdly announced that Habibie was his candidate for the vice-presidency. He did this in a successful bid to bring the Muslim modernists behind Habibie and the president, thereby splitting the opposition and pre-empting the establishment of an alliance of nationalists, Islamic traditionalists and modernists against his rule. However, its is doubtful that any tactical alliances—had they been forged in the first place—between these civilian leaders, who viewed each other as rivals for the presidency, would have continued for long. The second was that ABRI threw its support firmly behind Suharto and Habibie, extinguishing any doubts in the minds of competing elite members that the military leadership was divided over Indonesia's future leadership, or that it might countenance disruption to the general session of the MPR in March.[34]

Like his colleagues in ICMI, Amien therefore toned down his demands for reform when Habibie's ascent to the vice-presidency was imminent, and the prospects of ICMI gaining access to the corridors of power and influence over government policy-making, consequently, had improved. For example, just prior to the holding of the general session of the MPR, at the fifth-anniversary meeting of the ICMI think-tank CIDES held on 26 February, Amien acknowledged, what seemed then, the inevitable outcome of Suharto continuing in office. Flanked by ICMI luminaries, Amien insisted that all parties should give the government a 'fair chance' by allowing it a six-month to one-year grace period to prove itself (in overcoming the monetary crisis), and invited the participants to pray for a 'happy ending' for the government.[35] Amien's supporters in the student movement expressed concern that the Muhammadiyah chairman was moderating his tone, and might sell out on the reform movement, because he seemingly had struck some kind of deal with Habibie regarding the vice-presidency. Both Amien and the ICMI intelligentsia were hopeful that the Muslim intellectuals' association would bring them closer to power and, at this point, Amien gave tacit backing to Habibie's vice-presidency.[36]

It became increasingly clear that Amien's vacillation between confrontation with Suharto's government and conciliation depended on his assessment of the shifting balance of power. As such, Amien renewed his attack on Suharto's government in reaction to an interim list of proposed cabinet members (released to coincide with the MPR session of 1–11 March) and when conciliation had clearly provided no benefits to Muslim interests. The list created great consternation in ICMI circles as it had denied its intelligentsia ministerial posts and, instead, accorded several positions to ICMI bureaucrats who were considered to be unrepresentative of Muslim interests. Amien closely identified with the concerns of the ICMI intelligentsia and, on the 10th and 11th, visited the University of Indonesia and Gajah Mada campuses. Before thousands of student demonstrators, he proposed ten points of reform for clean government, criteria for the selection of cabinet members, and the setting up of an independent team to evaluate the future cabinet and to audit the personal wealth of ministers. He bemoaned the failure of the government to recruit Adi Sasono and other ICMI intellectuals into the cabinet, asserting that it was 'no longer appropriate that we mention ICMI. ICMI indeed has been abandoned.'[37]

At a rally 16 March in Jakarta, Amien sharply criticised the newly sworn-in seventh development cabinet. He singled out as corrupt and unprofessional new ministers such as Suharto's golfing partner and timber tycoon the Minister of Trade and Industry, Bob Hasan, and the Minister for Tourism, Culture and Arts, Abdul Latief. As labour minister, Latief had allegedly been implicated in a big corruption scandal. Amien also criticised as corrupt Haryanto Dhanutirto, the former transport minister and new Minister of Foodstuffs, Horticulture and Medicine—an ICMI official that the ICMI intelligentsia had earlier gone to great pains to defend from corruption charges. Amien exclaimed, 'this cabinet is like a political joke'. He called on Suharto's government to return its mandate to the MPR, if it could not solve the crisis within a period of six months.

By late March, the pendulum of Amien's stance again swung back in favour of conciliation and he announced that he would support Suharto's government if it overcame the crisis. The Army Chief of Staff, Gen. Subagyo Hadisiswoyo, with Gen. Prabowo at his side, declared that the recent attitude and comments made by Amien were 'sufficiently mature'. Amien's conciliatory approach was closely linked to his regular meetings with the military's top brass. He had cultivated close relations with Prabowo and spoke warmly of the general (a known supporter of Habibie) as well as meeting with senior officers of the rival camp under Gen. Wiranto's command. Amien understood, as did other civilian leaders, that for any future government to survive—whether it be one led by him, Habibie or another leader—it would require the backing of ABRI. He therefore proceeded carefully with his calls for reform and a change of government, it seemed, by trying to keep the military leadership on side, whilst seeking to draw them closer to the aspirations of the reform movement. In late February, Amien had talked of there being 'a strong understanding that the armed forces must not confront their own people, let alone shoot them'.[40] It is obvious that one of the results of negotiations with the military top brass was that Amien sometimes subdued his attacks against Suharto's government.

Overall, Amien's tactic regarding ABRI was to appeal to its senior leaders to side with the people-driven reform movement against the narrow interests of Suharto's regime. After the Trisakti shootings and the broad moral outrage sparked by it, Amien's plea to ABRI became more of an ultimatum. At a memorial service for the victims, he presented ABRI with two stark choices of either protecting the interests of the wealthy Suharto family or defending the people's interests.[41] A week later, however, he was forced to cancel a plan to bring his millions of supporters onto the streets of Jakarta on the anniversary of national awakening day (20 May). This, reportedly, was because a senior general had threatened to create a bloody Tienanmen Square incident in response.[42]

Thus, it appears that Amien's vacillation between condemning Suharto and giving Suharto a chance to undertake reform was influenced by his own search for a leadership role, amid a rapidly deteriorating and uncertain situation in which he adjusted his stance to the contingency of developments. He was acutely aware that for any reform to succeed it would require ABRI's imprimatur and the kind of reform he sought was not the 'total reform' enunciated by the more radical student activists. Rather, it was one of measured reform that would better locate him in future power configurations (of a more democratically elected government) after the anticipated political demise of Suharto. Amien was an ambitious politician who aspired to gaining, if not the presidency, a central role in the new government. Moreover, his removal as the head of ICMI's council of experts had not entirely precluded him from being an aspirant 'insider' who still supported ICMI against its opponents. In February and March, at least, his attitude towards Suharto did appear to be influenced by his assessment of the prospects of ICMI's intelligentsia entering government.

However, despite Amien's prevarications, state strategies of incorporation had never really succeeded in co-opting the Muhammadiyah leader. The most recent backdoor negotiations between state officials (Habibie and senior military

officers) and Amien failed to silence his dissenting voice. As a leader of ICMI
he had already levelled criticism against Suharto's rule. Since his sacking as
ICMI's head of the council of experts, and the exclusion of ICMI's intelligentsia
from power, Amien stepped up his attacks against Suharto and threatened to
bring a 'people power' movement onto the streets. The growing student-led
reform movement provided the necessary momentum for him to pursue his
objectives more aggressively. At the end of the day, as chairman of the
Muhammadiyah and popular Gajah Mada academic, he had sufficient means
and support to promote his leadership ambitions outside of state institutions,
once the ICMI option fell through.

THE ICMI INTELLIGENTSIA TURNS AGAINST SUHARTO

If Amien Rais was at the forefront (albeit equivocally) of the student-led
demonstrations, the more cautious ICMI intelligentsia also began to articulate
dissension from Suharto's rule. Before the holding of the MPR general session,
they tentatively expressed their support for reform but, at this stage, muffled any
criticisms they might have had for Suharto's presidency. The Secretary General
of ICMI, Adi Sasono, gave his support to the reform movement. He planned to
have CIDES sponsor a national dialogue on reform, to which he would invite
senior state and military officials as well as critics of the government,
Megawati, Amien Rais and Abdurrahman Wahid. Even Sasono's cautious
proposal was viewed as too much of a threat to the regime. Consequently, the
Chief of ABRI's Social and Political Affairs, Yunus Yosfiah, declared that he
saw no need for national dialogue outside of existing channels, as the parliament
was the appropriate forum for debate.[43]

Aspirations of the ICMI intelligentsia for change were constrained and, to
some extent, determined by their perceptions of relative advantage and
disadvantage in intra-elite competition for the spoils of office and patronage.
They subdued their calls for reform when they thought that they would be
rewarded with positions in government because of their loyalty to Habibie. This
is not to suggest that members of the intelligentsia were not committed to
democratic reform (see the discussion in chapter seven concerning ICMI
agendas). Thus, when the CIDES finally met on 26 February, participants
(including Amien Rais) discussed the need for reform, but used the occasion to
declare their support for Habibie's candidacy as vice-president and Suharto's
return to office.

Their main concern before March was to promote the prospect of their
Chairman Habibie becoming the next vice-president, a staging post many
believed to the presidency, and they realised this required Suharto's imprimatur.
With Habibie as Indonesia's future president, they could hope, as Habibie's
most trusted advisors, to exert real influence on government policy. Therefore,
senior ICMI leaders, Adi Sasono, Jimly Asshidiqie, and Achmad Tirtosudirjo,
and intellectuals like Dawam Rahardjo and Nurcholish Madjid, promoted
Habibie's credentials as a man of research and technology, with 'democratic'

leanings, a reform-minded man who was well qualified to lead Indonesia into a new era of 'global knowledge economy'.

They backed Habibie in tough competition with the technology minister's opponents in Golkar, who preferred the choice of Harmoko, Try Sutrisno or other candidates for the strategic post. Suharto's children, Siti Rukmana and Bambang Trihatmojo, the majority of Golkar MPs, and Golkar member organisations such as the Self-help Family Association (MKGR), the Total Self-help Cooperative (Kosgoro), and the Central Organisation for Indonesian Socialist Functionaries (SOKSI) strongly opposed Habibie's candidacy for the second-in-command.[45] Suharto's nomination of Habibie as the sole candidate for the vice-presidential post subsequently saw the power struggle spill over into competition for cabinet posts.

Contests for Cabinet Posts

This contest became obvious with the holding of the MPR general session, when the interim list of proposed cabinet members went into circulation (discussed above). With Suharto's close associates and family members gaining the lion's share of posts, finally it dawned on the ICMI intelligentsia that Suharto would not countenance their presence in government, or their direct input into policy. The state's strategy of incorporation no longer suited them and, consequently, they began to turn on Suharto's New Order. They were slipping inexorably from being aspirant insiders into an irrevocable position of disadvantaged outsiders who would have little stake in the current status quo under Suharto's leadership.

On 12 March, ICMI held a plenary meeting and outlined six points of concern over the proposed cabinet list then in circulation. A meeting at ICMI headquarters followed this on the 13th, at which Adi Sasono, accompanied by Habibie advisor, Marwah Daud Ibrahim, and ICMI intelligentsia, declared that 'I hope the cabinet list, which has been circulated, does not become reality'.[46] An editorial board of the magazine, *Ummat*, which included ICMI intellectuals and other reform minded luminaries, proposed an alternative 'wish list' of cabinet ministers in rejection of the interim list. The *Ummat*'s list gave prominent roles to ICMI members and figures sympathetic to the cultivation of small-scale, non-Chinese business interests. Topping the *Ummat*'s list was Adi Sasono, as Secretary of State, the pro-ICMI Muslim general, Syarwan Hamid, as Minister of Internal Affairs, and the ICMI moderate, Nurcholish Madjid, as Minister of Education and Culture. Another ICMI member and Gajah Mada academic, Mubyarto, would gain Minister of Cooperatives, Habibie's advisor, Marwah Daud Ibrahim, Minister of Social Development, and the economist and pro-Megawati PDI leader, Kwik Kian Gie, Minister of Industry and Trade.[47]

Yet, the aspirations of pro-ICMI Muslim interests were not accommodated, as the government's interim list turned out to be a close approximation of the cabinet announced by Suharto on the 14th and sworn in on 16 March. The hopes of the ICMI intelligentsia that, with Habibie as vice-president, their own access to power and influence over government policy would be enhanced were shattered. Consequently, they became openly critical of Suharto and his newly appointed cabinet, in which Suharto's children reportedly had played a role in choosing ministers and diminishing Habibie's influence.[48]

Prominent Muslim leaders announced their immense dissatisfaction over the fact that those ICMI leaders who had gained cabinet portfolios were government bureaucrats regarded as unrepresentative of the Muslim community's aspirations. They expressed regret that figures like Adi Sasono, Dawam Rahardjo, Marwah Daud Ibrahim and Jimly Asshidiqie—leaders who were considered to represent Muslim interests in ICMI—were overlooked. The general chairmen of Muhammadiyah, KISDI, Persis, Al-Irsyad, and PMII strongly articulated this viewpoint. A despondent Dawam Rahardjo best expressed the profound sense of betrayal. He complained that the ICMI intelligentsia had, until then, continually defended government officials against criticism and in return the government had simply abandoned them.[49]

ICMI's Secretary General was more stoic in his response but nonetheless admitted his disgruntlement at the results, whilst calling for patience of his co-religionists in order to avoid social conflict.[50] ICMI was not alone in expressing its disenchantment over the cabinet, as Indonesian's social-political organisations (including the parliamentary fraction of the Islamic-oriented PPP), which were not included on the cabinet, protested their exclusion.[51]

Events through to the middle of March, then, saw the ICMI intelligentsia shift its position from one of cautiously broaching the need for reform to one of open disaffection as they were displaced from power. Mutual displeasure and antagonisms between Suharto's circle and ICMI spilled over into a tug-of-war over the choice of the organisation's new chairman. At ICMI's plenary meeting held on 12 March for the election of a new chairman, the rumour circulated that Suharto wanted Azwar Anas, the former Coordinating Minister for Community Welfare, as ICMI's new head. The ICMI intelligentsia, not wanting a government bureaucrat in the top job, hurriedly collected signatures in support of their own candidate. Their choice was Gen. (ret.) Achmad Tirtosudirjo (a founder of HMI and former head of Bulog who was already in his seventies) as chairman in charge of the daily affairs of ICMI. Achmad was elected by acclamation. Habibie remained the *de jure* chairman until his election to the presidency.

The Muslim intelligentsia hoped that Achmad would provide the opportunity for ICMI to loosen its dependence on Suharto's circle and promote its own agendas. Meanwhile, Achmad promised that he would try to make the organisation a more independent and critically vocal forum for 'voicing injustices experienced by the people'.[52] Ongoing frictions and the battle for control of ICMI, between its bureaucrats and its reform-minded members, on this occasion were resolved in favour of the latter. Whereas Suharto's circle had promoted ICMI bureaucrats to cabinet rank, the cost of this uncompromising policy (of rewarding his closest loyalists with posts) was that ICMI's intelligentsia sought to unhitch the association from bureaucratic influence and control. Failing to gain inclusion in the power structure, they wished to make ICMI a much more autonomous associational expression of their interests, unfettered by the constraints and controls of corporatism.

Habibie tried to placate the discontent of the intelligentsia by appointing Adi Sasono and other ICMI supporters as advisors to the vice-president's office. In return, Achmad Tirtosudirjo and other ICMI figures talked optimistically of the organisation assuming the role of think-tank on government policy.[53] According to *Asiaweek*, Habibie's new reform-minded advisors believed that they could transform Habibie and 'remake him—in their own image', to become 'a Muslim who is progressive, sophisticated, market-oriented and media-savvy; someone who cares about social justice, democracy, human rights, the environment'.[54] Although, Adi cautioned, 'we can't expect dramatic changes while Suharto is in power'.[55]

Efforts to mollify ICMI aspirations did not prevent them from attacking Suharto's rule. However, they began to call for the president to step down only after the horror of the Trisakti incident, student abductions and ensuing anti-Chinese riots of 14–15 May. Elite opinion and public opinion began to turn resolutely against Suharto as it no longer tolerated such crude methods of terror—against Indonesia's most treasured youth, university students—as a means of managing dissent and instability. Reflecting this outrage and disaffection over their own displacement from power, ICMI's chairman and Secretary General became more outspoken in their support for the reform movement.

For example, after a meeting in mid-May of the central leadership council of ICMI, Achmad Tirtosudirjo and Adi Sasono announced that ICMI supported student demands for 'total reform'. However, it is doubtful that, at the time, they actually desired 'total reform', as they were not seeking a significant shift in power configurations but a realignment of them under Habibie's future presidency. ICMI still provided an important vehicle for achieving this. They proposed that a special session of the MPR be held and the cabinet be reshuffled, in an allusion to the need for Suharto's government to resign.[56] On 16 May, Adi Sasono gave a fiery anti-Suharto speech before an emotionally charged audience at Al-Azhar Mosque.[57] The press reported Achmad Tirtosudiro as calling for Suharto to resign before the 20th of the month.[58]

To conclude, Amien Rais had led the defection from Suharto; eventually some of ICMI's senior leaders and intelligentsia followed suit. Incorporation in the existing state structures no longer worked for members of ICMI's intelligentsia nor for a number of its leaders. The March cabinet appointments of Suharto loyalists proved beyond a doubt that Muslim interests in ICMI would not benefit politically from continued accommodation with Suharto. The cabinet composition also demonstrated that Suharto was not serious about implementing reforms.

Although Suharto had previously disappointed the intelligentsia by not giving its members cabinet positions in 1993, this had not led to their defection from the president. The difference this time was the political context of deep crisis and intensifying intra-elite rivalry before an anticipated post-Suharto period. The momentum of student-led public protest and societal activation provided much of the impetus for change. Only in mid-May 1998, however, when public sentiment had turned assuredly against Suharto, did more cautious ICMI leaders and intellectuals find the courage to call openly for Suharto to resign. It appears that some members of the intelligentsia hoped that under a Habibie presidency they would gain strategic positions in a reconfigured power structure and would be able to promote democratic reforms.[59]

Before the clear shift in public mood, members of ICMI's intelligentsia for several years had wished to see Suharto resign. However, with the exceptions of Amien Rais and Sri Bintang Pamungkas, most of them, before this time, had been unwilling to air their views publicly. They had long desired political reform but also realised that, through incorporation in ICMI, Suharto gave them protection from rival groups, especially from nationalist elements in ABRI. It was also too dangerous to oppose Suharto, with the imprisonment of Bintang having demonstrated this danger. Until this point, incorporation and the threat of sanctions had acted as relatively effective mechanisms for neutralising dissenting voices in ICMI.

SUHARTO LOSING CONTROL

The groundswell of student-led opposition (and emerging chaos) to Suharto's New Order thus far discussed created tremendous pressures on the political elite to call for the president's resignation. Confronted by crisis, corporatism and repression failed to contain societal demands for participation. From 18 May until their removal on the 24th, in an act of open defiance, thousands of students occupied the parliament building in the South Jakarta suburb of Senayan and met with the parliamentary fractions. A veritable cornucopia of student umbrella organisations crowded the parliamentary compound. Muslim leaders and organisations comprised a significant segment of the student-led reform movement pushing for change of government in the last days of Suharto's presidency. Representing Islamic organisational presence was the umbrella KAMMI, the Regional Corps of HMI Alumni (KAHMI), and the Indonesian Muslim Community Movement for Reform (Gemanusi)—an umbrella to organisations like HMI, the Muhammadiyah University Students Association, Muhammadiyah Youth, Indonesian Secondary School Students (PII), the Indonesian Muslim Youth Movement (GPII), and the NU's Ansor Youth. Also calling for Suharto to resign were the Muslim Community Co-ordinating Body (BKUI), Dewan Dakwah and KISDI.[60]

Some of the Muslim organisations had been established recently as vehicles specifically for the promotion of reform, indicating the fluidity of the situation and the tendency of groups to coalesce into larger associational units. Others had been staunch supporters of Suharto since the state–Islamic rapprochement, but now withdrew their support. In addition, the varied new organisational entities constituted an expression of greater pluralism as students, and Muslims, began to break out of state-imposed corporatist constraints. Indicative of this challenge to the hierarchical political order, was the appearance at parliament of different professional layers of society, including academics, intellectuals, NGO leaders and other middle-class elite to address the students and contribute to demands for Suharto's resignation. National leaders, including the chairman of Muhammadiyah, Dewan Dakwah leaders, representatives from the National Reform Movement, the former head of Indonesia's Legal Aid Institute, and former ministers and retired ABRI officers arrived outside parliament to address students with rousing messages of support.

This was the first time, since the founding of the New Order, that a cross-section of society had gathered *en masse* outside parliament to declare their common support for the struggle for change. At the time, some observers might have believed that they were witnessing a microcosm of a future civil society in Indonesia. However, as subsequent events proved, the unity deriving from the shared desire to remove Suharto soon dissipated, after the president stepped down. The opposition forces that were gathering outside parliament lacked any co-ordinated plan of action to bring about a change of regime, to take over power, or to build a new government. Many students were distrustful of politicians. The reform movement was weak and divided, but this did not prevent the different elite, middle class, and student activists from coming together at a critical point of political tension to assert their demands collectively.

The greatest surprise came with the bombshell announcement by the parliamentary speaker, Harmoko that the DPR leadership had decided, in the interests of national unity, that President Suharto should resign 'wisely' and with 'dignity'. Students were jubilant as one of the deputy speakers for parliament, Lt Gen. (ret.) Syarwan Hamid, thrust his fist into the air in a victory signal. Support for Suharto was rapidly crumbling, as loyalists and sycophants alike were caving in to public pressure and responding to the obvious dissipation of support for Suharto among elite circles, including the military hierarchy.[62]

The clear loss of legitimacy and support suffered by Suharto by mid-May caused a defection of New Order stalwarts from the president. Even members of Suharto's palace circle finally regarded the president's resignation as a necessary step in order to minimise the potential damage of the reform momentum to personal careers and established institutions. A major blow to Suharto was when on the 19th fourteen economics ministers refused to serve on his reshuffled cabinet. At the eleventh hour, the military also withdrew its support from Suharto in an effort to protect its own institutional interests and salvage a badly tarnished professional reputation. The fall of Suharto de-legitimised much of his New Order, which was already under challenge from broadening societal pressures, and created the conditions for the unravelling of authoritarian institutions. Yet, as much as this open defiance of Suharto by regime insiders might have seemed to represent a political breakthrough for pro-reform forces, much of the politics that finally brought Suharto down consisted of behind-the-scenes manoeuvring, backroom deals and pact-making. The circumstances of elite defections from Suharto and divisions in the military have been discussed by other authors and take us too far away from the central concern of the book.[63]

CONCLUSION

An analysis was made of the withdrawal of Muslim support from Suharto in the context of broadening dissent against his rule. Under circumstances of deepening political and economic crisis, students galvanised into an anti-regime movement in retaliation against two decades of exclusion from political arrangements. This gave greater impetus to disaffected elite members to oppose Suharto's rule. In this context, ICMI leaders and the intelligentsia were among the defecting elite interests that had lost out in recent power struggles to Suharto's family interests. However, it must be noted that throughout his presidency, Suharto had managed to maintain exclusionary corporatist barriers to Muslim access to power. The wider incorporation of Muslim interests in state structures in the 1990s also had succeeded in muffling much of the critical voice of Muslims, while still denying them real positions of power. Nonetheless, the shift in corporatist strategy to greater inclusion of Muslim interests raised expectations—among ICMI-linked interests at least—for greater representation of Muslims in the near future. The refusal of Suharto to provide ICMI members with cabinet posts at a time that elite opinion was turning against him lost the president the support of Muslims. The withdrawal of Muslim support from Suharto was not the decisive factor that brought his presidency to an end. The mounting pluralist challenges against the authoritarian regime followed by elite defections, however, did indicate that corporatist exclusion was no longer a viable strategy of social-political management.

NOTES

1. Indonesians realised that the refusal of Suharto's circle to implement meaningful political reforms and bring about a measure of responsiveness, accountability and transparency was greatly responsible for the government's failure to deal with the deepening economic crisis. It was widely recognised that Suharto and his family had siphoned off much of Indonesia's wealth through their own business monopolies and foundations, and that government corruption was at epidemic proportions. Confronted by growing domestic and international demands to undertake necessary reforms, Suharto surrounded himself with a tiny nucleus of loyalists and cronies in order to protect family business interests and power.
2. After thirty-two years of rule, the causes of Suharto's forced resignation from office on 21 May were, nonetheless, multi-stranded and complex. However, a discussion of these causes is beyond the central argument

concerning pluralist challenges to authoritarianism in general and to exclusionary corporatist structures in particular. Other authors have analysed most of these causes and, therefore, the international and economic dimensions, including the role of the IMF will not be specified here. Suryadinata, 'A Year of Upheaval and Uncertainty'; Hill, 'The Indonesian Economy: The Strange and Sudden Death of a Tiger'; McGillivray and Morrisey, 'Economic and Financial Meltdown'; Evans, 'Economic Update'.

3. See chapter four for discussion on campus normalisation.
4. There remains the question of how consistently was corporatist organisation applied to student activities? For instance, the student co-ordinating bodies did not channel the activities of students into corporatist arrangements in the manner that Golkar, PPP, and PDI channelled and constrained the interests of political parties. However, the establishment of administration dominated student bodies did conform to exclusionary corporatist ordering insofar as students had their political activities on campus restricted and students were prohibited from organising openly through alternative channels to the authorised student bodies. Students responded to the policy of campus normalisation by joining unmediated cell-like organisations and channelled their energies into mosque-related pursuits with goals that were not overtly political. Thus, corporatist exclusion of student interests had taken place but certainly there was no strict regime of corporatist organisations established with which to rechannel student interests. Most of the above analysis is drawn from my own general observations. Bhakti, 'Trends in Indonesian Student Movements', p.172.
5. *Ummat*, 20 April 1998.
6. *Suara Pembaruan*, 24 February and 5 March 1998; *Tiras*, 9 March 1998; *Ummat*, 9 March 1998.
7. *Suara Pembaruan*, 26 February–11 March 1998; *Ummat*, 16 March and 29 April 1998; *Tiras*, 23 March 1998; *Gatra*, 18 April 1998; *Forum Keadilan*, 20 April 1998.
8. *The Age*, 13 March 1998; *Gatra*, 14 March, 18 April–25 May 1998; *Ummat*, 13 April–11 May 1998; *Suara Pembaruan*, 12–25 March 1998.
9. *Forum Keadilan*, 6 April 1998.
10. *Suara Pembaruan*, 3–26 March 1998; *Tiras*, 23–30 March 1998; *Gatra*, 18 April and 2 May 1998; *Ummat*, 4 May 1998.
11. Interview with members of the Youth Islamic Study Club (YISC) at Al-Azhar Mosque on 18 October 1996; *Ummat*, 23 March 1998.
12. Although some of these groups were mutually exclusive entities with restricted memberships, others were organised by a hierarchy of *murabbi* (mentors, leaders). They provided a potential breeding ground for future political actions. The Secretary General of Dewan Dakwah, Hussein

Umar—a fiery preacher in his own right—was a senior *murabbi* who played a prominent role in organising Islamic groups on campus. Suharto's New Order state tried to counter the proliferation of unmediated student groups by co-opting preachers like Hussein and sponsoring them to press the government's message at universities. It also established state-guided *pesantren kilat* (fast-track courses in Islamic morality for students) on campus and organised children from their pre-school years onwards into *al-Qu'ran* recital clubs and other state approved social activities. Interviews with Ahmad Syafi'i (senior researcher at the Department of Religion), 7 April 1997; Imaduddin Abdulrahim, 15 February 1994 and 2 September 1996; Rosyad, 'A Quest For True Islam'.

13. Madrid, 'Islamic Students', p.21.
14. Aspinall, 'The Indonesian Student Uprising', pp.218–24.
15. Madrid, 'Islamic Students', pp.21–6.
16. Rosyad, for example, argues that, since the founding of ICMI, many members of the Muslim student movement later tended to gravitate into positions within the state bureaucracy and become co-opted. Rosyad, 'A Quest for True Islam'.
17. Rosyad, 'A Quest for True Islam'.
18. There was a notable tendency for Abdurrahman and Megawati to align themselves with nationalist causes for a religiously-neutral state against what they saw as the inclination of modernist Muslims associated with Muhammadiyah and ICMI to sponsor Islamic causes.
19. This line of argument, although containing a large element of truth, tends to underestimate the high degree of diversity of, and competition between, social-political interests well before the New Order was established. For example, during the 1950s' period of parliamentary democracy, factionalism within and between national political parties was rife and contributed to the denouement of constitutional democracy.
20. *Gatra*, 28 March 1998; *Suara Pembaruan Daily*, 13–20 March 1998; *Ummat*, 6 April 1998.
21. This might explain why Suharto, through his Coordinating Minister for Politics and Security, Feisal Tanjung, rejected student requests to meet directly with the president. Student meetings with Suharto would be an admission that political solutions could be found to the crisis and that student demands were legitimate.
22. *Suara Pembaruan Daily*, 27 March 1998. The Minister of Internal Affairs (ret. Gen.) Hartono also rejected outright any notion of holding dialogue between student representatives and Suharto. *Ummat*, 4 May 1998.
23. 'Indonesia: Impunity Versus Accountability', ICG Asia Report, pp.3–4.
24. *Gatra*, 2–23 May 1998; *Ummat*, 4–18 May 1998; Louise Williams, 'Protesters shot in police clashes', *The Age*, 4 May 1998; Louise Williams, 'Police shoot to quell rioters', *The Age*, 6–11 May 1998; Louise Williams, 'Defiant students take protests off campus', *The Age*, 13 May 1998;

Louise Williams and Gerrase Greene, 'Deaths rile PM', *The Age*, 14 May 1998; David Lamb, 'Campus deaths fuel protests', *The Age*, 15 May 1998; Louise Williams, 'Riots shake Soeharto', *The Age*, 15 May 1998.

25. *Ummat*, 20 April 1998
26. One LIPI researcher, Syamsuddin Haris, referred to the 'hegemonic party system' as part of the 'sterile condition of conventional instruments of politics'. The head of the LIPI research unit for politics, Mochtar Pabotinggi, rejected as ludicrous the notion that parliament represented the people. He instead called the DPR/MPR the 'Regime's' Representative and Deliberative Councils. *Ummat*, 6 April and 11 May 1998.
27. Aspinall, 'Opposition and Elite Conflict', pp.144–5.
28. Although, minority religious groups and NU youth groups were among those who remained distrustful of the Muhammadiyah leader because of his former involvement in ICMI.
29. According to Amien, the coalition would have to include all social forces including the armed forces, Golkar, the existing parties, mass organisations, business people, religious groups and NGOs. *D&R*, 10 January 1998; *Tiras*, 30 March 1998; Young, 'The Crisis: Contexts And Prospects', pp.120–1; Aspinall, 'Opposition and Elite Conflict', p.145.
30. Louise Williams, 'Muslim leader calls for alliance to end Suharto's grip on power', *The Age*, 6 January 1998; Louise Williams, 'Warning signs for Suharto', *The Age*, 28 February 1998; *Tiras*, 30 March 1998.
31. See chapter eight.
32. Among those at the gathering at the time were the former Minister of Internal Affairs, Rudini who, in 1996, had publicly defended the various forces for change coalescing around Megawti's PDI against Suharto. Other figures present at the gathering, later referred to as '28 October Group', included Suharto critics Ali Sadikin (Jakarta's former governor and leader of the 'Petition of 50'), Baharuddin Lopa (the Secretary General of Komnas HAM), and Sri Edi Sasono (elder brother of the gaoled Sri Bintang Pamungkas and avid supporter of the student-led reform movement). On the whole, these were people who had been pushed to the margins of power by earlier political struggles and had remained mild irritants as they continued to criticise aspects of Suharto's New Order. *Gatra*, 24 January and 14 February 1998; *Tiras*, 2 February 1998; *Asiaweek Online*, 16 March 1998; *Republika Online*, 26 January 1998–2 February 1998; Margot Cohen, 'Daring to Say No: Muslim groups search for alternative to Suharto', *Far Eastern Economic Review*, 8 January 1998, pp.18–20; Margot Cohen, 'Campus Crusaders: Students raise temperature of the protests', *Far Eastern Economic Review*, 26 March 1998, p.26.
33. *Tiras*, 2 February 1998.
34. Mietzner, 'From Soeharto to Habibie', p.71.

35. At the function, Habibie's advisor on military defence Sayidiman Suryohadiprojo spoke on the subject of constitutional and gradual reform, while another Habibie loyalist the Chief of Social and Political Staff, Lt Gen. Yunus Yosfiah, attended. Other members of ABRI's top-brass were present at the meeting, including Gen. Wiranto's senior advisor Lt Gen. Bambang Yudhoyono. They apparently had warned Amien to restrain his attacks against Suharto, to secure the MPR session against the possibility of mass unrest.
36. *Republika Online*, 27 February 1998; Margot Cohen, 'Campus Crusaders: Students raise temperature of the protests', *Far Eastern Economic Review*, 26 March 1998, p.26; *Suara Pembaruan*, 27 February 1998; *Tiras*, 23 February 1998.
37. *Ummat*, 23–30 March 1998; *Tiras*, 23 March 1998.
38. Margot Cohen, 'Campus Crusaders: Students raise temperature of the protests', *Far Eastern Economic Review*, 26 March 1998, p.26.
39. *Suara Pembaruan*, 26 March 1998; *Tiras*, 23 March 1998.
40. Louise Williams, 'Warning signs for Suharto', *The Age*, 28 February 1998.
41. Louise Williams, 'Muslim leader supports student protesters', *The Age*, 12 May 1998; Aspinall, 'Opposition and Elite Conflict', pp.146–7.
42. Young, 'The Crisis: Contexts and Prospects', p.107.
43. Margot Cohen identified public dissension of ICMI intelligentsia from Suharto's rule as early as December 1997. Margot Cohen, 'Daring to Say No: Muslim groups search for alternative to Suharto', *Far Eastern Economic Review*, 8 January 1998; *Gatra*, 17 January 1998; *Ummat*, 9 March 1998.
44. *Republika Online*, 2–27 February 1998; *Tiras*, 9 March 1998.
45. *Far Eastern Economic Review*, 26 March 1998.
46. *Forum Keadilan*, 6 April 1998; *Gatra*, 21 March 1998.
47. *Ummat*, 16 March 1998.
48. *Forum Keadilan*, 6 April 1998; *Tiras*, 30 March 1998.
49. *Ummat*, 16–30 March 1998; *Tiras*, 23 March 1998.
50. *Forum Keadilan*, 6 April 1998; John McBeth, 'Suharto's Way', *Far Eastern Economic Review*, 26 March 1998.
51. *Suara Pembaruan*, 19 March 1998; *Gatra*, 21 March 1998.
52. *Forum Keadilan*, 6 April 1998; *LKBN Antara* (Radnet), 12–14 March 1998; *Gatra*, 21 March 1998; *Ummat*, 23 March 1998; *Tiras*, 30 March 1998.
53. *Tiras*, 23 March 1998.
54. *Asiaweek*, 16 March 1998.
55. *Asiaweek*, 16 March 1998.
56. *Gatra*, 16 May 1998.
57. According to the *Far Eastern Economic Review*, Adi declared that '"God is the Supreme Power, and God can take power away from anyone. We must

change the entire system so that people can control their leaders".' *Far Eastern Economic Review*, 28 May 1998.

58. *Ummat*, 25 May 1998.
59. This point is discussed further in chapter ten on Habibie's presidency.
60. *Gatra*, 23–30 May 1998; *Ummat*, 25 May 1998; *Forum Keadilan*, 15 June 1998.
61. See previous footnote.
62. *Forum Keadilan*, 15 June 1998; *Far Eastern Economic Review*, 28 May 1998.
63. Aspinall, 'Opposition and Elite Conflict'; Young, 'The Crisis: Contexts and Prospects'; Vatikiotis, 'Romancing the Dual Function'.

Chapter 10

Habibie and Party Pluralism

INTRODUCTION

President B.J. Habibie's 'reform development government' represented a significant, but not complete, departure from the authoritarian legacy of Suharto's thirty-two-year period of rule. During his short tenure (May 1998–October 1999), Habibie delegated to a 'team of seven' advisors, within the jurisdiction of the Ministry of Internal Affairs, the task of drafting a series of new political laws on parties, elections and the composition of legislative bodies. The reforms were to lay the ground for multiparty democracy to be realised with the holding of Indonesia's first democratically contested general elections in forty-four years. Consequently, as curbs were lifted on party organisation, unrepresentative political arrangements that had been the mainstay of Suharto's rule were progressively dismantled or rendered irrelevant. The lifting of restrictions on press freedom opened the floodgates to public criticism and scrutiny of Habibie's government, the military, authoritarian political institutions and corrupt practices.

The chapter examines how ICMI and Golkar fared during Habibie's presidency once the corporatist and other curbs were lifted on political organisation. An analysis is made of the splintering of group interests as members of the political elite left corporatist organisations and formed or joined new political parties with which to contest the elections. An examination also is made of the state's mobilisation of Muslim groups against the 'pro-democracy' opposition as Habibie sought to stave off challenges to his rule. The argument is made that, although corporatist arrangements were dismantled, the president and his armed forces commander, Wiranto, still relied on the politics of exclusion—namely, the exclusion of opposition political parties from the MPR, and the use of state-directed intimidation and repression against dissent. Authoritarian habits and (coping) strategies remained a salient feature of politics, as they coexisted with, and sometimes were reinforced within the context of, the emerging multiparty politics.

CORPORATISM DISMANTLED

The ruling party, Golkar, lost its single-majority status and control over the authorised party system, which was eroded at the June 1999 election and then removed with the convening of the new parliament (the People's Representative Council, DPR) in October. The 'mono-loyalty' of public servants to Golkar, through their membership of the compulsory civil servants union, Korpri (otherwise guaranteeing their vote would go to the ruling party), was abandoned. Internal factional disputes resulted in some of Golkar's affiliate organisations and members splintering away from the party to re-group into new political entities. The military leadership gave public assurances that it would remain outside of partisan politics and would not, as in the past, campaign in the elections on behalf of a political party, namely Golkar. Finally, Golkar's supervisory board, and Suharto's controlling position over Golkar as head of the board, was eliminated.[1] In short, all of these measures cut the ruling party from its New Order moorings and threatened to leave it adrift in its own irrelevance within the newly-evolving political system. The challenge facing Golkar cadres was to refashion the organisation and turn it into a viable party with strong grassroots support to compete effectively in the scheduled elections. Like Golkar, the two subordinate, and emasculated members of the state-corporatist party system, the United Development Party (PPP), and the Indonesian Democracy Party (PDI), were struggling to find a role in the unfolding political system.

The lifting of restrictions on parties heralded a new phenomenon of 'wild-growth' democracy, as new parties proliferated. Many of the parties were formed on the basis of old affiliations or *aliran*—the primordial/communal sectarian loyalties long suppressed by Suharto's New Order—with Islamic, Christian, nationalist, socialist, Sukarnoist, and other parties coming into existence. The ethnic Chinese also were allowed to form parties after three decades of political exclusion and persecution as a pariah class. Forty-eight of the more than one hundred parties were registered to compete in the election in June. The five main parties to contend the elections were the Indonesian Democratic Party for Struggle (PDI-P) led by Megawati, the National Mandate Party (PAN) led by Amien Rais, the National Awakening Party (PKB), which served as a vehicle for Abdurrahman Wahid's presidential aspirations, PPP, and the renamed Golkar Party.

A striking feature of the proliferation of new parties was that the Islamic politics that Suharto and his military backers had fought so hard to stifle was reconstituted under Habibie's government and the political freedoms it spawned. Dozens of Islamic parties came into existence in preparation for democratic elections. There were new organisations like the Masyumi, the New Masyumi, and the Crescent Moon and Star Party (PBB), which were all descendants of the Masyumi party (banned by President Sukarno and suppressed by Suharto). There were two parties besides PKB representing different factions of NU, the Community Awakening Party (PKU) and the Nahdlatul Ulama Party (PNU).

The Muslim organisations and parties at a special session of the People's Consultative Assembly (MPR) in November 1998 successfully lobbied to have the *Pancasila* sole foundation law, requiring that all social-political organisations be based solely on the state ideology, rescinded.[2] The government followed this on 29 April 1999 with its announcement of the official withdrawal of *Pancasila* (P4) indoctrination courses and the liquidation of the BP-7 agency responsible for administering the courses. Consequently, Muslim parties once again were permitted to adopt Islamic ideology as their foundational principle. PPP, for instance, chose to return to Islam, in place of *Pancasila*, as its party ideology. The decades of state ideological control of Islamic, social and political organisations seemed to be over.

Although Habibie's reformers paved the way for multiparty democracy, the DPR was fashioned to include appointees and some corporatist (functional) representation. The 500–member DPR still included sixty-five appointees from special (functional) interest groups (especially Islamic minority groups), and thirty-eight ABRI-appointed seats. Although appointees to the parliament were greatly reduced, through its allocated seats, ABRI could hold the balance of power in the fragmented MPR and thus provide the decisive votes to ensure a presidential nominee and political system favourable to the military. In the regional parliaments, retired military officers joined different parties (especially Golkar and PDI-P) in an attempt to exert future influence on politics and tilt 'pluralist democracy' in their favour.

Although restrictions were lifted on political organisation, the biggest headache for Habibie's government was how to manage this resplendent burst of party pluralism in a manner that would reinforce national stability and stave off challenges to his own leadership. With few pundits believing that this apparent political lightweight would survive the distance of even a transitional period in office, Habibie seemed determined to prove otherwise as he sought to win domestic and international support for his presidency by demonstrating that his government could implement timely reforms. With the scheduling of new political and electoral laws, a distinct possibility existed that Indonesia's hitherto excluded citizenry would participate in a robust and healthy democracy.

MUSLIMS IN GOVERNMENT

Habibie's decision to surround himself with trusted loyalists in a reshuffled cabinet, and to deny posts to his traditional adversaries and new pro-democracy parties ensured that political rivalries would continue along old lines of conflict for the duration of his administration. Until the holding of planned presidential elections, the new parties were given no place or representation in the DPR, which was responsible for passing new laws. Habibie's political antagonist, Abdurrahman Wahid, and his supporters in NU were denied cabinet posts. For several months, therefore, the parties were unable to have direct influence on public policy and the political system remained, in significant measure, exclusionary.

The clear winners in the new cabinet were Habibie's closest advisors and aides, some of whom belonged to ICMI. Although there is nothing unusual about a president appointing his closest advisors and aides to cabinet posts, Habibie's administration still lacked the legitimacy of freely contested elections and surrounding himself with loyalists reinforced old lines of conflict (to be discussed). ICMI's Secretary General, Adi Sasono, achieved cabinet rank as the Minister of Cooperatives, with the mandate to give financial assistance to the economically devastated indigenous business class. The reform-minded ICMI intelligentsia formed the core of presidential advisors, almost a kitchen cabinet. Habibie also conferred cabinet rank upon his loyalist generals, the so-called 'green', or Muslim, officers. The pro-Habibie officer, Syarwan Hamid, was rewarded for his defiance against Suharto with the position of Minister of Internal Affairs, replacing Lt Gen. (ret.) Hartono (who was disliked for his role in establishing greater control over the ICMI intelligentsia). The former ABRI commander and Suharto loyalist, Gen. Feisal Tanjung, was retained as Coordinating Minister of Politics and Security. Lt Gen. Yunus Yosfiah was rewarded for his loyalty with the position of Minister of Information.

The change of government saw the realisation of a strategy long propounded by some of the ICMI intelligentsia. That is, they had maintained that, if they waited patiently in the wings, under the protection of Suharto and Habibie's patronage, eventually they would outlive Suharto's presidency and inherit a major share of influence and power. Suharto's strategy of incorporating Muslim interests in ICMI, in the long run, had benefited a few members of its intelligentsia by bringing them into the corridors of power. This was an unintended consequence of New Order political arrangements, which had sought to neutralise Muslim political interests and exclude them from power arrangements.

FRAGMENTATION OF GOLKAR

The new administration was driven by the need to consolidate power behind Habibie's weak presidency and to project his authority, in the face of many adversaries who wished to see his transitional leadership foreshortened. In particular, the privileging of Habibie's Muslim aides and bureaucrats in the political structures ensured that power contests would continue, and sharpen, along pro-Habibie and anti-Habibie 'nationalist' lines that had characterised the last years of Suharto's rule. As politics was inexorably shifting to a more open, democratic culture, old political rivals positioned themselves to take best advantage of the new arrangements.

This section of the chapter considers how Golkar underwent a process of fragmentation, as the party became polarised between supporters of Habibie and his adversaries. This fragmentation was the consequence both of the re-play of earlier power struggles and of new pressures caused by multiparty politics, as the freedom to join any number of new parties undermined the rationale of a person's incorporation in Golkar. The first contest between the Habibie camp and rival interests in Golkar occurred in the lead up to an extraordinary congress in July 1998.

The Golkar Congress of July 1998 Causes Split

The congress was vital to Habibie's political survival as the president's backers in Golkar, most of them associated with ICMI, sought to gain control of the party and have their candidate, the State Secretary, Akbar Tanjung, replace the Suharto sycophant, Harmoko, as new Party Leader. Control over Golkar was still important because the party could use its parliamentary majority to influence the direction of political reforms, either to the benefit or detriment of the governing elite. Meanwhile, different factions representing Suharto's family, retired military officers, and nationalist elements in Golkar sought retaliation against the president. They backed former Defence Minister Edi Sudrajat, a long-time rival of Habibie, for the chairmanship. Suharto's children, Siti Rukmana and Bambang Trihatmodjo, former Indonesian Vice-President Try Sutrisno (also the chairman of the association of retired ABRI officers, Pebabri) and retired officers campaigned for Edi. With Akbar winning a comfortable majority, his military detractors in Golkar began to cry foul by accusing both Habibie and Wiranto of engaging 'New Order methods' to bring about a victory.[3]

One of the immediate consequences of the internal struggle for control of Golkar was that some of the defeated elements left Golkar and founded the Barisan Nasional (National Front) as a publicly vocal, but politically emasculated, anti-Habibie power bloc. Following this, some of them established their own political party under Edi Sudrajat's leadership, the Unity and Justice Party (PKP), with which to contest the general elections. In a bid to defeat Habibie's anticipated leadership of Golkar, they also lent their support to PDI-P's election campaign. This splintering away from Golkar reflected the growing dynamism of party-based pluralism, which permitted disaffected elements to re-channel their interests through alternative political vehicles. It also represented a polarisation along old lines of conflict. That is, many of the Barisan and PKP's leaders were figures who had been sidelined since Golkar's 1993 congress, had subsequently joined the pro-Megawati opposition alliance in 1996 and supported the nationalist organisation, the National Brotherhood Reconciliation Foundation (YKPK).[5] With the faces of political adversaries remaining constant, the political struggles of 1998–1999 under Habibie's leadership recalled the pattern of winners and losers in power contests of the mid-1990s during Suharto's rule.

The winners on this occasion clearly were Habibie's Muslim supporters as Golkar positions were filled by the president's advisors and bureaucrats from ICMI and by cadres from the Islamic university students and alumni associations, HMI and KAHMI. As a former HMI Chairman, the new Golkar Chair, Akbar Tanjung, drew a lot of support from these last two organisations.[6]

Golkar's National Work Meeting of March 1999: Further Schisms

A second division in Golkar occurred in the lead up to the party's national work meeting scheduled for 8–12 March 1999. Habibie's colleagues in ICMI promoted their mentor as Golkar's sole presidential candidate for the MPR election in November, while HMI/KAHMI interests backed Akbar Tanjung in competition with Habibie.[7] At one level, the rift illustrated the difficulty Golkar cadres faced in reforming the party and making a clear break with its corporatist past. That is, Akbar represented entrenched interests in Golkar that were alienated by efforts of the Internal Affairs Minister, at the behest of Habibie, to push through election law reforms. Akbar was indignant over a new regulation on the neutrality of civil servants, which sought to prohibit government ministers and senior officials from campaigning in the elections and freed civil servants (Korpri and the association for the wives of civil servants, Dharma Wanita) to vote for any party. Such measures were perceived as greatly hurting Golkar's election machine. Under the new regulations, as cabinet minister, Akbar no longer would be able to retain his position as Golkar chairman.

The new chair of the Golkar parliamentary faction and Akbar supporter, Marzuki Darusman, declared that if government officials were banned from campaigning, Golkar would withdraw its support from Habibie. As the Deputy Chairman of Indonesia's National Commission on Human Rights, Marzuki's threat sat awkwardly with his image as a reformer, who might have been expected to welcome an end to Golkar's days of pork-barrelling. This point considered, the issue was resolved when Akbar bowed to the requirement that bureaucrats no longer campaign for the party, resigned as minister, and chose to devote his energies to his own presidential ambitions as Golkar chair.[8]

Despite its reform agenda, Habibie's team of ministers and aides also engaged Golkar's traditional machinery and well-worn practices of pork-barrel politics. Habibie's team embarked on an all-out vote-buying campaign in the provinces. Initially only ten out of twenty-seven provinces backed Habibie as sole candidate. However, within twenty-four hours of the final session of the national meeting, amid accusations by party insiders of massive vote buying, twenty provinces had swung in favour of Habibie's sole candidacy for president.[10] Reliance on such tactics reflected attempts by Habibie's government (including ICMI interests) to consolidate their political advantage and translate it into enduring power before the holding of elections. It also brought into question the government's commitment concerning its restrictions on the practice of bureaucrats campaigning for Golkar at the elections.

Golkar–ICMI Tensions

A third rift in Golkar occurred between its Chairman, Akbar Tanjung, and the Minister of Co-operatives and ICMI Secretary General, Adi Sasono. Sasono, who had originally entered Golkar to defend Akbar's candidacy for party chair against Edi Sudradjat's 'nationalist' group, backed Habibie against Akbar for the presidential stakes. Sasono and ICMI supported the unsuccessful candidacy of Habibie's adviser, Marwah Daud Ibrahim, for chair of Golkar's parliamentary faction against the final victor, Marzuki Darusman. Members of Akbar and Marzuki's team retaliated by calling on Sasono to resign from Golkar for refusing to campaign in the general elections for the party.[11] Sasono responded by insisting that he decided not to campaign for Golkar because, as Minister of Co-operates, he would be accused of using government facilities to buy votes. However, by this stage Sasono had been isolated within Golkar by Akbar's faction.

Following this, there were signs that the Minister of Co-operatives was preparing an alternative vehicle to that of Golkar and ICMI with which to realise his political ambitions. Sasono was widely viewed as the man responsible for launching the new People's Sovereignty Party (PDR), whose leaders were known protégés and confidants of Sasono from the ICMI think-tank, CIDES, the Bandung Institute of Technology (where Sasono received his engineering degree) and the co-operatives department. Although Sasono denied any links with the party, analysts conjectured that the party would become an alternative political vehicle to Golkar for the Minister, and possibly for President Habibie should Golkar prove an insufficient political machine. The East Java chapter of PDR strengthened such speculation when it announced that Habibie and Sasono were its choice of 'national leaders'.[12]

There were signs that support for Habibie and Golkar might disintegrate even further, as the ICMI membership increasingly was split between support for Golkar and support for the new, mostly Islamic, parties such as PPP, PBB, PKU, and the more nationalist-oriented PAN. Although the Muslim parties initially considered forming a coalition with Golkar and supporting Habibie, many party leaders eventually withdrew their support and sought a separate 'Islamic' alliance.[13]

This fracturing of support for Habibie within ICMI and Golkar reflected a natural progression as the new Islamic parties offered more autonomous vehicles through which competing politicians could pursue their political aspirations and agendas. This splintering of support occurred during a pre-election phase that was in extreme flux, as different party leaders manoeuvred into a series of shifting 'potential' alliances of contending parties in anticipation of forming a governing coalition. At one stage, there was speculation that Golkar might form an alliance with PDI-P and PKB. This sparked retaliations from Muslim modernists, who then sought to establish a rival coalition of Islamic parties, which most likely would include Amien Rais's PAN, and threatened to withdraw their support from Habibie.[14]

In summary, there was a progressive slippage of support for Golkar, on the one hand, and Habibie, on the other, as competing factional interests entered into general election mode and fiercely contested the presidential stakes. This slippage was a consequence of pluralist politics heralded by the proliferation of parties. Both Golkar and ICMI, then, were fracturing along lines of new political entities and old political loyalties, with the future of these two organisations cast in doubt, unless they could transform themselves successfully into highly competitive grassroots parties. In retrospect, the political reforms promoted by Habibie in order to maintain his own presidency contributed to an erosion of his already tenuous hold on power, as the dynamism of party-based competition chipped away at the shibboleths of authoritarianism. The New Order under Habibie's leadership was being demolished from within, seemingly with the president's blessing.

THE POLITICS OF SURVIVAL: A RETURN TO NEW ORDER TACTICS

The political system was moving in the direction of greater political pluralism as elite interests organised to contest elections. Although the exclusionary corporatist arrangements had been dismantled, sobering counter trends to the democratic opening also were at play as the authoritarian habits of the past three decades were brought into tension with the emerging democratic pluralism. Habibie's administration still came to rely on the politics of exclusion—namely the intimidation and repression of opposition—in order to stave off challenges to his presidency. These counter trends became most evident with the holding of an extraordinary session of the MPR on 10–13 November to debate and pass the government's new laws on elections, parties and the composition of parliament. The extraordinary session became the focus of anti-government student demonstrations, state-organised counter-demonstrations, and military repression, which created a cycle of violence and replay of politics reminiscent of the late-Suharto period.

The extraordinary session of the MPR had provided a renewed common purpose to an otherwise fragmented student and pro-democracy movement, which had contributed to Suharto's downfall and once again resolutely articulated a range of political and economic concerns. Students and other advocates of 'total' political reform viewed Habibie's government as little more than a continuation of Suharto's New Order legacy, lacking the will or popular mandate to implement democratic change successfully. The demonstrating students, who sought to march on and occupy parliament in protest over the passing of the political laws, formed loose coalitions of cross-campus and pro-democracy groups. These included the Unified People's Action (Akrab), which comprised the Jakarta Communication Forum of Student Senates (FKSMJ), the Satgas Student Family of ITB, the University of Indonesia Larger Family, and the National Coalition for Democracy (KND). There were student coalitions like City Forum (Forum Kota), the Student Action Front for Reform and Democracy (Famred) and the Student and People Committee for Democracy (Komrad).[15]

Many student leaders were disheartened by, in their eyes, the slow pace and limited scope of the government's program for constitutionally measured change. They suspected that the drafting of new political laws and regulations were aimed at facilitating the government's re-election at fresh polls. They were uncompromisingly opposed to the government's retention of ABRI seats in parliament, as they called for an elimination of *dwi-fungsi*, and were disappointed that the assembly proceedings did not pass a separate law for the investigation and trial of Suharto. Of particular threat to Habibie's government was the prospect that students, supported by nationalist politicians from Edi Sudrajat's camp, would call for the government's replacement with a provisional presidium or people's council until the holding of elections. The Barisan leader, Kemal Idris, stated that he was 'prepared to die' in the fight against Habibie, 'He's a Suharto crony.'[16]

Another threat to Habibie was Megawati Sukarnoputri who was making a powerful comeback to politics after she had legalised her PDI faction's existence with a change of name to PDI-P and held a party congress in Bali (8–10 October 1998). Old opponents of Habibie, including Barisan leaders, regrouped under Megawati's party banner as the PDI-P's escalating popularity threatened to swamp the president's prospects for re-election. PDI-P declared the MPR proceeding invalid in protest over the fact that it, along with the other pro-reform parties, was denied participation at the extraordinary MPR proceedings.[17] In short, the main forces that Suharto's authoritarian government had suppressed were re-emerging as a clear threat to Habibie who, in order to consolidate power in the interim period before elections, also largely excluded political opposition from decision-making processes in the MPR. In this way, his administration tried to exert as much control as it could over the drafting of new laws and constitutional amendments.

Finally, Habibie's government was fearful of mobilisations of grassroots causes against his leadership, as Jakarta's residents and urban poor joined the student protesters on several occasions. Popular discontent had been deepening against the incumbent government because of its apparent failure to convincingly tackle the problem of widespread corruption of government officials or to alleviate the tremendous hardship and deprivation experienced by millions of Indonesians as a consequence of economic collapse earlier ,in the year. In the vacuum of legal uncertainty, peasant farmers and urban unemployed were among those who had taken matters into their own hands. They made raids on food stocks and crops, reclaimed vast tracts of land that had been alienated by the state, and sought retribution against regional, district and local government officials and agencies.[18]

It was under these circumstances of growing challenge that Habibie, with the backing of Wiranto, returned to a reliance on familiar New Order tactics. Such tactics included counter-mobilising Muslim interests against student demonstrations, deploying civilian vigilantes, thugs and paramilitary groups in the streets as a form of extra-legal crowd control, and using outright military repression of opposition. The New Order phantom of authoritarianism appeared to be making a ghastly but predictable return. Islam also was becoming a more politicised commodity, following on from mobilisations of Muslim interests against pro-democracy forces during Suharto's last years in office.

State Directed Mobilisations Against Opposition

Pro-Habibie Muslim interests allied to formerly corporatised organisations like ICMI and the Indonesian Council of Ulama (MUI) played a central role in providing manpower and logistical support to the establishment of civilian security militia (Pengamanan Swakarsa) for the safeguarding of the SI MPR proceedings. With an elevated position in ABRI doctrine and practice, civilian security militias like Pam Swakarsa were a creation of the state (military).[19] It appears, however, that there were misgivings within the military over the use of Pam Swakarsa and the role of Wiranto in supporting the militias is unclear. Nonetheless, it is doubtful that the militias could have operated so brazenly as they did without tacit approval from Wiranto. Thus, in tandem with the growth of multiparty politics, New Order elements that still dominated government were digging their heels in and employing state-orchestrated violence in order to fend off the multiplying challenges of democracy.

The difference this time, was that an estimated thirty thousand Pam Swakarsa, bearing sharpened bamboo poles, entered the Jakarta streets in public view to intimidate and battle demonstrators in order to defend the MPR session. As such, the New Order policy of utilising civilian militias to do its dirty work was much more in the open than on previous occasions. The Pam Swakarsa comprised several different elements, with the largest contingent being Muslim recruits plus the usual component of state-funded Pancasila and Pancamarga youth, unemployed and school dropouts who were recruited from the streets. There were Muslim storm troopers recruited by radical Muslim organisations like KISDI and new entities established for the occasion, Furkon (Forum for Upholding the Constitution and Justice) and FUNGSI (Muslim Supporters of the Constitution Forum).[20]

MUI created, and held leadership position in, Furkon, which based its *swakarsa* operations at Istiqlal Mosque in Central Jakarta, where MUI also had its headquarters.[21] Various other Muslim groups not linked to Furkon, going under such names as 'Batalyon Al-Ghifari', 'Banten army', and 'Istiqlal army', were organised separately as civilian volunteers. In addition, the Minister of Co-operatives, Adi Sasono, and his underlings at CIDES (ICMI), Eggy Sudjana (an experienced agitator behind an array of mass actions), Moh. Jumur Hidayat, and Edhi Santoso were attributed with having organised Muslim militias to confront student demonstrators.[23]

There were some strong indications that Pam Swakarsa was an army-backed operation. For example, the Chairman of Furkon, Faisal Biki, claimed that he had distributed Rp. 50 million to more than 20 *swakarsa* units and insisted that Gen. Wiranto and Golkar's Deputy House Speaker, Abdul Gafur, supplied his funds.[24] Claims of direct ABRI involvement in creating the *swakarsa* units also came from other militia members and informants.[25] Maj.-Gen. Kivlan Zein (the former Chief of Staff of Kostrad under Gen. Prabowo Subianto's command, before both officers were dismissed) was identified as one of the officers involved in organising Muslim recruits. Although Wiranto denied any association with the Pam Swakarsa operations, he defended their existence and rejected public calls to disband them. Under new restrictive laws on holding demonstrations, *swakarsa* units obtained police permits to conduct their operations, yet student demonstrators were withheld permission. The civilian militias also formed a front guard before lines of anti-riot police in their clashes with pro-democracy demonstrators.[26]

Military officers reportedly gave Muslim units of Pam Swakarsa pre-field briefings on the righteousness of their struggle against the students.[27] Consequently, as a result of military briefings, in its slogans and statements, the Muslim contingent of the militia claimed to be fighting an Islamic Holy struggle to defend the state and to safeguard the constitutional processes of the MPR against the students. Pro-MPR SI Muslim organisations, such as Furkon, had begun their propaganda campaign against the student movement as early as September and espoused ABRI's *kewaspadaan* (vigilance-security) approach, which had been developed by ABRI's National Resilience Institute (Lemhanas) during the New Order period. This approach had commonly identified the 'extreme left' (communism) and the 'extreme right' (political Islam) as threats to national stability, and frequently branded opponents of the regime with these appellations.[26] This time, however, ABRI had mobilised the 'extreme right' against regime opponents, identified as the 'extreme left'.

Muslim politicians and leaders joined the government initiated propaganda campaign against the state's 'enemies' and in defence of the MPR proceedings. These leaders were mostly drawn from the Islamic modernist stream of Islam and non-Abdurrahman Wahid aligned members of NU's traditionalist stream, and were affiliated with ICMI and MUI. They perceived themselves as being under threat from nationalist politicians who were backing Megawati's presidential ambitions and wanted to oust Habibie and Islam from power.[29]

The deployment of civilian militias was evidence that the army, even after the formal liquidation of its social-political affairs posts, still exercised a formidable social and political role underwritten by its *dwi-fungsi* doctrine. Many of the pro-Habibie/pro-MPR Muslim leaders and organisations earlier had participated in state-directed counter-mobilisations against Megawati's PDI coalition in 1996. This is not to suggest that Muslim leaders did not mobilise grassroots support independently of the state against the opposition. As mentioned in chapter eight, these Muslim leaders had considered Megawati to be a threat to the political interests of Islam. On this occasion, Muslim interests were mobilised in defence of Habibie's presidency against student groups and nationalist interests deemed hostile to Muslim political interests. In an attempt, once again, to dissipate and neutralise the energies of the student-led pro-democracy movement, the military had tried to consolidate behind the government status quo groups and anti-democratic forces. Central to the defence of the MPR proceedings was defence of the military's dual function and its allocated seats in parliament against student-led opposition that had pushed for revocation of the doctrine in order to realise fully civil and political liberties.

The main significance of the Pam Swakarsa phenomenon was that it constituted another state-directed mobilisation of anti-democratic forces for the purpose of preventing other social groups from engaging in political mass actions. Arguably, this might have been necessary for an interim period in order to permit the government to prepare the ground for Indonesia's elections. Had student-led demonstrators occupied the parliamentary (DPR/MPR) building during this crucial session, they might successfully have disrupted the political process and jeopardised the very reforms they claimed to defend. Both the government and opposition were faced with the dilemma of how to end old habits of mobilisation and counter-mobilisation so that a healthier process of political participation could be instituted.

Government Strong-Arm Tactics Backfire

The street stand-offs reached a climax with the so-called *Semanggi* incident or 'Black Friday' the 13th. Members of Indonesia's urban educated classes were shocked that Habibie's administration repressed student demonstrators in a manner reminiscent of the Tri Sakti shootings before Suharto's downfall. This time anti-riot troops opened fire with rubber bullets and live rounds on crowds outside Atma Jaya University, killing at least fifteen protesters and wounding hundreds.[30] The *Semanggi* incident brought Habibie's government into disrepute as a broad range of political organisations and community groups demanded government accountability over the deaths. Calls for Habibie to sack Wiranto as Defence Minister and ABRI Commander intensified in the days and weeks after the incident. ICMI leaders in cabinet and on Habibie's staff were among those demanding that Wiranto resign. There were also calls for Habibie to step down, and students led mass protests to strategic locations in Jakarta (Freedom Palace, parliament, Attorney General's Office) and other cities. Public reaction grew over the black Friday bloodshed. Even Habibie's Muslim supporters criticised the government for its use of force. The pro-Habibie Muslim leaders might have supported the MPR proceedings, but they were unprepared to condone the state's latest bloody suppression of innocent civilians.

On 16 November, three days after the *Semanggi* incident, a forum of religious scholars and community figures from Jakarta, Bogor, Tanggerang and Bekasi organised a Muslim community mass gathering (*Apel Akbar Umat Islam*) at Al Azhar Mosque in South Jakarta. Following on the heels of a third Muslim congress, Muslim leaders at the gathering again endorsed the MPR proceedings and issued a statement denouncing those who wished to bring about its defeat. The difference this time, was that the Muslim leaders called for an immediate government response to the black Friday incident, criticised the security forces, requested a full investigation into the shootings, and questioned whether Wiranto should continue as commander of the armed forces and minister of defence. A number of Muslim university students associations, HMI, KAMMI, IMM, Forma Indonesia and Forum Salemba issued a joint statement urging Habibie's government to immediately rescind ABRI's *dwi-fungsi* doctrine and its seats in parliament and place Suharto on trial.[32]

As a direct beneficiary of Habibie's presidency, ICMI, however, more or less endorsed the regime's standpoint. It released a statement of twelve demands, which called for a reduction of ABRI seats in the parliament rather than the elimination of *dwi-fungsi* and requested students to stop demonstrating. It sought specific concessions for Muslim political interests such as recognition that reform should be based on Islam's moral culture.[33]

It can be concluded from the fallout from the *Semanggi* incident, that the attempts by Habibie's government to organise pro-regime Muslim interests, thugs, state violence and intimidation against political opposition and dissent, to a great extent, had backfired. Such New Order instruments of coercion were not equipped to deal with the fluidity of post-Suharto politics. The existence of dozens of political parties and independent monitoring bodies, an increasingly independent parliament, press freedom and deep community distrust of the government all militated against the quiet acquiescence of Indonesia's citizenry. The result was that Habibie and Wiranto were forced to make a hasty retreat as they promised to take firm measures against the military officers responsible for the bloodshed and sought to mend fences with their main detractors among the national elite.[34] Even more than on the prior occasions of 27 July 1996 and May 1998, the ground had worn thin beneath military-backed coercion. Broad public opinion condemned the transparent efforts by ABRI to bolster its own security operations with civilian stooges. These developments—of societal demonstrations, counter-demonstrations, and regime repression—were reminiscent of cycles of protest and repression that occurred during the New Order, in the pre-election climate of 1996 and 1997.

THE GENERAL ELECTION OF 1999: DEMOCRACY PREVAILS?

Compared to the storm of *Semanggi*, the general election was conducted in an atmosphere of relative calm as the political elite turned to the business of contesting office. For the first time in forty-four years, Indonesians had the opportunity to participate freely in the political system and help determine the next government. The election also provided the first litmus test of political organisation in Indonesia since the lifting of authoritarian controls. The question arose as to whether corporatist organisations like ICMI, MUI, PPP and Golkar would drift into irrelevance and finally disband? The Golkar party sought to renovate its image and transform its organisation in order to attract grassroots support, but its links with Suharto's New Order left it publicly maligned. Serious doubts arose as to whether Golkar would survive the elections as a viable party, as public rage and dismal turn-out of party supporters forced it to cancel numerous campaign rallies in Java. The PPP also assumed again the Islamic *Kabah* as its party symbol, and sought to portray itself as a victim, rather than agent, of the New Order in a concerted effort to distance itself from Suharto's legacy and win support.

At the polls, Megawati's PDI-P picked up the largest bloc of votes, achieving 34 per cent of the votes cast. The Golkar party had consolidated with some success behind Habibie as the second largest vote-winner, but well behind PDI-P with 22 per cent of the votes. Abdurrahman Wahid had been in the political wilderness throughout much of the Habibie period because of a stroke. His PKB received the third largest bloc of votes, but well below the other two parties at 12 percent. PPP won 11 per cent of the vote and Amien Rais's PAN came fifth with 7 per cent.[35] The parties that ran on a self-consciously Islamic ticket—except PPP—were all but decimated, and would be unable to contest future general elections because they did not meet eligibility requirements under new electoral laws. This came as a major blow to Muslim leaders who had believed that democracy would bring about a majority victory for political Islam. Whereas ICMI had provided little if any representation of Muslim interests under Suharto—although it did offer some representation within Habibie's power structure—Muslim parties had now demonstrated their ineffectiveness as vehicles for channelling the interests of Muslim politicians. If the general election could be considered a test of Islam's political appeal and strength, the poll results demonstrated that Muslim constituencies did not care much for the political cause of Islam.

International and domestic election watchdogs gave the election a clean bill of health for democratic transparency. In contrast to the 1997 election campaign, which recorded the greatest levels of violence for an election campaign during the New Order, this time the campaign was surprisingly peaceful and without significant violent incident. However, one striking feature of the democratically contested elections was that Megawati's overwhelming lead did not translate directly into her election to the top executive post of Indonesian president. This was largely because of her inability to consolidate her advantage by failing to secure support behind her candidacy in the intervening period between the general election and the MPR general session. Instead, through clever behind-the-scenes horse-trading and compromise between Islamic minority parties, Habibie's faction of Golkar and PKB, Abdurrahman Wahid was elected as Indonesia's fourth president. Abdurrahman received much of the support by default. That is, after the MPR had rejected Habibie's report on his tenure as president, his faction—not wanting to see Megawati as president—instead backed Abdurrahman. The Islamic minority parties threw their weight behind Abdurrahman because they preferred a Muslim cleric in the top executive post to a woman, who seemed to represent the interests of nationalism against political Islam. They had cried foul of the general election results and dragged their feet on endorsing them. They had sought, instead, inclusion in the MPR based on their special status as a minority interest. Megawati had to settle for the much less influential position of vice-president.[36]

CONCLUSION

Political developments during the period of Habibie's transition administration confirmed a number of democratic trends and anti-democratic counter-trends. Political reforms paved the way for multiparty democracy, which resulted in a proliferation of new parties that competed in democratic elections. In this competitive climate, corporatist institutions unravelled, became irrelevant, or, as was the case for the Golkar party and PPP, sought to reinvent themselves so that they could participate in the new arrangements. The days of corporatist exclusion were over. However, Habibie and Wiranto still relied on the politics of exclusion (denying representation in the MPR to opposition parties, intimidation, and repression) in an unsuccessful effort to defeat opponents before the holding of elections. As part of intimidation, Muslims were organised into Pam Swakarsa militias and counter-demonstrations against student and pro-democracy demonstrators. Although much of the contest during Habibie's administration was conducted along the lines of multiparty politics, old power conflicts also continued to colour political competition. As such, national political leaders perceived the contests largely in terms of these rivalries (between the forces of Islam and the forces of nationalism) in a winner-take-all endgame. Several ICMI leaders also found a key role in Habibie's government either as close advisors or cabinet ministers. Habibie's leadership and patronage of ICMI had therefore benefited a number of the organisation's members, who had hoped that their limited inclusion in state structures under Suharto would provide them with political power.

NOTES

1. *Forum Keadilan*, 22 February 1999; *Gatra*, 20 March 1999; John McBeth, 'The Empire Strikes Back: As Golkar strives to reinvent itself, Suharto loyalists watch and wait', *Far Eastern Economic Review*, 9 July 1998.
2. *Forum Keadilan*, 16 November 1998.
3. *Far Eastern Economic Review*, 29 October 1998; *Kompas CyberMedia*, 14 July 1998; *Tempo*, 26 October 1998.
4. Long-time affiliate member organisations also left Golkar, with MKGR establishing its own party and Sons-Daughters of ABRI Pensioners' Communication Forum (FKPPI) and Kosgoro joining Barisan Nasional. *Gatra*, 20 February 1999; *Tempo*, 19–26 October 1998; *Tempo Interaktif*, 12 February 1998; *Republika*, 2 December 1998; *Tajuk*, 1–15 October 1998; *Forum Keadilan*, 22 February 1999.
5. For the past decade, they had remained unreconciled to Habibie's aspirations for the vice-presidency, his close relations with Suharto, and the state–Islamic accommodation represented by the ICMI phenomenon. Some of them were fresh recruits to the 'reform' ethos, who had been the New Order's most hardline generals from the 'nationalist' mainstream.

Prominent among this group were disaffected figures like Sembiring Meliala and Harsudiono Hartas, who had backed Try Sutrisno's vice-presidency against Habibie's candidature in 1994. Another figure joining Barisan was Gen. (ret.) Kemal Idris, who had been responsible for the 'half-coup' against President Sukarno in 1952, was instrumental to Sukarno's ouster in 1966, and had been a thorn in President Suharto's side for much of the New Order period. Sacked by Habibie for opposing Akbar Tanjung's candidacy, the former Transmigration Minister, Siswono Yudohusodo, and the Secretary General of Golkar (the former Environment Minister), Sarwono Kusumaatmadja, also became leading Barisan members. These two ministers had earlier, in the mid-1990s, sympathised with YKPK and Megawati's PDI against Habibie. David Jenkins, 'Habibie flogging a lame horse', *The Sydney Morning Herald*, 17 November 1998; *Tempo*, 12 October 1998; *Ummat*, 16 November 1998.

6. *Tempo*, 8 March 1999.

7. *Forum Keadilan*, 23 May 1999.

8. Marzuki was an old Golkar cadre for fourteen years who Suharto (Golkar's Chairman of the Board of Patrons) removed from Golkar over an interview statement in which Marzuki declared that he 'wanted to be president'. Keith Loveard, 'Test of Strength', *The Bulletin*, 24 November 1998; Margot Cohen, 'No Fear or Favour: Golkar will have to play by new election rules', *Far Eastern Economic Review*, 11 February 1999; John McBeth, 'Little Choice: Golkar finds no alternative to Habibie', *Far Eastern Economic Review*, 27 May 1999; *Tempo*, 5 April and 24 May 1999.

9. The newsweekly *Tempo* identified the ICMI leaders Achmad Tirtosudiro, Jimly Asshidiqie, Marwah Daud Ibrahim and Dewi Fortuna Anwar as senior advisors to Habibie, who had a role in organising support for the president. 'Pertarungan: Satu Nol buat Rudy', *Tempo*, 24 May 1999.

10. The Minister of Justice, Muladi, and Golkar leader, Slamet Yusuf Effendi, were identified as fund dispensers as they lobbied the head of Golkar's Central Java chapter. The State Minister for Youth and Sports lobbied the Jakarta chapter, the Head of the Supreme Advisory Council and strong Habibie supporter, Ahmad A. Baramuli, lobbied Eastern provinces, and other ministers and Golkar leaders were identified as lobbying other provinces.

11. Adi Sasono was Golkar's campaign co-ordinator for the Central Java province. *Forum Keadilan*, 22 February 1999.

12. *Tempo*, 14 December 1998; *Gatra*, 23 January 1999; *Forum Keadilan*, 25 April 1999.

13. The ICMI leader, Dawam Rahardjo, a former, if somewhat disgruntled, supporter of Habibie reportedly declared that 50 per cent of ICMI cadres backed Amien Rais's PAN and not Golkar *SiaR* (apakabar@ saltime.radix.net), 19 May 1999; *Gatra*, 23 January 1999.

14. Habibie's close adviser, Dewi Fortuna Anwar, also seemed to dissent from the president when she cautioned that 'conservative forces' associated with Golkar, PDI-P and PKB—the three largest parties as votes were being tallied—were most likely going to govern Indonesia, and that they were not inclined to push through essential political reforms. She bemoaned the fact that, in her opinion, Amien Rais's PAN was the most reform-oriented party that had consistently defended democratic change, yet was unlikely to have much influence on the future direction of government policy. ICMI's chairman, Achmad Tirtosudiro, announced that the Muslim intellectuals' association officially backed Habibie for president. Nonetheless, even he suggested that Adi Sasono, Amien Rais and the Chairman of PBB, Yusril Isha Mahendra, were acceptable presidential candidates. *Republika*, 15 June 1999.
15. For details on the student movement, see Aspinall, 'The Indonesian student uprising', pp.212–38; *Forum Keadilan*, 16 November 1998.
16. *Tempo*, 9 November 1998.
17. *D&Rá17 October 1998; Forum Keadilan*, 16 November 1998.
18. Soetrisno, 'Current Social and Political Conditions', pp.163–9.
19. As Bourchier has illustrated, the establishment of civilian militias in collaboration with the military was uniquely located in Indonesian defence doctrine, with the term 'Sistem Keamanan Swakarsa' (Civil Security System) in parlance since at least 1982; Bourchier, 'Skeletons, Vigilantes', p.157.
20. *SiaR News Service*, 4 November 1998; *Ummat*, 23 November 1998; *Tempo*, 30 November 1998.
21. For example, MUI's Secretary General Nazri Adlan was one of Furkon's leaders from MUI. *Tempo*, 16–23 November 1998.
22. The head of FUNGSI was an identified gangster. KISDI Chairman, Achmad Sumargono, had fostered close ties with the discredited former commander of Army Strategic Reserves (Kostrad), Lt Gen. Prabowo Subianto, and had been a member of Ali Murtopo's clandestine Special Operations in the 1970s. Sumargono acknowledged his former close relations with Prabowo in an interview by the Dateline program. Dateline, 8.30 report, SBS television, 9 February 2000.
23. *SiaR News Service*, 25 September–16 November 1998; *Tempo*, 14 December 1998.
24. *Tempo*, 30 November 1998.
25. *Detikcom*, 11 November 1998; *Tempo*, 30 November 1998.
26. *Tempo*, 23–30 November 1998; Crouch, 'Wiranto and Habibie', p.133.
27. *Tempo*, 30 November 1998; *Detikcom*, 11 November 1998.
28. In line with the vigilance approach, Furkon arranged a mass 'Alert' meeting (Apel Siaga) of approximately 25,000 Muslims at Istiqlal Mosque on 30 September, at which leaders invoked hysteria of the communist threat

and identified the cross-campus City Forum and the People's Democracy Party (PRD), as 'communist-infiltrated organisations'. On a separate occasion, a banner written by the state-corporatised mosque organisation, Indonesian Mosque Communication Body (BKPRMI), proclaimed: 'PKI-Style Riots, Pillage, Terror, Instability, Sabotage'. *Tempo*, 12 October and 30 November 1998.

29. They gave an early endorsement of the SI MPR at the Third Indonesian Muslim Congress, held from 3–7 November at the Stadion Utama Senayan (Grand Senayan Stadium) in Jakarta. Prominent modernist leaders such as Anwar Harjono and Hussein Umar of the anti-Christian propagation council, Dewan Dakwah, Yusril Ihzra Mahendra of PBB, and Achmad Sumargono (KISDI), and pro-government leaders of Nahdlatul Ulama, KH Ali Yafie, Syukron Makmun, and KH Ilyas Ruchiyat (also leaders of ICMI and MUI), participated in the congress, which was attended by an estimated 1,500-strong crowd from 30 Islamic organisations. Among its declarations, the congress reinforced a ruling by MUI (issued on 29 October) that Indonesia's future president must be a Muslim male and, therefore, their political rival from the nationalist camp, Megawati, could not legally become Indonesia's next president under Islamic law. The Muslim leaders had sought to draw upon quasi-religious justification as a way of de-legitimising her candidacy. The congress was an early example of mounting opposition of a coalition of Islamic parties and interests (including PPP) in their vehement rejection of the growing prospect of Megawati becoming Indonesia's next president. In a clear sign that Megawati was the most popular candidate, mass rallies in support of PDI-P, held in Jakarta and other main cities on Java and Bali were beginning to dwarf the rallies of other parties. Thus, the congress was an early sign of the closing of ranks between the government and its Muslim supporters in reaction to the mounting calls from students and nationalist politicians for a presidium government to replace Habibie and in reaction to Megawati's growing popularity. *Republika*, 15 November 1998; *Tempo*, 2 November 1998; *Antara*, 6 November 1998; *Kompas*, 9 November 1998; *Tempo*, 23 November 1998; *Ummat*, 16 November 1998.

30. Whereas the Trisakti incident had precipitated Suharto's fall, Habibie's administration weathered the mounting challenge to his rule after the Atma Jaya shootings, largely because Indonesians anticipated a fundamental change of political system through general elections.

31. *Kompas Cybermedia*, 3 December 1998; Louise Williams, 'Jakarta on the "edge of chaos"', *The Age*, 15 November 1998; Keith B. Richburg, 'Riots Follow Peaceful Jakarta Protest', *Washington Post Foreign Service*, 15 November 1998.

32. *Kompas*, 16 November 1998; *Ummat*, 16 November 1998.

33. *Republika Online*, 7 December 1998; *Tempo Interactif*, 12 May 1998; *Tempo Interactif*, 7 December 1998.

34. *Suara Pembaruan Daily*, 23 November 1998; *Ummat*, 23 November 1998; *Kompas CyberMedia*, 18 November 1998; *Kompas*, 27 November 1998.
35. 'Indonesia's Crisis: Chronic', p.3.
36. 'Indonesia's Crisis: Chronic', p.4.

Chapter 11

Conclusion: The Failure of State Corporatism?

As part of regime maintenance and survival strategy, the Suharto regime organised state–society relations along exclusionary corporatist lines. Islamic organisation was a major target of exclusionary arrangements. The exclusionary strategy served three main purposes. One was to inhibit the autonomous organisational capacity and demand making of group interests so that people's participation in the formal political system would be greatly restricted and challenges to the regime's exercise of power would be minimised. Another was to provide an institutional means of communication and linkage between state and societal interests. This was done in order to ensure that communication with the state occurred on the regime's own terms, through these formal mechanisms, and not through alternative political vehicles. These mechanisms mostly served to transmit government messages downwards to communities, but also as an information gathering mechanism to monitor society in order to identify communal antagonisms and political dissent before they threatened stability. A third was to mobilise communities for various political and economic development objectives, which included mobilising support for Suharto's presidency whilst neutralising the potential of that support to engage in independent political action.

In line with these purposes, corporatised interests had their energies and program activities diverted from overtly political concerns into New Order development-oriented projects. Exclusionary corporatism, therefore, served a dual, but inter-related, purpose of insulating the state from societal demands whilst helping furnish the Suharto regime with support and legitimacy derived from targeted political mobilisations of the populace and from the development orientation of organisational activities.

Beyond Suharto's strategies and objectives, the book examined Muslim responses to Suharto's political management of Islam and queried the extent to which different Muslim interests embraced, became co-opted by, and/or resisted capture by the state. An analysis was made of whether capture resulted in significant political benefits and opportunities for the incorporated interests, or whether these interests were mostly denied strategic access to political goods (i.e., representation, policy input, and governmental office). Certainly from the 1970s to the mid-1980s, there was a significant level of resistance to corporatist capture (especially from NU) when relations between Suharto and Muslim political interests largely were antagonistic. For those interests that had been captured in a variety of arrangements, corporatism mostly served to shut them out of power-sharing arrangements. However, this situation changed in the late 1980s, with a rapprochement occurring between Suharto and Muslim leaders. There was a discernible shift in state corporatist strategy in general from an exclusionary one to one that appeared, on the surface at least, to be partially inclusionary. An indication of this shift was that Suharto widened the scope of incorporation as he sought to co-opt strategic middle-strata elite (especially Muslims) into existing power arrangements behind his presidency. To this end, Golkar underwent a number of civilianisation and recruitment campaigns, and ICMI was established as a new vehicle of Muslim support.

In large numbers, Muslim leaders embraced ICMI as a sign of improving relations between Suharto and Islam. However, as Suharto expanded incorporation of new groups and extended state jurisdiction over Muslim community organisation, he tried to maintain exclusionary corporatist barriers to people's participation in the political system. Muslim leaders discovered that their incorporation did not translate into commensurate political goods. Although ICMI leaders did gain some representation in the MPR and DPR, most of its members were effectively denied meaningful participation in the political system and were not rewarded with strategic positions in government. Nevertheless, ICMI members felt that, through incorporation, they had achieved substantial progress—in terms of less military supervision of Muslim organisational activities, more freedom to organise and publicise Islamic ideas, and greater access to patronage and decision-makers.

NU was divided in its responses to corporatist capture. On the one hand, several NU leaders and components of the organisation were drawn into state structures, through Golkar, PPP, MUI, ICMI and other entities. On the other, the NU chairman represented orientations which resisted corporatist capture and strove for NU's political independence from the state.

A central concern of the book was whether Suharto's corporatist strategies worked successfully as a mechanism for obstructing the growth of associational pluralism. From the 1970s until the mid-1980s, it appears that strategies of corporatist exclusion did indeed inhibit associational pluralism. The enforcement in 1985 of *Pancasila* as the sole ideological foundation of organisational existence was the pinnacle of these efforts backed by arrests of extremists. However, after 1988, the partial shift to inclusionary strategy had the effect of re-politicising group interests after two decades of de-politicisation and corporatist exclusion. State capture of Muslim interests contributed to the organisation and counter-organisation of competing group interests and to a concomitant increase in associational pluralism.

Before elaborating this conclusion, however, there are a number of political and economic contexts which have to be considered in assessing the role of corporatism in facilitating societal pluralism in the post-1988 period. The political context from the late 1980s until, at least, the mid-1990s was one of a deepening intra-elite rivalry (especially between Suharto and segments of the military leadership) during a protracted succession crisis, coinciding with economic liberalisation followed by a limited political opening. The net effect of these factors was to generate greater autonomous activity within society, including increased associational capacity and pluralism. This impacted on authoritarian structures as demands for political participation, civil liberties, reform and democracy intensified.

Suharto tried to deal with challenges to his presidency. The shift in corporatist strategy was in response both to his conflict with military leaders and to growing demands for participation. He continued, as he had in the past, to sow division and fragment group interests. First, he exploited internal organisational rifts (e.g., NU and PPP), and rivalries between organisations (e.g., segments of NU and ICMI) with corporatism providing one of the means of splitting group interests through segmental capture of organisational components, and by alternately favouring one (incorporated) constituency over another (excluded) constituency. Second, corporatism helped regulate the access of state and non-state interests to patronage and power opportunities, which resulted in not only winners and losers but supplied one of the arenas in which struggles for position took place.

Corporatism helped Suharto to readjust the balance of competing interests as he played off different aspirants for power whilst seeking to remain the senior patron and final arbiter of disputes. In particular, incorporated Muslim interests were drawn into partisan struggles that facilitated Suharto's tactics of sowing division and circumventing potential threats to his power. He brought Muslim (civilian) interests into state structures in an attempt to offset his reliance on the military, as well as tried to absorb and neutralise the rising Muslim middle-class aspirations for change. He later sought to redress imbalances once he had more fully subordinated the military to his authority by placing a military loyalist, two former vice-presidents, and family members in supervisory roles over ICMI. In other words, Suharto used the corporatised Muslim interests to help him maintain a shifting disequilibrium of forces as rival interests competed for political predominance at the time of growing public perceptions of an impending succession crisis.

However, Suharto's tactics proved an insufficient means of dampening societal demands and challenges from opposition. Although Suharto was a recognised master of divide-and-rule, in the new context of political openness and growing pluralist pressures for change, there were distinct risks associated with this partial shift to a more inclusionary strategy, which had implications beyond previous experiments with state corporatism.

To begin with, several ICMI members constituted a potential counter-elite or opposition to Suharto from within these state structures. The intra-elite conflict and the period of political openness encouraged them to pursue the fulfilment of their own agendas for increased representation for Muslims, Islamisation of state and society, and reform of the political system including a process of demilitarisation. This brings us to the observation that the broader the interests absorbed into state arrangements, the more likely it is that those interests would make demands for their full representation in the system. Correspondingly, this would produce pressures for a change in the nature of the political system as an increasing number of interests competed for access to political goods.

Second, although Suharto neutralised the most outspoken ICMI members who criticised his presidency, the mobilisation of Muslim support behind his presidency and against opponents created a reaction from disaffected members of the elite, especially from those who had been displaced from power by the newly-incorporated Muslim interests. An increasing number of the sidelined members of the elite and regime opponents began to organise alternative vehicles for their political participation outside of the corporatist arrangements, for re-inclusion in a 'reformed' political system, and in protest against the state–Islamic accommodation. In short, corporatist inclusion of Muslim interests had contributed to a re-politicisation and multiplication of organised group interests demanding participation.

Consequently, the institutions of authoritarianism were showing signs of decay, because they were no longer able to contain, channel, neutralise, or co-opt effectively the diversifying demands and challenges of society. Suharto's counter-mobilisation of incorporated Muslim interests and other pro-regime groups against dissent had the effect of further politicising state–society relations. In these circumstances, the hardline military clampdown on dissent created deep social resentment and dismay, which, in the context of the 1997–1998 economic collapse, triggered further oppositional mobilisations against Suharto's rule. Recourse to crude state repression and terror was a clear sign that corporatism was failing as a strategy for the containment of society's latest associational dynamism.

In light of the political and economic crises, an analysis was made of whether captured Muslim interests contributed to anti-regime organisation, or whether they reinforced the authoritarian structures of the Suharto regime. To what extent were Muslim responses to pluralist challenges conditioned by their own location inside or outside of the state corporatist arrangements? The simple answer is that Muslim responses both to Suharto's rule and to the growing pluralist challenges were conditioned, but not wholly determined, by their location inside corporatist arrangements insofar as Muslim leaders perceived that they could gain political advantage from their incorporation. More broadly, calculations of relative advantage and disadvantage vis-à-vis rival political interests in contests for power in an anticipated post-Suharto period greatly influenced the positions adopted by incorporated (and unincorporated) interests.

Thus, Suharto was able to mobilise Muslim political opinion against the pro-democracy/pro-Megawati forces in 1997, not just because of the state-military's sophisticated propaganda campaign, but also because Muslim leaders at the time perceived Megawati to be a threat to their own political ambitions. In particular, these Muslim leaders felt the state–Islamic accommodation to be endangered by Megawati's rising star. On several occasions, ICMI leaders and members also were drawn into struggles in support of their chairman against his rivals until their support clearly failed to furnish them with much-hoped-for positions in the 1998 cabinet. Until this time, most ICMI members remained compliant supporters of Suharto, or were unwilling to voice their criticism too openly. They began publicly to support the student-led reform movement only after they had become disaffected by their failure to gain political appointments. Another crucial factor was that ICMI figures, including its most senior leaders, became emboldened to attack Suharto's rule once the tide of opinion had resolutely turned against the president in his last days of office.

Thus, the critical voice of Muslims was greatly constrained by their capture in state structures in a manner that reinforced authoritarian institutions. ICMI members did not significantly contribute to anti-regime mobilisations or to growing pluralist challenges, although, as argued, the creation of ICMI did trigger the counter-organisation of group interests outside of corporatist structures.

Our answer to the above questions shifts somewhat when we consider the role of the corporatised parties in anti-regime struggles. Until the 1997 general election, PPP and PDI had been mainly compliant components of the established political system—this was despite moments of resistance from PPP at earlier elections. However, from the mid-1990s until the pre-campaign period in 1997, PDI under Megawati's leadership became a major rallying point for opposition and anti-regime coalition-building initiatives as illegal and underground organisations and quasi-parties coalesced behind Megawati's campaign banner. Numerous politically sidelined (non-ICMI) Muslim interests also supported Megawati at the time. After the political decimation of PDI, PPP assumed the mantle of opposition party against Golkar during the election campaign, largely because of disaffection over Golkar's heavy-handed tactics (backed by the security forces) to win over voters. In short, opposition to Suharto emerged both from outside and inside the state corporatist party arrangements as increasing numbers of people became disaffected with his rule.

The NU chairman, who had remained at the political margins outside of state structures, also initially supported Megawati and the forces for change. However, Suharto managed to bring the chairman behind the Golkar campaign of Suharto's daughter. The NU chairman, in fact, appeared to assume stances according to his own calculations of relative advantage and disadvantage vis-à-vis rivals for power. In particular, the divide-and-rule tactics pursued by Suharto provided much of the framework of the chairman's retaliations and reconciliation, as the NU chairman sought to bring NU into a better bargaining position with state power and to displace the political influence of ICMI.

In the final chapters of the book the argument was made that exclusionary corporatism backed by repression was failing to keep group interests and opposition suppressed. Can we attribute the failure of corporatism in Suharto's last years to this form of coerced organisation or to external factors such as intra-elite conflict and economic crisis? The answer to this question has largely been provided by the above points—namely, state corporatism was part of the authoritarian institutional nexus (which included patronage games, divide-and-rule strategy, and repression), which proved unable effectively to respond to multiplying pluralist challenges, internal fragmentation of the state, and societal mobilisations.

The effectiveness of exclusionary strategy lies in the co-optation of strategic allies who collaborate with the regime against excluded groups. A shift in strategy to more inclusionary forms of state corporatism reflects the growing demands for participation from diversifying group interests. However, this kind of incorporation appears unable to satisfy those demands and contributes to pluralist challenges to regime survival. The problem was compounded for Suharto, once his power had sharply narrowed—based on mostly family interests and Suharto loyalists—with ever increasing regime members being sidelined from power-sharing arrangements. In these circumstances, exclusionary (and inclusionary) corporatist strategies became superfluous because the careful balance between regime collaboration and exclusion was shattered. Economic crisis acted on the political crisis and exposed the weakness of authoritarian institutions, including corporatist structures, and forced Suharto's resignation.

BROADER QUESTIONS

What does this study tell us about Suharto's management of state–Islamic and state–societal relations? Did Suharto get his management strategy wrong? In particular, was his downfall mostly the result of political and economic factors outside of his control, or did he precipitate his own demise through the kinds of strategies he pursued? Was the shift in corporatist strategy, however partial, in retrospect, a mistake on Suharto's part?

In effect, the shift to greater inclusion of Muslim interests—however controlled—helped undermine a major pillar of Suharto's institutional control: namely, the exclusion of most societal interests from participation in the formal political system. The consequent re-politicisation of group interests, with ICMI significantly contributing to organisation, counter-organisation and mobilisations of group interests, was one of the factors that appeared to hasten an end to Suharto's rule. Suharto's use of incorporated Islam with which to offset his reliance on the military and his harnessing of Muslim interests against opposition contributed to the re-politicisation process. The political opening, which was a result of economic liberalisation and intra-elite rivalry, was, nonetheless, an underlying factor sparking anti-regime societal mobilisations.

The question arises as to whether it was wise strategy for Suharto to use Muslim support as a means of offsetting his reliance on the military. After all, he had other well established mechanisms (such as army reshuffles and patronage games) at his disposal for dealing with over-ambitious military officers, without entailing the far-reaching social consequences implicit in the substantial incorporation of Muslim political interests. From a regime survival perspective, would Suharto have been wiser to continue a strict framework of exclusion of all Muslim political and organisational interests? Restated in broader terms, did the demise of Suharto's authoritarian rule lie in the liberalising moments rather than in the weakness of its institutional structures? Are the lessons to be learnt from Suharto's management of state and society relations in his last years of office that, if they wish to survive, authoritarian regimes should maintain an iron grip on social organisation and keep group interests suppressed?

An answer to this question is that, in the 1990s, social, political and economic change was creating a dynamic beyond the control of Suharto, and his authoritarian institutions and survival strategies were poorly equipped to deal with the fundamental nature of the change. In particular, state corporatism failed as a mechanism to contain the new burst of societal activation and corresponding state fragmentation. Comparative studies (Latin America, East Asia, and Africa) of state corporatism inform us that such systems of interest exclusion have broken down in the face of liberalising and democratising processes. This is notwithstanding that sometimes countries experience regime reversal to something approaching authoritarianism. In the final analysis, although Suharto's restructuring of the corporatist framework contributed to the breakdown of the regime, this restructuring was a response—among many other responses—to much broader challenges facing the regime.

A final question arises. What, if anything, can studies of state corporatist organisation vis-à-vis other group interests and societal movements tell us about state–societal interactions? Chapter 10 concerning the Habibie presidency possibly throws some light on this question, as corporatist arrangements quickly unravelled or were rendered irrelevant as a diverse range of independent political parties were established in preparation for democratic elections. A splintering of group interests occurred as the political elite left the enforced corporatist amalgams and joined the new parties. Thus, the emerging multiparty system provided the context for new lines of contest, which had largely been suppressed by exclusionary corporatism. However, a great deal of political contest was still conducted along the lines of earlier struggles, especially between political Islam and 'nationalists'. The Islamic–nationalist rivalries, as did the traditionalist–modernist rivalries internal to Islam, in fact, pre-dated the New Order period and had their roots in the colonial period. Quite clearly, Suharto's management strategies of divide-and-rule and corporatist fragmentation were not primarily responsible for political and communal cleavages. To a large extent, the corporatist framework aimed to reduce 'traditional' lines of division as well as to help demarcate future political contests to the greater benefit of regime maintenance and survival.

The usefulness of the analytical framework of state corporatism is that it brings attention to some of the specific ways by which Suharto sought to exploit and further fragment political divisions to the benefit of regime survival. The analytical framework identifies the actual linkages constructed between the state, Islam and other group interests and the particular kinds of group interactions in response to this linkage system. Analysis of state corporatism does not seek to explain an entire social-political reality. Instead it focuses on these specific configurations or linkages of power relations in seeking to explain the evolving state–societal interactions leading to both political stasis and change.

References

BOOKS, MANUSCRIPTS, MONOGRAPHS, AND JOURNALS

Acharya, Amitav. 'Southeast Asia's Democratic Moment', *Asian Survey* 39(3) (May/June 1999): 418–32

Adnan, Zifirdaus. 'Islamic Religion: Yes, Islamic (Political) Ideology: No!, Islam and the State in Indonesia', Budiman, Arief (ed.), *State and Civil Society in Indonesia*, Clayton, Centre of Southeast Asian Studies, Monash University, 1990

Ahmad, Haidlor Ali. 'Kelompok-Kelompok Keagamaan di dalam dan di Sekitar Kampus ITS', *Penamas: Beragama Cara Mahasiswa*, Jakarta, Balai Penelitian Agama dan Kemasyarakatan,1995

Anlov, Hans and Cederroth, Sven. 'Introduction', and Antlov, Hans. 'The Village Leaders and the New Order', Antlov, Hans and Cederroth, Sven (eds), *Leadership On Java: Gentle Hints, Authoritarian Rule*, Surrey, Curzon Press, 1994

Anshari, Saifuddin. *The Jakarta Charter 1945: The Struggle For An Islamic Constitution in Indonesia*, Kualar Lumpur, Muslim Youth Movement of Malaysia, 1979

Anwar, Dewi Fortuna. 'The Habibie Presidency', Forrester, Geoff (ed.), *Post-Soeharto Indonesia: Renewal or Chaos*, Indonesian Assessment 1998, Research School of Pacific and Asian Studies, Australian National University, Bathurst, Singapore, Crawford House Publishing Pty Ltd, Institute of Southeast Asian Studies, 1999

Aqsha, Darul et al. (eds), *Islam in Indonesia: A Survey of Events and Developments from 1988 to March 1993*, Jakarta, INIS, 1995

Aspinall, Edward. 'Opposition and Elite Conflict in the Fall of Soeharto', Forrester, Geoff and May, R.J. (eds), *The Fall of Soeharto*, Bathurst, London, Crawford House Publishing Pty Ltd, 1998

— 'The Indonesian Student Uprising of 1998', Arief Budiman et al. (eds) *Reformasi: Crisis and Change in Indonesia*, Clayton, Monash Asia Institute, 1999

Azis, Abdul. 'Meraih Kesempatan Studi Kasus Kelompok Keagamaan Mahasiswa University Indonesia', *Penamas: Beragama Cara Mahasiswa*, Jakarta, Balai Penelitian Agama dan Kemasyarakatan, 1995

Baretta, Silvio Duncan and Douglas, Helen E. 'Authoritarianism and Corporatism in Latin America: A Review Essay', Malloy, James M. (ed.), *Authoritarianism and Corporatism in Latin America*, Pittsburgh, London, University of Pittsburgh Press, 1977

Barton, Greg and Fealy, Greg (eds), *Nahdlatul Ulama, Traditional Islam and Modernity in Indonesia*, Clayton, Monash Asia Institute, Monash University, 1996

Barton, Gregory James. 'The Emergence of Neo-Modernism; a Progressive, Liberal, Movement of Islamic Thought in Indonesia: A Textual Study Examining the Writings of Nurcholish Madjid, Djohan Effendi, Ahmad Wahib and Abdurrahman Wahid 1968–1980', Thesis (Ph.D.), Clayton, Department of Asian Languages and Studies, Monash University, 1995

Bhakti, Ikrar Nusa. 'Trends in Indonesian Student Movements in 1998', Forrester, Geoff and May, R.J. (eds), *The Fall of Soeharto*, Bathurst, Crawford House Publishing, 1998

Bianchi, Robert. *Unruly Corporatism: Associational Life in Twentieth-Century Egypt*, New York, Oxford, Oxford University Press, 1989

Binder, Leonard. *Islamic Liberalism: A Critique of Development Ideologies*, Chicago, London, The University of Chicago Press, 1988

Boland, B.J. *The Struggle of Islam in Modern Indonesia*, The Hague, Martinus Nijhoff, 1982

Bourchier, David. 'Crime, Law and State Authority in Indonesia', Budiman, Arief (ed.), *State and Civil Society in Indonesia*, Clayton, Centre for Southeast Asian Studies, Monash University, 1990

— 'Skeletons, Vigilantes and the Armed Forces' Fall From Grace', Budiman et al. (eds) *Reformasi: Crisis and Change in Indonesia*, Clayton, Monash Asia Institute, 1999

— *Lineages of Organicist Political Thought in Indonesia*, Thesis (Ph.D.), Clayton, Department of Politics, Monash University, June 1996

Bowen, John R. 'On the Political Construction of Tradition: Gotong Royong in Indonesia', *The Journal of Asian Studies* 45(3) (May 1986): 545–59

Burke, Edmund and Lapidus, Ira M. (eds), *Islam, Politics, and Social Movements*, Berkeley, University of California Press, 1988

Burns, Peter. 'The Post Priok Trials: Religious Principles and Legal Issues', *Indonesia* 47 (April 1989): 61–88

Cahyono, Edi. 'The Unjuk Rasa Movement', Lambert, Robert (ed.), *State and Labour in New Order Indonesia*, Perth, University of Western Australia Press, Asia Research Centre, Murdoch University, 1997

Cahyono, Heru. *Peranan Ulama Dalam Golkar, 1971–1980: dari Pemilu sampai Malari*, Jakarta, Pustaka Sinar Harapan, 1992

Chalmers, Douglas A. 'Corporatism and Comparative Politics', Wiarda, Howard J. (ed.), *New Directions in Comparative Politics*, Boulder, London, Westview Press, 1985

Chazan, Naomi. 'Engaging the State: associational life in sub-Saharan Africa', Migdal, Joel S. et al. (eds), *State Power and Social Forces: Domination and*

Transformation in the Third World, Cambridge, New York, Melbourne, Cambridge University Press, 1994

Collier, David and Collier, Ruth Berins. 'Who Does What, to Whom, and How: Toward a Comparative Analysis of Latin American Corporatism', Malloy, James M. (ed.), *Authoritarianism and Corporatism in Latin America*, Pittsburgh, London, University of Pittsburgh Press, 1977

Crouch, Harold. 'The Indonesian Army in Politics: 1960–1971 Thesis (Ph.D.), Clayton, Department of Politics, Monash University, 1975

— 'Wiranto and Habibie: Military-Civilian Relations Since May 1998', *Democracy in Indonesia? The Crisis and Beyond*, Melbourne and Monash Universities, 11–12 December 1998

— *The Army and Politics in Indonesia*, Ithaca, Cornell University Press, 1988

Darmaputera, Eka. *Pancasila and the Search For Identity and Modernity in Indonesian Society: A Cultural and Ethical Analysis*, Leiden, New York, Kobenhavn, Koln, E.J. Brill, 1988

Dauvergne, Peter. 'Weak States, Strong States', Dauvergne, Peter (ed.), *Weak and Strong States in Asia-Pacific Societies*, St Leonards, Canberra, Allen & Unwin, Research School of Pacific and Asian Studies, Australian National University, 1998

Deyo, Frederic C. *Beneath the Miracle: Labour Subordination in the New Asian Industrialism*, Berkeley, Los Angeles, London, University of California Press, 1989

Dhofier, Zamakhsyari. *Tradition and Change: In Indonesian Islamic Education*, Jakarta, Office of Religious Research and Development, Ministry of Religious Affairs, 1995

Diamond, Larry et al., 'Introduction: Comparing Experiences with Democracy', Diamond et al. (eds), *Politics in Developing Countries: Comparing Experiences with Democracy*, Boulder, London, Lynne Rienner Publishers, 1990

Diamond, Larry. 'Beyond Authoritarianism and Totalitarianism: Strategies for Democratization', *The Washington Quarterly* 12–1) (Winter 1989): 141–61

Ding, X. L. *The Decline of Communism in China: Legitimacy Crisis, 1977–1989*, Cambridge, New York, Cambridge University Press, 1994

Djatiwijono H.R. SH. 'Kesan dan Kenangan Semasa Membantu Bapak H. Alamsjah Ratu Prawiranegara', Sempurnadjaja, Krisna R. *H. Alamsjah Ratu Prawiranegara 70 Tahun: Pesan dan Kesan*, Jakarta, Pustaka Sinar Harapan, 1995

Effendi, Bahtiar. 'Islam and the State in Indonesia: Munawir Sjadzali and the Development of a New Theological Underpinning of Political Islam', *Studia Islamika* 2(2) (1995): 97–121

Eldridge, Philip J. *Non-Government Organisations and Democratic Participation in Indonesia*, Oxford, Singapore, New York, Oxford University Press, 1995

Emmerson, Donald K. 'The Bureaucracy in Political Context: Weakness in Strength', Jackson, Karl D. and Pye, Lucian W. (eds), *Political Power and*

Communications in Indonesia, Berkeley, Los Angeles, London, University of California Press, 1978

Esposito, John L. *Islam and Politics*, New York, Syracuse University Press, 1984

— *The Islamic Threat: Myth or Reality?* New York, Oxford, Oxford University Press, 1992

Ethier, Diane. 'Introduction: Processes of Transition and Democratic Consolidation: Theoretical Indicators', Ethier, Diane (ed.), *Democratic Transition and Consolidation in Southern Europe, Latin America and Southeast Asia*, Basingstoke, London, The MacMillan Press Ltd, 1990

Evans, Kevin. 'Economic Update', Forrester, Geoff (ed.), *Post-Soeharto Indonesia: Renewal or Chaos* (Indonesian Assessment 1998), Research School of Pacific and Asian Studies, Australian National University, Bathurst, Singapore, Crawford House Publishing Pty Ltd, Institute of Southeast Asian Studies, 1999

Evers, Hans-Dieter and Siddique, Sharon. 'Religious Revivalism in Southeast Asia: An Introduction', *Sojourn* 8(1) (February 1993): 1–10

Fealy, Greg. 'The 1994 NU Congress and Aftermath', Barton, Greg and Fealy, Greg (eds), *Nahdlatul Ulama, Traditional Islam and Modernity in Indonesia*, Clayton, Monash Asia Institute, Monash University, 1996

— 'Indonesian Politics, 1995–96: The Makings of a Crisis', Jones, Gavin W. and Hull, Terence H. (eds), *Indonesian Assessment: Population and Human Resources*, Canberra, Research School of Pacific and Asian Studies, Australian National University, 1997

Federspiel, Howard M. 'The Muhammadiyah: A Study of an Orthodox Islamic Movement in Indonesia', *Indonesia* 10 (10 October 1970): 57–79

— *Persatuan Islam: Islamic Reform in Twentieth Century Indonesia*, Ithaca, New York, Modern Indonesian Project, Southeast Asia Program, Cornell University, 1970

Feillard, Andree. 'Traditionalist Islam and the Army in Indonesia's New Order: The Awkward Relationship', Barton, Greg and Fealy, Greg (eds), *Nahdlatul Ulama, Traditional Islam and Modernity in Indonesia*, Clayton, Monash Asia Institute, Monash University, 1996

Feith, Herbert. *The Decline of Constitutional Democracy in Indonesia*, Ithaca, New York, Cornell University Press, 1962

Forrester, Geoff. 'Towards March 1998, with Determination', Hill, Hal and Thee Kian Wie (eds), *Indonesia's Technological Challenge*, Canberra, Singapore, Research School of Pacific and Asian Studies, Australian National University, Institute of Southeast Asian Studies, 1998

— 'A Jakarta Diary, May 1998', Forrester, Geoff and May, R.J. (eds), *The Fall of Soeharto*, Bathurst, Crawford House Publishing Pty Ltd, 1998

Fuaduddin TM. 'Kelompok Keagamaan di IKIP Negeri Jakarta dalam Perspektif Gerakan Keagamaan Kampus', *Penamas: Beragama Cara Mahasiswa*, Jakarta, Balai Penelitian Agama dan Kemasyarakatan, 1995

Gaffar, Afan. 'Indonesia 1995: Setting the Tone for Transition Towards the Post-Soeharto Era', Barlow, Colin and Hardjono, Joan (eds), *Indonesian Assessment 1995: Development in Eastern Indonesia*, Canberra, Singapore, Research School of Pacific and Asian Studies, Australian National University, Institute of Southeast Asian Studies, 1996

Giner, Salvador. 'Political Economy, Legitimation, and the State in Southern Europe', O'Donnell, Guillermo et al. (eds), *Transitions from Authoritarian Rule: Prospects for Democracy*, Baltimore, London, The Johns Hopkins University Press, 1986

Hadiz, Vedi R. 'Challenging State Corporatism on the Labour Front: Working Class Politics in the 1990s', Bourchier, David and Legge, John (eds), *Democracy in Indonesia: 1950s and 1990s*, Clayton (Monash Papers on Southeast Asia No.31), Centre of Southeast Asian Studies, Monash University, 1994

— *Workers and the State in New Order Indonesia*, Perth, London, New York, Routledge, Asia Research Centre, Murdoch University, 1997

— 'The Sekneg Experience and New Order Politics', Pangaribuan, Robison. *The Indonesian State Secretariat 1945–1993* (translated by Hadiz, Vedi), Perth, Asia Research Centre on Social, Political and Economic Change, Murdoch University, 1995

Haris, Syamsuddin. 'PPP and Politics under the New Order', *Prisma* 49(31) (June 1990): 31–51

Hasan, Mohammad Kamal. *Muslim Intellectual Responses to 'New Order' Modernization in Indonesia*, Kuala Lumpur, Dewan Bahasa dan Pustaka, 1980

Hasyim, Umar. *Toleransi dan Kemerdekaan Beragama Dalam Islam Sebagai Dasar Menuju Dialogue dan Kerukunan Antar Agama*, Surabaya, Pt. Bina Ilmu, 1991

Hefner, Robert W. 'Islam, State, and Civil Society: ICMI and the Struggle for the Indonesian Middle Class', *Indonesia* 56 (October 1993): 1–35

Heryanto, Ariel. 'Indonesia: Towards the Final Countdown?' *Southeast Asian Affairs 1997*: 107–26

Hill, Hal. 'The Indonesian Economy: The Strange and Sudden Death of a Tiger', Forrester, Geoff and May, R.J. (eds), *The Fall of Soeharto*, Bathurst, Crawford House Publishing, 1998

Honna, Jun. 'The Military and Democratisation in Indonesia: The Developing Civil-Military Discourse During the Late Soeharto Era', Thesis (Ph.D.), Canberra, Department of Political and Social Change, Research School of Pacific and Asian Studies, Australian National University, June 1999

Hoogvelt, Ankie M. M. *Globalization and the Postcolonial World: The New Political Economy of Development*, Basingstoke, London, The MacMillian Press Ltd, 1997

Hooker, M.B. *Islamic Law in Sutheast Asia*, Singapore, Oxford, New York, Oxford University Press, 1984

Hunter, Shireen T. (ed.), *The Politics of Islamic Revivalism: Diversity and*

Unity, Washington, D.C., The Centre for Strategic and International Studies, 1988

Huntington, Samuel P. *The Third Wave: Democratization in the Late Twentieth Century*, Norman, London, University of Oklahoma Press, 1991

Imawan, Riswandha. 'The Evolution of Political Party Systems in Indonesia: 1900 to 1987', Thesis (Ph.D.), Dekalb, Illinois, 1989

'Intellectual Engineering in IAIN', *Studia Islamika* 2(1) (1995): 1–6

Ismail, Faisal. 'Pancasila as the Sole Basis for all Political Parties and for all Mass Organizations; an Account of Muslims' Responses', *Studia Islamika* 3(4) (1996): 1–92

Israeli, Raphael and Johns, Anthony H. (eds), *Islam in Asia: Volume II Southeast and East Asia*, Boulder, Colorado, Westview Press, 1984

Jenkins, David. *Suharto and His Generals: Indonesian Military Politics 1975–1983*, Ithaca, New York, Cornell Modern Indonesia Project, Southeast Asia Program, Cornell University, 1984

Johns, Anthony H. 'Islamization in Southeast Asia: Reflections and Reconsiderations with Special Reference to the Role of Sufism', *Southeast Asian Studies* 31(1) (June 1993): 43–61

Jones, Sidney. 'The Contraction and Expansion of the Umat and the Role of the Nahdlatul Ulama in Indonesia', *Indonesia* 38 (October 1984): 1–20

Kaufman, Robert R. 'Corporatism, Clientelism, and Partisan Conflict: A Study of Seven Latin American Countries', Malloy, James M. (ed.), *Authoritarianism and Corporatism in Latin America*, Pittsburgh, University of Pittsburgh Press, 1977

King, Dwight Y. 'Indonesia's New Order as a Bureaucratic Polity, A Neopatrimonial Regime or a Bureaucratic-Authoritarian Regime: What Difference Does It Make?' Anderson, Benedict and Kahin, Audrey (eds), *Interpreting Indonesian Politics: Thirteen Contributions to the Debate* (Interim Reports Series No.62), Ithaca, New York, Cornell Modern Indonesian Project, Southeast Asia Program, Cornell University, 1982

Kingsbury, Damien. *The Politics of Indonesia*, Oxford, Auckland, New York, Oxford University Press, 1998

Kohli, Atul and Shue, Vivien. 'State Power and Social Forces: On Political Contention and Accommodation in the Third World', Migdal, Joel S. et al. (eds), *State Power and Social Forces: Domination and Transformation in the Third World*, Cambridge, New York, Melbourne, Cambridge University Press, 1994

Kristiadi, J. 'The Future Role of ABRI in Politics', Forrester, Geoff (ed.), *Post-Soeharto Indonesia: Renewal or Chaos* (Indonesia Assessment 1998) Bathurst, Singapore, Research School of Pacific and Asian Studies, Australian National University, Crawford House Publishing Pty Ltd, Institute of Southeast Asian Studies, 1999

Liddle, R. William. 'The 1977 Indonesian Election and New Order Legitimacy' (unpublished manuscript), Canberra, The Australian National University, Menzies Library, 1977

— 'Politics 1992–1993: Sixth Term Adjustments in the Ruling Formula', Manning, Chris and Hardjono, Joan (eds), *Indonesian Assessment 1993, Labour: Sharing in the Benefits of Growth?*, Canberra, Department of Political and Social Change, Research School of Pacific and Asian Studies, Australian National University, 1993

Linz, Juan J. 'An Authoritarian Regime: Spain', Allardt, Erik and Rokkan, Stein (eds), *Mass Politics: Studies in Political Sociology*, New York, Free Press, 1970

Lowry, Robert. *The Armed Forces of Indonesia*, St Leonards, Allen & Unwin, 1996

Ludjito, H. 'Kenangan Bersama Bapak H. Alamsjah Ratu Prawiranegara', Sempurnadjaja, Krisna R. *H. Alamsjah Ratu Prawiranegara 70 Tahun: Pesan dan Kesan*, Jakarta, Pustaka Sinar Harapan, 1995

Ma'shum, Saifullah and Zawawi, Ali (eds), *50 Tahun Muslimat NU Berkhidmat untuk Agama & Bangsa*, Jakarta, Pucuk Pimpinan Muslimat Nahdlatul Ulama, 1996

MacIntyre, Andrew. 'Organising Interests: Corporatism in Indonesian Politics' (Working Paper No.43), National Library of Australia (August 1994)

Mackie, Jamie and MacIntyre, Andrew. 'Politics', Hill, Hal (ed.), *Indonesia's New Order: The Dynamics of Socio-Economic Transformation*, St Leonards, Allen & Unwin Pty Ltd, 1994

Madrid, Robin. 'Islamic Students in the Indonesian Student Movement, 1998–1999: Forces for Moderation', *Bulletin of Concerned Asian Scholars* 31(3) (1999): 17–32

Malley, Michael. 'The 7th Development Cabinet: Loyal to a Fault?' *Indonesia* 65 (April 1998): 155–78

Malloy, James M. 'Authoritarianism and Corporatism: The Case of Bolivia', Malloy, James M. (ed.), *Authoritarianism and Corporatism in Latin America*, Pittsburgh, London, University of Pittsburgh Press, 1977

Mardjoned, H. Ramlan. *KH. Hasan Basri 70 Tahun: Fungsi Ulama Dan Peranan Masjid*, Jakarta, Media Dakwah, 1990

May, Brian. *The Indonesian Tragedy*, London, Boston, R & K Paul, 1978

McGillivray, Mark and Morrisey, Oliver. 'Economic and Financial Meltdown in Indonesia: Prospects for Sustained and Equitable Economic and Social Recovery', Budiman, Arief et al. (eds), *Reformasi: Crisis and Change in Indonesia*, Clayton, Monash Asia Institute, Monash University, 1999

McIntyre, Angus. 'Working Paper No. 103: In Search of Megawati Sukarnoputri', Clayton, Monash Asia Institute, Centre of Southeast Asian Studies, Monash University, 1997

McVey, Ruth T. 'Faith as the Outsider: Islam in Indonesian Politics', Piscatori, James P. (ed.), *Islam in the Political Process*, Cambridge, Cambridge University Press, 1983

Mietzner, Marcus. 'From Soeharto to Habibie: the Indonesian Armed Forces and Political Islam During the Transition', Forrester, Geoff (ed.), *Post-Soeharto Indonesia: Renewal or Chaos* (Indonesia Assessment 1998), Bathurst, Singapore, Research School of Pacific and Asian Studies, Australian National University, Crawford House Publishing Pty Ltd, Institute of Southeast Asian Studies, 1999

Migdal, Joel S. 'The State in Society: an Approach to Struggles for Domination', Migdal, Joel S. et al. (eds), *State Power and Social Forces: Domination and Transformation in the Third World*, Cambridge, New York, Melbourne, Cambridge University Press, 1994

— 'Why Do So Many States Stay Intact?' Dauvergne, Peter (ed.), *Weak and Strong States in Asia-Pacific Societies*, St Leonards, Canberra, Allen & Unwin, Research School of Pacific and Asian Studies, Australian National University, 1998

— 'Strong States, Weak States: power and Accommodation', Weiner, Myron and Huntington, Samuel P. (eds), *Understanding Political Development*, Boston, Toronto, Little, Brown and Company, 1987

Milne, Stephan. 'Corporatism in the ASEAN Countries', *Contemporary Southeast Asia* 5(2) (September 1983): 172–84

Montgomery-Watt, William. *Islamic Political Thought: The Basic Concepts*, Edinburgh, Edinburgh University Press, 1968

Morfit, Michael. 'Pancasila Orthodoxy', MacAndrews, Colin (ed.), *Central Government and Local Development in Indonesia*, Singapore, Oxford, New York, Oxford University Press, 1986

Mudzhar, Atho, M. *Fatwas of the Council of Indonesian Ulama: A Study of Islamic Thought in Indonesia, 1975–1988*, Jakarta, INIS, 1993

Mulder, Neils. *Mysticism and Everyday Life in Contemporary Java: Cultural Persistence and Change*, Singapore, Singapore University Press, 1978

Munhanif, Ali. 'Islam and the Struggle for Religious Pluralism in Indonesia: A Political Reading of the Religious Thought of Mukti Ali', *Studia Islamika* 3(1) (1996): 79–126

Murtopo, Ali. *Strategi Politik Nasional*, Jakarta, Centre for Strategic and International Studies, 1974

Muzani, Saiful. 'Mu'tazilah and the Modernization of the Indonesian Muslim Community: Intellectual Portrait of Harun Nasution', *Studia Islamika* 1(1) (1994): 91–129

Nafis, Muhammad Wahyuni et al. (eds), *Kontekstualisasi Ajaran Islam: 70 Tahun Prof Dr H. Munawir Sjadzali*, Jakarta, Paramadina, Ikatan Persaudaraan Haji Indonesia, 1995

Nakamura, Mitsuo. 'NU's Leadership Crisis and Search for Identity in the Early 1980s: From the 1979 Semarang Congress to Situbondo Congress', Barton, Greg and Fealy, Greg (eds), *Nahdlatul Ulama, Traditional Islam and Modernity in Indonesia*, Clayton, Monash Asia Institute, Monash University, 1996

References

Nasution, Adnan Byung. *The Aspiration for Constitutional Government in Indonesia: A Socio-legal Study of the Indonesian Konstituante 1956–1959*, Jakarta, Pustaka Sinar Harapan, 1992

Nasution, Harun. *Islam Ditinjau dari Berbagai Aspeknya*, Jakarta, Bulan Bintang, 1977

Noer, Deliar. *Administration of Islam in Indonesia* (Monograph Series, 58), Ithaca, New York, Cornell Modern Indonesia Project, Southeast Asia Program, Cornell University, 1978

— *Modernist Muslim Movement in Indonesia, 1900–1942*, Kuala Lumpur, Oxford University Press, 1973

— *Partai Islam Di Pentas Nasional, 1945–1965*, Jakarta, Grafiti, 1987

Nordlinger, Eric A. 'Taking the State Seriously', Weiner, Myron and Huntington, Samuel P. (eds), *Understanding Political Development*, Boston, Toronto, Little, Brown and Company, 1987

O'Donnell, Guillermo A. 'Corporatism and the Question of the State', Malloy, James M. (ed.), *Authoritarianism and Corporatism in Latin America*, London, University of Pittsburgh Press, 1977

— *Modernization and the Bureaucratic-Authoritarianism: Studies in South American Politics*, Berkeley, University of California, 1973

Pangaribuan, Robison. *The Indonesian State Secretariat 1945–1993* (translated by Hadiz, Vedi), Perth, Asia Research Centre on Social, Political and Economic Change, Murdoch University, 1995

Parikesit, Suparman G. and Sempurnadjaja, Krisna R. *H. Alamsjah Ratu Prawiranegara: Perjalanan Hidup Seorang Anak Yatim Piatu*, Jakarta, Pustaka Sinar Harapan, 1995

Patty, Semuel Augustinus. '"Aliran Kepercayaan": A Socio-Religious Movement in Indonesia', Thesis (Ph.D.), Ann Arbor, 1986

Peacock, James L. *Purifying the Faith: The Muhammadiyah Movement in Indonesian Islam*, Benjamin/Cummings, Menlo Park, California, 1978

Pei, Minxin. *From Reform to Revolution: The Demise of Communism in China and the Soviet Union*, Cambridge, Massachusetts, London, Harvard University Press, 1994

'"Pesantren Kilat": Building a Better Muslim Youth', *Studia Islamika* 3(3) (1996): 1–6

Polomka, Peter. *Indonesia Since Sukarno*, Harmondsworth, Penguin Books, 1971

Pour, Julius. *Laksamana Sudomo: Mengatasi Gelombang Kehidupan*, Jakarta, PT Gramedia Widiasarana Indonesia, 1997

Rahman, Fazlur. *Islam* (Second Edition), Chicago, London, University of Chicago Press, 1979

Ramage, Douglas E. *Politics in Indonesia: Democracy, Islam, and the Ideology of Tolerance*, New York, Routledge, 1995

Rasyid, Ryaas M. 'Indonesia: Preparing for Post-Soeharto Rule and its Impact on the Democratization Process', *Southeast Asian Affairs 1995*: 149–63

Reeve, David, 'The Corporatist State: The Case of Golkar', Budiman, Arief (ed.), *State and Civil Society in Indonesia*, Clayton, Centre of Southeast Asian Studies, Monash University, 1990

— *Golkar of Indonesia: An Alternative To The Party System*, Singapore, Oxford University Press, 1985

Refleksi Pembaharuan Pemikiran Islam: 70 Tahun Harun Nasution, Jakarta, Panitia Penerbitan Buku Dan Seminar 70 Tahun Harun Nasution Bekerjasama Dengan Lembaga Studi Agama Dan Filsafat, 1989

Robison, Richard. 'Organising the Transition: Indonesian Politics in 1993/94', McLeod, Ross H. (ed.), *Indonesian Assessment 1994: Finance as a Key Sector in Indonesia's Development*, Canberra, Research School of Pacific and Asian Studies, The Australian National University, 1994

Rosyad, Rifki. 'A Quest For True Islam: A Study of the Islamic Resurgence Movement among the Youth in Bandung, Indonesia', Thesis (Masters), Canberra, Australian National University, February 1995

Ruechmeyer, Dietrich and Evans, Peter B. 'The State and Economic Transformation: Toward an Analysis of the Conditions Underlying Effective Intervention', Evans, Peter B. et al. *Bringing the State Back In*, Cambridge, Cambridge University Press, 1985

Ryter, Loren. 'Pemuda Pancasila: The Last Loyalist Free Men of Suharto's Order?' *Indonesia* 66 (October 1988): 45–73

Salam, Solichim. *Sedjarah Partai Muslimin Indonesia*, Jakarta, Lembaga Pejelidikan Islam, 1970

Samson, Allan A. 'Conceptions of Politics, Power, and Ideology in Contemporary Indonesian Islam', Jackson, Karl D. and Pye, Lucian W. *Political Power and Communications in Indonesia*, London, University of California Press, 1978

— 'Islam and Politics in Indonesia', Thesis (Ph.D.) (Microfilm), Berkeley, University of California, 1972

Schmitter, Philippe C. 'An Introduction to Southern European Transitions from Authoritarian Rule: Italy, Greece, Portugal, Spain, and Turkey', O'Donnell, Guillermo et al. (eds), *Transitions from Authoritarian Rule: Prospects for Democracy*, Baltimore, London, The Johns Hopkins University Press, 1986

— 'Modes of Interest Intermediation and Models of Societal Change in Western Europe', Schmitter, Philippe C. and Lehmbruch, Gerhard (eds), *Trends Toward Corporatist Intermediation*, Beverly Hills, London, Sage Publications, 1979

— 'Still the Century of Corporatism?' Pike, Frederick B. and Stritch, Thomas (eds), *The New Corporatism: Social-Political Structures in the Iberian World*, Notre Dame, London, University of Notre Dame Press, 1974

Schwarz, Adam, *A Nation in Waiting: Indonesia in the 1990s*, St Leonards, Allen & Unwin Pty Ltd, 1994

Sempurnadjaja, Krisna R. (ed.), *H. Alamsjah Ratu Prawiranegara 70 Tahun: Pesan dan Kesan*, Jakarta, Pustaka Sinar Harapan, 1995

Shue, Vivien. 'State power and social organization in China', Migdal, Joel S. et al. (eds), *State Power and Social Forces: Domination and Transformation in the Third World*, Cambridge, New York, Melbourne, Cambridge University Press, 1994

Sjadzali, H. Munawir. *Islam: Realitas Baru Dan Orientasi Masa Depan Bangsa*, Jakarta, Universitas Indonesia Press, 1993

— *Bunga Rampai Wawasan Islam Dewasa Ini*, Jakarta, Penerbit Universitas Indonesia, 1994

— *Islam dan Tata Negara: Ajaran, Sejarah dan Pemikiran*, Jakarta, University of Indonesia Press, 1990

Soerojo, Soegiarso. *Siapa Menabur Angin Akan Menuai Badai: G30S-PKI Dan Peran Bung Karno*, Jakarta, C.V. Sri Murni, 1988

Soetrisno, Loekman. 'Current Social and Political Conditions of Rural Indonesia', Forrester, Geoff (ed.), *Post-Soeharto Indonesia: Renewal or Chaos* (Indonesian Assessment 1998), Research School of Pacific and Asian Studies, Australian National University', Bathurst, Singapore, Crawford House Publishing Pty Ltd, Institute of Southeast Asian Studies, 1999

Soewondo, Nani. *Kedudukan Wanita Indonesia: Dalam Hukum Dan Masyarakat*, Jakarta, Ghalia Indonesia, 1984

Southwood, Julie and Flanagan, Patrick. *Indonesia: Law, Propaganda and Terror*, London, Zed, 1983

Stepan, Alfred. *The State and Society: Peru in Comparative Perspective*, Princeton, New Jersey, Princeton University Press, 1978

Sullivan, John. *Local Government and Community in Java: An Urban Case-study*, Singapore, New York, Oxford University Press, 1992

Sullivan, Norma. 'Master and Managers: A study of gender relations in urban Java' (unpublished manuscript), Singapore, National University of Singapore, Central Library, 24 February 1995

Sundhaussen, Ulf. 'The Military: Structure, Procedures, and Effects on Indonesian Society', Jackson, Karl D. and Pye, Lucian W. (eds), *Political Power and Communications in Indonesia*, Berkeley, Los Angeles, London, University of California Press, 1978

Suryadinata, Leo. 'A Year of Upheaval and Uncertainty: The Fall of Soeharto and Rise of Habibie', *Southeast Asian Affairs 1999*: 111–41

— *Military Ascendancy and Political Culture: A Study of Indonesia's Golkar*, Athens, Ohio, Monographs in International Studies, 1989

— *Political Parties and the 1982 General Election in Indonesia*, Singapore, Institute of Southeast Asian Studies (ISEAS), 1982

Syamsuddin, M. Din. 'Religion and Politics in Islam: The Case of Muhammadiyah in Indonesia's New Order', Thesis (Ph.D.), Ann Arbor, Los Angeles, University of California, 1991

— 'The Muhammadiyah Da'wah and Allocative Politics in the New Order Indonesia', *Studia Islamika* 2(2) (1995): 35–71

Tamara, Nasir. 'Islam under the New Order: A Political History', *Prisma*: 49, 1990

Tanja, Victor. *HMI: Himpunan Mahasiswa Islam, Sejarah Dan Kedudukannya di tengah Gerakan-gerakan Muslim Pembaharu di Indonesia*, Jakarta, Penerbit Sinar Harapan, 1982

Tanter, Richard. 'Totalitarian Ambition: Intelligence and Security Agencies in Indonesia', Budiman, Arief (ed.), *State and Civil Society in Indonesia*, Clayton, Centre of Southeast Asian Studies, Monash University, 1990

Tasmara, H. Toto. *Etos Kerja Pribadi Muslim*, Jakarta, PT. Dana Bhakti Wakaf, 1995

— *Menjawab Tantangan Zaman II*, Jakarta, PT. Dana Bhakti Wakaf, 1995

'Teaching Children to Read the Qur'an', *Studia Islamika* 1(1) (April-June 1994): 1–5

The Editors, 'Current Data on the Indonesian Military Elite: October 1, 1995–December 31, 1997', *Indonesia* 65 (April 1998): 179–92

— 'Current Data on the Indonesian Military Elite: September 1, 1993–August 31, 1994', *Indonesia* 58 (October 1994): 83–102

— 'The Indonesian Military in the Mid-1990s: Political Maneouvring or Structural Change?', *Indonesia* 63 (April 1997): 91–105

The Limits of Openness: Human Rights in Indonesia and East Timor, New York, Washington, Brussels, Human Rights Watch, 1994

Tirtosudarmo, Riwanto. 'Indonesia 1991: Quest for Democracy in a Turbulent Year', *Southeast Asian Affairs*, 1992

Uhlin, Anders. *Indonesia and the 'Third Wave of Democratisation': The Indonesian Pro-Democracy Movement in a Changing World*, Surrey, Curzon Press, 1997

Unger, Jonathan and Chan, Anita. 'Corporatism in China: A Developmental State in an East Asian Context', McCormick, Barrett L. and Unger, Jonathan (eds), *China After Socialism: In the Footsteps of Eastern Europe or East Asia?*, Armonk, New York, London, M.E Sharpe, 1996

van Bruinessen, Martin. 'The 28th Congress of the Nahdlatul Ulama: Power Struggle and Social Concerns', Barton, Greg and Fealy, Greg (eds), *Nahdlatul Ulama, Traditional Islam and Modernity in Indonesia*, Clayton, Monash Asia Institute, 1996

— *NU: Tradisi, relasi-relasi Kuasa, Pencarian Wacana Baru*, Yogyakarta, LkiS, 1994

Van Dijk, C. *Rebellion Under the Banner of Islam: The Darul Islam in Indonesia*, Leiden, Koninklijk Instituut voor Taal-, Land en Volkenkunde, 1981

Vatikiotis, Michael R.J. *Indonesian Politics under Suharto: Order, Development and Pressure for Change*, London, New York, Routledge, 1993

Walters, Patrick. 'The Indonesian Armed Forces in the Post-Soeharto Era', Forrester, Geoff (ed.), *Post-Soeharto Indonesia: Renewal or Chaos* (Indonesian Assessment 1998), Bathurst, Singapore, Research School of

Pacific and Asian Studies, Australian National University, Crawford
Housing Publishing Pty Ltd, Institute of Southeast Asian Studies, 1999

Ward, Ken. *The 1971 Election in Indonesia: An East Java Case Study* (Monash
Papers on Southeast Asia), Clayton, Monash University, 1972

Williamson, Peter J. *Varieties of Corporatism: A Conceptual Discussion*,
Cambridge, London, New York, Cambridge University Press, 1985

Young, Ken. 'The Crisis: Contexts And Prospects', *The Fall of Soeharto*,
Forrester, Geoff and May, R.J. (eds), *The Fall of Soeharto*, Bathurst,
Crawford House Publishing Pty Ltd, 1998

GOVERNMENT AND NON-GOVERNMENT REPORTS AND PUBLICATIONS

'Anggaran Dasar dan Anggaran Rumah Tangga Ikatan Cendekiawan Muslim
Se-Indonesia (ICMI)', Jakarta, Januari, 1991

'Daftar Aliran/Ajaran Kepercayaan Masyarakat Yang Telah Dilarang/
Dibejukan Selama Periode April 1988 S/D Maret 1990' (register of banned
organisations supplied by MUI)

'Daftar Anggota Forum Komunikasi Ormas Islam Karya-Kekaryaan', Jakarta,
1996

'Hasil Keputusan Muktamar III Dewan Masjid Indonesia', Jakarta, Pimpinan
Pusat Dewan Masjid Indonesia, 1995

'Indonesia: Impunity Versus Accountability for Gross Human Rights
Violations', Jakarta, Brussels, ICG Asia Report No.12 (2 February 2001)

'Indonesia's Crisis: Chronic but not Acute', Jakarta, Brussels, ICG Indonesia
Report No. 2, 31 May 2000

'Instruksi Menteri Agama Nomor 8 Tahun 1979 Tentang Pembinaan,
Bimbingan Dan Pengawasan Terhadap Organisasi Dan Aliran Dalam
Islam Yang Bertentangan Dengan Ajaran Islam', *Buku Peraturan
Perundangan Tentang Pembinaan Penyelenggaraan Kehidupan Beragama*,
Departmen Agama R.I. Sekretariat Jenderal, 1990/1991

'Instruksi Menteri Agama Republik Indonesia Nomor 3 Tahun 1981 Tentang
Pelaksanaan Pembinaan Kerukunan Hidup Beragama Di Daerah
Sehubungan Dengan Telah Terbentuknya Wadah Musyawarah Antar
Umat Beragama', *Pembinaan Kerukunan Hidup Umat Beragama: 50 Tahun
Kemerdekaan Republik Indonesia*, Jakarta, Departmen Agama RI, Badan
Penelitian dan Pengembangan Agama, Proyek Peningkatan Kerukunan
Hidup Umat Beragama, 1995/1996

'Instruksi Presiden Republik Indonesia Nomor 14 Tahun 1967 Tentang Agama,
Kepercayaan Dan Adat Istiadat Cina Kami, Pejabat Presiden Republik
Indonesia', and 'Keputusan Bersama Menteri Agama, Menteri Dalam
Negeri Dan Jaksa Agung Republik Indonesia: No. 67 Tahun 1980; No. 224
Tahun 1980; No. 111/J.A/10/1980', *Peraturan Perundang-Undangan*

Kehidupan Beragama, Seri C, Pembinaan Aliran-Aliran Keagamaan, Jakarta, Departemen Agama RI, Sekratariat Jenderal, 1996

'Keputusan Menteri Agama Nomor 35 Tahun 1980 Tentang Wadah Musyawarah Antar Umat Beragama', Sujangi (ed.), *Pembinaan Kerukunan Hidup Umat Beragama: 50 Tahun Kemerdekaan Republik Indonesia*, Jakarta, Departmen Agama RI, Badan Penelitian dan Pengembangan Agama, Proyek Peningkatan Kerukunan Hidup Umat Beragama, 1995/1996

'Keputusan Menteri Agama Nomor 44 Tahun 1978 Tentang Pelaksanaan Dakwah Agama Dan Kuliah Subuh Melalui Radio', and 'Instruksi Menteri Agama Nomor 8 Tahun 1978 Tentang Pelaksanaan Dakwah Agama Dan Kuliah Subuh Melalui Radio', 'Surat Edaran Menteri Agama Nomor 3 Tahun 1978', *Buku Peraturan Perundangan Tentang Pembinaan Penyelenggaraan Kehidupan Beragama*, Departmen Agama R.I. Sekretariat Jenderal, 1990/1991

'Keputusan Pertemuan Lengkap Wadah Musyawarah Antar Umat Beragama Tentang Penjelasan Atas Pasal 3, 4 Dan 6 Serta Pembetulan Susunan Penandatangan Pedoman Dasar Wadah Musyawarah Antar Umat Beragama', Sujangi (ed.), *Pembinaan Kerukunan Hidup Umat Beragama: 50 Tahun Kemerdekaan Republik Indonesia*, Jakarta, Departmen Agama RI, Badan Penelitian dan Pengembangan Agama, Proyek Peningkatan Kerukunan Hidup Umat Beragama, 1995/1996

'Laporan Situasi Daerah Kodia dan Kabupaten Pasuruan Selama Kampanye Dalam Rangka Pemilu 1997', Pengurus Cabang NU, Kabupaten Pasuruan, Bangil dan Kotamadia Pasuruan, 7 May 1997

'Pelatihan, Penempatan dan Pembinaan Transmigran Da'i, Subit Pelayanan Transmigran Tahun 1997', Jakarta, Direktorat Jenderal Bina Masyarakat Transmigrasi, Direktorat Bina Sosial Budaya, 1997

'Penetapan Presiden Republik Indonesia Nomor 1 Tahun 1965 Tentang Pencegahan Penyalahgunaan Dan/Atau Penodaan Agama' and 'Undang-Undang No.5 Tahun 1969 Tentang Pernyataan Berbagai Penetapan Presiden Dan Peraturan Presiden Sebagai Undang-Undang', *Buku Peraturan Perundangan Tentang Pembinaan Penyelenggaraan Kehidupan Beragama*, Departmen Agama R.I. Sekretariat Jenderal, 1990/1991

'Penjelasan Atas Peraturan Pemerintah Republik Indonesia Nomor 18 Tahun 1986 Tentang Pelaksanaan Undang-Undang Nomor 8 Tahun 1985', *Peraturan Perundangan-Undangan Kehidupan Beragama Seri B (Organisasi Kemasyarakatan Dan Ketentraman Beragama)*, Jakarta, Departmen Agama, 1994

'Penjelasan Atas Undang-Undang Republik Indonesia Nomor 8 Tahun 1985', *Peraturan Perundangan-Undangan Kehidupan Beragama Seri B (Organisasi Kemasyarakatan Dan Ketentraman Beragama)*, Jakarta, Departmen Agama, 1994

'Peraturan Pemerintah Republik Indonesia Nomor 18 Tahun 1986 Tentang Pelaksanaan Undang-Undang Nomor 8 Tahun 1985', *Peraturan*

References

Perundangan-Undangan Kehidupan Beragama Seri B (Organisasi Kemasyarakatan Dan Ketentraman Beragama), Jakarta, Departmen Agama, 1994

'Petunjuk Bagi Umat Islam Kerukunan Hidup Antar Umat Beragama', Sekretariat Majelis Ulama Indonesia, Masjid Istiqlal Jakarta, 1986

'Pointers Pengarahan Panglima Angkatan Bersenjata Republik Indonesia Dalam Rangka Menerima Pengurus ICMI', Jakarta, 22 Februari 1991

'Sambutan Menteri Agama R.I. Pada Dies Natalis Ke XI IAIN Sulthan Toha Syaifuddin Tanggal 22 December 1978 Di Jambi', *Pembinaan Kehidupan Beragama dalam Pembangunan Nasional (Bagian II)*, Jakarta, Biro Hukum dan Hubungan Masyarakat, Departmen Agama Republik Indonesia

'Sambutan Menteri Agama R.I. Pada Dies Natalis Ke XII IAIN Imam Bonjol Tanggal 29 November 1978 di Padang', *Pembinaan Kehidupan Beragama dalam Pembangunan Nasional (Bagian II)*, Jakarta, Biro Hukum dan Hubungan Masyarakat, Departmen Agama Republik Indonesia

'Sambutan Menteri Agama R.I. Pada Dies Natalis Ke XIV IAIN Raden Fatah Palembang Tanggal 21 Desember 1978', *Pembinaan Kehidupan Beragama dalam Pembangunan Nasional (Bagian II)*, Jakarta, Biro Hukum dan Hubungan Masyarakat, Departmen Agama Republik Indonesia

'Seruan Bersama Dehubungan Dengan Kejadian Solo Dan Di Tempat-Tempat Lain Yang Telah Menimbulkan Keresahan Di Kalangan Masyarakat', *Pembinaan Kerukunan Hidup Umat Beragama: 50 Tahun Kemerdekaan Republik Indonesia*, Jakarta, Departmen Agama RI, Badan Penelitian dan Pengembangan Agama, Proyek Peningkatan Kerukunan Hidup Umat Beragama, 1995/1996

'Undang-Undang Republik Indonesia Nomor 8 Tahun 1985 Tentang Organisasi Kemasyarakatan Dengan Rahmat Tuhan Yang Maha Esa Presiden Republik Indonesia', *Peraturan Perundangan-Undangan Kehidupan Beragama Seri B (Organisasi Kemasyarakatan Dan Ketentraman Beragama)*, Jakarta, Departmen Agama, 1994

15 Tahun Majelis Ulama Indonesia, Wadah Musyawarah Para Ulama, Zu'ama Dan Cendekiawan Muslim, Penerbit: Sekretariat Majelis Ulama Indonesia, Masjid Istiglal Jakarta

1996: Tahun Kekerasan: Potret Pelanggaran HAM di Indonesia, Jakarta, Yayasan Lembaga Bantuan Hukum Indonesia, 1997

Da'i dan Petani Membagun Daerah Baru, Sekretariat Majelis Ulama Indonesia, Masjid Istiqlal Jakarta, 1993

Himpunan Keputusan dan Fatwa Majelis Ulama Indonesia, Jakarta, Sekretariat Majelis Ulama Indonesia, 1995

Kompilasi: Peraturan Perundang-Undangan dan Kebijakan dalam Pembinaan Kerukunan Hidup Beragama, Department Agama RI, Badan Penelitian dan Pengembangan Agama, Proyek Pembinaan Kerukunan Hidup Beragama, Jakarta, 1993/1994

Mimbar Penyuluhan Kepercayaan Terhadap Tuhan Yang Maha Esa: Jalur Pembinaan Penghayat Kepercayaan Terhadap Tuhan Yang Maha Esa,

Jakarta, Departemen Pendikikan Dan Kebudayaan, Direktorate Pembinaan
Penghayat Kepercayaan Terhadap Tuhan Yang Maha Esa, 1983/1984
Munawir Sjadzali and Baharuddin Lopa, *Keterangan Pers Tentang Laporan
Komnas HAM Mengenai Peristiwa 27 Juli 1996 di Jakarta*, 10 October 1996

Index

For Product Safety Concerns and Information please contact our EU
representative GPSR@taylorandfrancis.com Taylor & Francis Verlag GmbH,
Kaufingerstraße 24, 80331 München, Germany

Printed and bound by CPI Group (UK) Ltd, Croydon, CR0 4YY
11/04/2025
01844008-0017